International Protection
of Human Rights

Nobel Symposium 7

International
Protection
of Human Rights

Proceedings of the Seventh Nobel Symposium
Oslo, September 25–27, 1967

Edited by

ASBJÖRN EIDE and AUGUST SCHOU

Research Fellow of the
University of Oslo,
Norway

Director of the
Norwegian Nobel Institute
Oslo, Norway

INTERSCIENCE PUBLISHERS

A division of John Wiley & Sons, Inc. *New York London Sydney*

ALMQVIST & WIKSELL *Stockholm*

© 1968

Almqvist & Wiksell/Gebers Förlag AB

Library of Congress Catalog Card Number 68-9448

Printed in Sweden by

Almqvist & Wiksells Boktryckeri AB, Uppsala 1968

Contents

Summary of discussion

Nobel Foundation Symposium Committee

Ståhle, Nils K., Chairman, Executive Director of the Nobel Foundation

Hulthén, Lamek, Professor, member of the Nobel Committee for Physics

Tiselius, Arne, Professor, chairman of the Nobel Committee for Chemistry

Gustafsson, Bengt, Professor, secretary of the Nobel Committee for Medicine

Gierow, Karl Ragnar, Dr.Ph., member of the Swedish Academy (literature)

Schou, August, Director of the Norwegian Nobel Institute (peace)

The subject of the symposium *International Protection of Human Rights* was originally suggested by the Institute's adviser on international law, Professor Torkel Opsahl. The preparations were made by him and Director August Schou, in cooperation with Professor Frede Castberg. They were assisted by Mr. Asbjörn Eide and the staff of the Nobel Institute.

The papers are reproduced here as they were presented, with little or no modification. The discussions have been edited along these lines: Though interventions were made after the presentation of each paper, a number of the interventions covered subjects beyond those discussed in that particular paper. For that reason, and also in order to enhance the value of the summary, the interventions are *not* summarized in connection with each paper, but have been edited according to subject-matter and are all comprised in one section forming the last part of the volume. The summary has—with the exception of two cases where it was expressly requested—*not* been read by the participants before printing. The responsibility for the contents therefore rests entirely with the author of the summary, Mr. Asbjörn Eide.

List of Participants

LATIF O. ADEGBITE, University of Lagos, *Lagos*, Nigeria

JOHANNES ANDENÆS, University of Oslo, *Oslo*, Norway

RUDOLF BYSTRICKÝ, Charles University, *Prague*, Czecko-Slovakia

FRANCESCO CAPOTORTI, Università degli Studi, *Bari*, Italy

RENÉ CASSIN, European Court of Human Rights, *Paris*, France

FREDE CASTBERG, University of Oslo, *Oslo*, Norway

BIN CHENG, University College, *London*, England

ASBJØRN EIDE, University of Oslo, *Oslo*, Norway

FELIX ERMACORA, Universität *Wien*, Austria

J. E. S. FAWCETT, Oxford University, *Oxford*, England

C. W. JENKS, International Labour Office, *Geneva*, Switzerland

SEAN MACBRIDE, International Commission of Jurists, *Geneva*, Switzerland

A. B. MCNULTY, European Commission of Human Rights, *Strasbourg*, France

MILAN MARKOVIĆ, University of Beograd, *Beograd*, Yugoslavia

CARL AAGE NØRGAARD, Aarhus University, *Aarhus*, Denmark

TORKEL OPSAHL, University of Oslo, *Oslo*, Norway

STURE PETRÉN, The International Court of Justice, *Stockholm*, Sweden

ROGER PINTO, Université de Paris, *Paris*, France

ULRICH SCHEUNER, Universität, *Bonn*, West Germany

AUGUST SCHOU, The Norwegian Nobel Institute, *Oslo*, Norway

MARC SCHREIBER, Division of Human Rights, United Nations, *New York*, USA

EGON SCHWELB, Yale Law School, *New Haven*, Conn., USA

IMRE SZABÓ, Hungarian Academy of Sciences, *Budapest*, Hungary

TERJE WOLD, Supreme Court of Justice, *Oslo*, Norway

Address of welcome

By August Schou

The Norwegian Nobel Institute, Oslo, Norway

On behalf of the Norwegian Nobel Institute I have the honour and pleasure to welcome you to this Symposium.

Our Institute was founded in 1904 in connection with the activities of the Nobel Committee of the Norwegian Parliament.

One paragraph in our regulations reads as follows:

"The object of the Institute is to follow the development of international relations, especially the work for pacific settlement of them, and thereby councel the Committee with regard to the distribution of the Prize.

The Institute shall moreover work to promote mutual friendship and respect, peaceful intercourse, justice and fraternity between nations."

As you will see the last-mentioned section contains a very ambitious aim. It is not becoming to us to evaluate to which extent we have managed to realize these demanding objects, but frankly speaking I think we have to admit that it is not very much we have been able to achieve. In this respect, however, the Institute undoubtedly is in the same situation as other institutions of an international character. While the world with respect to technical achievements more and more is growing into a unity, it is still divided by grave political, national and ideological contrasts. In a period like ours it is indeed not too easy to make an essential contribution to realize Alfred Nobel's ideal of a "fraternity between nations".

In spite of this the Institute has tried to work along the lines of Nobel's intentions. Through educational work it has tried to make a contribution to the creation of an awake and unprejudiced public opinion in these fields.

With regard to the cultivation of international contacts the Institute has for many years been hampered by financial difficulties. It is in fact only a part of the interest amount which can be used for the administration of the institute, most of the money going into the Peace Prize. Therefore it was a very stimulating event when the board of the Tri-centennial Fund of the Bank of Sweden some years ago as a result of a petition from the Nobel Foundation in Stockholm granted an amount which made it possible to arrange international symposia within the fields represented by the five Nobel-prize groups—physics, chemistry, medicine, literature and peace-activity.

Up till now 6 Nobel symposia have been arranged in sciences and literature. The symposium which starts today is therefore the seventh in the range.

The reason why we have chosen as subject "The international Protection of Human Rights" is that in our opinion it is an essential part in the work to secure the world's peace and at the same time it seemed to us that it could be an appropriate rise for next year's jubilee for the UN's Declaration of Human Rights.

One may ask if not such a subject is of a particular utopian character. Every day we experience the whole world over gross violations of human rights, on political, ideological or racial basis. To this argument we could perhaps give the following answer: In any case the oppression will not be *less* if the doctrine of human rights and the discussions about it fell into oblivion.

It is important to go on with the work on the construction which one day may be a real bulwark for human freedom and dignity. If the work often may seem futile, it would be useful to remember those who throughout the centuries fought for human rights. Even if the outlook seemed dark they drew strength from the idea that the campaign was just about to start. Our country's great national poet Henrik Wergeland—who lived about 130 years ago—belonged to this type of clear-sighted dreamers. He was convinced that all the oppression he observed after all was of a passing nature. One important result of his own struggle for human rights was that the prohibition of immigration of Jews to Norway—a real stain on our constitution—was removed, if only after he himself had passed away. In Wergeland's opinion the human civilization had just started to grow. As he expressed it in his poetical language:

"The experiences from untold generations are just mankind's lullabies and its childhood's fairy tales."

I should think that a scientific approach to the problem of creating a more solid foundation for human rights is in the spirit of this great poet.

With these words I declare the VII Nobel Symposium to be opened.

Natural law and human rights.
An idea-historical survey

By Frede Castberg

University of Oslo, Oslo, Norway

Natural law in ancient times and the middle ages

The law of the gods and the ideas of justice in Ancient Greece. In the classical literature of Ancient Greece from the 5th century B.C. we come across a striking expression of the belief in the power exercised by the gods in a human society based on law. The gods establish a law which stands above the obligations and interdictions imposed by the rulers of the community. The oft-quoted proud words which Sophocles puts into the mouth of Antigone in her tirade against King Kreon are a condemnation of the King's commands based on the higher law of the gods:

"I did not think that these commands possessed such power that in their name mere mortals would wax bold enough to violate the gods' eternal unwrit laws; it lives for ever—not now and yesterday—and no-one knows when first it was revealed."

Here we have the *de facto* valid rules of those in power confronted with higher norms, i.e. with norms of the kind we call "natural law", to use a term which is now more than two thousand years old.

At an early stage in Greek philosophy we come across the idea of *justice,* as a guiding principle not only for the behaviour of the individual, but also for the organisation of society. The most outstanding among the Greek philosophers who speculated on the concept of justice was Aristotle (384–322 B.C.). As we know, one of the main ideas of Aristotle's ethics is that like shall be treated as like, and unlike as unlike. But what does this likeness, or unlikeness, which is supposed to be decisive in our search for justice, consist of?

The problem appears to be simplest when we are considering the exchange of one contribution for another. Aristotle speaks here of an "arithmetic" justice, which consists of a balance between contribution and countercontribution. Here, equality is the rule; however, when the question arises of sharing goods of various kinds between persons of varying qualifications, then the distribution must be proportional, based on the difference in qualifications.

Aristotle calls this justice of distribution "geometrical" justice. Positions and power, honours and riches should be distributed according to the degree of effort or the qualities that should be decisive. But what factors should be decisive? Naturally, Aristotle is unable to give any completely satisfactory answer to this question. Should power in society be distributed according to each individual's wealth, wisdom, and strength? On this point Aristotle makes it clear that the criterion should be based on expedience, without giving us any unambiguous solution.[1]

A few generations after Aristotle the school of philosophy known to us as Stoa is the most significant in the history of the development of natural law. The doctrine of the Stoics is characterised by the affinity it establishes between the regularity of Nature and the general regularity which is incumbent on human existence. The Stoics were subsequently to influence several jurists and statesmen in Ancient Rome, more particularly Marcus Tullius Cicero, whose doctrine of natural law will be mentioned in our next section.

The Roman jus naturale. The great Roman jurists were juridical technicians rather than legal philosophers.

The emperor Justinian's great legislative work contains in the résumé of Roman legal doctrine which he has called "Institutiones" (from 533 A.D.) a brief account of the fundamental concepts and distinctions involved. A distinction is made between Roman national law (jus civile) and the law which is actually common to all nations (jus gentium).[2] Jus naturale, on the other hand, is the law which Nature herself establishes. Slavery exists among all people, and in this respect is part of the jus gentium; but slavery conflicts with jus naturale, since all peoples are originally born free.

The term jus naturale is defined in greater detail by Cicero. He makes no sharp distinction between what is legally right and what the individual should respect as a moral injunction; but he does at any rate clearly express the idea that natural law is the same in Rome and Athens, both now and in future. There is one eternal and immutable law, which will apply to all peoples at all times. God is the source of this law.

The vagueness which at times exists in Roman legal philosophy between the law as a legal ideal and as a moral prescription is also expressed in the definition of the concept of justice to be found in the works of the great jurist Ulpian: Justice consists in "honeste vivere, alterum non laedere, suum cuique tribuere". Here, in fact, honest living, taking care not to harm one's neighbour, is equated with the typical principle of just law and verdict, viz. giving every man what he is entitled to.

The concept of natural law we come across in the work of the disciple of the Stoics, Cicero, is clearly a general, absolute natural law. Of necessity, it has a clearly abstract character; but in the original Roman juridical writings we also come across a less general, almost concrete natural law, in the sense of what is the "natural", that is to say the right solution of legal questions for which no answer is given in any definite legal provision. It is easy to find examples in Roman law of reasoning of this kind, based not on positive legal norms, but on "natural reason". Gaius mentions, for example, that what another man builds on my property becomes my property on the principle of "superficies solo cedit" (that is to say, the right to the buildings yields to the right of ownership to the ground). But if I lay claim to the buildings, he can protest, provided he is acting in good faith. All this is regarded as jus naturale.[3]

The ability of Roman jurists to solve legal questions in a way which is felt to be patently right, even without any explicit deduction from the principles of "natural" or other law, has been emphasized with good reason.[4] In this connection it might be opportune to recall the characteristic feature of jurisprudence familiar to all students of Roman law: "Jurisprudentia est divinarum atque humanarum rerum, justi atque injusti scientia." Another well-known characteristic describes "jurisprudentia" as "ars boni et aequi". Here, in fact, arriving at a good, fair solution is described as an art.

The Catholic doctrine of natural law in the Middle Ages. The concept of a natural law, a law raised above the positively established rules and regulations of the community, lives on in the Middle Ages in the works of the Church teachers, in the form of a belief in a law of God, above all human laws. St Augustine even goes so far as to consider that a law which violates justice is in principle invalid. "Mihi lex esse non videtur, quae justa non fuerit." But he has hardly drawn the logical conclusion of this adherence to principle, viz. that unjust laws should in no way be regarded as binding.[5]

The great authority of the Catholic Church in legal philosophy as well as in other spheres of ethical thinking, however, is St Thomas Aquinas.

Thomas Aquinas maintains that the legal rules of society only possess the quality of law if they conform with right reason; their validity is then derived from eternal principles of law. If a law deviates from the injunctions of reason, we are dealing with violence and not law. But even an unjust law borrows the validity of eternal law when it exists as a law by virtue of the authority of the lawgiver. This probably means that according to Thomas Aquinas positive law forfeits its validity and thus its binding power only if it grossly and irrefutably violates the demands of reason.

Thomas Aquinas maintains that the "speculative" (a word which appears to mean particularly the mathematical) reason is based on principles which are irrefutable, even though they are not known to all men.

Deductions derived from these principles provide unerring, irrefutable conclusions. "Practical" reason (which in this context seems to mean reason in the sphere of morals and justice) affects human actions. Here, the actual principles quite obviously apply with a certain degree of necessity; but in applying these principles, the closer one approaches the special cases, the more do these principles have to admit of exceptions. Reason, for example, demands that debts should be repaid. This applies in most cases. But what is the position if, for instance, the sum of money to be repaid is going to be used to wage war against one's own country?

Thomas Aquinas, in fact, is aware of the problems that will arise in applying principles in special cases; and his ideas of natural law have developed points of contact with the ideas in our own age of the varying contents of natural law, depending on time and place. Thomas Aquinas only regards wilful actions as ethically relevant. He appears to accept a certain freedom of will as a precondition for rational legal and moral evaluation. In the question of law and freedom of will, too, Thomas Aquinas is in harmony with various marked trends of law and value judgments on law in our own age.[6]

It is clear that the belief in natural law as a higher law, above positive systems of law, was a matter of *dead earnest* in the Catholic philosophy of law. Well into recent times Catholic Church teaching preached the right to the murder of tyrants. When the fanatical Catholic Ravaillac murdered King Henry IV in 1610 he claimed that he had acted in accordance with the law (justice). According to extreme Catholic notions Henry was not only a "tyran d'exercice", because of the way in which he ruled; he was also a "tyran d'usurpation". According to this view he had no right whatever to be king of France. He violated a higher law than the rules and regulations of secular rulers, because he had failed to protect the Church and the Catholic faith. The right to murder a tyrant was rooted in the traditional Church teaching of the Middle Ages, whose sources were both biblical accounts and the legal philosophy of the Ancient World.[7]

Natural law in recent times

Extreme doctrine of natural law, based on reason. Hugo Grotius is undoubtedly one of the great figures not only in the history of international law, but also in the history of natural law. His writings mark a clear break with the older doctrine of natural law, which sought to derive natural law, the higher justice, from the Holy Scriptures and the will of God. Grotius' natural law is a law of reason pure and simple. Admittedly, Grotius in no way assumes a standpoint opposed to Christianity; furthermore, he regards everything that exists, including human reason, as the work of God. But the commandments of natural law are not God's command, any more than mathematical propositions are. On this point Grotius makes a statement that is particularly characteristic. He writes in his work "De jure belli et pacis":[8]

"The law of nature, again, is unchangeable—even in the sense that it cannot be changed by God. Measureless as is the power of God, nevertheless it can be said that there are certain things over which that power does not extend; for things of which this is said are spoken only, having no sense corresponding with reality and being mutually contradictory. Just as even God, then, cannot cause that two times two should not make four, so He cannot cause that that which is intrisically evil be not evil."[9]

It has been said, not without good reason, that this bold, secularized view of the basic problem of natural law marks a turning-point in the history of thinking.[10]

The major representatives of the idea of natural law in the 17th century had on the whole a peculiar idea of certainty with regard to the viewpoints they maintained on law and morals, justice, and binding international law. Pufendorf declares with regard to deductions from principles of right and wrong that no person in his senses can doubt them.[11] He maintains the certainty and unassailability of ethical reasoning as compared with the un-certainty the historian encounters when he endeavours to establish the his-torical truth on the basis of the testimony of the past.[12]

In the Age of Enlightenment, and in the works of ideologists of the French Revolution, we come across the idea familiar to us from the Greek Stoics and from Cicero's philosophical authorship, that natural law—the "right" law —must be the same for all peoples and at all times.[13] Just as the world is governed by eternal laws of nature, so the laws and rules governing human society are eternal and immutable.

The doctrine of the social contract. In the doctrine of the state and of author-ity of the state organs the theory of the social contract plays a dominant role in both the 17th and 18the centuries. A legal philosopher who significantly influenced the development of this way of thinking was the German Johannes Althusius (c. 1600).[14] The doctrine of the social contract presupposes the irrefutable validity of the proposition that contracts must be kept. If the organisation of the state and the power of its ruler can be based on a contract, then the existing state system, is rooted in natural law. The social contract is not only the original basis for the state and the power of its ruler: it is also constantly renewed in one form or another, even though tacitly.

It is an argument of this kind that is assumed to justify absolute monarchy. It is significant, for example, that after 1660 the Dano-Norwegian absolute monarchy desired to establish its formal legality by obtaining the confirmation

of the assemblies of the estates—in Denmark from January 1661, and in the
case of Norway from August of the same year. The resolutions passed by
the assemblies of the estates were tantamount to popular recognition of the
autocracy that had in fact been established the year before.

Thus, in this way the doctrine of the social contract was to serve to legalise
the existing state regime. But the doctrine of the social contract played politically a still more important role in the ideological systems that demanded
a change in the status quo involving the sovereignty of the people and the
recognition of human rights.

In Jean Jacques Rousseau's book from 1762, Du Contrat Social, the social
contract is depicted as an agreement entered into between the various members of the community in an original state of nature, in which all enjoy equal
rights. This agreement, whereby all members of society subordinate themselves to the general will ("la volonté générale"), creates "the sovereign".
The general will is synonymous with the will of the majority, since all are
equal. My own will merges with this general will, which for Rousseau appears
to have been a mystic collective will; and this will is not only general, in the
sense that it is the will of all or the majority: it is also general in its form.
In other words, it is synonymous with the law, the general norm. And for the
will of the sovereign in its highest form, as a general law, no legal limits
could apply.

The doctrine of human rights

The new attitude. During the Age of Enlightenment, and the American and
French revolutions in the last quarter of the 18th century, we come across
a new manifestation of the concept of natural law. In ancient times and the
Middle Ages the concept of natural law had always envisaged the eternal
natural law, conceived as principles of a right law or as patently correct solutions of concrete legal questions.

The attention is now directed more to the rights of the individual than to
objective norms. This new trend in the reasoning of natural law finds its expression, as it has been said, rather as a "theory of rights" than as a "theory
of law".[15]

The universal principles of natural law which formed the basis in the
solemn declarations of the American and French revolutions were formulated
as the recognition of the eternal and inviolable individual rights of man and
the citizen.

The classical presentation of the ideology of natural law is the one produced as early as 1689, viz. in John Locke's essay on civil government. Locke
operates with the concept of an original state of nature, before any national

community or any state power had been organised, where all people have the same rights and obligations in common, and where everyone is entitled to defend his right to life, freedom, and property. The organised community is established by means of a social contract, whose primary object is to confirm and protect these individual rights. But the individual has not abandoned more of his original rights in the natural state than necessary for this purpose. To the extent that individual rights have not been abandoned, they still exist, and they are eternal, unforfeitable, and inviolable.

At times it is not quite clear to what extent Locke and other theoreticians of natural law in the 17th and 18th centuries imagined that a natural state of this kind had once existed, and that the state society had in fact arisen in this way. It is maybe just as probable that the theory of a natural condition and a social contract was intended to be accepted as a fiction—an imaginary construction whose aim was to provide a reason (origin) both for the power of the state and also for inviolable human rights. The historical importance of this theory for political development as well as for the evolution of constitutional law is at any rate indisputable.

The declaration of human rights of 1789. This "Declaration des Droits de l'Homme et du Citoyen", which was adopted by the French legislative assembly, remains to this day the classic formulation of the inviolable rights of the individual vis-à-vis the state. The remarkable thing that occurs with the adoption of this declaration is that the inviolable, natural-law human rights are set forth in a state document and thus, in so far as that goes, incorporated in national positive law.

At one time a lively argument was waged between scholars, especially French and German, as to what should be regarded as the ideahistorical background for this event. In actual fact, the English colonial settlements in North America had initiated their war of freedom against the Mother Country as far back as 1776 by invoking the principle of freedom and equality for all men. The opening words of paragraph 2 of the American Declaration of Independence of 4 July 1776 are well known:

"We hold these truths to be self-evident, that all men are created equal, that they are endowed by their Creator with certain unalienable Rights . . ."

In the same year that the Declaration of Independence was adopted in Philadelphia, one of the older colonies, Virginia, drew up a declaration of rights which, like the subsequent French declaration, professed eternal, inviolable human rights. The German constitutional law theoretician Georg Jellinek propounded in his famous thesis from 1895 the theory that the line of development runs from the Reformation and its demand for freedom of conscience to the struggle of the American colonies for religious freedom and independence, and then—and only then—to France and the Declaration of 1789.[16] Another scholar and authority of Imperial Germany, Otto v. Gierke, even goes so far as to say of the Declarations of Rights that their source is to be found in "die uralte und unausrottbare germanische Freiheitsidee".[17] French scholars[18] on the other hand maintain that the French Declaration of 1789 was derived primarily from the European literature of enlightenment.

It suffices to observe that here, as so often in history whether we are dealing with the history of ideas or political history, various forces and ideological trends act and interact on one another. It is obvious that the American War of Independence and the constitutional documents it produced proved a source of inspiration to a great many people, not least revolutionary France. At the same time it stands to reason that the English colonists in America also derived their ideas from inherited English traditions. The American declarations emphasize rights which Englishmen had maintained, in their disputes with the Stuarts, as rights of liberty inherited by all Englishmen.

However this may be, it is the French Declaration of 1789 which provides, from the point of view of literature, the most fortuitous formulation of the contemporary concept of the inviolable rights of man and citizen vis-à-vis the state. It is, furthermore, this declaration which has historically speaking played the most important role in the constitutional policy of subsequent ages. Jellinek is entirely right when he declares that political history of ideas must not be political literary history, but must always be considered in relation to the history of constitutional realities.

The Declaration of Human Rights of 1789 contains concise expressions of the principle of the sovereignty of the people, the principle of legality (that restrictions on the freedom of action of citizens can only be established by law), the principle of the distribution of powers, the principle of fair justice, and, furthermore, a number of inviolable rights to freedom. All subsequent republican constitutions in France have acknowledged these principles,[19] which has also influenced, directly or indirectly, a number of subsequent state constitutions in many other countries.

Human rights and the right to revolt. The right to revolt against a tyrannical ruler was, as already mentioned, recognised in Catholic Church teaching in the Middle Ages. In principle, the doctrine of the right to revolt is also to be found among the theoreticians of autocratic government. The celebrated champion of absolute monarchy, Jean Bodin, declares in his *magnum opus* from 1608[20] that a tyrannical monarch is one who violates the freedom of his subjects, "by trampling the laws of Nature beneath his feet".[21] A tyrant is someone who has seized power without warrant—"without being elected, without hereditary rights, without right acquired by drawing lots, or by a just war and without any special vocation from God". Even the murder of a tyrant of this kind was justified.[22] The ecclesiastical champion of absolute monarchy under Louis XIV, Bossuet,[23] deduced from the Scriptures a doctrine that God's punishment will visit the tyrannical monarch.

One of the results of the glorious revolution in England in 1688 was that Parliament in its Declaration of Rights of 1689 established the rights of people and parliament vis-à-vis the King. This declaration enumerates James II's many offences, which prove that he has "endeavoured to subvert and extirpate the protestant religion, and the laws and liberties of this kingdom". It was this which in the eyes of Englishman had justified rising and revolting against their king and driving him from the throne.

In the introduction to the American Declaration of Independence of 4 July 1776, the right to revolt is unequivocally established:

"But when a long train of abuses and usurpations, pursuing invariably the same object, evinces a design to reduce them [men] under absolute Despotism, it is their right, it is their duty, to throw off such Government, and to provide new Guards for their future security."

The right to revolt has been given a particularly precise and radical wording in the French revolutionary constitution of 1793, which admittedly never came into force:

"When the Government violates the rights of the people, revolt is the most sacred of all rights and the most unbreakable of all duties, not only for the people, but for every part of the people."[24]

Reaction against natural law

Traditionalism and the philosophy of utility in England. The doctrine of natural law at the turn of the century after the French Revolution was a doctrine on abstract, immutable principles and eternal, inviolable human rights. It is against this ideology of natural law that the reaction sets in with tremendous violence in many countries.

In England Edmund Burke, above all others, launches his attack against the assertion of the natural law doctrine of the eternal, abstract rights to freedom and equality. Burke is certainly no positivist, in the sense that he is prepared to accept existing systems of government under all circumstances; nor is he by any means an ethical "realist" in the modern sense that he is prepared to dispute the very principle of objectively valid moral assessments. He does not dispute "the *real* rights of man".[25]

It is the claim of the doctrine of the rights of man for equality that he attacks: he speaks of the contempt which the ideologists of human rights have for experience. No limitation is valid against their human rights; no agreement can be invoked against them, no comprise applies.

"Against these their rights of men let no government look for security in the length of its continuance, or in the justice and lenity of its administration."[26]

Thus Burke does not attack natural law *per se,* in the sense of norms which are higher than positive law; but he is "the main champion of the historical tradition of England".[27] And it was because of his violent attack on human rights and above all on the revolutionary ideas of equality that Burke provided the principal target for the attacks of contemporary ideologists of freedom and equality.[28]

Later on, it was the champions of the philosophy of utility in England who attacked the abstract doctrine of natural law and the ideology of human rights. Jeremy Bentham describes natural law as "nothing but a phrase". According to him there is hardly a single law which those who dislike it will not consider "repugnant to some text of scripture". The doctrine of natural law compels a man, on the dictates of his conscience, to take arms against any law which he may happen to dislike. Bentham leaves it to his opponents to explain what sort of government can survive in face of an attitude of this kind. "It is the principle of *utility* accurately apprehended and steadily applied, that affords the only clue to guide a man through these straits."[29]

This last sentence expresses in a nutshell the principle of the philosophy of utility in judging the legal order. Utilitarianism, too, contains an *a priori* principle, viz. that legislation should be of such a kind that it promotes the greatest possible happiness for the greatest possible number of people; but absolute norms and absolute human rights are rigorously rejected.

In the work of Bentham's disciple in the utilitarian ethics, John Stuart Mill, the *a priori* moral point of departure emerges clearly in the formulation of the demand for happiness, which the legal set-up is to satisfy: I regard utility as the ultimate appeal on all ethical questions; but is must be utility in the largest sense, grounded on the permanent interests of a man as a progressive being.[30]

The decisive goal, in other words, is not happiness such as men in fact desire, but such as they *ought* rightly to desire.

As we know, Mill was an outstanding champion of freedom in society, especially, intellectual freedom and the political and social emancipation of women. He makes a vigorous plea for intellectual freedom on the grounds of the usefulness of free speech to the community; but he also says: If all mankind minus one, were of one opinion, and only one person were of the contrary opinion, mankind would be no more justified in silencing that one person, than he, if he had the power, would be justified in silencing mankind.[31]

It is difficult to see how this last remark can be said to differ greatly from the standpoint of natural law, that we are faced with an inviolable, individual human right.

German legal positivism. In Germany, the reaction against the philosophy of natural law emerges first and foremost with the so-called "Historical School" of jurisprudence. The great name associated with this trend is Friedrich v. Savigny. In his well-known pamphlet from 1814, Vom Beruf unserer Zeit für Gesetzgebung und Rechtswissenschaft, he rejects the idea of giving permanent form to German law in the shape of a codification. The law lives in the consciousness of the people, it is a creation of the people's spirit. He regards any attempt to codify a country's laws according to the dictates of a universal "law of reason" to be "a grandiloquent, completely hollow idea".[32]

It is obvious that this represents a trend in the conception of the nature of the law, which is akin to the national-romantic view we also encounter in contemporary art, literature, and history.

Throughout the 19th century German legal theory was marked by a positivism that was often extreme. In legal theory and the practice of law the positively established legal norms, i.e. the rules of legislation and customary law became the only object of scientific study and practised application.

Any belief in objectively valid norms for right and wrong was regarded as metaphysical, and therefore rejected. It was the task of jurisprudence, by means of logical mental processes, to arrive at the correct solution of every question involving the application of positive law and right. It was precisely in German jurisprudence that formal logical way of reasoning was to prove particularly dominant.

At the same time, it is in German jurisprudence that we also first come across a vigorous profession of what the actual purpose of a legal rule inevitably involves in its interpretation and application. "Der Zweck ist der Schöpfer des gesamten Rechts", declares the great German jurist Rudolph v. Ihering in a work written in 1877.[33] v. Ihering is the enthusiastic champion of the sanctity of law—the valid, positive law. His quasi-religious attitude to the law in force gives him all the appearance of a sort of jurist of natural law, but in such a way that positive law is his natural law.

Sociological jurisprudence and legal realism. Other forms of intentionally anti-natural-law trends in the jurisprudence of the 19th and 20th centuries are the American so-called "sociological" legal reasoning, the German and Nordic "free-law" method, and the American and Nordic "realism" in jurisprudence. It would be impossible within the scope of this survey to give a detailed account of these partly purely methodological, partly markedly legal-philosophical theories. Space will only allow a brief glimpse at certain salient points.

Both the American "sociological" jurisprudence and the German "free-legal" reasoning are anti-methaphysical, focusing their interest on social realities. Both trends really start at the beginning of this century, marking a break with the generalising, formal-logical, so-called "conceptual jurisprudence" which was a typical feature of jurisprudence, especially in Germany, but also in a great many other countries in the 19th century. The aim now was to interpret the law on the basis of its reasonable aims, without being slavishly bound by the wording of the law or jurisprudential generalisations.

All these trends in the reasoning of legal positivism certainly run counter to natural law; but they also have one feature in common, viz. that they regard the rules of law—positive law—as norms which according to their intention place certain obligations on the members of society; and they operate with the concept of rights and duties, based on the rules of law. In term of ordinary legal interpretation these are not norms, rights, and duties identical with moral norms and demands: a congruity of this kind may—but need not—exist.

A more recent trend in jurisprudence also brands this traditional ideology of norms and rights as methaphysical and superstitious. American legal realism appears to be on the wane. In the Nordic countries a movement which has arisen completely independently of the American one, has played a dominant role ever since the discerning Swedish philosopher Axel Hägerström in 1911 held his inaugural lecture "On the truth of moral concepts". Hägerström's rejection of the jurists' ideology of obligations and rights was maintained, and an attempt made to carry it through in legal theory by the Swedish professors Vilhelm Lundstedt and Karl Olivecrona. In Denmark, the dominant figure in the struggle against the traditional so-called "legal idealism" has been Alf Ross. He considers that the *scientific* task of legal reasoning is to foresee how the courts and other authoritative bodies within the state are likely to act, entirely factually, in the future. Natural law has nothing to do with the science of law. The concepts "just" and "unjust" have no reasonable meaning in propositions on existing or proposed legal rules and regulations. To say that a law is unjust is a subjective expression of emotion and nothing else.[34]

Scandinavian and American "realism" may be regarded as the most extreme expression of the positivist and anti-natural-law juridical reasoning of our age.

Natural law once again—covert and overt

The covert natural law. Any appreciation of the law in force that claims to be objectively correct must necessarily be based on assessment premises which are assumed to possess objective validity. This applies, for example, clearly to the legal philosophy of the utilitarians or the philosophy of utility, when they assess legal rules on the basis of their ability to promote universal happiness. That it is right to promote the happiness of the greatest possible number of people is an ethical postulate of a kind that is regarded as indisputably correct. Furthermore, the actual weighing of conflicting interests presupposes a scale of values which is objectively right; and the "happiness" to be promoted is, as already shown, not the "happiness" that any person may choose himself, but on the contrary a "happiness" which it is right and justifiable for him to choose. An ethical appreciation which claims to possess objective validity accompanies the doctrine of utilitarianism so to speak at every step; even the basic reasoning of this doctrine is a principle to which is attributed universal, one might say absolute, validity.

Another kind of covert or unconscious natural law ideology is to be found among the "law positivists", who pursue their science in the spirit of the German historical school. The great German authority on constitutional law in the period between the Franco-Prussian War and the First World War, Paul Laband, possesses to a very high degree the style of "Begriffsjurisprudenz" (conceptual jurisprudence) in his scholarly *magnum opus* on German constitutional law. He emphasizes that the basic legal concepts are immutable in all legal systems. The creation of a new legal category, incapable in any way whatever of being subordinated to a higher, more universal concept of law, is just as impossible as it would be to discover a new logical category or for a new natural force to arise.[35] When all is said and done, this is a train of thought which is closely akin to the doctrine of natural law on eternal valid principles of law.

Jurisprudence in Germany in the 19th century, moreover, was greatly influenced by the interest in Roman law. The nuanced, logically fascinating legal reasoning of the Roman jurists was considered by v. Savigny and other Germans as "die Fleisch-gewordene Vernunft".[36] It was precisely the natural law feature of the reasoning of Roman jurists that appeared so brilliant and created a school of following.[37]

The renaissance of natural law in Germany after the Second World War.
When Hitler's National Socialist tyranny had collapsed, German law philosophy and legal science underwent an abrupt change of course. In the
opinion of a great many people, German legal positivism was now shown
to have been a fatal mistake. Many people took the view that the unreserved
acceptance on the part of German jurists of the regime introduced by the
de facto rulers of the country was closely related to their legal-philosophical
positivism.

A great many jurists and law philosophers in Germany have adopted the
natural law idea after the war, and in many cases drawn far-reaching conclusions from this standpoint. Very many have taken Christianity as their basis.
This is true both of Germany and Austria. Professor Gerhard Leibholz, who
was forced to leave Germany when Hitler came to power, resumed his pro-
fessorship after the war, and also became a member of the newly established
constitutional tribunal in Karlsruhe. In his article "Politics and Natural Law"
he professes his belief in a natural law "which flows from the eternal law
of God".[38] It is the right of a Christian person and his duty towards God
to resist tyranny in order to overthrow its regime.[39] The connection between
natural law and Christianity is emphasized by all participants in the natural
law discussion published in the Österreichische Zeitschrift für öffentliches
Recht, 1963, Fascicule No. 2.[40] Others appear to base their natural law
standpoint on non-religious foundation.

It is particularly interesting to note the profound influence which the conviction of "supra-positive" law has left in German constitutional legislation
and in constitutional law court practice. The Bonn Constitution of 1949 is
to a very considerable degree marked by a desire to build on fundamental
principles which must never be violated. Art. 1, paragraphs 1 and 2 of the
Constitution, declares:

"1. Man's dignity is inviolable. It is the duty of all state authority (power) to
respect and protect it.
2. For this reason the German people accepts the inviolable and immutable
human rights as the basis of every human society, of peace and justice in
the world."

The most important principles of freedom and democratic government cannot in any way be altered according to the very rules of the Bonn Constitution itself.[41] Even the state organ which is competent to alter the Constitution
is thus prevented from undertaking any such changes that violate these
principles. This was expressly stated by the Federal Constitutional Court in
Karlsruhe in a judgment of 1951. The Bavarian Constitutional Court has
established in a celebrated judgment from 1949 that there are fundamental
principles of justice which are also binding on the legislator, and provisions

in the Constitution which violate these principles may be regarded as invalid.[42]

In a number of cases the courts have refused to accept as valid German law Nazi rules and regulations of the kind that violated elementary principles of humanity and justice. With this in mind it is easy to understand the statement that German law set the principle: "Naturrecht bricht positives Recht."[43] (Natural law supersedes positive law.)

This provides the basis for several German judgments on German war criminals, in full agreement with what might be described as popular opinion in both the democratic West and the Communist East. German war criminals are convicted even though they acted on the orders of officials of the Nazi regime. The extermination of the Jews has been regarded as murder, irrespective of the fact that it was organised as a result of decisions taken up by the highest authority in the state.[44] The courts have declared illegal the act of obeying Hitler's notorious "Catastrophe Orders" from the last period of the war to the effect that every deserter should be executed without a trial.

On the other hand there is no denying that the courts have also made decisions which it would be difficult to explain except by the fact that a somewhat extreme form of Christian sexual morals has been raised to the status of universal "natural law". In a judgment of 1954 the Supreme Court of the Federal Republic convicted a mother for procuring, because she had not prevented a daughter, who was living at home, from indulging in an affair with a married man.[45] It may safely be said that millions of enlightened and decent people throughout the European-American cultural community today would be in profound disagreement with this kind of viewpoint.

Natural-law reasoning in the United States. Not only, as we have already seen, was the American Declaration of Independence of 1776 based on the natural-law doctrine of man's innate right to freedom and equality, and not only was the actual revolt against English colonial government based on the right to revolt which is deeply rooted in natural law, but a whole series of central human rights were expressly established, some in the actual constitution of 1787, and some in the ten amendments adopted by Congress in 1789, and usually called "the Bill of Rights".

Of special interest is the rule that no one shall be deprived of his freedom or property except by due process of law.

During a period of about one hundred and fifty years after the Constitution was adopted, the rule of "due process" has been used by the courts to reject as unconstitutional a great many laws involving the right of property or regulating the freedom of contract. There is no space here to give an account of this interesting aspect of the constitutional and political history of the United States. But in order to throw light on the history of natural law it is of interest to mention that through long periods the judges have seemed to regard the right to property and liberty as pre-existent human rights in relation to state legislation. This way of thinking appears to lie at the root of a judgment from as far back as 1815 on a private licensing right.[46] However, the view of the right of property as a right rooted in natural law, preceding all state power, has been particularly noticeable at times when the courts have gone a long way to override radical, social, and economic legislation.

It is, at the same time, striking that the courts of the United States in this century should have shown a tendency to base their decisions rather on considerations of utility and justice than on the basis of an expressed doctrine of rights which is to be regarded as applying prior to and independently of the Constitution. The "due process" articles have often been interpreted on the basis of the judges' conception of social utility and justice. At the beginning of this century the desire was to maintain the domination of private property right and far-reaching freedom of contract. Subsequently—and especially after the sensational struggle between the Supreme Court and President Franklin D. Roosevelt in 1936–37—the federal courts appear to have altered radically their social views and with them the application of the Constitution in the field of the policy of economic regulations. Both the Supreme Court in Washington and other courts have exercised their authority to supervise the legislative power with a much greater degree of caution. In dealing with economic and social legislation the federal courts practise a clear judicial restraint.

In return, the powerful court in Washington has proved all the bolder in its interpretation of the Constitution with regard to legislation—particularly state legislation—concerning freedom of expression, religious freedom, freedom of assembly, and the right to racial equality. Here, there are certainly few signs of judicial restraint, but rather a marked "judicial activism". The Supreme Court has protected freedom of expression and freedom of assembly in numerous judgments, primarily against the ruling of state legislative assemblies. However, it is not the concept of freedom of expression and freedom of assembly as inviolable, individual human rights that has been the leading viewpoint; it is rather the belief in these rights as necessary conditions for an effective democratic government. Time and again in Supreme Court judgments in cases of this kind we come across the observation that the community needs free discussion and full access to an expression of opinion. For only in this way can the best results, from the point of view of community interests, be achieved.[47]

With regard to the Supreme Court's defence of religious freedom and particularly racial equality, social-psychological investigations play an important role in the interpretation of the Constitution. When the Supreme Court, in its celebrated judgment of May 17, 1954, unanimously denounced the segregational principle of "equal but separate", great emphasis was attached to the fact that excluding Negroes from white schools would involve psychologically detrimental effects, irrespective of whether they could be sent to Negro schools which formally were just as good.

However, the fact that the reasoning in these matters of rights could be given such a sociological slant, does not mean that the belief in objective justice and innate human dignity does not lie at the root of many of the court decisions that have been handed down in recent times in defence of the rights we have mentioned. By and large, it is striking how much American political reasoning is still influenced by the ideology of natural law, both among progressives and among conservatives. Most frequently it is the tradition from the Revolution of 1776 that is invoked. Extreme conservatism and nationalism can march beneath the banner of "the Sons of the Revolution", or "the Daughters" thereof. But even the progressive idealism which always forms part of the picture of American politics is anchored in the natural law tradition. In President John F. Kennedy's inaugural address on January 20, 1961, the following passage occurred:

"And yet the same revolutionary beliefs for which our forebears fought are still at issue around the globe—the belief that the rights of man come not from the generosity of the state but from the hand of God."

Natural law and human rights in the international community

International law as positivised, classical natural law. The international-law framers who formulated the doctrine of international law in the 17th and 18th centuries, Hugo Grotius, Pufendorf, Vattel, and many others, based themselves entirely on the tradition of natural law. They took as their starting point principles whose validity was considered beyond doubt, such as the right to life and freedom, the idea of equality, and the rule that agreements shall be kept (pacta sunt servanda). From these principles they derived a doctrine of the basic rights of states in the international community. Sovereign states were legally equal, independent in their relations to other states, not bound by other obligations than those they had themselves assumed, and in all respects they were free to rule their own territory. These principles came to be recognised in international practice to highly general and vague fundamental principles, which it would be difficult to describe as anything but as natural law. This is especially the case with the IV Hague Convention of 1907 on the rules of war, which declares in its introduction that, apart from the rules of international law, states are bound by "the demands of humanity and public conscience".

The position of the individual in international law. According to traditional international law theory states have been regarded as the only legal subjects in positive international law, that is to say, in the system of international rules based in treaty and custom. It is in accordance with this somewhat rigid doctrine that, when one state treats the subject of another state in a manner that violates international law, then this is regarded as a legal offence committed against the state of which that person is a subject, and not against the person who has suffered injury.

During the last three or four decades, however, there has been a tendency in this sphere to regard private individuals, too, as having certain rights and obligations according to various norms of international law. It is characteristic that even the German authorities during the Occupation of Norway did not venture to reject the invocation of the IV. Hague Convention by Norwegian individuals and organizations, on the pretext that only states could invoke international law. In this connection it is beside the point that the invocation of the Hague Convention or any other form of international law seldom produced any concrete results.

A much-disputed question in European politics has been whether or to what extent states are entitled to intervene in the affairs of other states on a purely humanitarian basis. The great English liberal statesman, Gladstone, conducted a violent political struggle in the 1870's in order to secure British intervention to prevent the cruelties inflicted by the Turkish authorities on their Bulgarian subjects. His opponent, Disraeli, won in the struggle about intervention. But the question of humanitarian intervention had been raised; no other basis existed apart from moral and international natural law.

After the First World War came the provisions of the League of Nations Charter, as well as a whole series of special agreements for the protection of national minorities and of the population in the so-called mandated territories.

In this way international protection of individuals and groups of people had secured a not unimportant foothold in positive international law; but the great and sensational advances in this area belong to the period after the Second World War.

The United Nations Charter and the Declaration of Human Rights of 1948. Several provisions of the United Nations Charter[48] deal with inviolable human rights, and in 1948 the General Assembly adopted "the Universal Declaration of Human Rights", which sets out in detail the nature of these internationally recognized rights.

In the introduction to this declaration the underlying motives are mentioned. It declares that the recognition of "the inherent dignity" of all men and of their "equal and inalienable rights" constitutes the basis of freedom, justice, and peace. This recognition is said to be necessary in order to avoid a state of affairs in which men are compelled to have recourse as a last resort, to rebellion against tyranny and oppression.

Furthermore, the aim is to promote progress and cooperation between the nations.

The basis of these somewhat vaguely formulated aims and objects is actually highly varying moral and religious ideologies. In the debate in the United Nations Assembly in 1948 strictly Christian postulates of belief were confronted with the economic materialism of East European Marxists. Nevertheless, the declaration, with its introduction and thirty-six articles, was unanimously adopted.

No-one will deny that in its essence the declaration is a document involving moral obligations; but from the very first the question as to whether it is also of significance in the domain of international law has been disputed. It has been maintained that it will inevitably have a bearing on the interpretation of the specific articles of rights of the U.N. Charter and on the competence of the General Assembly in questions involving the violation of these articles. Others have expressed the opinion that from the purely legal point of view the declaration has no effect whatever.

Again and again assertions in the United Nations of alleged violations by certain states of human rights have been countered by quoting Art. 2, § 7, of the Charter, which guarantees member-states the right to arrange their own internal affairs. Nevertheless, it can safely be stated that to an increasing extent the General Assembly of the United Nations has tended to attach greater importance to considerations of human rights than to the assertion of the state's independent jurisdiction in its own domestic affairs. In this connection the declaration of 1948 has been of great significance, despite the fact that it is not a binding agreement of international law but a proclamation of morally binding norms. The General Assembly, for example, in 1949 expressed its condemnation of the Soviet Union's refusal to allow Russian women, married to foreigners, to leave the country. In 1954, 1961, and 1966 it has repudiated racial discrimination in South Africa, and in 1960 adopted a declaration on the granting of independence to colonial peoples and countries.[49] Here, the right of nations to self-determination is clearly regarded as a consequence of the natural law claim to freedom and equality.

The European Convention on Human Rights of 1950 and the Protocol of 1952. The motives underlying this convention, which are mentioned in its introduction, are unusual, in so far as they characterize the maintenance and development of human rights and fundamental freedoms as one of the ways and means of achieving the aims of the European Council, viz. greater unity among its members. At the same time the signatories to the convention affirm "their profound belief in those fundamental freedoms, which are the basis of justice and peace in the world".

This convention sets up a system for dealing with, and under certain circumstances for making binding decisions on complaints—including those lodged by private individuals and groups—of alleged violations of the provisions of the convention (or the supplementary protocol). There are probably grounds for describing the arrangement as an attempt to create a positive-legal, international protection of human rights, on the lines generally agreed on today.

While this is not the place for a juridical analysis of these treaty provisions, it should suffice to mention two contrary tendencies which are apparent in the preparatory work of the convention, and which may also be said to arise in the interpretation of these provisions. These tendencies are not only apparent in the literature, but also to some extent in the practice adopted by the judicial and quasi-judicial organs established in Strasbourg in compliance with the rules of the convention.

In the preparatory work in the different instances in the European Council one comes across the idea that the aim of the convention is to protect and maintain a number of minimum demands of legislation, administration, and judicial procedure in member-states. The object is to prevent the development, anywhere within the sphere of the European Council, of oppressive and inhumane tendencies. The convention aims to promote the maintenance of a sort of minimum of natural law in democratic Europe. But there is also evidence that the convention and its institutions are intended to place such obligations on national legal systems that states are obliged to reform existing codes and proceed still further than they have done hitherto in ensuring the individual's rights and freedom.[50]

Here we come across signs of the contrast existing between the minimum demands that the ideology of natural law makes of the legal system, and the ideals for future development which are at all times an effective factor in the life of the community.

Reform, in the shape of new rights, over and above the old classical rights, cannot be realised in positive law merely by an interpretation of the Convention of Human Rights and by the first supplementary protocol. In order to ensure further development, and to oblige states to submit to new international obligations, new supplementary protocols to the Convention of Human Rights have been drafted. As yet (summer, 1967) they have not come into force.

In 1961, however, a European Social Charter has been established. This lists a series of minimum demands for the social legislation of treaty signatories. This charter can be adopted wholly or partially. In order to become a party to the treaty, a state need only adhere to a certain number of the articles of the Charter.[51] We are here confronted with principles which do not express the minimum demands of natural law. These are aims to be realized in the future, the ideal demands of social policy.

NOTES

[1] Of the wealth of literature on Aristotle's concept of justice, I would like to mention: Villey, *Leçons de l'Histoire de la Philosophie de Droit* (1962), p. 28.

[2] The expression "jus gentium" develops in more recent times into the concept for the rules of law regulating relationships between states, i.e. international law.

[3] Gaius, *Institutiones,* Book 2, pp. 73–76. Cf. the *Digests,* Book 9, II-50.

[4] See particularly Fritz Schulz, *History of Roman Legal Science,* pp. 70–71, and, by the same author, *Prinzipien des römischen Rechts* (1934), p. 24. Cf. also D'Entrèves, *Natural Law* (1951), pp. 29–30 and 24–26.

[5] Friedrich, *The Philosophy of Law in Historic Perspective* (1958), p. 39.

[6] Cf. K. E. Tranøy: *Thomas av Aquino som moralfilosof* (Thomas Aquinas as Moral Philosopher), pp. 29–51 and 92–96; Batiffol, *La Philosophie de Droit* (1960), p. 63.

[7] The case of Ravaillac and the ideological problems it raised are dealt with by Roland Mousnier in *L'assassinat d'Henri IV* (1964).

[8] This difference between Grotius's view and the attitude of the Catholic medieval philosophers has in my opinion not been fully recognized by Kelsen in an article he wrote in the *Österreichische Zeitschrift für öffentliches Recht* (1963), pp. 34–35.

[9] Book 1, chapter 1, 5.

[10] D'Entrèves, *Natural Law* (1951), p. 70.

[11] Pufendorf, *De jure naturae et gentium* (1672), Book 1, chapter 2, 8.

[12] Op. cit., chapter 2, 9.

[13] See Batiffol, *La Philosophie du Droit* (1960), p. 58.

[14] On Althusius, see Otto v. Gierke, *Johannes Althusius* (1904).

[15] D'Entrèves, *Natural Law* (1951), p. 59. Cf. also Schulz, *Prinzipien des römischen Rechts* (1934), pp. 110–111, on the supreme power of the state inconformity with the theoretical view of Roman law on the relationship between the individual and the state in Roman law.

[16] G. Jellinek, *Die Erklärung der Menschen- und Bürgerrechte.*

[17] Otto v. Gierke, *Johannes Althusius,* p. 346.

[18] Boutmy *et al.* Cf., *inter alia,* my article in Festschrift Verdioss (1960) and Oestreich, Die Entwicklung der Menschenrechte und Grundfreiheiten, in the work: *Die Grundrechte* (ed. Bettermann, Neumann, and Nipperday), I (1966), p. 1 et seq., especially pp. 52–53.

[19] With regard to the political struggle centering round the principles of the "Declaration of Human Rights" Léon Blum has written (1935) a short but interesting article published in *L'Œuvre de Léon Blum,* IV, pp. 497 et seq.

[20] *Six livres de la République.*

[21] p. 287.

[22] pp. 297–98.

[23] *Politique tirée des propres paroles de l'Écriture Sainte,* Liv. VIII, IIe art., IVe prop.

[24] Art. 35.

[25] Burke, *Reflections on the Revolution in France, Works,* II, pp. 331–332.

[26] p. 331.

[27] Ernest Baker, Burke on the French Revolution. In *Essays on Government* (1946), p. 221.

[28] A typical example of this is Thom Paine. See, for example, Paine, *Works,* I, p. 81, and II, p. 5.

[29] J. Bentham, *A Fragment on Government,* chapter 4.

[30] J. St. Mill, *On Liberty.* (People's edition) (1880), p. 6.

[31] Op. cit., p. 10.

[32] Op. cit., p. 18.

[33] *Der Zweck im Recht I,* Vorrede, p. VI.

[34] On Law and Justice (1958), p. 274.

[35] P. Laband, *Das Staatsrecht des Deutschen Reiches* (1876), I Preface, pp. II–III.

[36] Mitteis, *Über das Naturrecht* (1948), p. 27.

[37] Fritz Schulz, *Prinzipien des römischen Rechts* (1934), pp. 24–25.

[38] Collection: *Politics and Law,* p. 22.

[39] The article "Memoir of Dietrich Bonhoeffer" in the collection quoted, pp. 150–151.

[40] p. 1 et seq. Cf. p. 117.

[41] This point is elaborated in my book *Freedom of Speech in the West* (1960), pp. 347–348.

[42] These judgments are dealt with by Ernst von Hippel in his article: "The role of Natural Law in the legal decisions of the German Federal Republic, *Natural Law Forum* (1959), p. 114.

[43] Heinrich Mitteis: *Über das Naturrecht* (1948), p. 38.

[44] Cf. the thesis, quoted above, by E. von Hippel in the *Natural Law Forum* (1959), pp. 116 et seq., and H. Rommen, in the same periodical, same volume, p. 1 et seq.

[45] Cf. Arthur Kaufmann, Zur rechtsphilosophischen Situation der Gegenwart. *Juristenzeitung* (1963), p. 143, col. 1.

[46] See Wilh. Friedmann, *Legal Theory* (1953), 3rd ed., p. 58.

[47] Examples that can be mentioned from recent years include the Supreme Court judgments in the following cases: The New York Times Company *versus* L. B. Sullivan, of 9 March 1964, and B. Elton Cox *versus* the State of Louisiana, of 18 January 1965. With regard to the arguments in favour of freedom of speech, see my book: *Freedom of Speech in the West* (1960), especially, pp. 269–276 and 413.

[48] Art. 55c, 56, and 62, 1.

[49] For this development in the practice of the United Nations, see Elihu Lauterpacht, Some concepts of human rights, *Howard Law Journal* (1965), pp. 264 et seq.; Egon Schwelb, *Archiv des Völkerrechts* (1966), pp. 1 et seq.

[50] In the preparatory work to the convention, published by the Secretariat of the European Council, one encounters particularly often the idea that the aims of the convention shall be to prevent any attempt to "undermine" our democratic way of life; its purpose is to "maintain intact" existing rights and freedoms in member-states, etc., see e.g. statements by Lord Layton (VI, p. 21) and by the chairman of the Consultative Assembly, Professor Teitgen (VI, p. 25). The expression is also used that the aim is to protect "our common inheritance" (VI, p. 41) or "le dénominateur commun" (VI, p. 86). But it is also stated that the aim is to promote reform and further development of human rights. The political organs in the European Council have particularly maintained this view. See, for example, the statements quoted in the preamble, IV, p. 14, and V, p. 15.

[51] The reader is referred to an article by Peter Papadatos, The European social charter. *Journal of the International Commission of Jurists* (1966), III, no. 2, pp. 214–242.

The theoretical foundations of human rights

By Imre Szabó

Hungarian Academy of Sciences, Budapest, Hungary

1

We are living in an age when human rights have not only found a positive expression in national laws, but have been embodied in international law as well. This broadening of their scope explains—among other things—why next year will be internationally celebrated as the Year of Human Rights under the sponsorship of the UNO all over the world.

The incorporation of human rights in international law has, to a certain degree, brought about an approach of the various concepts relating to them; more precisely, it has enabled those starting from different approaches to arrive at a harmony in the legal definition of human rights. Thus, on the one hand it can be said that after the adoption of the Universal Declaration of Human Rights and of international treaties relating to human rights, it seems of minor interest, whether believers in the different social systems, respectively in the different theories and philosophical trends organize their scientific approach to the human rights in this or that manner, since the diversity of theories has been balanced by the unity of positive law. In this, special tribute is due to those who have played a signal role in the elaboration of the international documents on human rights, because by positive-law regulation they have succeeded in bridging over the theoretical controversies,—but only to a certain degree. On matters of principle there is not —and there cannot be—any question of the theoretical controversies being eliminated by positive international law. Incidentally, these antagonisms—or shall we say discrepancies—make themselves felt also in positive international law, because it is always the theory which provides a basis for the formation of a practice, a starting point of interpretation, and guiding principles for implementation. Thus, it could be just as well pointed out that the human rights having become positive international law will kindle the disputes about the theories of citizen's rights, as the practical significance of such disputes is now receiving added emphasis.

2

Without any attempt to completeness: in general, the theories relating to human rights can be divided into three large groups. The first group would include the various natural-law tenets. The second group represents the main line of the positivist trend which would identify the human rights with the rights granted by the state, so that on the national plane it treats them as citizens' rights, while on the interntaional plane it will only admit them as international positive rights. The third group comprises the socialist concept. There are authors who pretend to differentiate between various kinds or shades within the socialist camp, thus speaking of a western and an eastern socialist standpoint. Without going into discussions I would like to express my opinion: the only course to be accepted as the socialist course is the one based on the teachings of Marx. Undoubtedly, it is in the socialist countries that these have widened into a socially recognized trend: therefore, in our opinion, the theory, as professed there, should be accepted as an authentic interpretation. This is the theory we profess, and upon which we will base our further arguments.

It is common knowledge that the socialist concept is sharply opposed to any kind of natural law. Maybe I should say that in doing so it has detached itself not so much from "nature" as from the concept of "law". For instance in the case of human rights it does not dispute their being natural—more accurately human—phenomena, but it denies them the character of *rights*. The phenomenon commonly called natural law is obviously loaded with a moral content expressing a determined standpoint. This standpoint is, partly, determined by other social phenomena, partly a factor determining the latter. The moral content expressed in the shape of natural law is nothing but the consequence of the objective conditions of the latter. In the last analysis, through the intermission of various factors not listed here, it derives from these conditions. Historical experience seems to show that the moral element condensed into natural-law concepts refers to principles acting through the ages and regarded as almost timeless. In reality, however, even this is subject to change, to development. A striking example of this is provided by the extension of the catalogue of human rights in the last fifty years or so. The moral content expressed in the concept called natural law consists, essentially, of the summary of ideas which, though not rights in themselves, can influence legislation and are subsequently expressed by it. Thus, the human rights embodied in natural law are neither laws nor rights, but moral ideals, or shall we say: pretensions conceived of as rights, formulated in respect of the law-to-be-created; accordingly, they should not be called rights at all. Para-doxically, one is tempted to say that natural rights are rights only as long as they are not converted into positive law, that is: civic rights; in the latter case their purely "human rights" character—as a pretension—is completed by their becoming genuine statutory laws which involves the eventual trans-formation of their character.

Nowadays, since their admission to international positive law the scope of validity of human rights, and of course their path to effectiveness has undergone a change. In international life human rights are first manifest as claims, postulates, in the wake of the citizens' rights passing into positive international law. Thus we first encounter them as international legal claims, next turning into incomplete positive international law in the Universal Declaration of Human Rights, and subsequently into complete ones in the international treaties relating to human rights. In international relations the term "rights" is applied both to the pretensions demanding to be recognized in positive international law, and to the positive international law in which such "rights" are already substantiated. This may create complications as regards the definitions, but will not alter the situation.

That some trends are "forced" even today to call human rights as rights, although they are only (or yet) pretensions, has other reasons beside theoretical-philosophical ones. One of the reasons is found, for instance, in the efforts at "pure" science—an effort which closes its eyes to the ultimate reasons of the legal phenomena which are to be found in metajuridical phenomena, but wants to find them at all costs within the law itself, any kind of law. Because of this the said trends denote those social conditions existing prior to law and rationally explainable—including the social ideas derived from the former—as human rights though these are no more than postulates, as to the law to be enacted. They will recognize the postulates, but not their derivation from economic, political, moral, or other factors, not their intrinsic character. True, if they did so, they would carry the science of law beyond the narrow boundaries of law. However, this is unavoidable if the real conditions are to be taken into account. Otherwise the name of rights should be accorded both to the social factors influencing law, and the claims, titles deriving therefrom: in other words we should have to call rights, even human rights, something which is not right—or not yet.

The aforesaid explanation is based on the assumption that the natural-law trends, although recognizing the connection between the law and the metajuridical social phenomena, yet regard the latter as falling outside the scope of the *science* of law and, therefore, do not deal with them. At the same time the natural-law concept may have another cause, namely that it denies the very possibility of a rational explanation of the elements which may effect the law (and can be regarded as natural law), conceiving of these factors as *a priori* existing ones. This tenet, however, fails to provide an explanation of the human rights themselves, or rather renounces to the investigation of their scientific foundations.

3

The positivist standpoint is relatively simpler and does not allow of so many interpretations. In positivism—briefly speaking—only those rights are acknowledged as human rights which are positive rights—part and parcel of the positive legal system; that is, they are either incorporated in the national laws as citizens' rights, or appear in international positive law. In other words, the positivist concept professes the will of the state to be the direct cause of human rights. On the international plane, it is held that human rights derive from the congruent wills of several states. Human rights are not recognized unless expressed in statutory rules. However, the positivist theories are no longer content to stop at this conclusion, but attempt to explain the formation, the origins of the state's will. Such explanations, however, usually fall short of the investigation of the deeper reasons of the state will, reaching —as they do—at most the factors directly provoking the state will. Nowadays the science of politics is making efforts to describe the elements directly leading to, or motivating, the normative positive-law decisions of the state or states. This science, also engaged in studying the day-to-day politics, includes in its investigations the evolution of the power-relations among the major power groups etc. In this manner, the traditional—purely positivist— concept has recently been somewhat extended, is expanding its horizons; the question remains, however, whether it can and will get far enough scientifically by this method.

The departure from the strict positivist standpoint, from the traditional grounds, indicates a definite change. We think, however, that it has still remained on the plane of positivist practicism and has not become the real theory of human rights since it has failed to dig into the deeper causes and theoretical foundations of law—probably it does not even wish to do so. The positivist standpoint arrives at the science of politics by searching for the moving forces behind the political activity culminating in law, instead of looking for the essence of law and human rights. One could say that nowadays legal positivism bases its theory on the science of politics, whereas the latter is really no more than the applied science—or practice of its own theory: which is the science of state and law or the philosophy of law.

Thus, the current authorities of the positivist concept of human rights support their argument by the science of politics. When elevating certain requirements to the level of human rights they do so by drawing empirical conclusions from the political situation—both domestic and foreign. In other words, in looking for the factors leading to human rights they restrict themselves to the analysis of the domestic or foreign international political conditions. Now as regards human rights this standpoint necessarily bears the stamp of a practitioner. When, further, the political conditions are evaluated without the suitable theoretical foundations, subjectivist elements will unavoidably slip in.

4

The third main trend concerning human rights—to be outlined here—is the socialist concept based on Marxism. This concept is alternately branded as being of the natural-law or the positivist type, although in fact it is neither. A few analogous elements may be found in it, but basically it is a radically new, different theory. Its starting point is criticism, which is applied partly against the aforesaid trends and partly—more emphatically—against the duality which can be found in the constitutions of the states differentiating between human rights and citizens' rights, respectively. The declared reason for such a division is to separate those rights which—allegedly—derive from man's quality as such, and those deriving from man's quality as citizen. In fact, however, these are not the real reasons. Differentiation is based on the social conditions upon which the given types of rights are built up. Let us take a closer look at them.

The said standpoint—as is known—uses the term "human rights" to denote those rights which, allegedly, are due to mankind even in the absence of the state, yea even preceding the existence of the state. These should be regarded as inalienable rights, born with man. As against this: citizens' rights derive from the state and their character is essentially political. While human rights were supposed to be unconditional (i.e. guaranteed in any case), citizens' rights were dependent on the type of the state, its political system and other conditions. As against this, the socialist standpoint declares that there is no difference between the origins of the said two types of rights, because all right is derived from the state;—at most their social preconditions may differ. Those fighting for bourgeois society under the slogan of "enligthenment" called human or eternal and inalienable rights those rights which expressed or protected the fundamental institutions of the social system based on capitalistic private ownership: private property, the freedom of enterprise. These, then, were conceived of as human rights because they were of fundamental importance for the said social system. Therefore they tried to lay down such basic social institutions and conditions under the shape of rights which—supposedly—did not originate from the state, but had existed previously. On the other hand the rights connected with the *political* system of the bourgeois society—equality before law, the political freedoms—were regarded as citizens' rights; in other words: such rights which the political power *may* grant to man in his quality as a citizen but which are not necessarily granted under every state structure. One of these twofold categories, i.e. the human rights—which were "inalienable"—required to be explained by natural law. In the case of the other type—citizens' rights—a strictly positivist interpretation seemed appropriate. Subsequently these two types of rights and two kinds of explanations were to be mixed up, and both types were uniformly accompanied by either a natural-law motivation, or a positivist one.

The socialist theory denies the double origin of human rights both in respect of the social systems based on private ownership and in respect of those based on social ownership of the means of production. It recognizes *the priority* of the property relations in both systems (in fact in any system); it recognizes their existence "preceding" that of the state, even the social pretensions that these be regulated. However, it does not "project" such claims or pretensions into rights, much less human rights. The less so, because the property relations—being the fundamental institution of the society—ultimately determine even the rights called human rights. The socialist concept will speak in a uniform manner of citizen's rights, because it considers every positive right as being created by the state. This is why some of its critics accuse the socialist concept of making the citizens' rights directly dependent on the will of the state-power, in other words they accuse it of unbridled positivism. The fact is, however, that the socialist concept does not regard the constitutional expression of the citizens' rights as being dependent on the arbitrariness of the state. Why? Because it considers this will itself to be determined by objective circumstances, and therefore it makes efforts to reveal the factors determining and influencing the state will.

Everybody will probably agree that the citizens' rights have been formulated as a result of a complicated process—conditioned and influenced by several factors. Opinions, however, differ concerning the role played by the ideas about citizens' rights, or generally about human rights, in this process. According to the socialist theory these ideas are nothing but social pretensions expressed in a particular form and relating to the citizens' rights-to-be-created. It is necessary to reveal the social conditions leading to, affecting and creating, such claims. These social conditions and the sequence of circumstances have of course also their own causality. There is, however, no time to analyse them here. We merely wish to refer to the tenet—one of the foundations of the Marxist theory—according to which social pretensions to human rights, and the evolution and formation of citizens' rights are ultimately determined by the material living conditions of the society. The types of prevailing forms of the latter will, ultimately, fill in the contents of the human rights, respectively of the citizens' rights of a given system or of a given age. All this happens through the intermission of the prevailing political, moral and cultural conditions and in interaction with the latter. The fact that human rights are permanent (as said before) and that certain types emerge in different social systems (which makes them appear to be above-society), does not alter the truth of the thesis.

5

The socialist concept of human rights—briefly outlined in the foregoing—focuses in the first place on the fundamental rights within the state, that is: the genuine citizen's rights. Although this conclusion is not reached through the positivist interpretation of human rights, it is by analysing the facts and taking into account the diversity of the social systems, that the socialist theory draws the dividing line between the various types of citizens' rights. Incidentally, these are also characterized by their differing statutory guarantees and the varying degree of effectivity. However, this will still not provide a theoretical answer to the question, what is the basis of the human rights incorporated in positive international law, or put differently, what is the origin of the claims which are postulated as human rights on the international plane? The answer will obviously depend also on the concepts about the essence, creation and guarantees of international law, but it must be understood that we are unable to deal with this in detail here.

It goes without saying that it is more difficult to find the theoretical explanation and the common ground of the definition of human rights as an *international category,* than for human rights *within the state*—i.e. citizens' rights. It should also be taken into account that on an international plane human rights are still incompletely developed: they still lack definite outlines, solid guarantees, their validity is not supported by any permanent structure. Thus, it can be said that they are still more or less in formation. This applies not so much to their categories under international law, as to their international implementation and safeguards. The catalogue of the human rights already recognized (or approaching recognition) has been developed on the model of the citizens' rights recognized (or postulated) within the state. They are no more than the projection of municipal legal institutions of citizens' rights, on the international plane. One of the objectives of the international declaration of such rights and their inclusion into treaties is to prompt the states to lay down these rights in their national legal systems. To this and to their national validation they will attach international guarantees as well, thus expressing the postulate that the system of these rights should act directly also in international law. Of this consists the new feature of the international aspects of human rights—this new and slowly unfolding realization of their guarantees. This side of things is indeed of international-law origin, and accordingly is the source of just as many problems as are generally concomitant with international law.

Now if the more or less accepted types of human rights in international law are no more than a classification—international standardization—of the various types of citizens' rights known in various countries—then the question, what is the international significance of these rights, types, or groups, will obviously depend on the social system of the individual groups of states. Everyone has probably heard about the current dispute—partly also manifest in international treaties—about the relative importance of the so-called classical human rights and the economic, social and cultural rights. It is also common knowledge that the socialist states and the socialist jurisprudence stress the priority of the economic, social and cultural rights as against the so-called classical rights; whereas in the western countries the authors generally profess the opposite view. It is further self-evident that the differences of opinion relating to the origins and essential features of human rights also exist on the international plane, and also in the science of international law. There are as many respective comments as there are views concerning citizens' rights within the state. In consequence it would be premature to expect the emergence of a universally accepted international theory; last but not least owing to the differences, even antagonisms, between the existing social systems. The theoretical approach is necessarily different and is bound to be so. Nevertheless, in international life there is always some common meeting point leading to agreements concerning the internationally acceptable catalogue of human rights, as well as their guarantees under international law. But it is never the theory on which an agreement is reached.

The conditions for the international declaration of human rights and the creation of their safeguards are, generally, given and determined by international political conditions. It should be obvious without further proof that the postulate of an international enunciation and guarantee of human rights is the progressive demand of a democratic international community. One could say that the democratic elements, forces and factors active in international relations are the ones creating the basis of the international assertion of human rights. When examining these conditions under the scientific-theoretical aspect, it will be found that the study of international political relations—including the inherent progressive elements—is, primarily, not a theoretical but rather an empirical task. It should be left to the science of politics, or to the branch dealing with international relations. However, the empiricism which characterizes the science of politics (including its said branches) cannot be the empiricism of the lack of principles. When, for instance, it is said that the Universal Declaration of Human Rights is a characteristically pragmatic document, it does not mean that it had not been preceded by a thorough analysis of the balance of powers, by an extensive evaluation of the conditions and realities; in other words it does not mean that the scientific background had been lacking. What was really missing, was the uniform philosophical background, since the participants had started from opposing theoretical considerations. In spite—but not quite regardless —of this, the eventual agreement was reached on the ground of the practical conditions. Differing theoretical standpoints, or even outright antagonisms— and at the same time a compromise on certain practical solutions: this current antithesis is characteristic not only of the international cause of human rights: identical situations are often encountered in international life in other domains as well.

It would seem from the foregoing discussions as if the science of politics had an important role in promoting the international cause of human rights, in elaborating the conditions of their implementation. However, for truth's sake it must be said that this conclusion was reached only in a conditional manner—in fact, in a manner conditional under more than one aspect. First of all it ought to be stressed that the said role of the science of politics will only come into question in connection with the international catalogue of human rights, with the *drawing up* of the said catalogue subject to international relations. However, when we come to the international *safeguards* of the said rights: the elaboration of the types and system of the safeguards will no longer be the task of the science of politics, but of the science of international law. Next: even under the first aspect, the question arises whether the drawing up of the types of human rights to be laid down internationally is the subject of an independent political science, or that of the science of international law. Finally, it is also disputed whether the science of international law, almost in its entirety (but anyway its branch devoted to human rights) will not merge into the science of politics; or vice versa whether the science of international law will develop an applied branch which will also include in its investigations the international-political conditions of its own origins and applications? Similar problems could be raised also in connection with the citizen's rights, or even in connection with constitutional law—in respect of relations within the state. There, too, both standpoints could be endorsed, namely that either the political sciences incorporate the whole of the science of constitutional law, or else that the science of constitutional law should be completed with political elements.

Currently all three theoretical positions have their own advocates—even if not expressly in connection with human rights. The discordant opinions can be polarized into two extremes. There is a conception which would like to fuse international law (or possibly its human rights aspect) into an independent science of politics or else into that branch of the latter which deals with international relations. This would mean that the emerging science of politics would take upon itself the task of expounding the actual international relations. On the other hand, in the literature of international law there can be found such a view which favours the stretching of the boundaries of this branch of science beyond the narrow normative aspects, and extending it also to its socio-political interconnections. In this case of course, with the widening of the concept of jurisprudence, the science of international law too might be completed with socio-political aspects. Currently rather the former standpoint seems to prevail in the East, though lately we have heard arguments also in the East in favour of introducing an independent science of politics.

I am afraid that, with all the foregoing, we have somehow stepped beyond the set of problems of international human rights; however, the question under discussion is connected with them. As to our own standpoint: we would say that the science of international law (just like any legal branch, or jurisprudence in general) must not get stuck with the dogmatic treatment of the positive law, restricting itself to the analysis of the texts and of case law. On the other hand, neither should jurisprudence be limited to a kind of general social analysis,—detached from the particularities of law. The science of law—both as a whole and its branches—should strive at the unity of these traits. Moreover, it should even fuse into itself the theoretical questions. Wide theoretical foundations, socio-political interconnections, finally positive-law analysis: these are the features adding up to the subject of each individual branch of jurisprudence, or of jurisprudence as a whole. Starting from such principles, the science of international law (conceived in this way) covers, in our opinion, the investigation (relating to human rights) of the question: "under given international conditions how large is the scope within which human rights can be internationally defined and provided with international safeguards in a realistic manner?" Thus, approaching the science of international law from the side of human rights, we must reach the conlusion that this science is not just the positivist science of human rights, but also includes the conditions and the theoretical aspects of the latter. We realize, of course, that for the moment the prospects of forming a *communis opinio* are not very favourable.

6

The preceding questions only appear to be taxonomical or methodological ones, because in fact they also involve considerations as to the subject-matter. So, for instance, if we regard the science of international law as a theoretical science engaged with the international aspects of human rights and going beyond the study of the conditions of the international assertion of human rights, the investigations of this science should also cover the question whether the catalogue of human rights can be extended by new types of rights. In fact, it ought to be examined whether new types of human right can be evolved—such rights which are par excellence and exclusively *international* human rights, taking their roots in international life and community. In fact, could we not, for instance, lay down as human rights (and provide them with international legal safeguards) such conditions which have already been admitted to international law as protected situations, without having become part and parcel of international law as yet? Allow me to refer to the example of genocide which is today an internationally prohibited act but still has not been worded as a right, due to racial or other groups, as are the rights due to human groups, under international law.

With this we have returned to the various concepts regarding the international aspects of human rights. As told before, under the present-day social and ideological conditions it is difficult to imagine a universallly accepted theory concerning the essence of human rights as an international institution. It is fundamentally a social question whether a given state will recognize the citizen's rights, and if so, what types and safeguards will be included in its constitution. Similarly, it is an equally fundamental question (closely linked with the former) whether a state advocates the citizen's rights internationally and to what degree it requests their protection on an international plane. And, of course, whether in connection with the former it supports the evolution of a democratic international community rallying under the flag of the protection of these rights. We believe that such a democratic international community could be built up and strengthened from various sides and under various theoretical aspects, all of which, however, must be characterized by a common endeavour to maintain peace and international security, to maintain peaceful coexistence. Such endeavours may—or should—include the demand of the creation of the international safeguards of human rights. On this basis, a certain common standpoint can be found also concerning the manner, degree and quality of the international vindication of human rights. This will subsequently engender international legal acts affecting human rights: declarations, pacts, treaties or other documents on human rights.

Controversial theories and different approaches exist as to the essence and nature of human rights on the one hand, and possibility of agreement concerning the actual international codification and safeguards of these rights on the other. In the simultaneous presence of these two opposing factors the cause of human rights is unfolding and ripening in international relations and on an international scale in our days.

Implementation of human rights and the domestic jurisdiction of states

By Milan Marković

University of Beograd, Beograd, Yugoslavia

When we start considering the various questions related to such a vast and spectacular area, comprising today two whole realms of law, penetrating through both international and national legal order, anyone more or less familiar with these questions must ask himself what does the ordinary, average man of today expect, "these particles dispersed throughout all the meridians" (in the words of one of our poets), from the resounding words: human rights and fundamental freedoms, implementation of these rights, embodied in the supreme constitutional act of the contemporary international community? How are these rights to be realized for him, how is that international guarantee going to reach him, what means are to be available to him, to this humble, common man, whose fundamental rights and freedoms had been constantly infringed, throughout history, and mostly by that clumsy, impersonal machinery called the State, constituted just by him and his fellow human beings, but which had turned, like many other things invented by him, from a helpful and necessary tool into something else, alienated, blind, slipped out of control, became an end in itself, and had deserved the denomination of a monster (Leviathan) long ago. In his small, narrow world, subjugated to that terrible power called the State, which wipes out individualities, how and by what means would it be possible for him to stand up and oppose the will of the State when it is oppressing and depriving him of his rights? These and similar questions we must ask ourselves for we are dealing with the matter concerned as experts and scientists. In other words, we have to ask ourselves what is our own role, as jurists and internationalists, when answering that ordinary, everyday man, to whose circle we belong, too, to satisfy his eternal striving towards more liberty, so humble and still so justified, by reason of which he deserves his name. For it is not enough to answer these questions as jurists only, as experts whose speciality is the interpretation of the rules of law cast in various moulds, i.e. as the exegetics. No, particularly in the field mentioned above, so definitely connected with human destiny, with the attainment of more liberty and dignity, we must not be only the jurists, but an amalgam of jurist, sociologist, philosopher and ethician, who will try, conclusively and with profound comprehension of the historical development and social basis of human condition in general, and human rights in particular, to answer all those various complex questions related to this area, questions that could be all reduced to one: how to realize human rights and fundamental freedoms and, at the same time, avoid States becoming the only omnipotent arbitrators. For, as is well known, even States with the most perfect institutions and with progressive social forces in power, as well as those with the most reactionary ones, are subject to making mistakes, heavy injustice and infringements of the rights of their own citizens, to usurpe their prerogatives, to overlook or to extort their will for objectives which are far from being general.

We are now faced with the results of hard work of nearly two decades concerning the elaboration of an appropriate instrument, or instruments for the protection of these rights on an international scale, accomplished by various organs of the United Nations, in the first place by the Commission on Human Rights, the Economic and Social Council and the General Assembly. Whatever these results might be, whatever objections might be raised against the text of these instruments, they are nevertheless, in spite of all their shortcomings, aiming at an end already mentioned, i.e. to enable our fellow human being, the man in the street, of whom all States are constituted, to struggle to secure his basic rights and freedoms beyond the frontiers of States (if necessary). We are all well aware, of course, of how things stand and may develop, and of the way they can develop, on which depends whether and to what extent the individual may attain such possibilities of protection of his rights as to be extended beyond the national frontiers of his State. That depends on the universal acceptance of the texts mentioned by the States and, of course, on their conscientious accomplishment. By this the States have the freedom of determination (as usually meant), so that it depends on their sovereign will whether they will commit themselves to such serious obligations.

According to Reference paper, No. 6, of June 1967 published by the UN Office of Public Information, in the attached survey of the state of signatures and ratifications of the International Conventions on Human Rights on May 15, 1967, only 12 States, members of the UN, have so far signed the Covenants on Human Rights (both the Covenant on Economic, Social and Cultural Rights and the Covenant on Civil and Political Rights) and only 7 States, members of the UN, the Optional Protocol to the Covenant on Civil and Political Rights, while none of them has yet ratified these instruments. In that number is not included Yugoslavia, which has also signed both Covenants at the UN Headquarters. It is obvious that some States are waiting to see the conduct of other States in that respect, especially of the Great Powers.

Therefore, the role of us internationalist jurists should be to influence public opinion by our spoken and written word in our respective countries in order to create a so-called juridical conscience (*opinio juris*) among the masses and among the individuals, particularly among decision-making groups, in favour of the signature and ratification of these instruments which, besides all the objections that could be raised, are important tools for accomplishing the noble end of the democratization of the human society. We are asked, of course, to carry out this task with full conscientiousness and responsibility, pointing out the merits as well as the shortcomings of the clauses in the instruments in question, the appropriate consequences and liabilities, the extent of the rules and rights involved, the respect for the sovereign rights and necessary prerogatives of individual States, etc. However, we must bear in mind not only the interests of our own countries, but the wider interests of humanity as a whole, too, the interests of that larger community to which we all belong without distinction as to colour, origin, sex, religion, nation, all of which distinguish us so little from each other, after all.

It appears to us that in this context we should consider also the question of the domestic jurisdiction of States relating to the implementation of human rights and fundamental freedoms. Under the latter category we have in mind the international as well as the national legal performance of these rights and freedoms, because it is obvious that the national implementation is supplemented by the international one, and *vice versa*; to both spheres it is possible to apply home jurisdiction of one State. On the other hand, and in connection with that, we also bear in mind both the concordance and completion of those notions and categories; implementation of human rights and the internal jurisdiction of States, and their contradiction, opposition and withstanding. It is quite understandable, when we are aware of the fact that the matter of human rights is of a twofold character *par excellence,* of dual legal nature, the internal as well as the international one. It comprises the vast area of international and internal legal order so that the question of implementation of human rights is to a large extent the question of relation between these two legal orders. It is evident, with regard to what we have already said about the concordance and discordance in the matter concerned, that we could find there elements of monism, i.e. of the concept of unity of the two legal orders, but also the elements of dualism, i.e. of the concept of the relative separation of these orders. We are led to such conclusions by every realistic study of the institutions of International Law and their manifestation in practice, especially in the field we are exploring here, though there is a movement towards unity with the tendency of a certain primacy in the international legal order (of course, not absolute).

When considering the complexity of relations of human rights confronted with domestic jurisdiction, we ought to start from the entity of the rules of international law concerning human rights, in the UN Charter as in the Universal Declaration of Human Rights, in the Covenants and in the Protocols, even the regional ones, embodied in the European Convention for the Protection of Human Rights for they are not of the same value and have different rank in the UN legal order—or are out of it. That is why this is having an influence on domestic jurisdiction, for somewhere the range of human rights is only in principle and not developed, though indicated, while in some regions the internal jurisdication is stronger and more noticeable depending on the kind of norms of human rights.

First of all, we must mention that the discussion depends on how we conceive the area of domestic jurisdiction envisaged by the UN Charter but not sufficiently defined, which refers not only to human rights but also to wider matters from the field of international law, and of the Charter. Further, even the very States, in accordance with their constitutional provisions, are determining the relation between international and national law, therefore accordingly the relation of domestic competence towards the norms of human rights. It is enough to recall the numerous debates where views have been presented whose effect are to have the provision of Art. 2, paragraph 7, of the UN Charter referal to internal competence and by which the Member States reserve what falls into "matters which are essentially within the domestic jurisdiction of any State". It must be pointed out that the provision of the paragraph mentioned in Art. 2 has a wider meaning and not only and not particularly regarding human rights—for this matter as such is not even mentioned—and that is why the question has been raised: are human rights something which could be included in that paragraph? The answer to that question depends on what place and what legal significance is being given to the category of human rights in the Charter, as well as what meaning and range can be given to the provision of paragraph 7 of Art. 2 itself. It could serve well to recall in this place what possible interpretations have been given in both directions in the doctrine and how practice has been explained by the doctrine.

The overwhelming majority of authors has accepted the opinion expressed by the great British lawyer Sir Hersch Lauterpacht, that the significance, the character of human rights as provided for in the UN Charter is not at all of a declaratory nature, as some would wish to see,[1] but it represents a legal obligation of the Member States in spite of the generalization of the duty to respect human rights and fundamental freedoms, without defining what is the consistance of these rights and freedoms and how they will be realized.[2] Such a standpoint is supported by many other writers who also consider that respect for human rights and fundamental freedoms as provided for by the UN Charter should be realized as a legal obligation for the States, and that its breach would represent the infringement of the Charter itself.[3] The fulfilment of commitments and sanctions imposed in case of their breach is another thing, governed by the rules about the breach of international treaties in general, bearing however in mind that here we are dealing with such a breach which has doubtless a more serious character, for the UN Charter represents not only the legislative but also constitutional act of an organized international community, in which there are many principles and rules constituting the international public policy, i.e. *jus cogens*. This is independent of the fact that these rules of a nuclear type might later be developed and elaborated, supplied by special prescriptions and sanctions relevant to the breaches, which then become even more subject to the application as the *lex specialis*.

But, in spite of learned interpretations of the significance and the extent of the UN Charter's provisions on human rights, given by numerous writers more or less categorically, it seems to us that the best and clearest proof in favour of the idea for which the majority of the writers quoted are pleading is in fact straight language of the provisions of the UN Charter. Thus, among the aims of the UN, put down in Art. 1, paragraph 3, which the UN will have to carry out, are the advancement and promotion of respect for human rights and freedoms for all without discrimination; in Art. 55 one of the functions of the UN is the advancement of the universal respect for these rigths and freedoms without discrimination; in Art. 76 one of the main purposes of the trusteeship system is again the respect for the same rights; Art. 13, 1 b, makes it the duty of the General Assembly to initiate studies and give recommendations for the purpose mentioned in Art. 62, paragraphs 1 and 2, the same things are provided for the ECOSOC; Art. 68 envisages the formation of a commission on human rights; Art. 87, in order to carry out the provisions foreseen in Art. 76, empowers the Trusteeship Council to consider the reports from the territories under trusteeship, to receive petitions, to send visiting missions etc. Apart from this, in Art. 24, paragraphs 1 och 2, the power by which the Security Council is equipped for the maintenance of international peace and security, is to be used in accordance with the purposes and principles of the UN (referring also to those about human rights); in Art. 34 the same organ can examine each dispute and situation (also those concerned with the respect for human rights) which would lead towards threats to international peace and security; according to Art. 39 the same organ shall determine the existence of whatever threats to the peace (i.e. even by violations of human rights), breach of the peace, or act of aggression and to make recommendations, or decide about measures to be taken according to Art. 41 and 42; finally in Art. 56 all Member States of the UN *pledge themselves* to undertake separate or joint actions in cooperation with the Organization to achieve the aims of Art. 55.

We had to point out more fully these articles precisely for their language; and particularly the wording of the last one speaks about how the question of respect for human rights and freedoms was decided upon in the Charter. It was solved on the basis of unbiased, even solemn obligations on the part of the Member States—in view of the place it has among the purposes of the Organization. When bearing in mind the constitutional character of an act such as the UN Charter, and especially the peremptory legal nature of certain principles and rules in the Charter, including human rights in general, that obligation is not a simple international legal obligation, subject to amendments and revocation; by its legal nature it represents a legal duty from which there is no derogation.

Therefore, all the Member States of the UN irrevocably commit themselves to give the Organization all possible support in its work on the promotion of respect for human rights by undertaking joint or separate actions in that regard. Such a work of the Organization and such action of its members represents no doubt the elaboration of Covenants on Human Rights and of the Optional Protocol related to one of them. Now, when questioning the relation of these members and the Charter itself towards the newly elaborated Covenant and Protocol, on the one hand, we can affirm that the signing and ratification, and accession respectively to those international instruments originated in the Charter, in the duty prescribed by it just in that respect, is not left to arbitrary judgment on the part of the individual Member States, Great Powers included, but that it should represent the execution of their former international legal obligation, namely of a coercive character, from which there is no derogation. On the other hand, this does not prevent us from making another assertion, if alternatively it comes about that one of the States does not sign or accede to the Covenants: in no way does it mean that such a State would be exempted from the fulfilment of all obligations in the UN Charter dealing with human rights and freedoms. We can go even further and state that they will be also bound, in principle, by the standards and rules embodied in the Covenants and Protocol in view of the effect of the imperative rules *erga omnes,* on the third parties, i.e. on the non-signatories, as certain rules and principles from the UN Charter, which are integral part of *Ordre public international,*[4] have affected the non-members of the Organization. It is our deep conviction that progress, voluntarily or involuntarily, is in that direction.

It remains to see the other side of the problem, i.e. how is it conceived and how can that notorious notion of domestic or internal, according to some even exclusive jurisdiction be conceived in relation to human rights? We have now reached the proper field of our examination, although still, in a way, in the sphere of a so-called initial, not to say classical linking or opposing that concept—as a barrier, reservation, assurance of States—towards the area of human rights as a possible motive for the UN action in respect to them. But it is clear how necessary was this introduction for the correct understanding of the whole problem. For, as already stated, the reservation in Art. 2, paragraph 7, of the Charter dealing with domestic jurisdiction, is provided for in a wider and more general way, having no express connection with the matters of human rights (though some people state that it was just because of the matter introduced).[5]

The principle of non-intervention in the internal affairs of a Member State represents, of course, a very positive guarantee of the State sovereignty rationally conceived, the barrier against the unlawful, unauthorized and unjustified interference in the area assigned and reserved only for the State's regulation. However, regarding the mode in which that important principle was formulated in the UN Charter—and it is well known that this formulation is not very successful, being subject to so many different and extreme interpretations in one or another sense—it seems that it would be better if it were left out of the Charter altogether since this reservation is already presumed, as in the case of treaties relating to the peaceful solution of international disputes, e.g. by means of arbitration, where it is understood that disputes involving the honour and dignity of States are exempted (since classical times), just as today the disputes where vital interests are in question are claimed as being expected. For it was important to define the functions and powers of the UNO, so that everything else, which is outside of them, cannot be considered their competence, but remain within the competence of the Member States.

Formulated as it is, that provision constitutes a stumblingblock upon which all those who justifiably defend themselves from interference rely, i.e. from intervention (as it has well discerned Lauterpacht)—as an imperative influence in order to achieve a certain desired conduct to be imposed, as well as those who wish to escape responsibility for breaking the basic purposes and principles of the Organization, e.g. the Union of South Africa.

It is rather well known, so we shall mention it only briefly, that in the Covenant of the League of Nations (Art. 15, paragraph 8) the reservation of the domestic jurisdiction of States was more satisfactorily formulated in binding it to the solution of disputes, or excluding from the competence of the Council of the League questions "which the international law leaves to the exclusive jurisdiction of one party". Comparing this formulation with the present one, from Art. 2, paragraph 7, of the UN Charter, where "matters which are essentially within the domestic jurisdiction of every State" are exempted from the competence of the UN organs, we can see two points in which the Charter is less efficient: in the first place, the sphere of international jurisdiction is less clearly defined, i.e. its limits regarding the wording used in the Covenant, and in the Charter, and secondly, leaving—in the Charter—to the States the possibility that they may themselves determine what is the matter falling into the area of domestic jurisdiction. Earlier, in the Covenant the exclusive domestic jurisdiction of States was indicated for certain affairs, which narrowed the whole area, though it remained disputable what was falling within it, but about which decision was brought according to international law, not by a unilateral act of the State concerned. Now, in the Charter there is no mention of the adjective *exclusive,* since only the words *domestic jurisdiction* are used, and thereupon this qualification has deteriorated, as many maintain, because of the uncertain expression *essentially,* which has contributed even more to a possible wider interpretation of that so flexible notion. Moreover, the determination of what falls within the scope of the notion is not subject to rules of international law, but it may be conceived, and even applied in practice, as being left to the States concerned.[6]

As to the possible interpretations of the domestic jurisdiction of States, as provided for in Art. 2, paragraph 7, of the UN Charter, in the first place we agree that by omitting the word "exclusive" the notion of what was meant to be kept out of the activities of the UNO was in a way extended, although it may be argued about it in the opposite sense, too. Indeed, seeing that practice tends to surrender many matters and questions, earlier considered internal, to examination and solution by international organs and bodies, we can maintain that from this domestic jurisdiction so easy and often subject to be transformed in an international one, not even a stricter category can be discerned as such an exclusive competence, which in no way could be questioned. On the other hand, even when we conceive the wording of the notion domestic jurisdiction without the adjective "exclusive", as enlarged, it seems that the expression "essentially" rather moderates the whole formula about domestic jurisdiction, for in our opinion it can be understood as related to the matters which are, in principle, *principally* subject to the reservation of the domestic jurisdiction—but not always and completely. It seems to us that such a narrower interpretation of the exception, which paragraph 7 of Art. 2 generally represents concerning the otherwise normal competence of the UNO, is more appropriate to the maxim: *exceptiones sunt strictissimae interpretationis.*

Who is authorized to determine whether some matter belongs to the sphere of internal or international jurisdiction, in this case of the UN Organs? We are of the opinion, despite the silence about this in the text of the reservation from paragraph 7, Art. 2 of the Charter, that it would hardly be conceded that the will and apprehension of one State could be competent, for that would mean that, in a controversial case, one interested party was at the same time the decision-making one, by the very fact of excluding it in advance from examination in general. This would violate the general principle of law: *nemo judex in sua causa (re sua)*.

There is, of course, one more question, a hard and complicated one: can the provision of paragraph 7, Art. 2 of the Charter be related to human rights at all? In the first place, let us set apart what is indisputable. It is unquestionable, being evident from the very text of the provision itself, that this reservation is immaterial when we are faced with such violations of human rights as might lead to a threat to or to a breach of peace and security in the world, or to aggression, according to Art. 39 of the Charter. In that case it is the competence of the Security Council which is engaged in action on the basis of Art. 41 and 42, where there is no possibility of invoking the reservation of non-interference in internal affairs.

It might be, following the reasoning developed by Lauterpacht, that if we proceed from the statement that "human rights and freedoms are not comprised within the category of matters essentially within the domestic jurisdiction of the State, then it would appear that the competence of the United Nations in respect of them is wholly unrestricted . . .".[7] Since human rights are really proclaimed as such being among the most important purposes of the UN and representing the subject of their various activities, to which the members of UN are in advance obliged to give support, it is evident that such a matter could not fall within the area of reserved rights (*domaine réservé*), provided for in Art. 2, paragraph 7, of the UN Charter. Such a concept of domestic jurisdiction has been reflected in the case of Spain, as well as in the case of the Union of South Africa before the General Assembly. In the first case, indeed, there was not exactly the question of human rights, but of a political régime which might threaten international peace and security. On that occasion the Australian delegate had already in San Francisco expressed the opinion that "once a matter is recognized as one of legitimate international concern, no exception to the general rule is needed to bring it within the powers of the Organization. The general rule itself ceases to apply as soon as a matter ceases to be one of domestic jurisdiction."[8] However, though the domestic jurisdiction was in such a manner conceived in the case of Spain, the case was not judged as being such to provoke an action by the Security Council, i.e. as leading to a threat to peace and security. Because of that, Lauterpacht concluded that certain measures of interference (primarily measures undertaken by the General Assembly in the form of recommendation, such as cancellation of diplomatic intercourse, etc.) are not really intervention, and that the questions within the domestic jurisdiction of a State are not in essence such when they are of international concern notwithstanding that they could contain no threat to peace at all.

In another case, dealing with the Union of South Africa, which at the beginning concerned only the treatment of Indians, but later concerned with the whole policy of racial discrimination in that country—*apartheid*—particularly regarding South-West Africa and still topical, the General Assembly declined even to request the consultative opinion of the ICJ, and declared itself as competent by its resolution of December 8, 1946, affirming that the treatment of Indians in that country endangers friendly relations between the Union and India, and that the treatment of Indians ought to be in accordance with the international agreements between the two governments and with *"appropriate provisions of the Charter"* (underlined—MM).

However, when drawing conclusions out of the foregoing statements, Lauterpacht stopped somehow half-way. He stated that the UN could be competent for the violations of human rights which were not covered by domestic jurisdiction, at least not "essentially", but he then concluded that the competence of the UN, except for the cases where the violations are of such a nature, i.e. "systematic" and "flagrant", as to become a source of danger to peace, and when the action of the Security Council is to be set in motion, results only in studies, recommendations of the application of Art. 6 of the Charter concerning exclusion from membership, etc., which he had designed as "short of enforcement". It must be admitted that he had good reasons for such a pragmatical solution: not only by interpretation of the wording of the Charter's provisions and by the extent of powers of particular UN organs, but also from the cited practice, confirmed in the subsequent work of the UN. Indeed, the main organs, invited to deal with the matter of human rights, are the ECOSOC and the General Assembly, their decisions having almost exclusively the character of recommendations. No one could deny that. We could hardly defend and plead for another distribution of competences because there would be no support therefore in the express provisions of the Charter. If we were to suppose that the exemption from the exception contained in the rule of paragraph 7, Art. 2 of the Charter refers to human rights even when their breach was not related to a menace to international peace, we would again land on the ground of an extensive interpretation, not in accordance with the above-mentioned principle concerning the exceptions. In effect, such an extensive interpretation might be extended to that sort of breaches of human rights, too, when we would try to cover it by the notion of security, viewing it from the concept of peace. Anyhow, even then it would be required that the breaches in question should be massive and drastic, since *de minima non curat praetor,* so that the whole matter is being reduced to shades, whereby it becomes clear that the isolated and individual cases of the violations of human rights are not appropriate for consideration by the UNO organs.[10]

In fact, that is why International Covenants on Human Rights and the Optional Protocol are being drafted and adopted. It does not mean that the Universal Declaration on Human Rights was not an important step in the same direction, i.e. to ensure that specific, not generalized rights be provided for, as might be known what kind of violations and of what actual rights will represent the real breach of law. That Declaration, which lacks sanctions in case of non-fulfilment and which was constructed as "the ideal for achieving", cannot be considered as deprived of any legal value.[11] It is growing in value at first substantially, for its source is to be found in the provisions of the UN Charter, from which and from relevant duties of States originates its general legal force (that is why some see it as the elaboration of the Charter, having the same rank, while others consider it an independent act but of the same value). Then, from the formal point of view, though this act was passed by the resolution of the General Assembly, having the character of a recommendation, nevertheless, many people ascribe today a certain legal force to such decisions of international organs which are brought by a great majority, or by unanimous vote (as, for instance, the Declaration on decolonisation), considering that they are expressing the legal conscience of humanity or the general principles of law. Moreover, reference to the Declaration of Human Rights in the constitutions of some new States or international agreements, such as the Memorandum of Understanding on Trieste, is further proof of a certain legal value of that important document.

But let us return to the Covenants and Protocol, which are, as we said, precisely tailored for the purpose of bringing individual breaches of human rights before international organs. This means that such breaches could not be considered so far by the UNO organs. To that assertion one could make the objection that there were cases of that sort submitted to the UN, as for instance the case of Soviet citizens—wives of foreign nationals—to whom the authorities denied the right to abandon the territory of their respective country, which was solved by a resolution of the General Assembly 285 (III) of April 25, 1949; the question of ten of the Greek maritime trade union leaders, sentenced to death, which was raised by Yugoslavian initiative, with many different decisions; further a similar question of the 24 Spaniards imprisoned in Barcelona, sentenced to death by a military court which disregarded the usual guarantees of defense, etc.[12] However, in all these cases the decisions had only the force of recommendations while the decisions which will be made under the Covenants and the Protocol should have a more far-reaching legal force (owing to the formal aspect of a treaty, as well as to the specified rules and the competences of the organs contemplated for action and decision-making).

The question now is what will be the position of domestic jurisdiction in respect of the obligations in the Covenants and the Protocol. Will States again have the possibility to invoke their domestic jurisdiction when breaches of human rights are concerned, as provided for and guaranteed by the Covenants and Protocol? It is our conviction that the States could not, even before the adoption of the Convents, call upon their national jurisdiction when drastic violations of human rights were involved, because it is a case of infringement of the UN Charter's provisions, where the Declaration on Human Rights might help in indicating which rights were to be dealt with, as infringed. The States have even less opportunity to invoke their domestic jurisdiction now that these provisions (on human rights) are specified in a form of perfect legal obligations, with defined competence of the organs established for examination, fact-finding and dealing with violations of human rights. All is now clearer than before.

There still remains the controversial question—though to a slightly less extent—who will be the arbitrator in a case of domestic jurisdiction invoked, i.e. whether the matter represents the violation of the right of an individual according to the Covenants, or does it still stay in the sphere of domestic jurisdiction, sanctioned by the Charter? For, Art. 2, paragraph 7, remains even here as the barrier dividing the area where international organs have the influence, from the one which is really left as sacrosanct to the sphere of the internal activities of States. Basically, one could here also apply, and even support by more arguments, the conclusion to which the Permanent Court of International Justice arrived in its Consultative opinion of February 7, 1923, in the case of nationality decrees in Tunis and Morocco, namely that the question whether a matter falls under internal or in international jurisdiction depends on the development of international relations and "that it will be necessary in each case to resort to international law" (which is in accordance with the resolution of the Institute of International Law in 1934). The Court found that this case in particular fell outside domestic jurisdiction because the matter has been regulated by international agreements.[13] However, we have already stated that even without special treaty provisions, the question whether, in a certain case, domestic jurisdiction should or should not prevail cannot be decided unilateraly by the State concerned.[14] Still less, *a fortiori,* is that possible when we are in the presence of international obligations fixed by a treaty.

Such a situation will arise when the application of the Covenants comes into existence, where there are international obligations of that kind. We maintain this conviction even more because the organs for the implementation of human rights (more exactly: civil and political rights), namely the Committee on Human Rights and the Conciliation Commission, are entitled, under the conditions of Art. 41,[15] to examine and to request not only the reports regarding the promotion of the respect for human rights in individual countries, but also the violations of the rights provided for and the disputes about those violations among the Member States, whereby the mentioned organs will have the power to decide upon the justification of the domestic jurisdiction as invoked by a State Party. The objection in that sense would always present a prejudicial question.

We must mention here that the provision of Art. 41 of the Covenant on Civil and Political Rights is rather disappointing and weakens the significance and efficiency of the measure of implementation in general. In fact, according to that provision, Member States may, if they find it opportune, declare their acceptance of the competence of the Human Rights Committee or of the Conciliation Commission, on the grounds of which these organs will be able to examine and suggest measures for the removal of the violations of human rights in the State concerned, if another State initiate the appropriate procedure. What does that really mean? It means, indeed, that for such actual implementation of human rights (for everything else, all that consideration of reports by States, studies, general recommendations, etc. are palliative measures) it is necessary to achieve some kind of compromise between two States or, better still, since such a possibility is allowed, it should be agreed upon in advance by unilateral statement of the will of a State party to the Covenant, what amounts to an *optional clause* like the one about the jurisdiction of the International Court of Justice. The presence of such a provision on the implementation in the structure of the whole text of the treaty is very astonishing, for it makes the implementation itself, and by this also the international protection of human rights, dependent on special consent, i.e. on a new agreement in an existing treaty. And, moreover, by the existence of a separate Optional Protocol, which is also conditioning the implementation, only in a specific aspect, and which is approaching the real protection of the rights of the individual by giving him some autonomous rights of the appearance on the international plan, certain *locus standi* (though not *in judicion*). Yet that weak international protection through the implementation of the right of individual to be able to address himself to an international body, when feeling that his human rights have been violated, has been reduced by this Protocol and its separation from the text of the Covenants to an ephemeral degree and made it dependent on the consideration of States Parties. No matter that they ought to make an entity, this separation, as well as that of the Covenants, are understandable and could be justified from the point of view of purposefulness.

Those are very serious imperfections in the whole system of the contemporary international protection of human rights and fundamental freedoms, for they prevent the system from making substantial headway compared with the classical one, in which the individual was not the active subject of international law, because States were his permanent tutors and he remained always some kind of minor under trusteeship in the international society and its legal order. It is certainly a paradox that, as compared with the individuals from territories actually under trusteeship, who enjoy the right to address themselves by means of petitions to the UNO by reasons of the violations of their rights, the individuals from other countries on a higher degree of development are unable to use the same means. This does not agree with the development of international society itself, with its technological advancement and economic unity, and specially with increased intercourse across frontiers. But we hope that use will be made of the provisions which provide for a possibility of amendments to the Covenants, in order to improve the mechanism of implementation, though it depends on the will of the parties.

Therefore, the domestic jurisdiction of States on which they can reasonably insist does exist, generally speaking, by the very fact that they exist by themselves as well as the matters and activities which they could and must settle autonomously, without interference from outside. As such matters there are considered to be: the condition of aliens; the organization of government and of State agencies, i.e. constitutional questions; the acquisition and loss of nationality; labour relations and the like. However, even these matters are only relatively in the scope of internal jurisdiction, as they might be, if not entirely at least partly, subject to international regulation and thereby to international jurisdiction, too, especially by way of international conventional norms—as is shown in the case of nationality decrees in Tunis and Morocco, or in the numerous peace treaties, which often regulate even the form of government in a defeated country, or by international labour conventions. That is why it is better to speak not about the exclusive jurisdiction, but simply about domestic jurisdiction of States, within the limits of its existence and as long as it exists, which is again someting that depends on their own will, at least from the formal point of view, since there are no other means to compel them to make concessions in the sphere than by social-economic necessities and lawful evolutive tendencies. If so far one could question international jurisdiction in the matter of human rights because of the general character of the UN Charter's provisions and of indistinct powers of the UN organs, especially with a view to the necessity of existing grave violations of human rights, so that they might be translated into threats to international peace and security, this kind of jurisdiction cannot be denied being definitely and precisely provided for by the stipulations of the Covenants.

This does not mean that in the matter of human rights domestic jurisdiction will discontinue. On the contrary, this jurisdiction will continue to be exercized parallelly with that provided for by international norms in such a large area regulated in more detail by national constitutions and laws, prescribing the competence of various organs and authorities in the matter of civil and political as well as of social, economic and cultural rights. The international jurisdiction is engaged only exceptionally in this bright field, not excluding the existing domestic jurisdiction, in case States and their organs ignore the international standards of individual rights of their citizens, when the infringements of these rights cannot be in final instances corrected by national legal mean. Up to this moment, and even after that, home jurisdiction does not cease to apply, and often the international organs will indicate, call upon it, when examining and settling the disputes between States or a State and an individual, in order to achieve improvement, to prevent or stop further violations, to attain the redress for the breaches committed. But the very prejudicial question: whether this border-line is transgressed where a breach of human rights emerges from the usual sphere of home jurisdiction and enters the international one, i.e. whether after all exhausted legal means, regular and extraordinary, there still remains the breach of one of the human rights provided for in the Covenants and invoked by the individual, that will be decided by the international organ, since it becomes internationalized. Besides the general principles of law and apart from considerations made already on the subject, it is evident from the very text of the appropriate provisions of the Covenants, particularly from Art. 41, where the so-called *local remedy rule* is established, i.e. the requirement that all available domestic means and remedies are exhausted (with the exception of a case where deliberately and unreasonably it is prolonging the application of these remedies on the part of the State agencies). Whether it is so and whether it has proceeded in such a way in the case under examination, the Committee will have to determine in dealing with the matter "in conformity with the generally recognized principles of international law". At any rate, the international law is the criterion of that judgment and proceeding.

Therefore, the domestic jurisdiction shall exist and can be reasonably and effectively invoked if the limits of the provisions and competences, set up by the Covenants and by the Protocol, are exceeded, transgressed. It is very important, since it shows that the sovereignty and sovereign equality are not denied and in no way diminished. The thing that really matters is that between State and the international community a certain compromise has been achieved, so that now the international community has been given the role of a new unselfish and impartial representative of the individuals. In fact this compromise still leaves to States the vast field of application of the internal legal rules and of domestic jurisdiction in this important sector, while only a smaller, exceptional part, though significant because of possible misuse and guaranties against it, is conceded to the international organs to which the individuals may address themselves and which proceed on their behalf.

That is why we regard that large field of human rights of such vital importance, as one where these two jurisdictions are supplementing themselves and where international collaboration might be developed. It appears to us that precisely in this field the implementation of human rights and fundamental freedoms must be conceived as constituting an integrated whole by its very nature, as we have already partly explained, like a vast area in which States jointly or through the Organization and even through the individuals would have to cooperate in the promotion of welfare and securing of justice and freedoms for all. The last categories inextricably connected, for there is no real freedom and no political and civil rights without secured material, economic conditions of life of the individual, and the other way round; without civil and political rights the individuals are devoid of the important means in the struggle for their economic emancipation. For, as has long since been ascertained,[16] States are not an end in themselves but instruments for the most rational organization of human society and safeguards of the interests of their citizens, for more and more emancipation of the individuals, i.e. for the achievement of more freedoms and rights, so that virtually at some stages of social development States might become perhaps redundant in all the functions and prerogatives which they actually possess (for instance, armed forces and other forms of constraint). This is the conception advocated also by the Marxist doctrine and political science.

Evidently, in this big field of accomplishment, i.e. of the implementation of human rights, so comprehensively conceived, a great many tasks, and still prevailingly, are relying upon the Member States of the organized international community. At last, that realization of human rights and freedoms cannot be imagined in the first place without State participation, because the States have to carry the burden of securing the economic and political prerequisites of the organization of human society today not only for the constitutional reasons mentioned, since their respective constitutions entrust and impose such a task upon them, but because it is in the spirit of the UN Charter, as it was construed on the occasion of its creation. In the report of the Subcommittee I/IA of the San Francisco Conference it is expressly said: "The Subcommittee held that assuring or protecting such fundamental rights is primarily the concern of each State. If however such rights and freedoms were grieviously outraged so as to create conditions which threaten peace or to obstruct the application of provisions of the Charter, then they cease to be the sole concern of each state."[17] That basic postulate, which can be understood solely as a *jurisdiction divided* between States and the organized international community, whereby States have a primary, prevailing role, including the responsibility, too, might be in a general way applied to-day also, when the specific provisions of the Covenants and of the Protocol exist, of course, not questioning the provisions themselves, but only the things which would overstep them. The international jurisdiction is thereby to some extent enlarged and specified, becoming more efficient, but still remains a vast area of the application of national jurisdiction in this matter. Besides that enlargement of the notion of control, and thereby of the implementation in itself concerning international commitments, is tending lately to comprise the internal measures and means (as for instance, by the Moscow Treaty banning nuclear experiments to be supplemented by banning such underground experiments where the control is to be realized by national means). It does not exclude different arrangements, too, where the measures of international control could be introduced (as by the Antarctica Treaty from 1959).

On the other hand, we do not believe that friendly relations among nations would be endangered by the existence of a possibility to consider the results attained by the States in the field, which is the first, rather modest role of the international organs according to the Covenants, or of their good offices and mediation in the quarrels between States about the maintenance of the human rights standards, which is certainly more active, though still modest role of these organs. It is rightly stated that every measure of international implementation is bearing certain risk. On that subject there were already too many bitter debates in the framework of the Human Rights Commission, as well as in the theoretical monographs and the like, where it was pointed out (as on the occasion of similar institutions in the League of Nations), that such instance might be used for attacks and defamation of a State for quite different reasons, often propaganda reasons, and that the new institution could be misused for the purposes quite opposite to those of the UN, etc.[18] However, when we consider the risks, shortcomings and advantages, we cannot deny that the organs called upon to act on the basis of the reports submitted or in disputes before them, when exercising responsibly their competence and considering only verified cases of drastic violations of the rigths of individuals and ignoring the irresponsible outbursts or actions inspired by propaganda, represent an impartial joint body, governed by general, not particular interests. As general interests we are having in mind those of all or of the great majority of States and of their fellow citizens. It appears so from the expression used in the text: "general recommendations", which indicates the character of measures to be primarily undertaken, as well as the mediatory and conciliatory nature in settling the disputes to which could be, optionally, proceeded. There is, of course, a main and grave remark which can be put to such means of solving and securing the implementation on the basis of so-called *State-to-State* complaints, namely, that States may but need not set in motion the mechanism of implementation on account of infringement of human rights of their citizen, that they could choose, having regard to the aims of foreign policy and momentary interests, not to be involved in a quarrel with a certain power, not to espouse a cause of their own citizen and to neglect arbitrarily the wrong he suffered.

Therefore, we are of the opinion that there is only the way of giving individuals the possibility to *petition* (in the texts the expression used is *communication*) from individuals, which is also weakening the nature and the efficacy of the means provided. In such an effective procedure there is less possibility for the States to manifest arbitrary conduct and taking as guidance the special interests of State policy and finally, their resentfulness to the acts of each other. All that can be avoided by the said means, though these acts of individuals could also be misused, inspired by the desire to make trouble and propaganda, just as by the State-to-State complaints, but it depends on the organs competent for such acts, as how they are to proceed (whether they would, strictly estimating, receive or refuse the acts). At the same time, this is the only mode to open slightly the door, a half-way to individuals to be able to appear before international bodies, since it was always affirmed that the individuals are those final "addressees" of international legal norms —as *omne jus hominem causa constitutum est*—and that they are anyhow subjects of international relations, becoming now subjects of the international legal order, too, although to a modest extent. This is only how can be bridled the omnipotence of States, those permanent tutors of individuals. In this way only can a certain democratization of the international society be achieved, enabling States to transform themselves from monsters—an end in itself— into the real tools of the human race. This is why the acceptance of the way by which individuals appeal to the international organs represents a *test* of democratism of particular States and governments. Those countries which are sure about their own rule and institutions do not have to fear, because if the rule and institutions are accepted by their citizens, there will be certainly no reasons and motives for complaints invoking violations of human rights within their jurisdiction, apart from the possible misuses of the means and frightenings of individuals, as two negative extremes.

By all these procedures wherewith the international jurisdiction may be engaged, it is to be started from the general rule about previous exhaustion of all available domestic legal means. This is expressly provided for in the Covenant on Civil and Political Rights as well as in the the Optional Protocol related to it, and it has to be interpreted as meaning that previously all regular legal means were used (as, for instance, complaint, appeal, revision) and extraordinary legal means (as, for instance, the instigation of a procedure on the request for the protection of legality), being at anyone's disposal. That pointing out of a precedent use of legal means from the internal legal order clearly shows the connection between the domestic and international jurisdiction in the implementation of human rights, since it is to start from the former as a necessary assumption and again come back to it, once the regulation has been achieved on an international scale about the question or dispute concerning the violations of a right, when it has to give redress for violation or otherwise to correct the condition by bringing proper decision, or to compensate for damage or loss, etc., because all this has to be executed within the internal legal order.

We believe that the very existence of the international legal norms about the standards of human rights and fundamental freedoms will have positive influence on their realization in internal legal orders of States, particularly the measures of implementation, even provided for in such minimal scope. The States will endeavour to harmonize their own standards of economic and political rights of citizens with the international ones. And we should not have illusions though the Covenants are dealing with average standards of these various categories of human rights, all States, big and small, developed and underdeveloped, even the superpowers, will have much to do in one or the other field of promotion of human rights. There are so many examples today when even the largest and most powerful countries may have grave internal disturbances if they do not pay enough attention to the economic and social rights of their citizens without discrimination.

We also believe that, inversely, many States will have an opportunity to transmit very much of their experience to each other in the matter of human rights and their implementation, from the sphere of domestic jurisdiction, either in the structure of organs and agencies, or in the guarantees of a judicial, or procedural nature, as well as in the socio-political organization and autonomies, which precisely in this field may be particularly favourable. We would like to mention in this connection that Yugoslavia has developed a rather new type of socialist relations through social and workers' self-management, which should not only lead to the improvement of human relations in the society by advancing the productivity in keeping the producers more interested in the management of their enterprises, plants and in the distribution of profit, but it is supposed to secure more democracy when deciding upon social and public functions, as in the education, culture, health, etc. These and other forms of the autonomous settlement are applied in various organs of power, from the elementary ones, as the municipalities, or communes up to the highest, as the federal units and the federation. Through all these forms there is an immanent possibility to achieve more safeguard for human rights, inscribed in the Constitution and in the statutes. In that way, the safeguard of the rights and freedoms becomes the matter of concern of the general public and the interested individual, so that the mechanism of the autonomy and self-management at work influence more immediately the efficiency of the accomplishment and protection of human rights, especially in the economic and social field, particularly in the area of the minority (nationality) rights, since the care about decisions and their execution is transfered from the classical state organs, subject to bureaucracy and neglecting the man, into the hands of broad masses of individuals, human beings, whereby more guarantees are given for their rights. This and many other experiences of States would contribute to the improvement of the international standards of human rights and to their implementation, in other words, in this way will be constantly renewed that historical process of the beginnings of this institution in international law: from the national constitutional acts and declarations to the international norms and standards, and inversely: constant reciprocal enrichment.

In connection with this, we consider that the establishment of national commissions on human rights, apart from other interior measures, recommended by the resolution of the UN General Assembly 2200 (XXI) C, by which the texts of the Covenants and of the Protocol were adopted,[19] would represent a very useful tool of transmission in both directions of the cooperation between the international competent organs ond the domestic organs of States parties in the field of safeguarding and realization of human rights. On the other hand, we do not consider it necessary to establish the post of a UN High Commissionary for human rights, who would be supposed to have certain competences intermingling and overlapping with those of the Committee on Human Rights under the Covenant on Civil and Political Rights. Therefore, we should not dissipate energies and establish substitution ("Ersatz") for organs which have normally to function.

Besides the ideas already pointed out on the imperative character of norms which derive from the UN Charter, which in itself imposes the duty to accede to the Covenants and to the Protocol and carry them out in good faith (*bona fide*), we are of the opinion that such duty and responsibility is specially incumbent to the Great Powers, from which no one (as we are informed) has so far signed the documents concerned. They are not only obliged to do so, as other countries are, having regard to their own constitutional provisions on the same matter, for it is supposed, or these States claim so, that they offer their citizens even more substantial standard of rights than in the international one, on the average. They should not only be compelled to accomplish their international legal duty, as the others, by the peremptory character of the norms in question, but the very position as great powers should induce them to do so; because they have many privileges in this world and also responsibilities, one of them consisting of the supposition that they should give good, not bad, examples to the others.

NOTES

[1] See, for example, R. Brunet, *La garantie internationale des droits de l'homme,* pp. 146 et seq., Genève, 1947; H. Kelsen, *The Law of the United Nations,* pp. 29–30, London, 1950.

[2] H. Lauterpacht, The International Protection of Human Rights, *Recueil des cours de l'Académie de Droit International de La Haye* (1947), vol. 70, pp. 15–16; *International Law and Human Rights,* pp. 34, 147–148, London, 1950.

[3] In that sense M. Ganji, *International Protection of Human Rights,* pp. 113–123, Paris and Genève, 1962; P. Guggenheim, *Traité de Droit International Public,* p. 301, Genève, 1953; S. Glaser, *Les droits de l'homme à la lumière du droit international positif, Mélanges offerts à H. Rolin,* pp. 110–114; H. Bokor, Human rights and international law, *Socialist Concept of Human Rights,* pp. 279, 283–289, Budapest, 1966; to some extent M. Moskowitz, *Human Rights and World Order,* pp. 13, 32–33, New York, 1958; and particularly R. Cassin, La Déclaration Universelle et la mise en œuvre des droits de l'homme, *Recueil des cours de l'ADI* (1951), p. 254. In the same sense M. Milojevic, *Položaj pojedinca i njegov aktivni subjektivite u medjunarodnom pravu* (La condition de l'individu et leur personnalité active en droit international), thèse, str. (p.) 256–259, Beograd, 1955, who is citing B. Jankovic, *Osnovi medjunarodno javnog prava* (Eléments de droit international public), I, str. (p.) 247, Sarajevo, 1958.

[4] According to previous, French draft of the Universal Declaration of Human Rights, submitted to the Commission on Human Rights, it (Declaration) also had to be conceived as the act of which application concerns the international public policy, so that the UN would be competent to deal with infringements of its provisions, R. Cassin, op. cit., p. 289.

[5] See H. Lauterpacht, *The International Protection of Human Rights,* pp. 18, 19; H. Bokor, op. cit., p. 284, citing the commentary of the UN Charter by Goodrich–Hambro, pp. 96–97.

[6] See the interpretations of the notions of domestic jurisdiction and of exclusive jurisdiction, etc. by H. Lauterpacht, op. cit., pp. 17–55; M. Ganji, op. cit., pp. 133–136; M. Moskowitz, op. cit., pp. 32–35; H. Bokor, op. cit., pp. 283–288.

[7] H. Lauterpacht, op. cit., pp. 29–30.

[8] Quoted by H. Lauterpacht, op. cit. p. 39.

[9] Ibid.

[10] There are some writers who categorically insist upon the conception that the relevant provisions of the Charter are in no way preventing the UNO organs from dealing with the safeguards of the respect for human rights, in other words, with all its possible violations, including such an organ, as the Security Council, too. Namely, it has been pointed out that the actions of the latter organ are something else, separated, insofar as the threatening or breaking of peace is concerned, from the situations where the violations of human rights are in question, which might but need not be connected (while in our opinion is precisely that which is hard to be discerned, so that usually here is only a matter of degree of endangering, depending on graveness and comprehen-

siveness of the violations). In that sense M. Ganji, op. cit., pp. 115, 117, 124, to some extent M. Moskowitz and H. Bokor.

[11] We wrote about that in our works and articles: *Zaŝnita manjina u sklopu medjunarodne qastite ljudskih prava* (The protection of minorities in the framework of the international protection of human rights), thèse, Beograd, 1958; Ljudska prava i zaŝtita manjina (Human rights and protection of minorities), in *Jugoslavenska revija za medjunarodno pravo,* 1959.

[12] J. F. Green, *The United Nations and Human Rights,* Washington, 1958.

[13] Decrees on Nationality in Tunis and Morocco. *PCIJ Series B* (1923), No. 4, p. 24.

[14] In that sense basically H. Kelsen, *The Law of the United Nations,* pp. 771, 783, London and New York, 1950, though he, in effect, has an opposite opinion regarding the competence of the UN for human rights.

[15] *Gen. Assem. Off. Rec., XXI Sess.,* Suppl. No. 16 (A/6316), pp. 49–60.

[16] H. Lauterpacht, op. cit., p. 9.

[17] *UNCIO,* Doc. 723 I/I A 19, p. 10, quoted by Kelsen, op. cit., pp. 29–30; H. Bokor, op. cit., p. 287; M. Ganji, op. cit., p. 134, however, rightly pointed out that the word "primarily" has to be interpreted, as different from Kelsen, like a matter in which, beside States, international organized community is interested.

[18] H. Lauterpacht, op. cit., p. 67; M. Ganji, op. cit., pp. 186 et seq.; J. F. Green, op. cit., p. 690 et seq.; M. Moskowitz, op. cit., p. 108.

[19] *Gen. Assem. Off. Rec., XXI Sess.,* Suppl. No. 16 (A/6316), p. 60. See also Resolution 2217 (XXI) concerning the International Year of Human Rights, with the recommendations D, F and H in the Annex.

African attitudes to the international protection of human rights

By Latif O. Adegbite

University of Lagos, Lagos, Nigeria

Acceptance of the idea of respect for human rights

Only four African states: Egypt, Ethiopia, Liberia and the Union of South Africa[1] took part in the discussion on the future Charter of the United Nations at San Francisco. Some 35 African states have since acceded to the Charter with its human rights provision. What do these states think of the provision? Do they see it as an alien notion unsuited to the needs and problems of Africa today?

The claim is often made that the idea of respect for human rights is rooted in European tradition. Therefore, people with non-Western cultural background can be forgiven if they lag behind in the due observance of human rights. Most African states in particular have just emerged from their tribal situation where the traditional of freedom was wholly non-existent.

Of course, these are fallacies; for the love of freedom is universal. But so is man's propensity to deny it to his fellow man. Pre-colonial Africa recognized this conflict, and provided remedies against tyrannical rulers who trampled on the rights of their subjects. Perhaps, the indigene in traditional Africa enjoyed greater freedom than his modern counterpart. Admittedly, his rights were not guaranteed by the state such that he could, at his own instance, enforce them against the whole world. He had to rely on his intimate group: the extended family or the clan, to manipulate the political and social forces to secure his rights. This group support was obligatory and could not be withheld from an individual unless he had been outlawed by the community. The group also afforded basic needs to its members. The citizen thus enjoyed a kind of social security which is the envy of modern states.

Slaves, serfs, aliens,[2] and to some extent, women enjoyed lesser rights. Mention must be made too of some stratified societies with their rigid status differentiations. Here only those who belonged to the ruling race enjoyed the benefits of full membership of society. The rest were treated as outsiders, tolerated only for the jobs they performed which members of the superior race could not or would not perform. *Ruanda* was an example of such an unequal society. Apartheid in South Africa provides a modern parallel.

A few dictatorships also thrived in traditional Africa. The *Kiganda* system in Buganda, now part of Uganda, was probably the highest form. Here, one man, the *Kabaka,* stood at the pinnacle of power controlling every section of the community and every sphere of life. This system was, however, *sui generis*. Even the much maligned *Chaka* of Zululand at no time matched a *Kabaka's* absolutism. But the *Baganda* killed many a Kabaka in defence of their rights and freedoms.

Elsewhere in Africa, there were recognised procedures for removing a ruler who violated the laws of the land and disregarded the rights of the people. Thus the *Akan* peoples of Ghana would prefer definite charges against their chief before de-stooling him. Among the *Yoruba* of Nigeria, the *oba* (king) might be called upon by his subordinate chiefs to poison himself if, in their judgment, he had lost the confidence of his people.

It may be argued that since in a traditional society hereditary chieftaincy was the rule, the rejection of one ruler meant a replacement by another of his kinsmen who would in any event continue his predecessor's policy. As a rule, however, royal kinsmen did not always see eye to eye; they rivalled one another for support among the kingmakers who were not bound (except among the *Bini* of Nigeria where the rule of primogeniture prevailed) to select the eldest eligible prince to accede to a vacant throne.

Moreover, no important decision affecting the community as a whole could be taken without a prior debate in the public assemblies—the *Basuto pitso,* for instance—which were a universal feature of indigenous African political systems. Egalitarian and democratic feeling was even stronger among the peoples of non-centralised societies like the *Nuer* in the Sudan and the *Ibo* of Nigeria.

Was it not the colonial masters who, for their convenience, destroyed the checks and balances surrounding the powers of a traditional ruler who was converted to a "Sole Native Authority" in the new scheme of things? In some chiefless societies, some men were even handpicked and made "warrant chiefs" with disastrous consequences.

We may add too that traditional African legal order recognised certain rights as fundamental and inalienable. Therefore, a law or an executive decision derogating from any of these rights would not stand. As the *Basuto* would put it, man-made law must not contradict *mulao*.

The purpose of the foregoing discourse is to refute the argument that the love of liberty was ingrained in some races and extant in others. We do not know enough about the traditional practices of the peoples of the world to rush to generalisations. Nazi Germany was, after all, European; so was Fascist Italy. Indeed, the regimes in South Africa and Rhodesia, which continue to defy world opinion by perpetrating racial discrimination, are headed by men of European stock who claim to be defending a European civilisation.

To arrogate the origins of the notions of human rights to a particular race is to deny their Natural Law basic and their inherent quality. Such racist thinking has regrettably done considerable disservice to the general effort to secure universal adherence to human rights. It has encouraged some African demagogues to dismiss the growing international concern for human rights as a new form of cultural colonialism. But such men are in a minority; most African leaders are genuinely committed to the realisation of human rights and freedoms for all, without distinction as to race, sex, language or religion, as laid down by Art. 13(2) of the United Nations Charter.

It is interesting to recall that but for the insistence of Egypt (as it then was) supported by other smaller states and some private organisations, the Charter provision on human rights would have been weaker. Egypt suggested amendments to the Dumbarton Oaks Proposals so as to state definitely the United Nations obligations "to promote respect for human rights and fundamental freedoms".[3] The General Assembly would supervise this policy of promoting international co-operation in political, legal, economic, social and humanitarian fields as well as the adjustment of situations likely to impair the general welfare. Because these economic and social problems are of the utmost importance, the Egyptian delegation further proposed that the Economic and Social Council should be one of the principal Organs of the Organisation to be placed on equal footing with the other Organs.

Ironically, the most eloquent speech in support of the international promotion of human rights was made by Field Marshall Smuts, the South African Prime Minister. Alluding to the War just ended, he declared:

"We have fought for justice and decency and the fundamental freedoms and rights of man which are basic to all human advancement and progress and peace. Let us in this new Charter of humanity give expression to this faith in us, and thus proclaim to the world and to posterity that this was not a mere brute struggle of force between the nations but that for us behind the mortal struggle was the moral struggle, was the vision of the ideal, the faith in justice and the resolve to indicate the fundamental rights of man, and on that basis to found a better, freer world for the future."[4]

He stressed that the peace they were striving for and which they were taking such pains to safeguard was "a peace of justice and honour and *fair dealing as between man and man,* as between nation and nation".

But three years later, the world was to know that the South African conception of man was not the same as held by most of mankind. During the debates on the draft of the Universal Declaration of Human Rights, the South African delegate to the General Assembly, Mr. E. H. Louw questioned the assumption[5] that all human beings were born free and equal in dignity and rights and should act towards one another in a spirit of brotherhood.

The South African voice was a solitary one, and the Universal Declaration of Human Rights was duly proclaimed on December 10, 1948. As M. Cassin of France explained:

"There could be no question of allowing the particular philosophy of one state or group of states to prevail."[6]

Mr. Charles Malik of Lebanon who took an active part in the drafting of the Declaration has also given us an insight into the pains taken by the Commission on Human Rights to ensure that the Declaration was universal in its formulation:[7]

"It could be said that the present declaration had been drafted on a firm international basis, for the Secretariat's draft was a compilation not only of hundreds of proposals made by Governments but also of the laws and legal findings of member states of the United Nations."

The Declaration was not intended to be legally binding, the vagueness of the rights defined attests to this. It was to be supplemented by a legally binding International Bill of Rights as well as by appropriate measures of implementation. Notwithstanding its hortatory character, however, the Declaration has made a remarkable impact on many countries, not the least on those of Africa.

All African constitutions provide for fundamental rights. The suggestion is not that every one of these constitutions was adopted with the Declaration in view. Indeed some of the constitutions predate the Declaration. For example, the Liberia Constitution with its Bill of Rights modelled on that of the United States of America, was issued on July 26, 1847. A number of recent constitutions have, however, adopted almost word for word the rights enumerated in the Declaration. The fundamental rights provision in the Nigerian Constitution was borrowed from the European Convention on Human Rights which was itself inspired by the Universal Declaration. All the anglophone African countries whose independence came after Nigeria's (with the exception of the former Tanganyika) have, in their turn, patterned their fundamental rights provisions on the Nigerian model.

Francophone African states do not only list a number of fundamental rights in their constitutions, they also incorporate by reference the Universal Declaration of Human Rights and the French Declaration of the Rights of Man and the Citizen.

The efficacy of these diverse constitutional provisions is examined in the third section. Meanwhile, we turn to a discussion of the role of the African states in the international efforts to promote or protect human rights.

Fulfilment of international obligations in the field of human rights

The emergence of a large number of African states coincided with a new development which was taking roots in the field of human rights. Nazi experience had awakened the world to the futility of entrusting the protection of human rights solely to the internal jurisdiction of a state. The need for an international action found expression in the United Nations Charter which, as we saw, assigned definite responsibilities to the Organisation and its Members for the promotion of human rights. The historic Universal Declaration followed, but the work on the draft of the Covenants on Human Rights took longer than expected. Perhaps the initial enthusiasm generated by the memories of the Second World War waned. Or did the impact of the new states alter the course of events?

These states began to challenge the assumptions of the framers of the Declaration which to their disappointment failed to provide for the right to self-determination as well as that of peoples freely to dispose of their natural wealth and resources. The draft covenants must fill these gaps which meant some delay both in drafting and in winning general support, for the insertion of the "new rights". The older powers considered these rights as inappropriate for inclusion in legally binding instruments. Their plea was not taken.

In collaboration with the Asian, some Latin American states and the socialist states of Eastern Europe, the African states succeeded in placing priority over the international protection of certain rights which they believed would uphold the dignity of the black race. In 1960, the Declaration on the Granting of Independence to Colonial Countries and Peoples was adopted. Certain forms of colonialism were denounced as contrary to the U.N. Charter and therefore a violation of human rights. Henceforth, inadequacy of political, economic, social or educational preparedness would not serve as a pretext for delaying independence. Immediate steps were therefore to be taken in Trust and non-self-governing Territories or any territory which had not yet attained independence, to transfer all powers unconditionally to the peoples of these territories if they freely express the desire to be independent. The Special Committee of 24 was constituted in 1965 to supervise the liquidation of outstanding colonial empires.

The Declaration on the Elimination of All Forms of Racial Discrimination was adopted in 1963. Increased African pressure produced a Convention on the same subject in 1965. Far-reaching measures of implementation were laid down. A committee was established (as well as an *ad hoc* Conciliation Commission). Reports on the legislative, judicial, administrative and other measures adopted by the States Parties to the Convention are to be forwarded to the Committee. The latter is empowered to make suggestions and general recommendations based on the examination of the reports. The Committee would also settle disputes among States Parties making use of the Conciliation Commission, if need be.

By far the most thorough provision is that which permits individuals or groups of individuals within the jurisdiction of States Parties of the Convention to petition the Committee if the latter's competence in this regard has been recognised by the State Party whose national is making the complaint.

There has, however, not been similar African readiness to strengthen the international protection of other human rights. Thus, the measures of implementation proposed for the International Covenant on Civil and Political Rights were, so to say, watered down by a largely African states' amendment which was carried. The explanation for this attitude is manifold:

Disharmony of state interests. African states are still suspicious of their ex-colonial masters. They fear that a potent implementation machinery would give the latter an undue advantage which would be seized upon to perpetuate past injustices. The experts who would enforce the Covenant would be drawn from the ranks of their former rulers, since they would easily qualify as persons with recognised competence in the field of human rights. Fiske's warning is apt: dispassionate decisions by experts are hardly possible. Ambassador Quaison-Sackey of Ghana expressed the fear quite frankly:

"What is more, we fear that any agreement on our part to a special group of experts would commit us in a large measure. Supposing the group came out advocating the partition of South West Africa—which we all oppose—what will be the position of African states in regard to such a recommendation?"[8]

This was precisely what happened in 1957 when the U.N. Good Offices Committee (consisting of U.S.A., Great Britain and Brazil) on South West Africa[9] suggested that South West Africa should be divided into black and white areas. Bantustan policy of South Africa within South Africa itself was thus approved by implication.

Then came the disquieting decision of the International Court of Justice of July 1966 in the South West Africa Cases[10] about which much has been written and said.[11] African states simply interpreted this decision as a European expression of support for South Africa even though the Court declined to pronounce on the merits of the case to which the issue of apartheid belonged, and notwithstanding the distinguished dissent of Judge Jessup of the United States of America and his country's official condemnation of the astonishing decision.

That case too, allegation of undue bias apart, was a defeat for the human rights crusade. The 1962 minority, now turned majority, judges had indicated in 1962 that if they were called upon to decide on the merits, they might decline to recognise human rights as having the force of legal norms. If, at best, human rights were international standards, they could only affect future situations and could not disturb existing rights. In other words, South Africa could not by some vague political, moral or humanitarian considerations be compelled to assume more onerous obligations than the prevailing conditions when the Mandate was accepted, required.

Although the majority did not adopt the foregoing arguments in their 1966 judgment, as they chose to rest their decision on a strange procedural technicality, the 1962 *dicta* have assumed a fresh significance. South Africa has drawn great comfort from them.

Breach of the international promise to recognise human dignity. The Universal Declaration of Human Rights in its Preamble affirms the inherent dignity of man. But nearly twenty years after this affirmation, the dignity of the black race is still assaulted with impunity in South Africa, Rhodesia, the Portuguese territories, and to a much lesser extent, in U.S.A. The Big Power Nations with the economic and military strength to curb these inhuman practices condemn them, but are not prepared to force the issue. African opinion interprets this attitude as one of condonation.

African disillusionment with the United Nations on this matter can hardly be put much stronger than the Secretary-General of the United Nations did in his 1965/1966 Report:[12]

"The most conspicuous and anachronistic mass violation of human rights and fundamental freedoms is that which continues to be enforced against the non-white majority of the people of the Republic of South Africa. The situation has shown no improvement . . . There is a growing disappointment among member states because of the ineffectiveness of the demand for stronger action."

The much needed economic aid which would enhance the material well-being of Africans has not flown in in the quantity expected. The gap between the rich and poor countries continues to widen. Economic inequality breeds indignity since those who are well off tend to look down on the less fortunate ones. Human rights cannot prosper in such a situation. If an international system of protection of human rights is to be effective, the international community must promote a brotherhood of mankind in which economic and other forms of inequality would be reduced to the barest minimum.

Domestic jurisdiction plea. It is true that many African states are still jealous of their newly-won independence and sovereignty, but except in a few instances, the plea of domestic jurisdiction has not been pressed too far.

When the U.N. Charter was being drafted, Liberia issued a caveat:[13]

"That in connection with the working out of details of whatever economic, social or other humanitarian problems, as may be projected at the Conference, care should be taken to see that definite and specific means be set out therefore; as otherwise unjustifiable interference in the internal affairs of nations might occur."

Recently, I.L.O. sought to place the allegation of violation of human rights by Burundi on the agenda of a meeting of the Commission on Human Rights.[14] The allegation was that some trade union leaders had been wantonly executed by the Burundi authorities. The latter protested but promised to disclose the facts leading to the trial, the procedure adopted and the execution of the trade unionists.

At one stage in the consideration of the draft Convention on the Elimination of All Forms of Racial Discrimination, Tanzania opposed a Ghana proposal for strong measures of implementation including recourse to the International Court of Justice in certain cases. It was the view of the Tanzanian delegate that since the feelings of states were still strong on the question of sovereignty, he did not see how the provision under which one state could lodge a complaint against another concerning internal matters could be accepted.[15] A similar reservation was expressed by some new states during the debates on the implementation machinery of the draft covenants on human rights.[16]

African revolutionary era. The African states further feel that in the present stage of their development, they cannot honestly be expected to fulfil the obligations spelt out in the Covenants. They are pre-occupied with the task of nation-building and may have to use stern measures to integrate the diverse communities making up the state, some of whose leaders would stop at nothing in their bid to disintegrate the state. The rapid economic development of the country may also lead to decisions which might detract from the high ideals expressed in the Covenants.[17]

Furthermore, it might be necessary to follow an unequal road to equality. For instance, some groups of people who had been unduly favoured in the colonial period may be discriminated against in order to correct unjust imbalances. Conversely, other classes of people who are handicapped may receive undue favours in the balancing process: special jobs for Africans in Kenya; quota system in the Nigerian public service (which dilutes the principle of merit but which has as its aim the maintenance of an ethnic equilibrium).

The African plea that all the difficulties discussed above would gradually disappear carried the day in the world community. A respite was thus given to the developing countries by making the reporting system the only obligatory measure of implementation for the Covenant on Civil and Political Rights as well as for the Covenant on Economic, Social and Cultural Rights. State-to-state complaints before the Committee on Human Rights would be progressively adopted by states in respect of civil and political rights. No time limit was fixed for the duration of this respite.

The proposal for individual petitions which was later embodied in the Protocol on Human Rights, was not popular with the African states. A guarded support came, however, from Nigeria whose Government listed two conditions which must be fulfilled: First, before any petition could be lodged with the appropriate body established for the purpose, all local, judicial and administrative remedies must have been exhausted; secondly, such petitions must be rooted through the Government of the aggrieved national whose comments on the complaint should be dispatched with the complaint itself to the Permanent Organ.[18]

African states have been participating actively in the other diverse actions of the U.N. to further the cause of human rights such as the definition of specific human rights in international instruments, collection and exchange of information, debates and recommendations by the various U.N. organs, ratification and appreciable observance of Conventions relating to human rights sponsored by the U.N. or its specialised agencies, especiallly I.L.O., U.N.E.S.C.O. and W.H.O.

African state action in the field of human rights

African insistence on a voluntary measure of implementation may suggest that a second best is good enough for the common man in Africa. This would be refuted by most African states whose periodic reports to the U.N. organs invariably lay claim to a high degree of adherence to human rights; as evidence, the constitutional instruments, legislative measures and judicial decisions of each state.

A close examination of African constitutional instruments and practices reveals, however, that in most cases the adherence to human rights is only formal.

The method employed by the constitution to protect human rights affords a good, though not conclusive, test of the effectiveness of the protection accorded. Three methods are distinguished:

Type "A" constitution. The rights are precisely formulated and entrenched. More pertinently, these rights are specifically made enforceable by the courts.

Examples of states with such a constitutional guarantee are Liberia, Nigeria, Sierra-Leone, Gambia, Uganda, Kenya, Malawi, Zambia, Botswana, Lesotho and the Somali Republic.

Type "B" constitution. Here the rights are declaratory and are usually phrased in general terms. Francophone states come within this category, as do the Arab-African states. The rights may be entrenched too, thus it may be prescribed that only an organic law can qualify the rights.

The personal presidential pledge of adherence to listed principles provided for in the former Republican constitution of Ghana was a *specie* of this type of human rights.

Type "C" constitution. Only Tanzania's constitution falls within this category. It provides for an *Ombudsman* type of institution. A three-men Permanent Commission of Enquiry is established to investigate complaints against public officers, including civil servants; party functionaries, officials of statutory bodies, and even officers of Workers' Unions.

There is no unanimity as to which classes of rights should be protected. The English-speaking countries, true to their British background, omit rights whose protection is desirable but not enforceable. The francophone states, on the other hand, bundle these economic and political rights together.

Civil and political rights are everywhere subject to restrictions which, in most cases, are so far-reaching as to make one wonder whether there is anything left of the rights purportedly protected. Thus, although the Constitution of Rhodesia, 1961, embodies a Declaration which provides for the enjoyment of human rights and fundamental freedoms of the individual whatever his race, tribe, place of origin, political opinion, colour or creed, the provision would not apply to anything done under a law in force immediately before the operative date of the Constitution. Instruments of oppression like the Land Apportionment Act and the Law and Order (Maintenance) Act, 1959, were thus saved.

In periods of public emergency many of the rights protected are derogated from, though some constitutions provide that the derogation shall not be more than is necessary to deal with the situation.

In the last resort, the efficacy of fundamental rights rests on an independent and fearless judiciary able and willing to enlarge rather than restrict the rights. African experience to date does not offer too much hope, though there have been a few bold judgments. The one-party phenomenon and the dominance of one party in the multi-party states are perhaps too intimidating for the judiciary. However, some of the most important decisions which are taken in Africa today, e.g. where a new town or industry should be sited, who is to be awarded, what contract, where should certain amenities go, etc., are not fit for judicial review. Yet these are decisions which affect the common man the most. To ensure that he is not denied his due share of the fruits of development, he needs a protector who would watch over his interests and to whom he can complain if he suspects that an abuse has been committed against him by the bureaucracy. In this regard, the *Ombudsman* institution deserves consideration by African states. But it should not be a substitute for the usual judicial review of laws as has been done in Tanzania.

The need for an African machinery of protection

Many African constitutions have collapsed in the last two years despite their fundamental rights provisions. Would the bush-fire of military *coups d'etat* have flared up had there been an international machinery for the protection of human rights? The present Greek situation belies such a conclusion.

The Scandinavian countries' unique espousal of the cause of the suffering Greek opponents of the military regime before the European institutions,[19] cannot force an immediate change; it would probably bring about a slowing down of repressive measures. By the time all the European remedies are exhausted, the Greek military rulers would have succeeded, maybe, in installing a puppet civilian government so that the human rights procedure would become academic.

This notwithstanding, it is submitted that an effective international machinery, however limited, for the promotion of human rights on the African continent, is necessary.

African freedom ought not to be restricted to state freedom. The impression is created by the Charter of the Organisation of African Unity that the Organisation exists primarily for the maintenance of the sovereignty of the respective African states and governments (the Charter expressly outlaws subversion, and "political assassination"). Individual Africans ought to benefit directly from the O.A.U. An African guarantee of his fundamental rights may afford such tangible benefit.

The idea is not new. It was first suggested by an unofficial body of African jurists who met in conference in Lagos in January 1961.[20] Similar call was recently made by francophone African jurists at another conference held in Dakar in January, 1967.[21] Only one African government, namely Somali, has echoed this call for an African Convention on Human Rights.[22] What is important about the Somali proposal is that it suggests a machinery for linking any regional arrangement to the U.N. system. It also recognises that further action would have to be taken to minimise the differences between regional approaches when a network of regional systems has been established.

The time is probably not propitious for an African solution in this matter. Relations between most African states are far from cordial. Border disputes abound. Allegations of one state harbouring and financing subversive elements against another are numerous. Language division has hardened into blocs coinciding with groupings based roughly on past common colonial experience. The immediate task before the O.A.U. therefore, is to normalise relations among its feuding members. This, it is hoped, would pave the way to the formulation of a definite programme in the field of human rights instead of resting content as now with a formal Charter affirmation of adherence to the Universal Declaration of Human Rights. It is a welcome sign that the O.A.U. has taken steps to find an African solution to the continent's burning refugee problem.

NOTES

[1] Other African states do not accept South Africa as an African state; she is, therefore not a member of the Organisation of African Unity.

[2] As in all ancient societies. Cf. Hans Blix, "Treatment of Aliens", a paper presented as background for discussion at an African International Conference in International Law, Lagos, March 14–18, 1967.

[3] *U.N. Conference on International Organisation,* vol. 3, pp. 453 et seq.

[4] Ibid., vol. 1, pp. 425–426.

[5] *U.N. General Assembly Official Records, 3rd Session,* p. 39.

[6] Ibid., pp. 61–62.

[7] Ibid., 858.

[7a] See Report prepared by Mrs. P. de Leon, Rapporteur for the Third Committee, on Draft International Covenants on Human Rights, A/6546, paragraph 33.

[8] U.N. Doc. S/P.V. 1077, December 3, 1963, pp. 17–20 quoted by A. C. Leiss and V. Mackay, The issues after two decades, *Apartheid and United Nations Collective Measures* etc. (ed. A. C. Leiss) (1965).

[9] Appointed under General Assembly Resolution 1143 XII. For the Report of the Committee see A/3900 of 1958.

[10] Second Phase, Judgment (1966) 1 C. J. Report 6; see earlier Preliminary Objections (1962) 1 C. J. Report 319.

[11] See Rosalyn Higgins, The International Court and South West Africa: the implications of the judgment, *International Affairs* (1966), vol. 42, p. 573; see also an adapted version of the same article in *Journal of the International Commission of Jurists* (1967), vol. 8; E. A. Gross, The South West Africa case; what happened?, *Foreign Affairs* (1966), vol. 45, p. 36; Elizabeth S. Lands, The South West Africa cases; remand to the United Nations, *Cornell Law Quarterly* (1967), vol. 52, p. 627; B. Cheng, The 1966 South-West Africa judgment of the World Court, *Current Legal Problems* (1967), vol. 20, p. 181; R. R. Falk, The South West Africa cases; an appraisal, *International Organisation* (1967), vol. 21, No. 1, p. 1.

[12] Introduction to the Annual Report of the Secretary-General of the Organisation June 16, 1965 – June 15, 1966, *General Assembly Official Records, 21st Session,* Supplement No. 1A.

[13] *U.N. Conference on International Organisation,* vol. 3, p. 464.

[14] *U.N. Monthly Chronicle* (1967), vol. 4, pp. 24–25. Cf. Liberian attitude to the Committee appointed under Art. 26 of the Constitution of the International Labour Organisation to examine the complaint filed by the Government of Portugal concerning

the observance by the Government of Liberia of the Forced Labour Convention 1930. See Supplement II to the *1963 I.L.O. Official Bulletin;* also *Report of the I.L.O. Committee of experts in the application of Conventions and Recommendations 1962.*

[15] *Official Records,* Third Committee of the General Assembly (*20th Session*), 1345th Meeting.

[16] A/65, 46 op. cit., paragraph 413.

[17] See more fully, *U.N. Seminar on Human Rights in Developing Countries held in Dakar from February 8–22, 1966,* U.N. Report ST/TAO/HR/25.

[18] *Governments observations on the Explanatory Paper on Measures of implementation prepared by the Secretary-General,* A/5411/Add. 2 of October 25, 1963.

[19] See Press Release No. C(67) 33 issued by the Directorate of Information of the Council of Europe on September 20, 1967.

[20] See *African Conference on the Rule of Law* (1961) (International Commission of Jurists Publication).

[21] The Conference of French speaking African Jurists. *Bulletin of the International Commission of Jurists* (1967), vol. 29, pp. 1 et seq.

[22] See A/5411/Add. op. cit.

The universality of human rights in a world of conflicting ideologies

By Rudolf Bystrický

Charles University, Prague, Czecho-Slovakia

1

The Universal Declaration of Human Rights claims to be universal according to its title and content.

The preparatory materials show that originally the intention was to draft an international rather than a universal declaration. The use of the term universal was not merely a change of words but an expression of a certain conception. Even in the past many declarations of human rights were formulated in a universal way, as, for instance, at the time of the French revolution when declarations spoke of the protection of men "de tous les temps et de tous les pays", but they as their predecessors (Habeas Corpus, Bill of Rights, The American Declarations) were in fact documents of internal law, whose aim was to protect the interests of certain classes and strata. The authors of these declarations were aware of the fact that by an appeal to principles of a universal character they would more easily win over the hearts of the population and gain their support for a certain political program. At the same time of course all these declarations contained some all-human elements in accordance with the achieved cultural level of the particular country.

The Universal Declaration is a novelty both as to its origin and content. It is a document of international law expressing the common will of sovereign states. This international character of the Universal Declaration was in no way affected by the novel idea of universality. To the authors of the Universal Declaration it was obvious that the international community rests on the existence of sovereign states and that the protection of human rights is essentially dependent on both the internal and foreign politicies of these states. It was not the intention that interstate relations on which today's international community rests be replaced by some other kind of relations; nor was it the intention to give international subjectivity to individuals, which would have had the result of loosening the ties of a citizen with his state, nor was it the intent to create some instrument of an exaggerated individualism, which would undermine the legal status quo.

The Covenants on Human Rights of December 1966 are entitled "International Covenants". They are international because humanity has organized itself in nations, but states must consider themselves to some extent as the agents of humanity. Thus one is able to talk of an international convention with universal character.

The international protection of human rights rests on two obligations of states:

Firstly, every state undertakes the legal obligation to assure on its territory the protection of human rights.

Secondly, by the signing of the Charter, states obliged themselves to an international cooperation in the interests of the promotion, protection and development of human rights and fundamental freedoms. Should some state refuse to cooperate, there would be a violation of its legal pledge under Art. 56 of the Charter.

Human rights and freedoms can be protected and guaranteed only in time of peace (*inter arma silent leges*) and on the basis of international cooperation. Hence it follows that the right to peace and the right to claim politics of peaceful coexistence are to be considered as fundamental human rights.

In what does the universality of the protection of human rights consist?

In short, human rights and fundamental freedoms should be available to every human being on our planet. In other words; the subjects of international law remain states, but the beneficiaries of all human rights are the inhabitants of the whole earth. In particular the universality manifests itself in the following ways:

(*a*) Firstly in the "personal" sense. All articles of the Universal Declaration begin with the words "everyone" or "no one" or "men and women". That means that human rights should be enjoyed by every human being without regard to citizenship or domicile. According to Art. 2 everyone is entitled to all rights and freedoms set forth in the Declaration.

In contrast to the past it is not a question of protection of a national or other minority, but protection of all men. The resolution of the General Assembly of the UNO (A/C3/307 Rev. I/add. 1) pointed out that with regard to the universality of the Declaration there is no need for specific protection of minority groups. For practical reasons it is necessary, however, to conclude conventions for the protection of certain groups like for instance the convention on genocide or the stipulation on the right of peoples to selfdetermination.

In three cases only, special rights for citizens as opposed to others are recognized: The right to return to his own country (Art. 13/2); the right to take part in the government of his own country and the right of access to public service in his own country (Art. 21).

The general tendency in the world is towards putting foreigners on an equal footing with nationals, at least in the field of private law. Reciprocity is required in most cases; in my country national treatment of foreigners is not necessarily dependent on reciprocity (Law No. 97/1963). This tendency to universality found its expression in Art. 2 of the International Covenant on Civil and Political Rights of 1966 which imposes the obligation on states to guarantee all rights to everyone on their territory.

This, however, does not mean that conditions have ripened to the extent where the difference between a citizen and a foreigner could be abolished entirely. All states of the world have special regulations for the entry of foreigners into their territory, for permission to remain, for employment and permanent residence. Neither the Universal Declaration nor the International Covenants on Human Rights do impinge on these rights.

(*b*) Secondly universality manifests itself in a "territorial" sense in that its territorial validity is unbounded. It is true that the Preamble of the Universal Declaration speaks only of member states and territories under their jurisdiction, but paragraph 2 of Art. 2 states that no distinction shall be made on the basis of the political, jurisdictional or international status of the country or territory to which a person belongs.

In the light of what has been said it is a regrettable departure from the principle of universality when some states and international organisations admit reservations to international conventions under which the operation of the convention does not automatically extend to the dependent territories. (Convention on Genocide, International Labour Conventions, Art. 63 of the European Convention on Human Rights and Freedoms etc.). It is a pity that even the International Covenants of 1966 are open to signature only for member states of the UNO, or the specialized agencies, or those states which are invited to do so by the General Assembly.

(*c*) A further feature of the universality of the Universal Declaration consists in an appeal not only to nations but also to every individual and every organ of society. The realization of human rights necessarily presupposes this full cooperation.

From this it follows that states should not allow any activity of individuals or associations whose aims and methods are in obvious contradiction to the spirit and letter of the Universal Declaration. It would be entirely incorrect to play off one article of the Universal Declaration against the other and to invoke for instance in this connection Art. 19 on the freedom of expression or Art. 20 on the freedom of association.

(*d*) A distinct feature of the universality of human rights and freedoms is that the organs of the UNO have a jurisdiction in their respect. According to Art. 2 paragraph 6 this is so even in the case of non-members because the Charter links the protection of human rights with maintenance of peace.

This jurisdiction of the organs of the UNO—including the International Court of Justice—is given under the same conditions as in other matters concerning peace and security. The recent verdict of the I.C.J. concerning violation of human rights in South-West-Africa was a big blow to the expectations of those who thought that if jurisdiction was to be given to an international tribunal, all questions of the protection of human rights would be solved.

One should always distinguish between institutional, consistent and continued violation of human rights by a state and individual and sporadic cases. Both are regrettable and have to be opposed, but the jurisdiction of international organs is given only in cases which are a threat to international peace and security. This legal situation was clearly expressed in the report of the respective sub-committee in San Francisco, where the following statement may be read:

"The subcommittee held that assuring or protecting such fundamental rights is primarily the concern of each state. If, however, such rights and freedoms were grievously outraged, so as to create conditions which threaten peace or obstruct the application of provisions of the Charter, then they cease to be the sole concern of each state." (U.N.C.I.O. Doc. 723. I/I.)

It follows from all that I have said that the universality of human rights is not in contradiction with the international character of the respective documents; on the contrary these two features are complementary. One may say that states should in all their activities—without infringing the sovereign rights of other states—keep in mind their universal responsibility in promoting and encouraging respect for human rights.

2

Varying conceptions of the world and man, conflicting philosophical doctrines, different opinions as to whether human rights are natural or social rights, conflicting ideologies—all these led to doubts as to the possibility of universality of human rights. At the time the Universal Declaration was being drafted opinions were expressed that it had little sense to formulate in an abstract way some splendid sounding principles, which would remain dead letters. However, the opinion prevailed that even if the Universal Declaration was nothing but a catalogue of rights which should be protected it would nevertheless be of great significance: The Charter of the UNO imposes a legal obligation to protect human rights and fundamental freedoms but does not indicate the kind of rights and freedoms to be protected.

In the course of the last 20 years this opinion has proved correct. The Universal Declaration had a great influence on the formulation of various municipal and international documents and this without regard to the discussions on the juridical nature of the Declaration. We can say without exaggeration that almost every state has at some time or other appealed to the articles of the Universal Declaration.

The protagonists of different doctrines and ideologies did not reach and seem unlikely to reach a consensus. This is true whether they are adherents of the different naturalist or positivist schools, or whether their approach is that of an idealist or rationalist or materialist. It is characteristic of the ideological struggle, that a theoretical reconciliation is not possible. The function of international law, however, has never been and can never be that of unifying opposing doctrines but rather to find and elaborate common rules of behaviour and thus to achieve in mutual understanding a practical goal. The adoption of the final version of the International Covenants on Human Rights on December 16, 1966 was a significant step forward in the development of progressive international law.

The achievement of practical goals rather than a consensus on ideological matters is the function of the UNO and the substance of its activities. If the states are able to agree on concrete actions, which in an objective sense strengthen human dignity, peace and security, then their motives are of secondary importance. What matters are practical conclusions; each partner to a common action is entitled to his own ideology and justification of his acts.

The authors of the Universal Declaration were aware of these facts: Nevertheless, opinions are repeatedly expressed that the development of international law and its tendency towards universality—especially in the field of the protection of human rights—is hindered by the existence of conflicting ideologies.

There are differences in conceptions of law, morality, justice and equally there is no unanimity on the notions of freedom and democracy. In my opinion, however, mistakes are made in several respects in emphasizing only the differences of doctrinal and philosophical attitudes:

Firstly, it is incorrect to consider every conflicting interpretation or application of a particular rule or principle as a manifestation of ideological struggle. We know from both municipal and international practice that it is not unusual for protagonists of the same ideology to put a different interpretation on a principle or a norm: Today's interpretation of the Code Napoleon is not the same as it was decades ago, nor is Belgium's interpretation entirely indentical to that of the Paris Cour de Cassation; and I would mention also the famous book of Charles Ch. Hyde, which is entitled "International Law Chiefly as Applied and Interpreted by the USA".

Secondly, it is mistaken to consider that conflicting ideologies are at the root of international tensions and conflicts. We are told that if there was a convergence of capitalism and socialism, all problems would be solved as a result of the disappearance of ideological conflicts. If, however, one examines the history of the last three or four centuries one can see that the causes of wars and tensions were in power politics and not in ideological divergencies. There were no essential differences in the social, political or economic systems of the European powers before the First World War; no socialist state existed at that time and in spite of it the First World War broke out; and even the Second World War did not start as a war of ideologies. We can see that coincidence of ideologies is not necessarily a guarantee of peace, nor are conflicting ideologies necessarily a cause of war.

Finally, it seems to me that it is a shortcoming in the theoretical work of lawyers, philosophers and sociologists that they mainly concentrate their attention on the differences, and neglect to stress the common human content of some notions and ideals.

It is indisputable—according to our views—that such notions as law, justice, morality, democracy, freedom etc. are historical categories, whose content is determined by the conditions of life of a people and by their social circumstances. As the conditions of life change, so the content of notions and ideas may change. The ruling ideas of an age are the ideas of its ruling class.

However, this approach does not deny the existence of ideals, principles, notions, which have—at least to some extent—a universal character and are a sort of common denominator for everyone within a certain historical period.

Karl Marx in his Inaugural Address to the International Movement of Workers wrote in 1864 of the necessity of observing between nations "the same simple rules of morality and justice" which ought to govern relations between individuals. It follows from these words that Marx recognized the existence of some a priori given universal rules of morality and justice, which were ignored by the ruling classes. These ideas of Marx were incorporated into the statutes of the International Association of Workers in 1864, which stated that "all individual members and associations recognize truth, justice and morality as a basis for their relations both mutual and vis-a-vis any other human individual".

These ideas were developed by Lenin who wrote that Marxism was not born in a vacuum away from the main stream of human civilization; on the one hand Marxism destroys all obsolete ideas and institutions, on the other hand it considers itself to be the heir of all the noble ideas and achievements of humanity.

Influenced by these ideas and in the light of past experiences the XXIIth Congress of the Communist Party of the Soviet Union adopted in 1961 a final resolution which—in the part dealing with ideological questions—repeats the words of Marx on the violation of the simple norms of morality and justice by the ruling classes and states among others that "communist morality includes all the basic human norms, which are the result of the struggle of the masses over thousands of years against social oppression and moral corruption".

I mention these things because in our legal profession we necessarily use some abstract notions, and the question is whether one can achieve—at least a partial—common understanding of these notions or whether they will always remain controversial.

As we know, there is no abstraction without some concrete bases. The sources of every abstraction are some concrete events on the base of which the abstraction has been made.

Thus, for instance, the Charter of the UNO uses the expression justice (Preamble, Art. 2/3); the statutes of the International Labour Organization speak of social justice etc.

What is meant by justice? So far nobody has defined this notion. The greek philosopher Epicurus pointed out over two thousand years ago that "only those provisions of law which are beneficial according to the experience of everyday life can be considered as just". Law and justice are not the same thing; law may be an instrument of justice and injustice as well (summum ius, summa saepe iniuria).

Why then do states employ the notion of justice in international documents? They do so because they rightly assume that in spite of ideological conflicts they may come to a common understanding of this notion in concrete cases.

Let us take another notion, democracy: Art. 29 of the Universal Declaration speaks of a democratic society. The preparatory materials show that because of ideological differences any hint as to the meaning of this notion was intentionally omitted. We find the notion of democracy in the Potsdam Agreement, according to which the German people should be given the opportunity to rebuild their life on democratic lines. Human rights on a democratic basis are guaranteed to the Vietnamese people in the final Declaration of the Geneva Conference on Indochina.

What kind of democracy is meant in these documents? History knows the Athenian slave democracy, the bourgeois democracy, liberal democracy, peoples democracy etc. But apart from these concrete types of democracy, one can speak in abstract terms of democracy and that was done by the authors of the documents mentioned before. They assumed that at least on some aspects of democracy a common understanding may be reached. Thus, for instance, under the present circumstances it will be clear to everybody that a fascist form of government or the policy of apartheid is contrary to the notion of democracy. On the other hand differences may arise as to whether free elections or plebiscite belong to the abstract notion of democracy; experiences have shown that these institutions can play in some circumstances a democratic and progressive role, while on other occasions they can become a weapon in the hands of tyrants.

By using such terms as democracy in international documents, states assume that in practice they will agree on some aspects of this notion, while they will try to reach a compromise on other aspects and remain divided on the rest. In other words, ideological divergencies will continue to exist as they are inherent in the development of human society; on the other hand there exist some pertinent contemporary standards, which correspond to the actual level of development.

According to the last paragraph of the Preamble of the Universal Declaration, a common understanding of human rights and freedoms is of the greatest importance for the full realization of the pledges of states. The original version spoke of a common understanding of "the nature of these rights"; the word "nature" was deleted during the preparatory work owing to ideological differences. The present wording of this paragraph seems to indicate that the authors were aware of the fact that for the time being there was no common understanding on all the aspects of human rights and freedoms, but on *some* aspects understanding existed and exists and in the course of the exchange of conflicting views further common understanding might be achieved. When abstract notions are to be put into operation and take a concrete shape, all views, experiences and attitudes of the contemporary international community must be taken into account.

3

I should like to mention one fundamental problem of contemporary world. While in the advanced countries human rights and freedoms are occasionally violated, in the developing (underdeveloped) countries these rights simply do not exist for a large section of the population. So for instance the statistics of the F.A.O. show that almost half of the world population lives in a permanent state of hunger. The reports of the W.H.O. state that millions of human beings never reach their 30th birthday. According to UNESCO many million of children have no opportunity to attend school.

This situation affects us all in that it constitutes a threat to international peace and security, the prevention and removal of which is the aim of the UNO.

It is evident that in these countries the problem of human rights and freedoms is somewhat different from that in affluent societies. We know that civil rights and freedoms on one hand and economic and social rights on the other hand, are inextricably linked and therefore the establishment of a hierarchy among them is not justifiable in the advanced countries; however, the lack of economic and social rights in the developing countries creates a different situation. There the main emphasis must be laid on the establishment of conditions under which human dignity can be guaranteed. The protection of human rights must be closely linked with speedy economic development.

This task is beyond the possibilities of our legal profession. Cooperation among jurists, economists and natural scientists is indispenable. They must seek and find a convenient solution for a planned fight against this great threat to humanity. The role of the jurist must not be limited to the formulation of some noble principles and rules. Jurists must collaborate in the exploration of the optimal solutions.

It is probably this situation which Art. 2 of the International Covenant on Economic and Social Rights had in mind, stating, that international cooperation in the technical, economic and legal fields could together guarantee human rights.

Special responsibility rests on the advanced socialist and capitalist countries, since more than two thirds of the worlds technical, economic and scientific potential is in their hands. Cooperation between them and the developing countries in a co-ordinated way could help the underdeveloped countries to the extent that they would then be in a position to help themselves. The elimination of the notion of an underdeveloped country would be the greatest contribution to the protection and promotion of human rights.

In conclusion I should like to point out that the problem of human rights and freedoms is once again a topic of penetrating debate in the socialist countries. The question is not one of having these rights embodied in the Constitution and other legislation, for that had been done quite some time ago. In my country it happened last in the 1960 Constitution and in a number of other legislative acts. Our society is seeking answers to new questions arising out of its development and the current scientific and technical revolution, and our political theory realizes that we can no longer operate with many of the existing concepts; it has therefore once again raised the question of the relationship between socialism and democracy, which also includes the question of civil and political rights and freedoms.

The tendency is to abandon the deep-rooted idea that there is a higher interest of society in contrast to the subordinate interests of the individual and that the purpose of law is to bridge these contradictory interests of the individual and society. As a matter of fact, in a modern society the interests of the individual and society should be in harmony rather than contradictory. Society can develop only if its individual members have the possibility of freely developing their creative ability, and it is therefore in the interest of society to protect individual rights and freedoms. On the other hand, the individual can develop his abilities and apply them only in a society which can adequately safeguard the rights and freedoms of its individual members. It is therefore in the individual's interest to protect the interests of society, just as it is in the interest of society to be a society of free individuals.

We realize that the attainment of such an ideal state of harmony goes beyond the legal sphere, nevertheless we believe that proper legislation can considerably influence the whole course of development of society.

Much of the debate is concerned with the question which I have discussed from a general viewpoint above, namely to what extent should we abandon the traditional concept of human rights and of civil and political freedoms, and to what extent should they be viewed as the common cultural heritage of mankind. We follow very closely developments in other parts of the world and we find that in some—but far from all—advanced non-socialist countries the content of the aforesaid rights and freedoms has somewhat expanded under the influence of the pressure exerted by the working class and progressive elements. In view of this trend, marxist theory and political practice in certain non-socialist countries—such as France, Italy or Finland—are elaborating the question of the possibility of a constitutional, parliamentary road to socialism. In my country—and I suppose that in other socialist countries as well—political theory has discarded its previous and erroneous views on the total discontinuity of the development of human and civil rights, and are closely following the trends in democratic world public opinion and political practice.

However, in doing so we do not in any way idealize the development in even the most advanced non-socialist countries, and we continue to hold firm to the positions of socialist humanism. We do not ignore the fact that in spite of all the achievements of civilization in the past decades, in spite of the tremendous technological progress, in spite of the unprecedented availability of consumer goods, human relations in the most advanced countries have not become better, more just, people are not happier and more balanced; on the contrary, they frequently suffer from disillusionment, a sense of frustration, nervous exhaustion and alienation from society.

We therefore seek new and our own ways of consolidating human and civil rights and freedoms in the period of the scientific and technical revolution. We are trying to find a system of rules and other regulators, which would govern objective economic, socio-political, psychological, cultural and other conditions so as to provide for man's comprehensive development. We believe that man's position in labour relationship is of key importance in this respect, because work constitutes the basic part of man's life, and it is within the process of work that man is most exposed to influences which shape his life both from the material and psychological points of view, and it is also the process of work which gives rise to the majority of objective factors of a dehumanizing character. This brings forth the question, how to organize the life of people in the process of work so as to promote their conscious cooperation and rid them of sensations of helplessness. These are extremely difficult questions involving the problem of how to secure the best socio-political and psychological medium for the work and private life of individuals, or how to place in harmony the demand of the participation of the public in the administration of the State, including production and the whole national economy, and the application of scientific methods of management.

The rights of individual citizens and the scope of their application are in most cases formulated rather generally and broadly, and the constitutions and laws use such terms as public order, interests of the workers and society, etc. We realize that such general terms cannot be avoided, nevertheless demands have been raised that the very constitutional provisions should be more detailed and specific, and where the use of general terms cannot be avoided, a stability of their interpretation should be secured. (For example, the Yugoslav Constitution specifies in Art. 40 the scope of the freedom of the press, speech, and association by providing for such limits as the prohibition to undermine the socialist democratic system, threat to equal international co-operation, incitement to racial, religious or national hatred, etc.)

We are fully aware that the *conditions* promoting human rights and freedoms and the *protection* of these rights are not one and the same thing. We continue to hold that the creation of favourable economic and social conditions constitutes a prerequisite of the aforesaid rights, but there is a growing trend of opinion calling for a broad social control of the observance of these rights through various democratic organizations, the press, radio and television, as well as for the possibility of judicial control.

I have outlined only a few of the problems which I believe exist in varying degrees in some other countries. An exchange of experiences and a confrontation of views will undoubtedly help us to find also in the legal sphere new solutions for newly arising situations.

The role of the United Nations in the protection of human rights—is it misconceived?

By J. E. S. Fawcett

Oxford University, Oxford, England

1

The question which I raise for discussion here is narrower than the title might suggest. I am not of course putting in issue the force and influence of the Universal Declaration and the two Covenants: on the contrary, it is precisely their almost legislative effect which has diverted the U.N. in certain ways from what I believe is its proper task in the protection of human rights. Again I am not questioning the usefulness and aim of the work of the Third and Fourth Committees, ECOSOC, the Trusteeship Council, the Human Rights Commission, and other U.N. bodies, not least among them the Secretariat.

My question concerns U.N. action in the field of self-determination. What I shall suggest is that, for a period at least since 1960, the U.N. has appeared to understand and apply the principle of self-determination for the protection of human rights in ways, which have in important cases failed to lead to that protection, and which have had political effects that are not in the long term in the interest of human rights. In short, I believe that in this period self-determination, which is and should remain a directive principle, has been given the status of a directly enforceable right; that it has come to be treated as one of the recognized "human rights"; and politically it is identified, not always with advantage, with independence. I want to examine in turn these three interconnected factors in the evolution of the principle, and then point to some of the results.

2

The U.N. Charter, in Art. 1 (2) and 55, treats self-determination as a directive principle. I borrow this description from Part IV of the Constitution of India, Art. 37 of which reads:

"The provisions contained in this Part shall not be enforceable by any court, but the principles therein laid down are nevertheless fundamental in the governance of the country and it shall be the duty of the State to apply these principles in making laws."

Though the field of operation of the Charter and Universal Declaration is not the same as that of the Constitution of India, there is I think sufficient common ground for the analogy of directive principles to be sound.

The Universal Declaration does not speak directly of self-determination but it declares that the will of the people shall be the basis of the authority of government (Art. 21 (3)), and that everyone is entitled to a social and international order, in which the rights and freedoms declared can be realized (Art. 28). Again General Assembly Resolution 637A–VII (16.12.1952) declared that

"the right of peoples and nations to self-determination is a prerequisite to the full enjoyment of all fundamental human rights";

recommended that U.N. members

"uphold the principle of self-determination of all peoples and nations"

and called for information under Art. 73 c of the Charter on

"the extent to which the right of peoples and nations to self-determination is exercised by the peoples of those (Non-self-governing) Territories, and in particular regarding their political progress."

I believe that these formulations of self-determinations as a directive principle were correct.

Nevertheless, it is to be noticed that Resolution 637A–VII, though it follows the lines of the Charter and the Universal Declaration speaks of a *right* of self-determination. This is repeated in Resolution 1188–XII, and finally prevails in the famous Declaration of 1960 (Resolution 1514–XV) which says in paragraph 2:

"All peoples have the right to self-determination; by virtue of that right they freely determine their political status and freely pursue their economic, social and cultural development."

It is possible to discern two forces which went to make this Declaration: first, the accelerating movement to end colonialism, reflected in the admission by the same Assembly which made the Declaration of seventeen newly independent countries; and second, the realization from experience of the political impact of the Universal Declaration, far greater than was foreseen in 1948.

The General Assembly did not set a time-limit or time scale for the exercise of self-determination by colonial peoples, and it did not accept a draft resolution by the Soviet Union that 1962 should be the year of "the end cf colonialism". Nevertheless paragraph 2, which I have quoted from the Declaration of 1960, now forms Art. 1 (1) of each of the two Covenants;

since it is not excluded from the scope of Art. 41 of the Civil and Political Rights Covenant, the right of self-determination may, it seems, be enforced through the Human Rights Committee equally with other covenanted rights; and this conclusion is confirmed by the provisions of Art. 7 of the Optional Protocol.

I would emphasize here that I am not saying anything so absurd as that peoples do not have a right to self-determination. But I am saying that it is a right of a second order: it stands behind the human rights set out in the Universal Declaration and Covenants as a *precondition* of their full exercise by individuals as members of collectivities, which I shall describe in a moment.

I would recall here what Professor Bystrický said yesterday, that at an early stage in the work of the U.N. there had been a shift from concern with the protection of minorities as such to the protection of every human being, and he pointed to the U.N. Charter call "to establish *conditions*". The principle of non-discrimination is to my mind a similar precondition. The drafters of the Covenants seem to me to have half recognized, but only half, the different character of self-determination and non-discrimination by placing them in separate parts from the substantive rights.

3

I have sketched the evolution of self-determination from its recognition as a directive principle to a place among the enforceable human rights of the Covenants. Even if I am wrong in regarding it as a precondition of the exercise of rights rather than a directly enforceable right, I shall now offer reasons for thinking that it is not a "human right" of the kind recognized and formulated in the Universal Declaration and the other Parts of the Covenants.

The subjects of human rights are essentially individuals; and, though we may extend the notion of individual to husband and wife, and also to the family, seen as units, we can only very exceptionally extend it to *collectivities* of individuals as such. Exceptions perhaps are the recognition that a legal person (persona moralis) may have a right or interest in property, or that trades unions may federate, though even here it is arguable that any human rights involved are really those of the natural persons, of which the legal person or association is ultimately composed. If we look through the human rights enumerated in the Universal Declaration and the Covenants, we find none that are not those of individuals; even the right to free and genuine elections which has something of the character of a collective right in Art. 21 (3) of the Universal Declaration is transposed into an individual right in Art. 25c of the Civil and Political Rights Covenant.

Now it is of course possible to speak of the self-determination of an individual, and to describe that as a human right. It is plainly not in this sense that the right of self-determination is described and used in U.N. instruments, which refer always to the self-determination of *peoples or nations*. These are collectivities: they may be whole peoples seeking freedom from colonial rule or substantial groups markedly distinguished from the remainder of the community in which they live, by physical characteristics, habitual language, religious belief or practice, or political affiliation.

By treating self-determination as equivalent to other recognized human rights, the U.N. can draw upon those political emotions and forces which the Universal Declaration and Covenants have so effectively focussed on human rights; but it is also led into the position, less obvious and more dangerous, of overstepping the bounds set by Art. 2 (7) of the Charter. Human rights are, apart from treaty, initially at least matters of domestic jurisdiction, as Professor Markovic pointed out, referring to the maintenance of the domestic remedies rule in Art. 41 (1)c of the Civil and Political Rights Covenant; nevertheless, it is now I think demonstrated in U.N. practice that the systematic denial of human rights to individuals as a matter of international concern justifying U.N. intervention: equally justified is intervention on the denial of self-determination to a people or nation. But by confusing self-determination with human rights proper the U.N. too often intervenes without achieving the protection of either.

This confusion is intensified by the tendency to identify self-determination with independence, a tendency manifest in the Declaration of 1960. In the rapid process of decolonization which for the U.N. began in 1947, the great majority of peoples in determining their own future, opted for independence; and the choice was perhaps obvious. But, though the U.N. has recognized from time to time the possibility that self-determination may take another course, for example, of continued association with another State without full independence,[1] it has in the last decade seen self-determination, not as the necessary precondition of the exercise and enjoyment of human rights, but simply as a mode of ending colonialism.

Few would dispute the need to end colonialism, if by that is meant unwanted alien rule, whether coming from the inside or the outside. But the ideology of anti-colonialism is not in itself a guarantee of the protection of human rights. Professor Bystrický made an important observation yesterday, when he said that, although ideological conflicts cannot be resolved on the theoretical plane, practical solutions can and should be sought for the protection of human rights and that the theoretical differences would become irrelevant. I wholly agree, but I am tempted to ask why, if these ideological principles can be so smoothly bypassed, we need ideologies at all; and I also know the brute fact that in the U.N. ideologies too often count for more than human rights.

4

I have finished my analysis of self-determination and its place as I see it in the U.N. system. It may be said that the kind of distinctions drawn cannot be made in the broad field of human rights, that we cannot separate the individual from the collectivity large or small to which he belongs, and that legal niceties about different kinds of rights are out of place. This criticism may well be sound, but it is a criticism of the whole conception of the Covenants which as I understand it is to place the human rights, set out in the Universal Declaration, within a framework of legal obligation. What then are some of the contemporary consequences for human rights?

Consider the situation in Southern Arabia. In the Yemen there was civil war between what sociologists have come to call the traditional elite and the nationalist elite: the latter supported by Egyptian arms have overthrown the old feudal regime. The South Arabian Federation was formed by the United Kingdom, out of old colonial habit and with seemingly little foresight, out of seventeen sultanates and the State of Aden. Between the Yemen and the Federation the boundary is uncertain over a long distance, and the Yemen has territorial claims. The civil conflict in Aden is well known—fifty-one civilians were killed between March and June 1967—as is the political differences between FLOSY and the NLF. Aden has been for some time a U.N. candidate for self-determination. But we may ask: self-determination for whom? The followers of FLOSY, of the NLF, the Federal government which has evaporated, or the Yemen as territorial claimant? In February 1967 the General Assembly adopted a resolution, which both committed the U.N. to intervention in the internal political struggle, which is not its proper function, and yet gave only secondary consideration to the protection of human rights, which was.

The resolution requested the Secretary General to send a special mission to determine, in consultation with the United Kingdom Government and the Committee of 24, not only

"the extent of U.N. participation in the preparation and supervision of elections"

but also

"practical steps for the establishment of a central caretaker government."

But at

"the reports issued by various international humanitarian organizations (Amnesty) on the maltreatment of political prisoners" the Assembly simply expressed concern and gave no directive. The U.N. mission visited political prisoners, but having made up its mind to have no dealings with the Federal Government abruptly left the territory.

It also expressed concern at what it called

"the continuation of military operations against the people of the territory".

But in the Committee of "Twenty-four" a motion was carried 14–7–3 to refuse even to accept for consideration evidence tending to show Egyptian support for acts of violence in the territory.

The U.N. has shown no greater response to the confirmed reports by the ICRC of the use of poison gas, probably mustard gas, against civilians in the Yemen campaign; Egypt again may have been involved. Despite the resolution passed in December 1966 by the General Assembly condemning in general terms the use of noxious gases, the U.N. has so far remained silent. It is a story of political muddle and dishonesty, and a failure to show real concern for human rights.

Resolutions adopted at the last General Assembly in December 1966 show similar practical confusions between the principle of self-determination for whole peoples, and the protection of human rights of individuals.

The formula of independence without delay was applied to Fiji, with a call for general elections, for the fixing of an early date for independence, and

"the abolition of all discriminatory measures so as to foster communal harmony and national unity".

But it is because each of the two communities in Fiji, almost equal in size, look for guarantees against discrimination as a precondition of independence, that the two parts of the resolution contradict each other.

The resolutions on the Falkland Islands and Gibraltar, adopted in the same context of self-determination, involve, like Aden, territorial claims. The Uniter Kingdom and Argentina were called on

"to continue negotiations to find a peaceful solution"

and

"the elimination of this colonial problem."

Would the problem be eliminated if sovereignty were simply transferred to Argentina, as that country demands? A similar question arises over Spanish claims to Gibraltar. But the United Kingdom has been condemned by the U.N. for asking the people of Gibraltar by referendum to make a choice as to their future political association. In these cases self-determination can apparently be negotiable; or is it really the self-determination of Argentina and Spain that is in issue?

5

I am not suggesting that all parts of the resolutions, which I have mentioned, are misdirected or unjustified, but only that the principle of self-determination has for a period been over-applied and sometimes misapplied. In conclusion I would say that

1. the principle of self-determination has an essential place in the Covenants, and the protection of human rights, and, though of a different order from other human rights, it embodies a basic obligation for the U.N. and its members, whether it is described as legal or political;
2. the U.N. should now direct its political effort to repair some of the fragmentation of the world, caused by the tide of independence, which has produced too many States, barely viable on their own;
3. the U.N. should also direct its interventions in the territories of its members more closely and more impartially to the protection of human rights as we find them in the Covenants.

NOTES

[1] Puerto Rico 748—VIII (27.11.1953); Greenland 849—IX (22.11.1954); Netherlands, Antilles and Surinam 945—X (15.12.1955); Alaska, Hawaii 1469—XIV (12.12.1959).

Some aspects of the International Covenants on Human Rights of December 1966

By Egon Schwelb

Yale Law School, New Haven, Conn., USA

Introductory

Paul-Henri Spaak, the Belgian statesman, at the time President of the Consultative Assembly of the Council of Europe, is reported to have announced the signing, on November 4, 1950, of the European Convention on Human Rights by the Foreign Ministers of the Member countries of the Council of Europe, in these words:

"The Convention of Human Rights will be signed by fifteen countries at 3 p.m. at the Palazzo Barberini. It is not a very good Convention, but it is a lovely Palace."[1]

And yet, the instrument signed in 1950 was to become the most important step, so far taken, to translate into reality the commitment of the international community and of everyone of its Members to protect the dignity and worth of the human person. The international machinery established by the European Convention has transformed the abstract idea of the international protection of human rights into a concrete, tangible, day-to-day task.

Some students of the International Covenants on Human Rights which were adopted and opened for signature and ratification on December 16, 1966 might be inclined to dismiss them as summarily as Mr. Spaak dismissed the European Convention. Whether the Covenants will be widely ratified and whether they will prove effective only the future can tell.

At any rate, the brief analysis I am submitting here of both the achievements and the weaknesses of these instruments will be undertaken in the spirit of the statement, that Lady Gaitskell made when, as representative of the United Kingdom in the plenary meeting of the General Assembly, she explained the affirmative vote of the United Kingdom in favour of the two Covenants and of the Optional Protocol. She said:

"This is not a time to give praise with one hand and take it away with the other; nothing can detract from the satisfaction and triumph of those delegations that have succeeded in obtaining the universal adoption of these covenants."[2]

Professor Capotorti who, as representative of Italy, played a distinguished role in the General Assembly proceedings relating to the Covenants will speak of the procedural aspects of the Covenants, the so-called "measures of implementation". I **will** therefore concentrate on substantive law. Considering the immensity of the subject, and the fact that the substantive articles have a legislative history stretching over nineteen years, I shall deal with a few selected topics only: with the general obligations which States undertake in becoming parties to the Covenants; with the limitations of the obligations States accept or, expressed differently, the restrictions on the rights they guarantee. I shall also deal with those provisions concerning specific questions by which the Covenants purport to make an original contribution to the law—for good, or, as in some cases, for bad.

Before entering in *medias res* I would like to recall that the adoption of the Covenants by unanimous vote of the Assembly was by no means greeted with a fanfare. The general public was hardly informed of it. Even those media of information which usually give a fair coverage to United Nations proceedings reported the event, if at all, at best in a short sentence or a hidden paragraph. For the international lawyer the proceedings concerning the Covenants were apparently overshadowed by other events which occurred during the 1966 session of the General Assembly, such as the convening of the international conference of plenipotentiaries on the law of treaties,[3] the commendation, by the General Assembly, of the Outer Space Treaty,[4] and the problem of South-West Africa.[5] To the legal profession, including teachers of international law, the signing of the Covenants appears to have come as a surprise. To mention one example which is not necessarily typical:

In the second edition of Hans Kelsen's Principles of International Law which reached the book market a month or two before December 16, 1966, Kelsen or the editor of the second edition, Robert W. Tucker, engaged in the metajuridical activity of prophecying and stated:

There is at present little prospect that these draft covenants will be approved by the General Assembly and opened for signature to member states.[6]

The origins of the International Covenants on Human Rights

A proposal to embody an International Bill of Rights in the Charter itself had been put forward but not proceeded with at the San Francisco Conference.[7] The idea of establishing an International Bill of Rights was, however, treated as inherent in the Charter. The "Preparatory Commission of the United Nations"[8] and its "Executive Committee",[9] meeting in the autumn of 1945, recommended that the work of the Commission on Human Rights should be directed, in the first place, towards the "formulation of an International Bill of Rights". The General Assembly agreed with this re-commendation at its first session in January, 1946.[10] Accordingly, when the terms of reference of the Commission of Human Rights were laid down in February 1946,[11] "an International Bill of Rights" was the first item on its work programme. As to the form which this Bill of Rights should take, the decision eventually emerged that the Bill should not be produced by one single, comprehensive and final act but that it should consist of two or more international instruments, namely a Declaration, a Convention (Covenant) and Measures of Implementation.[12] Later it was decided, for reasons which will be mentioned in due course, that there shall be not one, but two Cov-enants and that the provisions on the measures of implementation shall be embodied in the texts of the Covenants. This latter decision was modified somewhat in 1966 when the provisions regulating one specific aspect of the implementation arrangements, the right of petition (communication), were included in a separate Optional Protocol.[13]

The first part of this International Bill of Human Rights was adopted by the General Assembly in the form of a resolution as the Universal Declara-tion of Human Rights on December 10, 1948;[14] the remaining parts, viz. the International Covenant on Economic, Social and Cultural Rights; the In-ternational Covenant on Civil and Political Rights and the Optional Protocol to the International Covenant on Civil and Political Rights were adopted and opened for signature, ratification and accession on December 16, 1966, the two Covenants unanimously[15], the Optional Protocol by majority vote.[16]

One or two Covenants[17]

A problem, which, particularly in the first years, created a considerable amount of controversy, was whether the Covenant should set forth only those rights which traditionally have been embodied in national constitutions or catalogues of rights and which in United Nations parlance have been called "civil and political rights", or whether the Covenant should set forth also what has become known as "economic, social and cultural rights". The Com-mission on Human Rights was originally inclined to regulate in the first place the traditional civil and political rights and to deal with other groups of rights in additional instruments.[18] However, the majority of the General Assembly declared at its fifth (1950) session that the enjoyment of civil and political freedoms and that of economic, social and cultural rights "are in-terconnected and interdependent" and instructed the Commission on Human Rights to include in the draft covenant "a clear expression of economic, so-cial and cultural rights in a manner which relates them to civil and political freedoms proclaimed by the draft covenant".[19]

However, at the following session of the General Assembly in 1951/1952 the question was reconsidered and it was decided that two covenants shall be drafted, simultaneously submitted, simultaneously approved and opened for signature at the same time.[20] The reversal has sometimes been attributed to "pressure exerted by the colonial Powers",[21] or to the Western Powers.[22] This is not quite correct. The proposal to recommend to the Assembly the re-consideration of the decision of 1950 was first—unsuccessfully—made by the Indian member of the Commission on Human Rights at the latter's seventh session;[23] it was co-sponsored in the Economic and Social Council by India together with three Western States and one Latin-America State[24] and in the Third Committee of the General Assembly it was India and Lebanon who proposed the drafting of two Covenants together with Belgium and the United States.[25]

Between 1952 and 1966 repeatedly suggestions were made to revert to the original decision to have only one Covenant to cover both groups of rights. In spite of the change in the composition on the United Nations which in all probability would have resulted in a vote favouring a single Covenant, the view that a reopening of the question would delay the completion of the International Bill for some more years prevailed and a concrete proposal to reopen the question was not made. In view of all the work which, by 1966, had been done on the Covenants, the delegations critical of the 1952 decision resigned themselves to proceed on this basis in order to avoid further delay.[26]

The principal reason for having two diferrent instruments regulating the two groups of rights has, of course, been the fundamentally different character of the rights concerned which led some even to question whether the rights set forth in the Covenant on Economic, Social and Cultural Rights are, technically speaking, rights at all, rights in the sense of subjective enforceable and justifiable rights. This different character of the rights made it necessary to provide for a difference in the type of international obligations which States Parties undertake by accepting the one and the other of the two Covenants. Another consequence, it was thought, was the necessity to adjust the arrangements for international supervision, the "measures of implementation", to the different character of the rights.

By way of illustration of this fundamental difference I would like to list a few provisions from the one and from the other Covenant:

Art. 15 of the Covenant on Civil and Political Rights provides that no one shall be held guilty of any criminal offence on account of any act or omission which did not constitute a criminal offence, under national or international law, at the time when it was committed. Under Art. 19 (2) of the same Covenant everyone shall have the right to *freedom of expression* which, of course, is subject to certain restrictions. Similarly, Art. 21 and 22 provide for the right to *peaceful assembly* and the right to *freedom of association.*

In Art. 11 (2) of the Covenant on Economic, Social and Cultural Rights, on the other hand, States Parties recognize the fundamental right of everyone *to be free from hunger* and shall take, individually and through international cooperation, the measures which are needed: a) to improve methods of production, conservation and distribution of food by making full use of technical and scientific knowledge, by disseminating knowledge of the principles of nutrition and by developing or reforming agrarian systems in such a way as to achieve the most efficient development and utilization of natural resources. b) Taking into account the problems of both food-importing and food-exporting countries, to ensure an equitable distribution of world supplies in relation to need.

Another example is Art. 12 by which States Parties recognize the right of everyone to the enjoyment of the highest attainable standard of *physical and mental health.* The steps to be taken by the States Parties to achieve the full realization of this right shall include those necessary for:

(*a*) The provision for the reduction of the stillbirth-rate and of infant mortality and for the healthy development of the child;

(*b*) The improvement of all aspects of environmental and industrial hygiene;

(*c*) The prevention, treatment and control of epidemic, endemic, occupational and other diseases;

(*d*) The creation of conditions which would assure to all medical service and medical attention in the event of sickness.

In Art. 9 the States Parties "recognize the right of everyone to social security, including social insurance".

The difference in the type of obligation undertaken by States in the two Covenants. The obligations undertaken by States Parties by the two Covenants are accordingly different:

In the Civil and Political Rights Covenant (Art. 2 (1)) each State Party undertakes to *respect* and *to ensure* to all individuals within its territory and subject to its jurisdiction the rights recognized in that Covenant. The corresponding provision of the other Covenant (Art. 2 (1)) is to the effect that each State Party undertakes *to take steps,* individually and through international assistance and cooperation *to the maximum of its available resources,* with a view to achieving *progressively* the full realization of the rights recognized in the Covenant by all appropriate means. Subject to certain exceptions and modifications which I shall mention presently the Civil and Political

Rights Covenant imposes upon States Parties the obligation to maintain a defined standard. From the Economic, Social and Cultural Rights Covenant, the obligation results to promote a defined objective. By and large, it is, in a phrase coined by Jenks, a *"promotional convention"*.[27] The function of promoting an objective rather than setting an immediately applicable standard this Covenant shares with various other human rights and international labour conventions. The Equal Renumeration Convention, 1951, is an example.

Some of the recent conventions adopted to combat discrimination, the Discrimination (Employment and Occupation) Convention, 1958, the Convention against Discrimination in Education, 1960 and even the International Convention on the Elimination of All Forms of Racial Discrimination, 1965, contain "promotional" elements.[28] So does, in regard to one problem at least, also the Covenant on Civil and Political Rights. Art. 23 (4) of the latter provides that States Parties to it "shall take appropriate steps to ensure equality of rights and responsibilities of spouses as to marriage, during marriage and at its dissolution".[29] Apart from this concrete provision which has unmistakably a "promotional" character, in the view of some critics there are elements of progressive as distinct from immediate application implied in the Covenant as a whole. This view is based on the provision of Art. 2 (2) which is to the effect that where not already provided for by existing legislative or other measures each State Party undertakes to take the necessary steps to adopt such legislative or other measures as may be necessary to give effect to the rights recognized in the Covenant. In this regard it has been claimed that the "legislative and other measures" ought to be taken before a State becomes a party to the Covenant and not afterwards. A related element of "progressive implementation" can also be discerned in Art. 40 (1) where States Parties undertake to submit reports not only on the measures they have adopted which give effect to the rights recognized in the Covenant but also "on the progress made in the enjoyment of those rights".[30]

There are also some by no means unimportant exceptions to the general statement that the Covenant on Economic, Social and Cultural Rights imposes only the obligation to take steps to achieve the instrument's aims progressively:

In Art. 2 (2) of the Covenant on Economic, Social and Cultural Rights States *undertake* to guarantee that the rights enunciated in it will be exercised without discrimination of any kind as to race, colour, sex, language, etc. While it is permissible that the substantive aims may be fully realized only progressively according to the available resources, discrimination in their enjoyment is prohibited forthwith. This interpretation is, however, not borne out by the legislative history.[30a]

Art. 8 of the Covenant on Economic, Social and Cultural Rights which deals with the right of everyone to form and to join trade unions and with the rights of trade unions is, in my view, of immediate application. The words used are that States Parties "undertake to ensure" the right of everyone, etc. The other Covenant contains in Art. 22 a parallel and very similar provision on freedom of association including the right to form and join trade unions. In Art. 8 (1) (d) States Parties to the Covenant on Economic, Social and Cultural Rights also undertake to ensure (apparently effective immediately) the right to strike with the proviso that it is exercised in conformity with the laws of the particular country. From this it appears to follow that the municipal law of a State Party may limit and regulate the right to strike, but may not provide for an outright prohibition of strikes.

In Art. 13 (3) of the Covenant on Economic, Social and Cultural Rights, States Parties undertake to have respect for the liberty of parents to choose for their children schools, other than those established by the public authorities, which conform to approved minimum educational standards and to ensure the religious and moral education of their children in conformity with their own convictions. This is an immediately applicable undertaking. The same can be said of Art. 15 (3) by which the States Parties undertake to respect the freedom indispensable for scientific research and creative activity, a somewhat vague obligation but a legal obligation all the same.

The question whether the self-determination article (Art. 1 of both Covenants) is a "promotional provision" is treated on page 111 below.

Erratum

Eide-Schou, International Protection of Human Rights (Nobel Symposium 7)

The sentence at the bottom of page 108 reading: "This interpretation is, however, not borne out by the legislative history [30a]" should not be at the end of the last paragraph of page 108, but at the end of the first full paragraph of that page, i.e. after the words: "on the progress made in the enjoyment of those rights" [30].

ties as they
ts might be

State Party
territory and
. The words
ie Covenant
Convention
irties under-
jurisdiction".
ations Com-
eparate vote
iowever.[81]
in Art. 2 (1)

of the Covenant on Economic, Social and Cultural Rights to take steps "individually and through international assistance and cooperation, especially economic and technical, to the maximum of its available resources ... etc." the view was expressed that the provision might be construed as imposing a formal obligation upon States Parties to give to other States Parties economic, technical or other assistance.[32] Such an interpretation is not borne out by the text and the organization of the article. I believe that the Covenant imposes an obligation on each State to work towards the realization of the aims of the Covenant *within its own jurisdiction* and *to this end* to seek, when appropriate, international assistance and cooperation.

Art. 2 of the Covenant on Economic, Social and Cultural Rights contains, however, a provision, inserted by a narrow majority in 1962,[33] which is open to serious criticism. Paragraph 3 of Art. 2 reads as follows:

"Developing countries, with due regard to human rights and their national economy, may determine to what extent they would guarantee the economic rights recognized in the present Covenant to non-nationals."

It is not possible to enter into a detailed analysis of this paragraph in the context of this report. The following may be said, however: The Covenant on Economic, Social and Cultural Rights differs from the other Covenant in that it does not prohibit discrimination on the ground of nationality. It proscribes discrimination on the ground of *national origin,* the implication being that a State must not discriminate *among its citizens* on that ground. It is not admissible in the context to interpret the words "other status" to include (foreign) nationality.[34] A specific provision reserving to States Parties, whether developed or developing, the authority to distinguish in the application of the Covenant between nationals and non-nationals was therefore not necessary. The provision as adopted might, however, be interpreted to deprive developed countries of this authority. This is an irrational result which cannot have been intended.

The reservation in favour of developing countries applies only to "economic rights" as distinct from "social" and "cultural" rights. It does not therefore cover e.g., the right of access to schools. The sponsors of this clause[35] probably intended to exclude foreign investments in developing countries from the protection of the Covenant. They seem to have overlooked, however, that neither of the two Covenants—as distinct from the Universal Declaration of Human Rights and from the First Protocol to the European Convention on Human Rights—contains a provision protecting the right to own property.[36]

The self-determination Article. Both Covenants contain an article (identical in both instruments) on the right of self-determination of all peoples. This article was included in the Covenants by majority decision of the General Assembly taken at its 1951/1952 session.[37] Its final text was drafted by the Third Committee in 1955.[38] It is neither possible nor desirable to deal in this report with the involved legal and political arguments for and against this provision which occupied the organs of the United Nations for many years.

As far as the distinction between an immediately applicable, standard setting provision on the one hand and a promotional provision on the other is concerned, Art. 1 is in a special position: It is part of both the Covenant on Economic, Social and Cultural Rights which in general obliges States to take steps with a view to achieving the full realization of the rights set forth in it progressively. (Art. 2 (1)). It is also part of the Covenant on Civil and Political Rights by which States Parties undertake to respect and to ensure forthwith to all individuals within their territories and subject to their jurisdiction the rights recognized therein. (Art. 2 (1)). The self-determination article precedes the general provisions of either Covenant just paraphrased, which makes it doubtful whether it is governed by them. Art. 2 (1) of the Covenant on Civil and Political Rights which speaks of ensuring rights to *individuals* can hardly be interpreted to apply to the right of self-determination of *peoples*.

The first paragraph of Art. 1 contains the declaratory statement that "all peoples *have* the right of self-determination". It differs from the draft submitted by the Commission on Human Rights which would have provided that "all peoples ... *shall have* the right of self-determination".[39] The obligations of States Parties in regard to this right are spelled out in the third paragraph. The States Parties, including those having responsibility for the administration of Non-Self-Governing and Trust Territories, shall *promote* the realization of that right. They "*sont tenus de faciliter la réalisation*" of the right. Without entering, in the context of this report, into all the complexities of the self-determination article it might not be inappropriate to express the writer's personal opinion that the political difficulties assumed to flow from it for the acceptability of the Covenants by the so-called colonial Powers have been greatly over-estimated. In the light of the record of the last twenty years, surely such governments as those of the United Kingdom or of France cannot be accused of not having "promoted" the right of self-determination or of not having "respected" it.

Long before the Covenants were finally approved in 1966, paragraph 1 of Art. 1 as drafted by the Third Committee was made part of the Declaration on the Granting of Independence to Colonial Countries and Peoples.[40] The idea that all peoples may freely dispose of their natural wealth and resources which is reflected in Art. 1 paragraph 2 has also played a great role in proceedings of various organs and inspired, *inter alia,* the Declaration on Permanent Sovereignty over Natural Resources of 1962.[41]

The provision of Art. 1 (2) of both Covenants is a compromise text insofar as it proclaims that all peoples may freely dispose of their natural wealth and resources "without prejudice to any obligations arising out of international economic cooperation based upon the principle of mutual benefit, and international law". At the 1966 session of the General Assembly an article was inserted in both Covenants (Art. 25 and Art. 47 respectively) which is, in effect, a modification of the provision of Art. 1 (2). The added articles say that "Nothing in the present Covenant shall be interpreted as impairing the inherent right of all peoples to enjoy and utilize fully and freely their natural wealth and resources".[42] The whole question is far removed from the principal subject-matter of the Covenants. The article seems to mean that even obligations arising out of international economic cooperation and international law must not be interpreted to impair the right of all peoples to enjoy and utilize their natural wealth and resources.

The application to dependent territories. In the early years of the work relating to the Covenants one of the most controversial questions, causing very acrimonious debates, was whether their provisions should automatically apply to dependent territories of States Parties. In 1950 the General Assembly decided by majority vote to request the Commission on Human Rights to include in the Covenant an article to the effect that its provisions "shall extend to or be applicable equally to a signatory (sic!) metropolitan State and to all the territories, be they Non-Self-Governing, Trust or Colonial Territories, which are being administered or governed by such metropolitan State".[43] Accordingly, both draft Covenants which the Commission on Human Rights submitted to the General Assembly in 1954 contained an article to this effect.[44] In 1966 the representative of the Ukrainian S.S.R. whose delegation, together with those of the other Eastern European as well as of the Afro-Asian and most Latin American States, had strongly supported and voted for the inclusion of the territorial application article in 1950, moved *the deletion* of the article and the Third Committee so decided.[45] The arguments in favour of deletion were that after the adoption in 1960 of the Declaration on the Granting of Independence to Colonial Countries and Peoples[46] the acceptance of the article on the territorial application of the Covenants, would justify the perpetuation of the colonial system,[47] be a concession to the racist powers,[48] an anachronism.[49] The Covenant is, however, not quite consistent in regard to this non-recognition of the continued existence of non-self-governing territories. The self-determination article itself (Art. 1) speaks of States Parties having responsibility for the administration of Non-Self-Governing and Trust Territories and Art. 14 of the Covenant on Economic, Social and Cultural Rights which deals with compulsory primary education, mentions metropolitan territories and other territories under the jurisdiction of States Parties. Both the insertion, in 1950, and the deletion, in 1966, of the territorial application article were political demonstrations rather than moves to change the law on the queston. This law has been settled for a long time in the sense that the absence of a territorial application clause lays upon States Parties the obligation to apply it to their non-metropolitan territories, unless a different intention appears from the treaty or is otherwise established.[50]

The application to constituent units of federal States. A problem similar to that of the territorial application has been that of the application of the Covenants to the constituent units of federal States which has repeatedly occupied the United Nations and other inter-governmental organizations and in the solution of which the United States, Canada, Australia and India showed considerable interest. In 1950 the General Assembly addressed a request to the Commission on Human Rights to study a federal State article and to prepare recommendations which will have as their purpose the securing of the maximum extension of the Covenant to the constituent units of federal States, and the meeting of the constitutional problems of federal States.[51] Attempts at a compromise solution were subsequently made,[52] but the Commission on Human Rights adopted by a narrow majority[53] a Soviet proposal stipulating that the provisions of the Covenant shall extend to all parts of federal States without any limitations or exceptions. The article appeared in both draft Covenants submitted by the Commission in 1954[54] and was virtually unanimously approved in 1966.[55] The Covenants do not, therefore, in any way limit the international obligations of a State Party on the ground that it is a federal State.

Reservations to the Covenants. For almost two decades the question of reservations to multilateral conventions has occupied the attention of United Nations organs, both in its general aspects and in its application to concrete instruments. This is not the occasion to enter into this field of the law which is still in a rather fluid state and to which a generally acceptable and satisfactory solution has not yet been found.[56] It is not surprising that the organs involved in the preparation of the Covenants have also had to try to find an appropriate reply to the question in its application to the Covenants. At its sixth session in 1951/1952 the General Assembly devoted two resolutions to it: In the general context it recommended that organs of the United Nations, specialized agencies and States should, in the course of preparing multilateral conventions, consider the insertion therein of provisions relating to the admissibility or non-admissibility of reservations and to the effect to be attributed to them.[57] In regard to the draft Covenants it instructed the Commission on Human Rights to prepare, for inclusion in them, clauses relating to reservations, their admissibility and effect.[58] The Commission on

Human Rights did not agree on a provision on reservations and decided to transmit the various proposals which had been presented by its members to the General Assembly.[59] The attempt by the United Kingdom, repeated in 1966, to have an article on reservations included in the Covenants was not successful.[60] The General Assembly has not taken the advice it gave to all U.N. organs and to States in 1952 and the text of the Covenants is silent on the question. The absence of a provision does not mean that reservations to the Covenants are not admissible, but that the question is governed by the general rules of international law. These will be the object of the international conference of plenipotentiaries on the law of treaties which has been convened for 1968 and 1969.[61] The draft articles on the law of treaties prepared by the International Law Commission[62] which the General Assembly has referred to the Conference as the basic proposal for its consideration provide that in cases where the treaty contains no provisions regarding reservations, a State may formulate a reservation if the reservation is not incompatible with the object and purpose of the treaty. Under the International Law Commission's draft the decision whether or not a reservation is incompatible with the object and purpose is left to the decision by any two States themselves. Acceptance by another contracting State of a reservation constitutes the reserving State a party to the treaty in relation to that State. An act expressing the State's consent to be bound by the treaty and containing a reservation is effective as soon as at least one other contracting State has accepted the reservation. Without expressing here a view on the appropriateness of this solution in general international law—on this the conference of plenipotentiaries will have to make a decision—it is certainly open to doubt whether it fits into the scheme of a human rights convention. To give an admittedly extreme illustration: If South Africa were to decide to ratify the Covenants subject to the reservation that it does not accept those of their provisions which prohibit discrimination and if one single other State Party were to accept this reservation, South Africa would become a party to the Covenants with all the prestige and status this might imply.

The limitations of the rights set forth in the Covenant on Civil and Political Rights. Having dealt with the limitations of the obligations of States Parties which might be brought about by reservations, I now proceed to refer to the built-in limitations of the rights set forth in the Covenants, particularly those set forth in the Covenant on Civil and Political Rights. The formulation of these limitations differs, as far as details are concerned, from article to article. It can be said, however, that by and large the Covenant on Civil and Political Rights provides that such rights as that to freedom of expression (Art. 19), of peaceful assembly (Art. 21) freedom of association (Art. 22) and freedom to express one's religion or beliefs (Art. 18 (3)), shall not be subject to any restrictions except those which are provided by law and which are necessary to protect national security, public order, public health or morals or the protection of the rights and freedoms of others. The item "public order" is of particular interest. What is meant is not the absence of disorder but a concept for which the proper English expression would have been public policy. That this is so is proved by the fact that in five of the six articles where the limitation on grounds of "public order" is provided, the French term "ordre public" is added in brackets in the English text of the Covenant. The delegations responsible for this formula were not willing to admit to their public that freedom of the press, of assembly and association are limited by whatever public policy prevails in a State Party and one chose therefore the presumably less embarrassing French term. That the term "public order" is used in the sense of "public policy" is confirmed by the fact that both in the Commission on Human Rights[63] and in the Third Committee of the General Assembly[64] the term was interpreted as covering the right of a State to license visual or auditory devices. It was therefore considered unnecessary to insert a provision similar to that contained in Art. 10 of the European Convention on Human Rights that the article shall not prevent States from requiring the licensing of broadcasting, television or cinema enterprises.[65]

That the words "public order—*ordre public*" as used in the Covenant mean public policy is further demonstrated by the fact that amendments by the United Kingdom to replace the words "public order" by "prevention of disorder or crime" were consistently rejected.[66] The European Convention on Human Rights permits limitations on the rights to freedom of expression, assembly and association (Art. 10 and 11) not for reasons of public order i.e. public policy, but "for the prevention of disorder or crime". In connection with the right of States to limit fundamental rights on grounds of public policy, an extreme hypothetical case could again be used for the purpose of illustration: As *apartheid* is the *ordre public,* the public policy, in the Republic of South Africa, if that country became a party to the Covenant, it would be under the obligation to guarantee freedom of the press, of assembly and of association only subject to this public policy.

Derogation in time of public emergency

Apart from, and beyond, the restrictions on human rights, for which the individual articles provide, Art. 4 of the Covenant on Civil and Political Rights authorizes States Parties to take measures derogating from their obligations under the Covenant in time of public emergency. This right of States to derogate from the provisions of the Covenant is, however, subject to a series of conditions and limitations.

(a) The public emergency must be of such a character as to threaten the life of the nation.

(b) Its existence must be officially proclaimed.

(c) The emergency measures must not go beyond what is strictly required by the exigencies of the situation.

(d) The emergency measures must not be inconsistent with the State Party's other obligations under international law.

(e) They must not involve discrimination solely on the ground of race, colour, sex, language, religion or social origin.

(f) From some of the obligations no derogation is admissible even in time of public emergency.

(g) A State availing itself of the right of derogation shall immediately inform the other States Parties of the provisions from which it has derogated and of the reasons by which it was actuated.

Art. 4 corresponds to Art. 15 of the European Convention on Human Rights, which has already played a great role in cases which were considered by the European Commission and Court of Human Rights. It is to be expected or, at least, to be hoped that the jurisprudence of the European authorities will afford guidance to the authorities which will apply the Covenant when cases coming under its Art. 4 will come to be considered. I am referring to the position taken by both the European Commission and the European Court of Human Rights in the Lawless case that it was *their* task to determine whether the conditions for the exercise of the exceptional right of derogation have been fulfilled and whether the exceptional measures did not exceed the extent strictly required by the situation.[67]

The conditions for the application of emergency measures prescribed in the Covenant are somewhat stricter than those of the European Convention. The latter does not prohibit, as does the Covenant, emergency measures which involve discrimination solely on the ground of race, colour, sex, language, etc. The European Convention speaks of *war* or other public emergency and consequently while, like the Covenant, it prohibits derogation from the right-to-life article, it makes an exception in respect of deaths resulting from lawful acts of war. The Covenant, as an instrument established by the United Nations, does not mention war, because it does not wish to recognize the legality of war. A learned writer considers that the European Convention is, in this regard, more realistic than the Covenant.[68]

The catalogue of the rights from which no derogation is possible, which are "emergency-proof", *"notstandsfest"*, is somewhat longer in the Covenant than in the European Convention. Under either instrument no derogation is permitted, as already stated, from the article setting forth the right to life and further from the prohibition of torture or cruel, inhuman or degrading treatment or punishment (Covenant, Art. 7; Convention Art. 3); from the prohibition of slavery, the slave trade and servitude (Covenant, Art. 8 (1) (2)); Convention Art. 4 (1)); and from the prohibition of retroactive criminal legislation (Covenant, Art. 15; Convention Art. 7). In addition, under the Covenant the following provisions are also "emergency-proof": the prohibition of medical or scientific experimentation without free consent (Art. 7);[69] the prohibition of imprisonment merely on the ground of inability to fulfill a contractual obligation (Art. 11);[70] the right of everyone to recognition everywhere as a person before the law (Art. 16) and the right to freedom of thought, conscience and religion including the right to manifest one's religion or beliefs (Art. 18).

The human rights of those suspected of aiming at the destruction of human rights. Art. 5 of the Covenant corresponds to Art. 17 of the European Convention on Human Rights. Both are almost literal copies of Art. 30 of the Universal Declaration of Human Rights. "Nothing in the present Covenant", Art. 5 says, "may be interpreted as implying for any State, group or person any right to engage in any activity or to perform any act aimed at the destruction of any of the rights and freedoms recognized herein". Contrary to what I said a moment ago when I expressed the hope that the jurisprudence of the European authorities will afford guidance to the organs called upon to apply the Covenant provision on derogation in time of public emergency, I would like to express here, as far as Art. 5 is concerned, the contrary hope, namely that a precedent set at Strasbourg will not be followed in the interpretation of the Covenant. I am referring to the well-known decision of the European Commission in the case of the Communist Party of Germany.[71] The broad and sweeping language of this decision was not maintained by the European Commission itself in later cases and should not guide the Human Rights Committee which will be established under the Covenant.

General observations on the catalogue of Civil and Political Rights

As far as the catalogue of rights of the Covenant on Civil and Political Rights is concerned, it contains, with one or two exceptions, all those rights which are traditionally set forth in national constitutions and bills of right. In what follows I shall mention only a few examples where the Covenant differs from comparable national or international instruments:

Art. 6 which deals with the right to life does not outlaw the death penalty. It goes nevertheless in this regard somewhat beyond the corresponding provision of Art. 2 of the Europen Convention on Human Rights which appears to accept capital punishment as a permanent institution. The Covenant, while not prohibiting the death penalty, makes it clear that it looks upon it with disfavour. Nothing in this article, says paragraph 6 of Art. 6, shall be invoked to delay or to prevent the abolition of capital punishment by any State Party. Paragraph 2 refers to countries which have not, meaning *not yet,* abolished the death penalty and provides, *inter alia,* that it may be imposed only for the most serious crimes. Sentence of death shall not be imposed for crimes committed by persons below eighteen years of age and shall not be carried out on pregnant women (paragraph 5).

Art. 10 provides that all persons deprived of their liberty shall be treated with humanity and with respect for the inherent dignity of the human person. Some critics may question the legal value of a provision of this type. However, experience confirms the beneficial effect such general formulations have upon the application of the law in the hands of judges or administrative authorities who are ready to exhaust all possibilities to protect the rights and the dignity of the individual.

Art. 10 (2) provides that accused persons shall, save in exceptional circumstances, be segregated from convicted persons and that accused juvenile persons shall be separated from adults.

Art. 20 provides that any propaganda for war and any advocacy of national, racial or religious hatred that constitutes incitement to discrimination, hostility or violence shall be prohibited by law. These are controversial provisions which were adopted by majority vote against a strong opposition consisting mainly of most of the Western Powers.[72] As far as the prohibition of incitement to racial discrimination is concerned, the International Convention on the Elimination of All Forms of Racial Discrimination contains more farreaching provisions.[73]

Art. 23 (2) provides that the right of men and women of marriageable age to marry and to found a family shall be recognized. The Covenant does not define the marriageable age. This is a matter for the municipal legislation of the States Parties. In the United Nations Convention on Consent to Marriage, Minimum Age for Marriage and Registration of Marriages of 1962 the substantive provisions of which were drafted by the Third Committee at the same session of the General Assembly, i.e. at the 16th session in 1961, as what now is Art. 23 of the Covenant, it is provided that the States Parties to that Convention shall take legislative action to specify a minimum age for marriage.[74] In the *Recommendation* on Consent to Marriage, Minimum Age for Marriage and Registration of Marriages which the General Assembly adopted in 1965 it is stated that the minimum age for marriage shall not be less than fifteen years of age.[75]

From Art. 23 (2) together with the prohibition of discrimination contained in Art. 2 (1) it follows that laws prohibiting racially mixed marriages (so-called miscegenation statutes) as well as laws prohibiting inter-religious marriages are incompatible with the Covenant.[76] The International Convention on the Elimination of All Forms of Racial Discrimination of 1965 contains a provision to the same effect as far as racially mixed marriages are concerned.[77] The European Convention on Human Rights (Art. 12 and 14 read together) also prohibits racial or religious obstacles to marriage.[78]

Art. 23 (3) is to the effect that no marriage shall be entered into without the free and full consent of the intending spouses. Provisions to the same effect appear also in the Covenant on Economic, Social and Cultural Rights (Art. 10 (1)) and, with a certain amount of elaboration, in the Marriage Convention of 1962.[79]

Art. 24 which deals with the rights of the child was inserted comparatively late in the proceedings of the General Assembly.[80] Its first paragraph assures to every child the right to such measures of protection as are required by his status as a minor on the part of his family, society and the State. The word "society" which apears also in Art. 23 (1) is particularly vague. How and against whom can the right of the child which he has against society be enforced? The paragraph lists the prohibited grounds of discrimination. The legislative history[81] seems to indicate that it was not the intention to abolish distinctions between the rights of children born out of wedlock and of those born in wedlock.

No technical difficulty arises in regard to the second paragraph of Art. 24 which provides that every child shall be registered immediately after birth and shall have a name.

The third paragraph of Art. 24 is a provision of considerable importance. It raises, however, problems of interpretation and application of some complexity. It reads:

"Every child has the right to acquire a nationality."

It should be recalled that Art. 15 of the Universal Declaration of Human Rights provides that *everyone* has the right to a nationality and that the Covenant does not contain a corresponding provision. The Declaration of the Rights of the Child of 1959 contains the principle that the *child* shall be entitled from his birth to (a name and) a nationality.[82] The question is: this principle having been transformed into a legal obligation of the States Parties to the Covenant, which State Party is in a particular situation under the obligation to recognize a child as its national or to confer upon him its nationality. Paragraph 3 of the article was the object of controversy and was adopted by majority vote.[83] The opposition was based on the consideration that the problem of nationality was complex and on the assumption that States would not be willing to amend their nationality laws and would therefore not accept the obligation to do so. It was emphasized in this context that the Convention on the Reduction of Statelessness[84] had by the time of the proceedings in the Third Committee (1963) not been ratified by any State.[85]

However, the views opposing the provision did not prevail; it was approved and forms now part of the Covenant. As such it must be interpreted in good faith. It is probably legitimate to seek guidance in this task of interpretation from previous United Nations work on the subject. In the Study on Statelessness which the Secretary-General submitted at its request to the Economic and Social Council in 1949[86] one of the conclusions on the nationality of the child was that a child should acquire at birth the nationality of the country in which he is born, unless he has acquired the nationality of both or one of his parents. In the draft Conventions on the Elimination of Future Statelessness and on the Reduction of Future Statelessness which the International Law Commission prepared and submitted in 1953 and in 1954[87] the provision was contained that a child (or a person) who would otherwise be stateless shall acquire at birth the nationality of the Party in whose territory he is born. In the Convention on the Reduction of Statelessness of 1961 it is provided that a contracting State shall grant its nationality to a person born in its territory who would otherwise be stateless. The authority of these texts is, however, limited because the proposals of the International Law Commission were not, as such, approved by the General Assembly and only thirty States participated in the Conference which adopted the Convention of 1961, which is not yet in force. If the conclusion is justified that the child who is born stateless has the right to acquire the nationality of the State in which his birthplace is situated, then that State can, in its discretion, provide that its nationality will be granted at birth either by operation of law or upon application.[88]

Art. 24 (3) deals only with the nationality of the child and does not as such deal with the nationality of adults. It stands to reason, however, that among States Parties it will in due course contribute to a substantial reduction of statelessness.

Art. 25 deals with political rights in the narrower sense. It guarantees to every citizen the right and the opportunity without any of the distinctions mentioned in Art. 2, i.e. such as race, colour, sex, etc., and without unreasonable restrictions:

(a) to take part in the conduct of public affairs, directly or through freely chosen representatives;

(b) to vote and to be elected at genuine periodic elections which shall be by universal and equal suffrage and shall be held by secret ballot, guaranteeing the free expression of the will of the electors, and

(c) to have access, on general terms of equality, to public service in his country.

The article compares favourably with the corresponding provision in the European system, Art. 3 of the First Protocol to the European Convention, in regard to which the European Commission on Human Rights has stated that the States Parties have merely undertaken to hold free elections at reasonable intervals, but have not guaranteed an individual's right to vote.[89] Moreover, the European Convention and the protocols thereto do not regulate at all the right to have access to the public service.

The Covenant, as distinct from the Convention on the Elimination of All Forms of Racial Discrimination (Art. 2 (1) (d), does not impose an obligation on States Parties to prohibit discrimination in regard to rights other than those which are recognized in the Covenant. (Art. 2 (1)). The Commission on Human Rights had proposed a general prohibition of discrimination,[90] but the Third Committee, by a narrow majority, changed what now is Art. 26 of the Covenant in such a way that the general prohibition of discrimination disappeared from the provision.[91]

The Universal Declaration of Human Rights does not contain provisions on the "protection of minorities" as distinguished from the "prevention of discrimination".[92] In a resolution which the General Assembly adopted on the same date as the Declaration,[93] on December 10, 1948, it stated that it was "difficult to adopt a uniform solution of this complex and delicate question, which has special aspects in each State in which it arises" and that, "considering the universal character of the Declaration it had decided not to deal in a specific provision with the question of minorities in the text of the Declaration". Notwithstanding these difficulties, it was possible for the Commission on Human Rights and eventually for the General Assembly to agree on general provision on the problem. Art. 2 of the Covenant reads as follows:

In those States in which ethnic, religious or linguistic minorities exist, persons belonging to such minorities shall not be denied the right in community with the other members of their group, to enjoy their own culture, to profess and practise their own religion, or to use their own language.

This is a provision which is intended to be one of world-wide application. It is therefore less far-reaching and less elaborate than were, e.g. the provisions of the Peace and Minorities Treaties and Declarations of the post-World War I period and some of the existing bilateral arrangements. Its language is very cautious. It is not quite clear whether it is a condition for the enjoyment of the right formulated in Art. 27 that the members of the minority concerned are nationals of the State which they inhabit. Art. 2 (1) which ensures the rights recognized in the Covenant on Civil and Political Rights to all individuals within the territory of a State Party and subject to its jurisdiction would indicate that citizenship of that State is not a requirement. It might be recalled that the Minorities instruments of the inter-war period[94] guaranteed the protection of life, liberty and religious freedom to all inhabitants. Equality before the law, civil and political rights, the use of the minorities' languages, the right to establish charitable institutions and schools was guaranteed only to nationals. Only nationals were the beneficiaries of the undertaking to make appropriate facilities in the public educational system available to the minorities.

When Art. 27 speaks of the minorities' right to use their own language, the question arises whether the use of the language in private intercourse, in commerce, in the press and publications and public meetings is meant or whether the use of the minority language before the courts and authorities is also included.[95]

At this stage it is necessary to mention one right which is not covered by the Covenants. This is, as already stated, the right to own property. In the course of the consideration of the draft Covenants by the Commission on Human Rights the question of including an article on the right of property was the subject of considerable discussion. No agreement was reached on a text, however. At the tenth session of the Commission in 1954, i.e. the session at which the Commission completed its work of drafting the Covenants, it decided to adjourn *sine die* consideration of the question.[96] At the General Assembly level suggestions for the inclusion of an article on the right of property were made but none was pressed to the vote. It may be mentioned that the European Convention on Human Rights as signed in 1950 did not contain a provision on this institution so controversial in our time either; but the First Protocol to the Convention which was signed in 1952 contains an article guaranteeing the peaceful enjoyment of one's possessions.

Concluding observations

What I have presented to you was a very cursory and selective survey of some substantive law aspects of the Covenants. It is perhaps no exaggeration to say that at the present state in the development of international law and relations, the procedural arrangements, the measures of implementation, the international machinery are of greater importance and of greater interest than the re-statement of international human rights standards in treaty form. A meaningful evaluation of the Covenants requires therefore also the analysis of the measures of implementation to which Professor Capotorti will address himself.

At this state of our proceedings I would like therefore to stress only the following points:

Whatever the failing in some of the provisions may be, and admitting the comparative weakness of the measures of implementation, it is a noteworthy achievement that in a world so rent by strife 106 States from all parts of the world could give their unanimous agreement to a work of codification of this scope which touches upon the most delicate aspects and the whole range of problems of the relationship between the individual and society and between individuals and groups. Through eight years (1947 to 1954) were the Covenants under consideration by the Commission on Human Rights. The General Assembly went through the process of article-by-article drafting and re-drafting from 1955 to 1963 and again in 1966.

The impetus gained in 1965, when the Convention on the Elimination of All Forms of Racial Discrimination was opened for signature, was one of the motives which led the General Assembly to finish the work on the Covenants in the following year. In order that the momentum be not lost, the General Assembly abtained from another formal consultation of governments and from a revision of the texts from the point of view of drafting, coordination and consistency which would have made a further delay necessary.

The two Covenants and the Optional Protocol form, together with the Universal Declaration of Human Rights of 1948, the International Bill of Rights, one of the earliest undertakings of the United Nations and one of the most ambitious projects in the history of international law.

Critical writers will have no difficulty in finding faults in the drafting, inconsistencies, gaps and provisions which are not to their liking. However, if the Covenants are widely ratified and provided that Governments as well as the national and international organs which will have to apply them approach this responsible task in good faith and devote to the implementation of the Covenants ingenuity and tireless effort—and, I repeat, *provided* they do so—the positive contribution of the Covenants to the achievement of the aims of the Charter will outweigh their by no means negligible weaknesses.

NOTES

[1] *The Memoirs of the Earl of Kilmuir* (*Sir David Maxwell Fyfe*), *Political Adventure,* pp. 183–184, London, 1964.

[2] U.N. Doc. A/PV. 1496 (Provisional), December 16, 1966.

[3] General Assembly Resolution 2166 (XXI), December 5, 1966.

[4] General Assembly Resolution 2222 (XXI), December 19, 1966. Treaty on Principles Governing the Activities of States in the Exploration and Use of Outer Space, including the Moon and Other Celestial Bodies, subsequently signed on January 27, 1967.

[5] General Assembly Resolution 2145 (XXI), October 27, 1966.

[6] Hans Kelsen, *Principles of International Law* (1966), 2nd ed., p. 239 (rev. and ed. by Robert W. Tucker).

[7] 6 UNCIO Docs., p. 705.

[8] Report of the Preparatory Commission of the United Nations, PC/20, chapter III, section 4, paragraph 16, December 23, 1945.

[9] Report of the Executive Committee to the Preparatory Commission of the United Nations, PC/EX/113/Rev. 1, Part III, chapter III, section 4, paragraph 17, November 12, 1945.

[10] General Assembly Resolution 7 (I), January 29, 1946; in Doc. A/64 p. 12, Report of the Third Committee, U.N. Doc. A/17.

[11] Resolution 5 (I) of the Economic and Social Council, February 16, 1946, E.S.C. Official Records, First Session.

[12] Report of the Commission on Human Rights, Second Session, Economic and Social Council Official Records Supplement No. 1 (E/600), paragraph 18, December 17, 1947; General Assembly Resolutions 217 F (III), December 10, 1948; 421 E (V) December 4, 1950; 543 (VI), February 5, 1952.

[13] General Assembly Resolution 2200 A (XXI), December 16, 1966.

[14] General Assembly Resolution 217 A (III), December 10, 1948.

[15] The Covenant on Economic, Social and Cultural Rights was adopted by 105 votes to none; the Covenant on Civil and Political Rights by 106 votes to none. The difference in the figure has no significance. It is probably due to the fact that one delegation inadvertently failed to press the appropriate button of the voting machine. (U.N. Doc. A/PV. 1496, Provisional.)

[16] Ibid. There were 66 votes for, two against and 38 abstentions.

[17] At the request of the General Assembly the Secretary-General presented to it in 1955 a document entitled "Annotations on the text of the draft International Covenants on Human Rights". *General Assembly Official Records, 10th Session* (1955) Agenda Item 28, Annexes, Part II. These annotations summarize the history of the Covenants and annotate their individual provisions up to their presentation, in 1954, to the General Assembly. Thus they cover the time from 1947 to 1954.

[18] Report of the Commission on Human Rights, Sixth Session (1950). *Economic and Social Council Official Records, 11th Session,* Supplement No. 5 (E/1681).

[19] General Assembly Resolution 421 E (V), December 4, 1950. In the Third Committee of the General Assembly where the question was considered the vote on this instruction to the Commission was 23 for, 17 against, with 10 abstentions. *General Assembly Official Records, 5th Session,* Annexes, Agenda Item 63, Report of the Third Committee A/1559, paragraph 51. In the plenary meeting of the General Assembly the relevant part of the resolution was adopted by 35 votes for, 9 against with 7 abstentions (A/PV, 317).

[20] General Assembly Resolution 543 (VI), February 5, 1952. The reversal of the 1950 decision was decided upon in the Third Committee of the General Assembly by 30 votes to 24, with four abstentions (*General Assembly Official Records, 6th Session,* Agenda Item 29, Annexes, Report of the Third Committee A/2112, paragraph 50) and confirmed by the General Assembly in plenary by 29 votes to 25 with four abstentions (A/PV. 375, February 5, 1952).

[21] U.N. Doc. A/C.3/SR. 1396, October 17, 1966 (Saudi Arabia).

[22] Ibid. (U.S.S.R.)

[23] U.N. Doc. E/CN. 4/619/Rev. 1; E/CN. 4/SR. 248; Report of the Commission on

Human Rights, Seventh Session. *Economic and Social Council Official Records, 13th Session*, Supplement No. 9 (E/1992).

[24] U.N. Doc. E/L. 233; Resolution 384 C (XIII) of the Economic and Social Council, August 29, 1951.

[25] U.N. Doc. A/C. 3/L. 185/Rev. 1. *General Assembly Official Records, 6th Session*, Agenda. Item 29, p. 21, and Report of the Third Committee A/2112, paragraphs 49–50, ibid. p. 45.

[26] U.N. Doc. A/C. 3/SR. 1396, 17 October 1966 (Sudan).

[27] Jenks, The application of International Labour Conventions by means of collective agreements. *Zeitschrift für ausländisches öffentliches Recht und Völkerrecht* (1958), vol. 19, p. 203.

[28] See Schwelb, *International and Comparative Law Quarterly* (1960), vol. 9, pp. 671–672; *Archiv des Völkerrechts* (1959), vol. 8, p. 31; *International and Comparative Law Quarterly* (1966), vol. 15, pp. 1015–1016.

[29] The preparatory work leaves no doubt that it has been the intention of the General Assembly that Art. 23(4) might be interpreted as permitting Contracting States to take appropriate measures *progressively* to assure the equality of spouses. (Statement on behalf of the sponsors in A/C.3/SR. 1094; *General Assembly Official Records, 16th Session* (1961/1962), Annexes, Agenda Item 35, Report of the Third Committee, A/5000, paragraph 84.)

[30] See, in particular, *General Assembly Official Records, 16th Session* (1963), Annexes, Agenda Item 48, Report of the Third Committee, A/5655, paragraphs 21–23.

[30a] See the statements by Madagascar and Nigeria in U.N. Doc. A/C. 3/SR. 1427.

[31] U.N. Doc. A/C. 3/SR. 1259. *General Assembly Official Records, 18th Session* (1963), Agenda Item 48, Annexes, Report of the Third Committee A/5655, paragraphs 18 and 29. The words "within its territory" were adopted by 55 votes to 10, with 19 abstentions.

[32] U.N. Doc. A/C. 3/SR. 1455, December 12, 1966 (United States).

[33] *General Assembly Official Records, 17th Session* (1962), Agenda Item 43, Annexes, Report of the Third Committee A/5365, paragraphs 42 to 45, 65 to 70, 80 and 81. Paragraph 3 was adopted in the Third Committee by 41 votes to 38 with 12 abstentions. The motion for a separate vote on Art. 2 paragraph 3, made in the plenary meeting of the General Assembly was rejected by 67 votes to 16 with 23 abstentions. (U.N. Doc. A/PV. 1496, December 16, 1966.)

[34] The Covenant on Economic, Social and Cultural Rights prohibits discrimination of any kind *as to* race, etc. The Covenant on Civil and Political Rights (Art. 2(1)) prohibits distinctions of any kind, *such as* race, etc. The enumeration in the former is exhaustive, that in the latter exemplative. The French text of either Covenant makes the distinction very clear: In the Covenant on Economic, Social and Cultural Rights the parties guarantee the rights "sans discrimination aucune fondée sur la race, etc."; in the Covenant on Civil and Political Rights "sans distinction aucune, *notamment* de race, etc.". As drafted by the Commission on Human Rights the prohibitions in either Covenant were exemplative. (Report of the Commission on Human Rights, Tenth Session (1954) *Economic and Social Council Official Records, 18th Session*, E/2573, Annex I A and B (Art. 2).) The Third Committee changed this in regard to the Covenant on Economic, Social and Cultural Rights by replacing the formula "such as race, etc." by "as to race, etc.". (*General Assembly Official Records, 17th Session* (1962), Agenda Item 43, Annexes, Report of the Third Committee A/5365, paragraphs 44 and 78; amendment by Argentina, Italy and Mexico (A/C. 3/4. 1028/Rev. 2).) The Covenant on Civil and Political Rights protects all individuals within a Party's territory and subject to its jurisdiction irrespective of nationality. It distinguishes, however, between nationals and non-nationals in regard to freedom of movement (Art. 12) and political rights (Art. 25). The Convention on the Elimination of All Forms of Racial Discrimination (Art. 1(2)) does not apply to distinctions between citizens and non-citizens. The European Convention on Human Rights (Art. 16) does not prevent the High Contracting Parties from imposing restrictions on the political activity of aliens. See also Art. 2–4 of Protocol No. 4 to that Convention.

[35] Burma and Indonesia. U.N. Doc. A/5365 (note 28 above), paragraph 46; A/C. 3/4. 1027 Rev. 1.

[36] For governmental statements on Art. 2(3) see U.N. Docs. A/C. 3/SR. 1455 (U.S.A.) and A/PV. 1496 (France, Italy, United Kingdom, United States).

[37] General Assembly resolution 545 (VI), February 5, 1952.

[38] *General Assembly Official Records, 10th Session* (1955), Agenda Item 28 (Part I), Annexes, Report of the Third Committee A/3077, paragraphs 27 to 77. The Third Committee adopted the article by 33 votes to 12 with 13 abstentions.

[39] This difference between the Commission's draft and the final text as revised by the Third Committee in 1955 is, however, not reflected in the French text which in both cases reads "Tous les peuples . . . ont le droit de disposer d'eux-mêmes . . .".

[40] General Assembly Resolution 1514 (XV), December 14, 1960.

[41] General Assembly Resolution 1803 (XVII), December 14, 1962.

[42] The *travaux préparatoires* of Art. 25 of the Covenant on Economic, Social and Cultural rights will be found in U.N. Docs. A/C.3 SR. 1404 to 1406 and of the corresponding Art. 47 of the Covenant on Civil and Political Rights in Doc. A/C.3/SR. 1436. See also the Report of the Third Committee of the 21st session of the General Assembly, A/6546, paragraphs 95–101 and 553–556.

[43] General Assembly Resolution 422 (V), December 4, 1950. This resolution was adopted in the Third Committee by 30 votes to 11, with 8 abstentions and in plenary meeting by 36 votes to 11, with 8 abstentions. *General Assembly Official Records, 5th Session* (1950), Agenda Item 63, Annexes, Report of the Third Committee A/1559, paragraphs 14, 17 and 18; A/PV. 317.)

[44] Report of the Tenth Session of the Commission on Human Rights, note 34 above, E/2573, Annex I, A, Art. 28 and B, Art. 53.

[45] The amendment to delete the territorial application article was adopted by 92 votes for, none against, with 10 abstentions (U.N. Doc. A/C.3 SR. 1411, November 2, 1966; Report of the Third Committee, A/6546, paragraphs 131 to 138).

[46] See note 11 above.

[47] Ukraine in A/C.3 SR. 1411.

[48] Congo (Brazaville) ibid.

[49] U.S.S.R. ibid.

[50] The Legal Counsel advised the Third Committee that in the absence of a territorial clause a State, on becoming a party to the Covenant, would be bound in principle to apply the provisions of the Covenant to all its territories. He recalled also Art. 25 of the draft articles on the Law of Treaties presented by the International Law Commission in 1966 (*General Assembly Official Records: 21st Session*, Supplement No. 9 (A/6309/Rev. 1)). This writer expressed the same opinion in *American Journal of Comparative Law* (1963), vol. 12, p. 378. In 1962 and 1965 respectively the territorial application clause had been deleted from the drafts of what became the Convention on Consent to Marriage, Minimum Age for Marriage, and Registration of Marriages and the Convention on the Elimination of All Forms of Racial Discrimination respectively. (See the reports of the Third Committee A/5273 paragraphs 29 et seq. (1962) and A/6181 paragraphs 184 et seq. (1965).)

[51] General Assembly Resolution 421 (V), December 4, 1950.

[52] See, e.g., Report of the Tenth Session of the Commission on Human Rights (note 34 above), paragraphs 244–261. For the problem as it presented itself during the first years of the United Nations see Sørensen, Federal States and the International Protection of Human Rights, *American Journal of International Law* (1952), vol. 46, p. 195; also Jenks, *Human Rights and International Labour Standards* (1960), p. 142.

[53] The Soviet text received 8 votes for, 7 against, with 3 abstentions (ibid. para. 259). The result was due to the fact that the United States, which at the time was following the Dulles doctrine opposing "treaty coercion" and "formal undertakings" in human rights matters, abstained in the vote. For the attitude of the Eisenhower–Dulles Administration on international human rights matters see the letter from Secretary of State Dulles to the United States representative on the Commission on Human Rights of April 3, 1953, and his statement before the United States Senate Judiciary Committee of April 6, 1953, both reprinted in *Review of the United Nations Charter*, 83rd Congress, Document No. 87 at p. 263 and pp. 293 et seq.

[54] Art. 27 of the Draft Covenant on Economic, Social and Cultural Rights; Art. 52 of the Draft Covenant on Civil and Political Rights.

[55] U.N. Doc. A/C.3/SR. 1411; Report of the Third Committee A/6546, paragraphs 129–130. The vote was 72 to none, with 3 abstentions. The United States voted for the deletion. The representative of Australia explained his abstention with the difficulties arising under the Australian Constitution (A/C.3 SR. 1411 and 1437). The United States changed the position it had originally on the question of a Federal States clause in 1965, when it voted for the deletion of the Federal State clause from the draft to the International Convention on the Elimination of All Forms of Racial Discrimination (U.N. Doc. A/C.3/SR. 1386 paragraph 8, *General Assembly Official Records, 20th Session* (1965), Agenda Item 58, Annexes, Report of the Third Committee A/6181, paragraphs 195–196). In the case of the 1965 Convention the deletion of the Federal State clause was decided by 63 votes to 7, with 16 abstentions (ibid.).

[56] See the "Historical summary of the question of reservations to multilateral conventions" by Sir Humphrey Waldock, an Appendix to his First report on the law of treaties. *1962 Yearbook of the International Law Commission,* vol. II, p. 73.

[57] General Assembly Resolution 598 (VI), January 12, 1952.

[58] General Assembly Resolution 546 (VI) February 5, 1952.

[59] Report of the Tenth Session of the Commission on Human Rights (note 34 above) E/2573 (1954), paragraphs 262–305 and Annex II A.

[60] U.N. Doc. A/C.3/1353 Rev. 3; A/C.3/1378 (amendment by Chile); A/C.3 SR. 1410, 1412 and 1437; A/6546, paragraphs 139–146.

[61] General Assembly Resolution 2166 (XXI), December 5, 1966.

[62] Reports of the International Law Commission on the second part of its seventeenth session and on its eighteenth session. *General Assembly Official Records, 21st Session,* Supplement No. 9 (A/6309/Rev. 1), draft Art. 16–20.

[63] U.N. Docs. E/CN. 4/SR. 320–322; Report of the Commission on Human Rights, Eighth Session (1952), *Economic and Social Council Official Records, 14th Session,* Supplement No. 4 (E/2256) paragraph 241.

[64] U.N. Doc. A/C.3/SR. 1074, paragraph 42; *General Assembly Official Records, 16th Session* (1961), Agenda Item 35, Report of the Third Committee A/5000, paragraph 33.

[65] It should be noted, however, that Art. 1 of the Draft Convention on Freedom of Information as adopted by the Third Committee in 1959 sets forth the right to receive and impart information "by duly licensed visual or auditory devices", while the limitations article (Art. 2 as adopted in 1960), like the Covenant lists "public ordre (ordre public)" as one of the grounds for permissible restrictions. *General Assembly Official Records, 14th Session* (1959), Agenda Item 35, Report of the Third Committee, A/4341, Annex and *15th Session* (1960–1961), Report of the Third Committee A/4636, Annex.

[66] Report of the Commission on Human Rights, Eighth Session, *Economic and Social Council Official Records, 14th Session,* Supplement No. 4 E/2256), paragraphs 192, 207, 236, 242, 249 and 255.

[67] For the attitude of the Commission see, in particular, the statement by Sir Humphrey Waldock, its Principal Delegate before the Court, *Publications of the European Court of Human Rights,* Series B, Lawless Case, p. 281 (hearing of April 8, 1961); for the ruling of the Court, Lawless Case (Merits), Judgment of July 1, 1961, paragraph 22, reprinted also in *Yearbook of the European Convention on Human Rights* (1961), vol. 4, p. 472. See also *Austria v. Italy* op. cit. (1958–1959) vol. 2, p. 176.

[68] Partsch, *Die Rechte und Freiheiten der europäischen Menschenrechtskonvention* (1966), p. 77.

[69] This case is, however, probably covered by Art. 3 of the European Convention (inhuman treatment).

[70] When Art. 15 of the Convention was drafted the provision that no one shall be deprived of his liberty merely on the ground of inability to fulfill a contractual obligation was not contained in the European Convention. It will be added to its catalogue when Protocol No. 4 to the Convention (signed in 1963) enters into force.

[71] The Communist Party of Germany, Max Reimann and Walter Fisch *v.* The Federal Republic of Germany, Decision of July 20, 1957, *Yearbook of the European Convention on Human Rights,* vol. 1, pp. 222 et seq. For a recent critical comment see Partsch, op. cit., note 68, p. 82; see also Schwelb in *XVIII International Organization* (1964), pp. 567 et seq., and literature referred to ibid., p. 570.

[72] U.N. Docs. A/C.3 SR. 1078–1084; *General Assembly Official Records, 16th Session* (1961/1962), Agenda Item 35, Annexes. Report of the Third Committee A/5000, paragraphs 36–50. The vote on what now is Art. 20 (then 26) as a whole was 59 to 19, with 12 abstentions.

[73] See Schwelb, *International and Comparative Law Quarterly* (1966), vol. 15, pp. 1021–1025.

[74] The Convention was adopted and opened for signature and ratification by General Assembly Resolution 1763 (XVII), November 7, 1962. For the references to the drafting of its substantive provisions, see *General Assembly Official Records 16th Session* (1961/1962), Agenda Item 85, Report of the Third Committee, A/5035, December 14, 1961. See also Schwelb, *American Journal of Comparative Law* (1963), vol. 12, pp. 337 et seq.

[75] General Assembly Resolution 2018 (XX), November 1, 1965.

[76] This is borne out by the *travaux préparatoires:* Commission on Human Rights, Ninth Session, Docs. E/CN.4/SR. 382–384 (1953) and A/C.3/SR. 1090, paragraph 47, 1091 paragraphs 14, 19 and 37 (Third Committee, 1961); *General Assembly Official Records, 16th Session* (1961/1962), Agenda Item 35, Report of the Third Committee, A/5000, paragraph 86.

[77] Art. 5(d)(iv) (racial discrimination in regard to the right to marriage and choice of spouse).

[78] Partsch, op. cit., note 60, pp. 214–215; Robertson, *Human Rights in Europe* (1963), p. 31. However, such obstacles to marriage, contained in legal systems of States not Parties to the European Convention on Human Rights, may, it has been held by Courts in the Federal Republic of Germany, be applied if under the rules of private international law of a State Party to the Convention the law of the State non-Party is applicable. See Scheuner in Proceedings of the Second International Colloquy on the European Convention on Human Rights, Vienna, October 1965 (so far available only in its German version under the title *Menschenrechte im Staatsrecht und im Völkerrecht,* Karlsruhe, 1967) at p. 226.

[79] Note 74 above.

[80] Working paper by Poland, U.N. Doc. A/C.3/L. 943, November 3, 1961, *General Assembly Official Records, 16th Session,* Agenda Item 35, Annexes, p. 1; *17th Session* (1962), Agenda Item 43, Annexes, Report of the Third Committee A/5365, paragraphs 5–30; General Assembly resolution 1843 A (XVII), December 19, 1962; Report of the Commission on Human Rights, Nineteenth Session (1963), *Economic and Social Council Official Records, 36th Session,* Supplement No. 8, E/37/43, paragraphs 157–179; *General Assembly Official Records, 18th Session* (1963), Agenda Item 48, Annexes, Report of the Third Committee A/5655, paragraphs 57–85; Docs. A/C.3/SR. 1262, 1263, 1265, 1266.

[81] U.N. Doc. A/C.3/SR. 1262, November 13, 1963, paragraph 32. "The sponsors of the draft ... had taken out of it ... the question of children born out of wedlock, which was too controversial" (Poland).

[82] General Assembly Resolution 1386 (XIV), November 20, 1959.

[83] U.N. Doc. A/C.3/SR. 1264, paragraph 64, November 15, 1963. The vote was 51 for, 4 against, with 16 abstentions.

[84] U.N. Doc. A/CONF.9/15; also in *Yearbook on Human Rights for 1961,* p. 427.

[85] As of today the Convention has been ratified by one State (the United Kingdom).

[86] *A Study of Statelessness,* E/1112 and E/1112/Add. 1. U.N. Publication Sales No. 1949. XIV. 2; p. 161.

[87] *Yearbook of the International Law Commission* (1953), vol. II, p. 223; (1954), vol. II, p. 143.

[88] The sponsors of what now is Art. 24 proposed originally a text under which every child would have "the right ... to ... a nationality" (A/C.3/L. 1174). "To make the provision applicable under all legal systems" (A/C.3/SR. 1265 paragraph 3) the text was changed to "the right *to acquire* a nationality" (A/C.3/4. 1174/Rev. 1). The Convention of 1961 is to the same effect (Art. 1(1)(a) and (b)).

[89] X *v.* the Federal Republic of Germany, Decision of January 4, 1960, *Yearbook of the European Convention on Human Rights,* vol. 3, p. 184, at p. 190; X and others *v.* Belgium, Decision of May 30, 1961 same Yearbook, vol. 4, p. 260 at p. 268; X *v.*

Belgium, Decision of September 18, 1961, ibid. p. 324 at p. 338. In a decision of January 4, 1961, relating to elections in West Berlin, *Collection of Decisions of the European Commission of Human Rights,* vol. 5, the Commission seems to have taken a somewhat different view.

⁹⁰ Report of the Tenth Session of the Commission on Human Rights, note 34 above, E/2573, Annex I B, draft Art. 24.

⁹¹ *General Assembly Official Records, 16th Session,* Agenda Item 35, Annexes, Report of the Third Committee, A/5000 paragraphs 99–115. For a description of the incident see Schwelb, *International and Comparative Law Quarterly* (1966), vol. 15, pp. 1018–1019.

⁹² The United Nations Sub-Commission on Prevention of Discrimination and Protection of Minorities adopted at its first session in 1947 a decision on terminology in which it explained the term "prevention of discrimination" as "the prevention of any action which denies to individuals or groups of people equality of treatment which they may wish". With regard to the term "protection of minorities" the Sub-Commission stated that it was "the protection of non-dominant groups which, while wishing in general for equality of treatment with the majority, wish for a measure of differential treatment in order to preserve basic characteristics which they possess and which distinguish them from the majority of the population. The protection applies equally to individuals belonging to such groups and wishing the same protection." (*Economic and Social Council Official Records, 6th Session,* Supplement No. 11, E/CN.4/52, December 6, 1947.) There is, however, no hard and fast distinction between "prevention of discrimination" and "protection of minorities". They are, as the Permanent Court of International Justice has stated, "indeed closely interlocked". (Minority Schools in Albania, Advisory Opinion of April 6, 1935, Series A/B, No. 64 p. 17.)

⁹³ General Assembly Resolution 217 C(III), December 10, 1948.

⁹⁴ See, e.g., The Treaty between the Principal Allied and Associated Powers and Poland, signed at Versailles, June 28, 1919.

⁹⁵ Ibid. Art. 7.

⁹⁶ Report of the Tenth Session of the Commission on Human Rights, note 34 above, E/2573, paragraphs 40–71.

The international measures of implementation included in the Covenants on Human Rights

By Francesco Capotorti

Università degli Studi, Bari, Italy

1

The expression "international measures of implementation" is generally used today to indicate the collective legal instruments through which the States Parties to a multilateral agreement, or the Organisation which has promoted the stipulation of agreements among its Members, try to ensure the fulfilment of the obligations undertaken by each contracting State. These instruments are in most cases established by means of relevant clauses of the agreement, whose implementation is to be ensured, as is the case for the Covenant on Economic, Social and Cultural Rights (Art. 16–23) and for the Covenant on the Civil and Political Rights (Art. 28–45). Further examples are the Convention on the Elimination of all Forms of Racial Discrimination (Art. 8–16), the European Convention for the Protection of Human Rights (Art. 19–59) and the European Social Charter (Art. 21–29). Sometimes, implementation measures are set forth in a separate complementary agreement, such as the Optional Protocol to the Covenant on Civil and Political Rights, and the additional Protocol to the UNESCO Convention against discrimination in education (1962). In other cases it is the Constitution of an international organisation to provide for implementation measures with regard to all or part of the agreements concluded within its sphere. The most important example of this group is that of the Constitution of the International Labour Organisation (Art. 22–34), but also Art. VIII of the UNESCO Constitution and Art. 87–88 of the United Nations Charter concerning trusteeship agreements can be mentioned in the same context.

There are three main types of implementation measures, each of a very different nature. The most frequent is the consideration of periodic reports, which the contracting States undertake to submit regarding the action performed to fulfil their obligations. Such an examination can be made by an already existing body or by an *ad hoc* organ, with or without the co-operation of subsidiary organs; it is generally followed by recommendations inviting the States Parties to make further efforts for the full observance of the agreement. The second type of measure is a procedure for the settlement of disputes between the States Parties relating to the implementation of the agreement: the main purposes of this kind of procedures is to have the facts ascertained by an impartial body, and to find a reasonable basis for compromise; however in some instances the claimant State is also entitled to bring its case before an international court. Lastly, and more rarely, a special organ is authorised to receive and examine communications or petitions by individuals claiming to have been victims of a violation of the agreement. In these cases, the function of the organ can be limited to the expression of its opinion, or include the formulation of recommendations, or be similar to the function of an international judge.

From the point of view of a correct terminology, the legal instruments described should be defined as international measures for the control on the observance of the agreements, or as measures intended to promote such observance, rather than as "implementation" measures. There is in fact no doubt that the implementation of the agreements, in the sense of an action aimed to put in practice the obligations undertaken, is left with each single State Party. More particularly, so far as human rights are concerned, each State Party has to adopt a series of measures in its domestic sphere in order that the individuals under its jurisdiction might really enjoy those rights. This is clearly stated in Art. 2 of both Conventions.

In this regard, it should be noted that the Convention on the Civil and Political Rights imposes the obligation to adopt legislative or other measures giving priority to legislative measures. On the other hand, in the Convention on the Economic, Social and Cultural Rights, the realisation of these rights is to be achieved by "all the appropriate means, including particularly the adoption of legislative measures". It is in fact known that, for the realisation of civil and political rights, it is generally sufficient that the law recognize them and the State administration observe them; while for the realisation of the economic, social and cultural rights, all those financial and technical means are needed which make economic development and social progress practically possible. For this reason, the implementation of the Covenant on Civil and Political Rights is the *exclusive* responsibility of each State, while the steps which are necessary for the implementation of the Covenant on Economic, Social and Cultural Rights must be taken according to Art. 2 no. 1 "individually and through international assistance and co-operation, especially economic and technical". Having regard to the above assistance and co-operation, it might then be correct to speak of international measures for the implementation of the Covenant; however, the expression has now, as we have seen, a different meaning.

The characters of each category of human rights influence the implementation measures, both internal and international. According to Art. 2 No. 3 of the Covenant on Civil and Political Rights, the individuals whose rights and freedoms are violated shall have an effective remedy and shall have their rights thereto determined by competent judicial, administrative or legislative authorities. Nothing of the kind is provided for in the Covenant on Economic, Social and Cultural Rights because a judiciary or administrative decision would not be sufficient to ensure or re-establish the enjoyment of one of these rights. Consequently, the Covenant on Civil and Political Rights includes two implementation measures which cannot be put in operation if all available domestic remedies have not been exhausted in the matter: namely, the conciliation machinery and the system of communications from individuals. The Covenant on Economic, Social and Cultural Rights, on the other hand, includes the only measure which is consistent with the progressive rhythm of its implementation: the examination of the States Parties' reports. The same situation occurs in the European field, with regard to the implementation measures provided for in the Convention for the Protection of Human Rights, and in the European Social Charter, respectively.

The tendency to include implementation measures in the most important conventions on human rights is amply justified. In fact, the purpose of these conventions is to compel the contracting States to regulate in a uniform way the constitutional position of the individual by according him the same fundamental rights and freedoms in spite of great differences in the historical, social and economic conditions of each State. Naturally, when the moment comes to fulfil the international obligations through domestic measures, a certain resistance by the various domestic legal systems is to be expected. This resistance might assume the form of a delay in the adoption of such measures, or of an attempt to interpret the international obligations in the most convenient sense to the single State, in order to avoid substantial changes to the existing system. The international implementation measures must then serve as a stimulus for the States Parties to each Convention, urging them to take, as soon as possible, the steps required for the fulfilment of their obligations; and must promote the uniform interpretation of the convened clauses by hindering prevalence of national interests.

It should also be considered that one of the main problems with regard to civil and political rights is to protect the individual from abuses by the State authorities. For this reason, it is very important that these authorities be bound to give account of their action to international bodies, and it is particularly to be hoped that this might take place on petition by individuals. Finally, it must be underlined that the matter of human rights is obviously dynamic, and that new situations or new problems do not always fall in the abstract frame of already existing provisions. The organs which are responsible for the international implementation measures are confronted with these concrete problems: therefore the adjustment to reality of the legal provisions concerning human rights is an important aspect of their task. Thus, the function of control on the observance of the agreements contributes also to the development of those principles by which the matter of human rights is regulated.

2

According to both Covenants, the States Parties are obliged to prepare and submit to the Secretary-General of the United Nations periodic reports on the domestic measures of implementation adopted and the progress made in the realisation of human rights; reports may indicate factors and difficulties affecting the fulfilment of the obligations undertaken. However, different organs shall examine the reports on the basis of different procedures. The Covenant on Economic, Social and Cultural Rights entrusts the task of examining reports to the Economic and Social Council of the United Nations, which can avail itself of the co-operation of the Commission on Human Rights. In the Covenant on Civil and Political Rights, the competent organ is the special Human Rights Committee, elected by the States Parties and composed of eighteen persons acting in their individual capacity. The procedure established by the Covenant on Economic, Social and Cultural Rights has a dual aim: to promote the observance of the obligations undertaken by each State Party and to strengthen international co-operation. In order to achieve the first aim, the Economic and Social Council (acting on its own initiative or adopting draft resolutions of the Commission on Human Rights) can submit to the General Assembly recommendations of a general nature. In connection with the second aim mentioned above the Economic and Social Council may bring to the attention of the organs concerned with furnishing technical assistance, any matters arising out of the reports; it can also promote consultation, studies, or the conclusion of further agreements. Moreover, arrangements with the specialized agencies may provide for their reporting to the Council on the activities through which they contribute to the realisation of the purposes of the Covenant.

All this proves that the implementation machinery created by the Covenant on Economic, Social and Cultural Rights is closely linked with the general action of the United Nations and specialized agencies in the same field; it aims to promote and direct such action on the basis of the available information. This might be found to be more concrete and to give better results than the control on the fulfilment of the obligations undertaken by each State Party. On the other hand, the procedure concerning report examination provided for by the Covenant on Civil and Political Rights aims only to supervise and stimulate the contracting States: the Human Rights Committee makes certain general comments and transmits them to the States Parties to the Covenant, which may in turn submit their observations to the Committee. The United Nations do not, however, keep completely out of this procedure: copies of the Committee's comments can be transmitted to the Economic and Social Council, and in any case the Committee shall submit to the General Assembly an annual report on its activities. Therefore, the Council and the Assembly will be enabled to express their appreciation of the work of the Committee, if they deem it convenient. It should, however, be noted that the Covenant on Civil and Political Rights does not provide for a direct intervention of the United Nations organs towards the contracting States, unlike what we have seen with regard to the Covenant on Economic, Social and Cultural Rights.

To what extent are the reporting systems set forth in the two Covenants really apt to promote and control the respect for human rights? To give an answer to this question five aspects of the system should mainly be considered: the form of the reports, the composition of the organ to which they must be submitted, the participation, if any, of other organs in their examination, the nature and results of such examination.

With regard to the form of the reports, it is evident that if the control organ can determine it by drawing a list of questions and clearly stating what information is required from the States Parties and how it shall be supplied, the procedure will be more efficient, as it will avoid the exclusion of any important subject or its being dealt with too superficially. For this reason the Constitution of the International Labour Organisation and the European Social Charter entrust the power of establishing the form of the reports to the Governing Body of I.L.O. and to the Committee of Ministers of the Council of Europe, respectively. No provision of this kind can be found in the Covenant. It should, however, be born in mind that according to the Covenant on Economic, Social and Cultural Rights, reports must be furnished "in stages" in accordance with a programme to be established by the Economic and Social Council. In my opinion, such a programme might also deal with the form of reports, or at least with the subjects to be dealt with. As to the Covenant on Civil and Political Rights, it provides for reports to be submitted within one year of its entry into force and then gives the Human Rights Committee the faculty of requesting them whenever it deems it convenient. It seems to me that the power to request submission of reports includes the power to request supplementary information, and this is tantamount to determine the questions to which the States are asked to answer. Of course, such an interpretation of the Covenants leads to an extension of the powers expressly conferred to the Economic and Social Council and to the Human Rights Committee; however, I believe that this is consistent with the supervision aim which is the *ratio* of any reporting system.

With regard to the structure of the organ to which reports must be submitted, it is known that a body composed of government representatives must take into account considerations of prestige and respect of State sovereignty. This might make such a body reluctant to examine the treatment dealt by each State to the individuals under its jurisdiction, especially if the investigation has no political interest from the point of view of international relations. A body composed of individuals independent from governments is on the contrary exclusively bound to general interests: its members will enjoy larger freedom of initiative and will be capable of assuming a critical position, if they think it necessary, with greater objectiveness. For this reason the solution adopted in the Covenant on Civil Political Rights seems to be far better than that adopted by the Covenant on Economic, Social and Cultural Rights. It is also to be noted that the Economic and Social Council and the Commission on Human Rights are already burdened with work and will be able to devote only a small part of their time to the new tasks entrusted to them by the Covenant. However, as the States reports on economic, social and cultural questions must also help to promote international co-operation, especially in the field of technical assistance, the Economic and Social Council is still the best qualified organ for this kind of "implementation" of the Covenant.

With regard to the number of organs taking part in report examination, it is easy to understand that the examination is deeper and more accurate when the reports are discussed by one or more technical organs before they are submitted to the political organ, entrusted with the power of addressing recommendations to the States. In this respect the most interesting example is given by the International Labour Organisation: reports are examined by an expert Committee and are then summarised and transmitted to the relevant Committee of the General Conference with the observations of the experts. The latter Committee discusses the conclusions of the first examination and finally submits its own detailed report to the Conference in plenary meeting. It is for the Conference to adopt this report and to formulate appropriate recommendations. The European Social Charter establishes an even more complex procedure: reports are examined by an expert Committee; the Committee's conclusions are transmitted both to the Assembly of the Council of Europe, for its advice, and to a Sub-Committee of the Social Committee of the Council of Europe. The Sub-Committee reports to the Committee of Ministers and the latter may address its recommendations to the States after further consultation with the Assembly. The advantage of these procedures is that the specific competence, the independence of judgement, and the critical aptitude of the technical organs are combined with that sensitivity to political interests of the States which is peculiar to political bodies. The Covenants have not followed this road: the Human Rights Committee is the only competent body for examination of reports, according to the Covenant on Civil and Political Rights, while the Commission on Human Rights, which the Covenant on Economic, Social and Cultural Rights calls on to co-operate with the Economic and Social Council, is also a political, even though specialised, organ. One might ask whether the Commission will establish a subsidiary organ for the examination of the reports provided for by the Covenant. It is doubtful whether this might be lawfully made, as there is no clause in the Covenant allowing for it, in any case the creation of a subsidiary organ composed of experts should be excluded, as this would considerably alter the characters of the procedure.

With regard to the nature of the examination it should be underlined that it varies especially according to the elements of evaluation and comparison which the controlling body is permitted to use and to the enquiry powers entrusted to it. The reports by the States will furnish the official version of the facts, and obviously it is the interest of each government to present these facts under the most favourable light. The availability of other sources of information, of an unofficial character together with the faculty of the competent organ to verify, and eventually complete, the information transmitted by the governments are essential aspects of a really efficient control. Both the aspects are fulfilled in the frame of the International Labour Organisation, not only because the reports by the States Parties must be communicated to the most representative industrial associations of employers and workers which can submit their observations to the control organ, but also because the latter has the power to verify the contents of legislative and administrative measures of each State directly. Moreover, the well-known tripartite structure of the General Conference makes it possible for a debate between representatives of the governments and of industrial associations to take place. The situation is much different so far as the Covenants are concerned: apparently, the only available elements will be the information furnished by the governments, nor does it appear that the control organs have any direct investigation powers. There is only one possibility, regarding the Covenant on Economic, Social and Cultural Rights: it is that non-governmental Organisations, having a consultative Status within the United Nations, be admitted to intervene in the discussion on the reports. But there is no ground for such an intervention in the relevant clauses of the Covenant; we must see whether the praxis of the Council will step over the text of these clauses. In spite of the legal difficulties, an extension of the Council's powers would certainly foster a more efficient control.

We are now left to consider the formal results of report examination. The Covenant on Economic, Social and Cultural Rights provides for general recommendations to be submitted from ECOSOC to the General Assembly; the Covenant on Civil and Political Rights limits the powers of the Human Rights Committee to the formulation of general comments (it was probably thought that an expert organ might not have the political authority of addressing recommendations to governments). Both these expressions aim to exclude the possibility of specific recommendations, namely of recommendations addressed to a single government and concerning its attitude in the field of human rights. But, evidently, only specific recommendations might be efficient instruments to promote respect of the Covenants. If the concrete cases of non-observance could be pointed out and the attitude consistent with the Covenant obligations be brought each time to the attention of the State concerned, this might help to prevent further violations much better than general exhortations to all Parties. On the other hand, a specific recommendation presumes an accurate verification of the circumstances; it is not by chance that recommendations of this type are possible according to the Constitution of the International Labour Organisation and to the European Social Charter, that is to say in two instances in which the verification machinery is well devised. Thus, wherever examination of reports is superficial—as it is unfortunately in the Covenant system—the only possible outcome consists in general recommendations: and these have the function of means for political pressure, rather than of true instruments for supervising the observance of the agreements.

3

As we have already noted the Covenant on Civil and Political Rights, in addition to the reporting system, includes a second implementation measure, that is to say a procedure for the settlement of disputes between the States Parties on the fulfilment of their respective obligations. But this part of the Covenant does not affect all the States Parties; it affects only those States which have declared that they recognize the competence of the Human Rights Committee to receive and consider their claims. With regard to each dispute, the Committee shall have competence to intervene as long as both States Parties have previously accepted its intervention. Therefore, Art. 41–42 of the Covenant are equivalent to another optional protocol which shall come into force only when ten States Parties have made the special declarations of acceptance described in Art. 41.

The procedure we are dealing with consists of three stages. The first is a preliminary contacting stage, during which efforts are made to establish a direct dialogue between the two States concerned: the State Party claiming that another State Party is not fulfilling its obligations may, by written communication, bring the matter to the attention of the latter; the State Party receiving the communication has to reply within the three following months furnishing explanations and making also reference to domestic remedies already taken or still available. After this, the States Parties dispose of further three months to adjust their controversy to the mutual satisfaction.

In the second stage, the matter is referred to the Human Rights Committee: either State shall have the right to ask for its intervention, when six months have elapsed after the receipt of the initial communication and no friendly solution was achieved, provided all domestic remedies have been exhausted. The Committee shall make available its good offices to the States Parties; it may request any relevant information from them and is bound to take account of their respective points of view. These points of view may be expressed orally or in writing when the matter is being considered in the Committee. Within six months from the beginning of the second stage, the Committee shall submit to the Parties its report which must include in any case a brief statement of the facts: if a friendly solution has been reached, the Committee shall mention it, otherwise it shall attach to the report the Parties' written submissions and the record of their oral submissions.

The third stage will take place only if the dispute is still unsolved one year after the receipt of the initial claim; moreover, it requires a new manifestation of consent by the States concerned. On this base, the Committee may appoint an *ad hoc* Conciliation Commission, consisting of five persons (who shall serve in their individual capacity). These five persons shall be selected either by mutual agreement between the Parties of the dispute or, failing such agreement, by the Committee which must elect them among its members. The Conciliation Commission may collect further information from the States Parties and must take into account their written and oral submissions. Its main task is of course to promote a friendly settlement of the matter. Within twelve months, its report must be submitted to the Chairman of the Human Rights Committee. If the consideration of the matter has not been completed, the report will be confined to state this situation; if, on the contrary, a friendly solution has been achieved, the Committee shall compile a brief statement of the facts and of the solution reached. Finally, if the question has been thoroughly examined but no agreement has been reached, the Commission's report shall embody its findings on all relevant questions of fact and its views on the possibilities of an amicable settlement. In the latter case, the States Parties, to which the report must be communicated, will have three months at their disposal to notify the Chairman of the Committee whether or not they accept the contents of the report.

The procedure described above has precedents which can be used for comparison purposes. The Constitution of the International Labour Organisation, the European Convention on Human Rights and fundamental freedoms, the additional Protocol to the UNESCO Convention on Discrimination in Education and the Convention on the Elimination of all Forms of Racial Discrimination provide for a similar implementation measure. In all these cases, the procedure starts with a claim being brought up by a contracting Party, complaining that another State Party has violated its obligations; the aim of the implementation measure is to solve this international dispute in such a way that the value of the obligations undertaken is re-affirmed. There are, however, considerable differences from case to case and the degree of effectiveness of the procedure established by the Covenant on Civil and Political Rights may be evaluated just on the light of these differences.

Let us begin by considering the first stage of the procedure set forth by the Covenant: the direct contacts between the Parties in controversy to explore the possibilities of reaching a friendly solution. The UNESCO Protocol and the Convention on Racial Discrimination include similar provisions, but nothing of the kind could be found in the Constitution of the International Labour Organisation or in the European Convention. According to these agreements, the claim by a State Party shall be immediately followed by action of the organ entrusted with the responsibility of ascertaining the facts and of verifying whether the claim is well-founded (the Governing Body of I.L.O. and the European Commission on Human Rights). This already demonstrates that according to the I.L.O. Constitution and the European Convention the function of enquiry and ascertainment of the violation prevails in respect of the purpose to conciliate the Parties to the dispute; while the contrary happens within the Covenant. Moreover, in the Covenant the success of the procedure depends essentially on the consent of the States Parties, while, according to the Constitution of I.L.O. and the European Convention, the organ to which the claimant State applies has the power to reach a result independently of the consent of the States Parties.

A further evidence of the same circumstances emerges from the consideration of the powers and duties of the Human Rights Committee in the course of the second stage. Its main duty is undoubtedly to put its good offices at the disposal of the Parties; its power to call upon them for information is clearly instrumental to the task of bringing the diverging points of view close together. The brief statement of the facts, which the Committee is asked to submit within six months, must be found on the information and submissions from the two States directly concerned: therefore it cannot have the character of an objective ascertainment.

With regard to the possibility that the procedure makes a further step forward through the appointment of a Conciliation Commission, we have seen that this will depend on the consent of the Parties. No similar provision can be found in any of the above mentioned agreements. The second stage of the procedure set forth in the Covenant is partially similar to that laid down in the Convention on Racial Discrimination, but this Convention entrusts the Chairman of the Committee of Experts with the task to nominate a Conciliation Commission, without asking for the consent of the Parties. In the UNESCO Protocol no distinction is made between the second and third stage: if the initial efforts to reach a direct agreement are unsuccessful, each State Party may apply to a conciliation and good offices Commission. With regard to the I.L.O. system and the European Convention the difference is much deeper. In I.L.O. the Governing Body may, if it thinks fit, communicate with the government accused of inobservance of a Convention, but only to ask for explanations, and failing a satisfactory reply, it may appoint a Commission of Inquiry to consider the complaint. In the European Convention, the Commission shall put itself at the disposal of the Parties to reach a friendly solution of the dispute, but its main function is that of finding the facts and of forming its advice about the violation of the Convention through a wide inquiry which is very similar to judiciary proceedings.

A comparison between the results of the different procedures when a friendly settlement could not be reached is also interesting. The final issue is always a report which shall obviously include in any case a statement of the facts. According to the UNESCO Protocol and the Convention on Racial Discrimination, the conclusions of the report consist in recommendations substantially aiming to promote conciliation between the States Parties; while the Covenant makes reference only to the views that the Conciliation Commission may express on the possibilities of an amicable solution of the matter (Art. 42, no. 7(c)). On the other hand, in the I.L.O. system the Commission of Inquiry may formulate such recommendations as it may think proper, regarding the steps to be taken to meet the complaint and the time within which these steps should be taken; in the European Convention system, the Commission shall express its opinion as to whether the ascertained facts represent a violation of the Convention. One must conclude that the final report provided for by the Covenant is essentially a basis for compromise afforded to the States Parties, which are invited to use it; the report provided for by I.L.O. Constitution and by the European Convention decides whether the claim was well founded or not, even if it is not a final or binding decision.

A last point which is worth considering is the possibility of a further stage, subsequent to the report by the *ad hoc* organ. There is no possibility of this kind within the Covenant and the UNESCO Protocol. Obviously, the States Parties to a dispute shall always be able to refer it, if they agree, to the judgements of an arbitral tribunal or of the International Court of The Hague, but this judgement would be based on a separate agreement and would have no relation to the measure of implementation we have described so far. On the contrary, the Convention on Racial Discrimination and the I.L.O. Constitution include a clause by which a State Party may apply to the International Court of Justice, failing the acceptance of the recommendations made by the *ad hoc* organ. In this case, according to the I.L.O. Constitution, each State Party should inform the Director General of the International Labour Office as to whether it proposes to refer the complaint to the Court. In the frame of the European Convention, the Commission's report is always transmitted to the Committee of Ministers of the Council of Europe, which shall normally decide whether a violation of the Convention took place, and order appropriate measures to redress the injury; however, if both Parties have previously accepted the jurisdiction of the European Court of Human Rights, either may ask the Court to solve the dispute by its judgement. Thus, in conclusion, the systems of I.L.O. and of the Convention on Racial Discrimination offer the possibility to reach a binding judicial decision, as long as one of the States Parties to the dispute asks for it; the system of the European Convention secures a binding decision in any case, but normally refers it to a political organ, and provides for the possibility of a judicial decision only on the basis of an optional system.

The higher effectiveness of systems including a clause of compulsory jurisdiction of an international court needs not to be underlined: only such clauses, in fact, ensure a final solution of the dispute, even though one of the States Parties is interested in obstructing any legal solution. Moreover, the fact that the State Party which failed to fulfil its obligations can be bound to redress the injury, is a concrete measure to guarantee the implementation of the agreement. In other systems, as we have seen above, the accent is on the possibility to conciliate the Parties to the dispute. This sounds as ambiguous, since conciliation is a typical instrument for compromise between the particular interests of single States, while the interest for respect of human rights is of a general and absolute nature. In the field of human rights, conciliation has to face the limit of certain principles which cannot be a subject for compromise; for this reason, the Covenant on Civil and Political Rights expressly requires that any friendly settlement should be founded on the respect for human rights and fundamental freedoms. However, it is clear that there is a certain margin or at least a risk of contradiction between this requirement and the traditional nature of compromise solutions. Therefore it is important to reaffirm that the reaction by the States Parties to any failure to observe the provisions of the Covenant should be prompted by the general interest for respect of human rights. If each government had to be interested only in the enjoyment of human rights by its own subjects in foreign countries, the meaning and the value of the international regulation of human rights would be completely altered. This confirms that a judiciary solution, apt to safeguard the interests of a general and objective nature, should be preferred to the agreed settlement of international disputes concerning the respect of human rights.

4

The Optional Protocol to the Covenant on Civil and Political Rights is entirely devoted to another measure of implementation, which in principle might be considered as the most advanced form of guarantee for the respect of human rights: that is to say, individual petitions. Any individual claiming to be victim of a violation of the Covenant may, on the basis of the Protocol, submit a written communication to the Human Rights Committee. In the first place, the Committee shall find out whether the communication is admissible: it must not be anonimous or be considered to be incompatible with the provisions of the Covenant, or to be an abuse of the right to submit such communications. Naturally, another condition for admissibility is that the State which is being accused of a violation of the Covenant and the State to whose jurisdiction the individual is subject should both be States Parties to the Covenant and the Protocol. If the communication is considered as admissible, the Committee shall bring it to the attention of the State alleged to be violating the Covenant and this State, within six months, shall submit to the Committee its explanations or statements in writing, to clarify the matter and to indicate the remedy, if any, that it has taken. Both the individual and the State Party concerned may transmit to the Committee any document containing useful information. To proceed to the consideration of the matter, the Committee shall also ascertain that the same matter is not being examined under any other international procedure of investigation or settlement, and that the individual has exhausted all available domestic remedies. Having examined the communication, together with the information submitted by the State Party concerned and the individual, the Committee will then be in a position to form its "views" on the matter; these views shall be forwarded to the State Party and to the petitioner.

The described system is closely similar to that set forth by the International Convention for the Elimination of all Forms of Racial Discrimination (Art. 14) which is also of an optional character. The most interesting difference is that the Committee for the Elimination of Racial Discrimination has more restricted powers to declare an individual communication admissible; in particular, the Convention does not make reference to any abuse of the right of petition. At the end of the procedure, the Committee may transmit its "suggestions and recommendations" to the State concerned and to the individual: these terms are more precise than the word "views" used in the Protocol, and imply a greater degree of authority on the part of the Committee. It is also to be noted that each Party to the Convention may entrust a new or existing domestic body with the task of a preliminary consideration of individual petitions.

If we think of the deep reluctance on the part of the governments to be placed on the same level as the individuals, before an international body, we shall fully realize the importance of the petition procedure, and at the same time the difficulty to make it more efficient. This difficulty is even greater because the said procedure could bring to a comparison between the point of view of a State Party and that of one of its nationals, both of which must be equally and carefully considered by the competent international body, when all the State's domestic remedies have been exhausted without giving satisfaction to the individual. If we bear this in mind, it will be easy to understand the optional character of the petition machinery. On the other hand, it is true that the results of the procedure we have described seem to be modest, because even when a violation of human rights actually did take place, the responsible government shall only be subjected to a recommendation from the competent international organ. But were individual petitions to be followed by more adequte international acts, including the condemnation of the State which has failed to observe its obligations, it would be absolutely necessary to ascertain the facts and to implement the relevant clauses of the agreement through a judiciary proceeding. In fact, as long as the examination of the petitions is entrusted to a non-judiciary organ and is carried out on the basis of a restricted investigation, without the guarantees connected with judicial proceedings, it will logically be concluded only with suggestions and recommendations, or with the expression of "views" from the competent organ, which have a political more than a legal value.

These observations are confirmed if we look to the petitions system provided for in the I.L.O. Constitution, and in the European Convention on Human Rights. There is no doubt that, when considered on the whole, the measures of implementation set forth in I.L.O. Constitution are very efficient, as I had many occasions of pointing out. Nevertheless, there is no system of petitions on the part of individuals, whose interests are protected by the Conventions promoted by I.L.O. Only the industrial associations of employers and workers of the Member States may submit to the International Labour Office "representation" concerning the non observance of a Convention. In this case, the Governing Body may (but is not bound to) communicate the representation to the government against which it is made, and may invite that government to make such statements on the subject as it may think fit. If there is no reply, or if the Governing Body considers the statement received as being unsatisfactory, the Governing Body may publish the representation and any statement made in reply of it. The procedure ends at this point; but naturally the publicity given to the representation might induce any other Member State to file a complaint, whose developments would be those described in the previous paragraph.

It should also be noted that the right to file a complaint of non observance of a Convention is recognized, by I.L.O. Constitution, not only to the governments, but also to each delegate to the General Conference, and therefore, also to those delegates representing the employers and the work people of each of the Members. According to this provision, the complaint submitted by an individual in its capacity of delegate to the Conference has the same effects of any complaint submitted by governments. Such a possibility is, naturally, related to the official quality of a delegate to the Conference, which implies direct participation in the activity of the Organisation. Therefore, this is a very different case compared with the right of petition recognized to all individuals for the safeguard of their respective interests.

With regard to the European Convention for the Protection of Human Rights, its optional clauses on individual petitions are well known. The most important feature of this procedure is that it leads to the same result as the complaints filed by governments: that is to say, a binding decision by the Committee of Ministers or a judgement by the European Court of Human Rights, if the matter is referred to the Court by the State concerned or by the Commission itself. In other words, the petitions provided for in the European Convention, are the starting point of proceedings which may lead to condemn the State which has failed to respect human rights; such a condemnation would really meet the complaint of the individual. However, the greater practical effectiveness of the Convention is linked with two additional features:

1. The conditions for admissibility of petitions are very limited.
2. The powers and duties of the Commission are similar to those of an international Tribunal on the point of deciding whether the Convention has been violated or not.

Without entering here into details, I will confine myself to point out that the European Commission is afforded the discretional faculty of refusing to admit a petition if it considers it as incompatible with the Convention, evidently unfounded, or abusive. Moreover, the petition must not be anonimous, all the available domestic remedies must have been exhausted, no more than six months must have elapsed after a final domestic decision was reached, and no claim having the same content must have been previously submitted to the Commission or to any other international organ. Once the petition has been admitted, the Commission will then have wide powers of investigating the facts, and will at the samt time collect all the legal elements in order to establish whether the ascertained facts represent a violation of the Convention. Thus, even if the case is not referred to the European Court of Human Rights, its consideration by the Commission is sufficiently accurate to determine whether the claim was founded, or not.

5

The analysis of the international measures of implementation included in the Covenants and in the Optional Protocol has revealed the deficiencies of the system. Let us recapitulate the most serious:

(*a*) The periodic reports by the States are the subject of a superficial consideration which shall lead only to recommendations of a general nature.

(*b)* The procedure for the settlement of disputes is essentially based on goodwill of the states can be interrupted by either State Party to the dispute before the Conciliation Commission has been appointed, and does not include any possibility of unilateral application to a judiciary organ.

(*c*) Individual petitions can easily be considered as unadmissible by the receiving organ, and even if they are admitted, they are not followed up by an investigation of the facts or by the ascertainment of the alleged violation: the Human Rights Committee shall confine itself to express its views.

It might be worth noting that these deficiencies are not brought to light through a merely theoretical criticism; on the contrary, they emerge from a comparison with the measures of implementation included in other international agreements. We might say, on the whole, that the reports set forth in the two Covenants, rather than control measures, are a means of information; for this reason the reports on economic, social and cultural matters, a field in which the information might really help to improve the international assistance and co-operation, will be found to be most useful. As to the procedure for the settlement of disputes provided for in the Covenant on Civil and Political Rights, its is nothing but a prolonged attempt of conciliation, while the examination of petitions provided for in the Optional Protocol represents only a means for political pressure, which is far from being too strong.

In this respect, it is to be recalled that reports and petitions are already being used within the United Nations as means for a political pressure, on the basis of certain resolutions by the General Assembly and the Economic and Social Council. In particular, a system of periodic reports on human rights was established by the Economic and Social Council as early as in August 1956, and tends now to increase in importance: the governments of Member States are asked to submit periodic reports on the measures taken to put the principles of the Universal Declaration into practice and these reports are then examined by a special Committee of the Commission on Human Rights. The General Assembly has also requested the Member States to submit reports on the measures adopted both in the struggle against racial prejudice and national and religious intolerance (Resolution no. 1779, 1962) and for the realisation of the principles of the Declaration on the Elimination of all Forms of Racial Discrimination (Resolution no. 1905, 1963). Member States are not under a legal obligation to submit these reports, but the Organisation aims to stress in this way the concrete value of some particularly important Declarations. For this reason, the request that Member States should submit their reports is a part of the political action aiming to ensure the respect of those Declarations.

With regard to the petitions under the present United Nations practice, they can be submitted by the nationals of still dependent territories and by those of South Africa, victims of apartheid: the former shall be examined by the Special Committee of Twenty-Four, whose task is to promote the observance of the Declaration on the granting of independence to colonial countries and peoples; the latter shall be received by the Special Committee on the Apartheid policy of the Government of the Republic of South Africa. In both cases, the system functions independently of the consent of the Member States to the jurisdiction of which the claimants are subject. This happens because the system is related to the different activities for political direction and pressure, developed by the United Nations with regard to dependent and South African territories. In substance, this special system of petitions is an aspect of the United Nations efforts to promote a change in the political regime of certain territories. Now, it is obvious that any intention of this kind is alien to the general policy of protection of human rights. But we have to recognize that the United Nations practice is able to make rapid progress in the interest of oppressed individuals and peoples with regard to limited territorial situations which are politically condemned by the majority, while innovations of a general nature, in the field of human rights, which might be prejudicial to deep-rooted principles concerning the sovereign relations between the States, are making very slow progress.

The inadequacy of the implementation measures included in the Covenants and in the Protocol is partly a result of the excessive attachment most States continue to have for the traditional idea of sovereignty. The power of an international organ to supervise in the name of human rights the behaviour of States in respect of individuals within their jurisdiction is still considered by many Members of the United Nations as an intolerable interference in their domestic affairs. The developing countries are particularly diffident towards international action, as they fear that behind such an action there might be the hidden interests of the stronger States. These diffidences are still more considerable in the case of international organs consisting of a few members, and above all in the case of organs consisting of experts, whose attitude might less easily be controlled and forecast. There is no need to recall here the recent wave of mistrust against the International Court of Justice, as a consequence of its final judgement in the case of South West Africa. It is owing to this circumstance that any reference to the Court was cancelled in the final text of the Covenant on Civil and Political Rights, while the draft Covenant had given to the Court an important role.

All these difficulties must not lead to a sterile discouragement but only inspire patience and cautiousness. The approval of the Covenants and of the optional Protocol by the General Assembly after so many years from the beginning of the debate was certainly an important step: what is needed now is an increasing number of signatures, accessions and ratifications. The optional machineries of conciliation and petitions should also start functioning as soon as possible. We must wait for the experience that will be gathered by the new Human Rights Committee and make it the object of careful consideration. It should also be given a wide support in public opinion, in order that the Committee might develop a large and effective action for control and guarantee of human rights. On the other hand, international organs and competences should be prevented from becoming too many: one of the most serious problems in contemporary international life is the number of legal instruments overlapping one with the other.

The system aiming to supervise and promote respect for human rights at the universal level, as set forth in the Covenants and the Optional Protocol, is very far from being perfect, but is probably the most advanced among possible systems, bearing in mind the real conditions which still prevail in the international Community. Our vote is that these conditions might improve, and that the system for the protection of human righs might improve along with them. The road to peace and that of the effective realisation of these rights are largely coincident.

The strengthening of international machinery for the protection of human rights

By Sean MacBride

International Commission of Jurists, Geneva, Switzerland

Introductory

In considering methods that could be adopted for strengthening the international machinery for the protection of human rights, one point of a general nature needs to be made at the outset. It is that, having regard to the tremendous revolution—material, political and philosophical—which has taken place over the last twenty years, a revolution which is probably the most far reaching revolution in the history of mankind, we have to think not so much in terms of historical precedents or of theories based upon past experience, but rather in the light of the new situation resulting from this revolution. A number of resultant factors make a revolutionary approach necessary.

The first of these, of course, is the fact that a full-scale war must involve the destruction of a large segment of the human race. One need not be an idealist or a traditional pacifist to realise that self-preservation, if nothing else, dictates that an alternative to wars must be found. The chief concern of world leadership must be the elimination of war as a method of settling both internal and international conflicts.

The second of these factors arises from the ending of colonialism and the now generally accepted concepts of democracy. The creation suddenly of some 40 new sovereign states, with little or no preliminary experience or preparation, has posed tremendous problems for a world that was not prepared for this rapid transition.

The third factor arises from the stupendous increases in the world populations, particularly in those areas least well equipped to sustain their existing populations, let alone a rapidly increasing population.

The fourth of these factors arises from the fact that we live in a world in which frontiers to thoughts and ideologies have nearly ceased to exist. Mass media of communications and lightning means of transport, coupled with universal education, are levelling national barriers to such an extent that even authoritarian states can no longer insulate their populations from the outside world.

These factors have changed radically the political and economical ecology of the world in which we live; they also give a new dimension to the importance of providing international machinery for the protection of the dignity and rights of the individual. The effective protection of human rights is closely linked with the question of world peace.

Therefore, at the outset of our discussions, I would urge, that we should approach the problems arising out of my subject in a completely revolutionary way and not limit our thinking to the ideas which have dominated legal theory and practice in the past. To do this we must eradicate some taboos immediately. First of all we must try to eradicate the idea that supranational jurisdiction cannot be considered because it infringes the outdated narrow concept of absolute national sovereignty. Likewise, I think we have to eradicate from our minds the idea that the individual cannot be the subject of international law or cannot have recourse to international law.

For centuries the legal doctrine was that "The King can do no wrong". In the world in which we live, the old concepts of "absolute leave and licence" to rulers to act as they wished without regard to the rights of the human beings over whom they rule, cannot subsist. This concept of "absolute leave and licence" is in reality what governments often glibly encompass when they euphemistically refer to "infringements of national sovereignty". Every conventions, treaty or even trade agreement involves a limitation on absolute national sovereignty. Every military alliance treaty, be it NATO or the Warsaw Pact, is a limitation on absolute national sovereignty. It is noteworthy that some of the very sovereignty-conscious States of Europe have agreed to limit their absolute sovereignty in the domain of human rights by adhering to the European Convention for the Protection of Human Rights and Fundamental Freedoms. An even greater limitation of national sovereignty has been accepted by the States that compose the European Economic Community, which many other European States now are seeking to join.

Some of those governments which still cling to the old doctrine of "absolute leave and licence" for themselves also argue that the individual can never have rights under international law. This is quite an erroneous view: this concept was abandoned after World War I, when the Upper Silesian Treaties specifically gave individuals the right of petition. The European Convention as well as the International Convention on the Elimination of Racial Discrimination and two International Covenants on Human Rights all recognise the right of individual petition under international law.

In considering the mechanism that is needed to protect human rights it is necessary in the first instance to consider what are the main types of breaches of human rights that are taking place in the world. I have listed six different types, which I shall examine very briefly.

Firstly, I would list what could be termed *massive but temporary wholesale violations of human rights in international armed conflicts.* Inadequate attention has thus far been devoted to the protection of human rights in armed conflicts; yet, they are probably responsible for the most massive destruction of all human rights. Vietnam is a topical example of such a situation. Human rights should be protected in such situations as well, as well as in peace time. The Red Cross Conventions do make some very meritorious attempts to deal with such situations; but they are inadequate and are often ignored or evaded.

Secondly, there are *massive but also temporary wholesale violations of human rights in internal conflicts,* as distinct from international conflicts. An instance of this was, for example, the situation in Indonesia, where at least 600,000 people were massacred without any form of legal sanction. Unfortunately, there have been many other instances of this kind, in the last ten years.

Thirdly, there are what I would term *massive, systematic and permanent violations of human rights* arising out of the policies adopted by regimes as part of their political doctrine. South Africa and Rhodesia are cases in point. These cases differ from the massive violations of human rights that take place in international or internal armed conflicts in that they arise out of the deliberate political philosophy of certain states; in such cases violation of the most elementary human rights forms part of the inherent policy of the State machine. I have referred to the position in Southern Africa; to this could be added the most recent example which is Greece; there, the regime is deliberately suppressing democratic liberty because it is conscious that it could not survive otherwise. The same type of situation can also be said to have existed in Eastern Europe during the Stalinist period.

Fourthly, there are what I would term the "medium" but also semi-permanent violations of human rights, such as occur in a number of countries where the ordinary democratic rules do not operate and where the rule of law is made subject to the demands of a dictatorship; Spain and Portugal are obvious instances.

Fifthly, we have systematic violations of particular rights, such as freedom of association, freedom of expression, freedom of criticism. Of course, these rights are totally suppressed in the four previous categories of countries mentioned; but in some countries where there may be comparative freedom otherwise, these particular rights are constantly under attack. Some Eastern European countries at the moment come within this category.

Sixthly and finally, we have what I term the "marginal" violations that occur in every country; no matter how well run a country is, no matter how good its legal system may be, there is nevertheless always the possibility that human rights may be violated in individual cases on a marginal basis.

This may happen at a time of political stress or it is sometimes due to bureaucratic inaptitude.

Any implementation machinery to protect human rights must be capable of dealing with each one of these six different situations. The fact that in some of these situations the violations may stem from ideological or political factors in no way excuses them. We must try to avoid brushing under the carpet cases which stem from ideological or political factors.

Protection of human rights in armed conflicts

Before dealing with the type of machinery which could be utilised, it is necessary to deal with the protection of human rights in armed conflicts. There are the Geneva Red Cross Conventions, but they are quite inadequate to deal with the modern practices adopted by major powers of either initiating or supporting an armed conflict in another country.

It seems to be often forgotten that the Red Cross Conventions do bind the signatory States not only to respect the Conventions themselves but also to "ensure their respect in all circumstances". There is therefore a responsibility imposed on all signatory States to ensure that their provisions are respected even when they are not "directly" involved in a conflict but merely exercise "remote control". It is no answer to say: "We are not at war", or "This is an internal conflict in which we are not directly involved." Nations which participate however remotely in an armed conflict by supplying arms, technicians or finance have a definite responsibility to ensure that their indirect agents respect the Geneva Conventions.

The only Convention that seeks to protect civilian population from aerial bombardments is the Hague Convention of 1907, which was concluded at a time when there were no planes capable of bombing attacks, no thermonuclear weapons, no napalm bombs and no bacteriological or chemical warfare. This is a ludicrous situation. There is a reluctance on the part of the Governments of the major powers to remedy this lacunae. They presumably wish not to limit their freedom of action regardless of how many defenceless civilians may be slaughtered by such new means of destruction. Indeed, part of modern military strategy seems to be destruction of population centers and the killing of civilians in order to create chaos and inspire terror. These are problems which governments, probably at the instance of their military advisers, seek to avoid, so that world public opinion will not insist on a more humanitarian approach to armed conflicts.

One of the terrifying features of the world situation, in the present era, is the extent to which brutality has come to be accepted as a norm of our so-called civilisation. Man becomes accustomed to brutality and brutality becomes nearly a contagious disease. Brutality engenders counter brutality. One would have thought that after the horrors of the last world war, after the methodical extermination carried out by the Nazi regime, the world would have set its face firmly against the systematic brutality which is regularly taking place in different parts of the world today. One would have thought that it would have been impossible for 600,000 people be massacred in Indonesia—which I merely take as an example. One would have thought it would have been impossible to have a situation in which forty percent of the members of the parliament of a small country could be executed without trial in one week. One would have thought that the bombing of civilian populations with toxic gases or napalm, be it in Yemen or be it in Vietnam, would not have been regarded as possible. Yet these things are happening, with the tacit acceptance of governments. There is no machinery under international law to deal with such cases. We have in our respective countries elaborate penal codes that deal with murder, manslaughter, robbery etc., but when it comes to mass-murder of populations we have no machinery to deal with it.

As the most massive destruction of human rights occur in times of internal or armed conflicts, it is essential to deal with this aspect. Three particular steps suggest themselves:

International jurisdiction to deal with crimes against humanity. Most countries have laws making acts of cruelty and brutality criminal offences. Should not such acts also be made offences under international law? After all, international law does operate successfully in such relatively less important fields as extradition, communications, crime detection, commerce, shipping and consular relations. Has the time not come for the United Nations to create an international jurisdiction to deal with crimes against humanity? For a start, violations of the United Nations Covenants and Conventions and the Red Cross Conventions could be made indictable offences before an International Tribunal to punish crimes against humanity. Such a Tribunal could, in addition, be given general power to pass judgment on crimes that violate ". . . the law of nations, derived from the usages established among civilised peoples, from the laws of humanity and from the dictates of the public conscience" (Hague Convention). The list of offences triable by such a Tribunal could be added to at a later stage.

At the end of World War II a bold new concept of international jurisdiction was adopted under the Charter of the International Military Tribunal that dealt with crimes against humanity. Accepting the principle upon which this new jurisdiction was founded, Professor Lauterpacht (in the 7th edition of Oppenheim) rightly says that:

"... if affirmed the existence of fundamental human rights superior to the law of the State and protected by international criminal sanctions, even if violated in pursuance of the law of the State."

This jurisdiction suffered from one major defect: it was a trial of the vanquished by the victors. If this was a defect, is there any good reason for not creating now a permanent judicial tribunal to deal with all crimes against humanity? Such a permanent judicial tribunal would not suffer from the inherent defect of being set up on an *ad hoc* basis to deal *ex post facto* with a particular situation. The decisions of such a tribunal might remain temporarily unenforceable in some regions. But behind every act of cruelty there is an individual who perpetrates or inspires the act of cruelty. That individual could at least be identified and branded as an outlaw. Such a sanction would have restraining influence and would reduce the trend towards the brutalisation of mankind.

In protecting human rights, it is not sufficient to enunciate and define the rights involved; it is essential to provide a judicial remedy accessible to those affected. In curbing cruelty and crimes against humanity it is not sufficient to deplore them; it is essential to pass judgment and if necessary outlaw the individuals responsible.

Application of the Hague and Geneva Red Cross Conventions. A major feature of the Geneva Conventions of 1949 was the inclusion of Art. 3 requiring that, in the case of armed conflict *not of an international character,* occuring in the territory of one of the High Contracting Parties, each Party to the Conflict shall be bound to apply, as a minimum, provisions which require *inter alia* the humane treatment of persons taking no active part in the hostilities including members of the armed forces who have laid down their arms, and also of wounded, sick and detained persons. Also prohibited is "violence to life and person, in particular murder of all kinds, mutilation, cruel treatment and torture and the taking of hostages".

Whilst these Conventions, including Art. 3, contain provisions limiting their operation to conflicts within the territory of the Party or Parties concerned, and also defining the particular types of persons to be protected by them, it is considered that the Conventions do constitute a binding code of human conduct in all circumstances.

In regard to the Hague Convention of 1907, the position was clearly set forth by Lord Wright:

"The Hague Convention has consistently and on all sides during the Second World War, and substantially during the First World War, been held binding as an expression of the recognized principles of the law of war. Accordingly, it has a scope beyond that of a mere treaty or agreement between the actual parties, subject to denunciation at any time by any one of them. For this reason it is not necessary to consider whether the belligerent nation, whose conduct is impugned as being a breach of the Convention, is or is not entitled to dispute its authority on the ground that it never was a party to the Convention or, if it was, to denounce it. It is binding as a customary or established rule of law on every member of the community of nations." (Lord Wright: British Year Book of International Law, Vol. XXV, 1948, p. 303.)

It is considered that these remarks are also applicable to the Geneva Conventions of 1949.

Art. 3 of these Conventions imposes obligations not only upon the Contracting Parties but upon ". . . each *Party* to the conflict". To that extent the Convention, in keeping with other developments in modern International Law, treats persons and entitles other than States as subjects of international rights and duties. "The observance of fundamental human rights is not dependent upon the recognition of a specific status. Neither is it affected by the circumstance that the insurgents have risen in rebellion against the legitimate authority" (L. Oppenheim, *International Law*, supra, at p. 211 and Siordet in *Revue Internationale de la Croix-Rouge*, 3 (1950), No. 8, pp. 132–145).

No argument could be upheld which endeavours to justify inhuman treatment, on grounds either that a particular country is not a party to a Convention, or that the particular belligerent, regime, participant or individual persons responsible for such treatment did not have the status of a nation of was not bound by the treaty obligations of the States of which they are nationals.

Has the time not come, when it would be desirable, that whenever an internal conflict or disturbance arises in any part of the world the Secretary-General of the U.N., or some other U.N. authority, should specifically and unequivocally bring to the notice of the belligerents the provisions of the "law of nations" as elaborated by the Hague and Geneva Conventions as well as the provisions of the Universal Declaration of Human Rights. In cases where the belligerents are receiving active support from outside States, these States should also be requested to use their best endeavour to ensure the proper application of these minimal humanitarian rules. They should be reminded that by Art. 1 of the Geneva Conventions they have bound themselves not only to respect the Conventions themselves but *to ensure their respect in all circumstances*. If a procedure of this nature were adopted it would minimise some of the brutality which is so prevalent in internal conflicts; it would be essential that this machinery should operate automatically wherever an international conflict is anticipated.

Finally it may be said that the spirit and terms of the Declaration of

Human Rights of 1948, which appears to be gaining authoritative recognition as a code binding on all nations under international law, would clearly support the principles discussed above. It is only by constant recognition and promotion of these principles by the world community that human rights in this field can achieve utmost realisation. Thus mankind would be spared the horror and sufferings caused by the mass brutality which has caused our era to be one of neo-barbarism.

The adoption of a new Red Cross Convention to deal with aerial bombardments and new scientific methods of warfare. The Hague Convention of 1907 is the only international Convention which deals specifically with the bombardment of population centers. It is an admirable Convention but since 1907 new and worse means of destruction have become the weapons of war. The existing provisions of the Hague Convention should not be whittled away in any respect but a new Convention is essential to extend its scope to include the new methods of destruction now in use.

International machinery for the protection of human rights

The ideal system would, of course, be one in which a standard code of human rights based on the Universal Declaration of Human Rights would be universally adopted and be made enforceable at national, regional and universal level. Appeals from decisions of National Courts on Human Rights issue would in the first place go to Regional Courts of Human Rights and in certain specified cases to a Universal Court of Human Rights.

Protection at national level. This, of course, is the most effective where it is effectively realisable and can be relied upon. The effectiveness of domestic remedies, however, depend in the final analysis not only upon the laws but also upon the independence, courage and objectivity of the Courts in each country.

Unfortunately, we know only too well that in many countries the Courts are not as independent or courageous as they should be; the political authorities in some countries tend to use patronage, pressure and even coercion to secure a subservient judiciairy. Even in well regulated countries, at times of political or ideological stress, complete objectiveness on the part of courts cannot always be expected or assured. Hence, experience has taught that it is essential to have international judicial protection of human rights. It is significant that this need was recognised and provided for by the 16 countries of Western Europe which signed the European Convention for the Protection of Human Rights and Fundamental Freedoms (Austria, Belgium, Cyprus, Denmark, France, Germany, Greece, Iceland, Ireland, Italy, Luxembourg,

Netherlands, Norway, Sweden, Turkey and the United Kingdom). Comparatively, speaking, these countries are among the ones in which the Rule of Law operates reasonably well. The fact that these 16 countries recognised themselves the need for international judicial supervision of their own judicial systems in matters relating to human rights, is in itself significant. *A fortiori* this need is all the greater in areas of the world where the Rule of Law is less firmly implanted or in only a formative stage.

Protection at regional level. At the international regional level, the only valid system which exists so far is that provided by the European Convention for the Protection of Human Rights and Fundamental Freedoms. The International Commission of Jurists has repeatedly urged the adoption of analogous Conventions in other regions—Latin America, Africa, Asia, Eastern Europe and the Caribean region. Interest is not lacking, and even drafts exist, but progress has been very slow.

The European Convention goes a long way towards providing the sort of international judicial implementation machinery that is required. It suffers from two defects. These are dealt with in some detail hereunder because they have a bearing on the whole problem of implementation machinery.

The first defect is that the two optional clauses which give the right of individual petition (Art. 25) and which accept the decision of the European Court of Human Rights as binding and conclusive (Art. 46) have not yet been accepted by all the signatory States. Art. 25 has been accepted by Austria, Belgium, Denmark, W. Germany, Iceland, Ireland, Luxembourg, Netherlands, Norway, Sweden and the United Kingdom. Art. 46 has been accepted by the States enumerated with exception of Sweden. Accordingly in the case of Cyprus, France, Greece, Italy, Malta, Switzerland and Turkey an individual has no international remedy.

The second defect stems from the fact that there is no automatic procedure whereby a signatory State which commits obvious violations of the Convention—such as Greece since the Military Coup d'Etat—is required to appear before the European Commission or the Court of Human Rights.

The Colonels' coup d'Etat in Greece last April highlighted the need for some such automatic and mandatory provision. Greece had not adhered to either Art. 25 or 46, accordingly no individual could bring a case against the Greek Government for its obvious and public violation of the most elementary Human Rights guaranteed by the Convention which Greece had signed and ratified. Here was a case of gross, obvious and public breaches of a solemn obligation undertaken by Greece, yet there was no automatic machinery that could operate without the formal lodging of a complaint by another signatory State.

The ICJ requested the Committee of Ministers, jointly or severally to lodge a complaint against Greece for obvious and public violations of the Convention; it also requested the individual governments to do so. For some unexplained reason which is not easy to understand, the Committee of Ministers did not act. Also for some unaccountable reason the Secretary-General of the Council of Europe did not request Greece, as he could have under Art. 57, to furnish an explanation. Finally, the Governments of Denmark, Netherlands, Norway and Sweden with a proper sense of their international and moral responsibility did lodge the complaint which is now about to be heard before the European Commission of Human Rights.

The measures taken at the Consultative Assembly level and at the Commission and Court of Human Rights level (thanks only to Denmark, Netherlands, Norway and Sweden) have saved the European Convention on Human Rights from being a dead letter. Had the Council of Europe machinery remained inoperative and passive while thousands were being jailed and newspapers and trade unions suppressed in Greece, the value of the Council of Europe would have been irretrievably damaged and the valuable work done by it so far would have been destroyed. The International Commission of Jurists and other NGOs played a really leading role in activating the Council of Europe and in saving it from its own intertia.

Very important lessons have emerged from the Greek episode at the Council of Europe in regard to international regional implementation machinery. They are:

(a) The need to ensure that the necessary judicial machinery will be set in motion automatically and will not be dependent on the initiative of governments.

(b) The value of independent judicial machinery as opposed to governmental or political committees. If the protection of human rights in Greece had depended on the Committee of Ministers of the Council of Europe, their silence and quiesence would have condoned the destruction of human liberty and democracy in Greece. Not to mention that this would have amounted also to a tacit acceptance that a signatory to a solemn Convention could violate it at will. There is a strange sort of "There but for the Grace of God go I" psychological attitude on the part of governments in dealing with complaints against another government in regard to human rights. They are always afraid of creating a precedent that might be used against themselves should they, too, feel inclined to imprison their opponents or censor their own newspapers. In addition, political alliances and political expediency rather than objective judicial considerations, dominate the political approach of governments to such problems.

(c) The right of individual petition is vital. It enables the actual person injured to bring his case himself in his own way and to recover compensation. The payment of compensation to individuals who have been imprisoned or otherwise damnified is not only necessary to do justice but it is a useful deterrent.

(d) As national judicial process requires international regional judicial supervision so does regional judicial process require supervision by a Universal Court. If there had been in existence a Universal Court of Human Rights within the framework of the United Nations, the Council of Europe would have moved much more decisively and rapidly. The knowledge that if it did not move some other State would have filed a complaint at the U.N. Court would have acted like magic in persuading the European Governments to act.

The failure of the Council of Europe to deal effectively and swiftly under the European Convention with Greece does not minimise the value of the Convention. It was the first massive violation of the Convention by one of its signatories that it had to face: if it failed to deal with it at first, it is at least now dealing with it. However, it now becomes essential to learn from this episode. It is absolutely necessary to provide machinery which will operate automatically whenever there is an obvious and open violation of the Convention by one of the signatory States. It should not be left to the discretion, whim or political inclination of a few States within the secret meetings of the Committee of Ministers. The Committee of Ministers seldom meets at Ministerial level; hence, such decisions are usually taken by a "Committee of Ministers" consisting only of officials, some of whom are rather junior. Such automatic machinery will probably require the appointment of an Attorney-General or Ombudsman who would be charged with the duty of bringing any "obvious and open violation of the Convention" before the Commission and if necessary before the Court. He should have a completely independent status and be a judicial officer responsible only to the Court. He should in no way be a creature of the Committee of Ministers and should be quite independent of their direct or indirect control. Quite apart from this specific duty, he should be given the general function of acting as an Ombudsman on the Swedish pattern and should report, at least annually, to the Committee of Ministers and to the Consultative Assembly on all matters pertaining to the observance of the Convention by its signatories. He could also be available to advise *bona fide* complainants as to their rights under the Convention. He should be of a stature sufficient to enable him to discuss human rights problems at top level with governments.

Provisions should also be made to make the powers granted to the Secretary-General to request a government to furnish an explanation of the manner in which its laws ensure the effective implementation of any provision of the Convention under Art. 57 mandatory at the request of any signatory State, the Court, the Commission and the Attorney-General or Ombudsman. This article is not a mere piece of surplusage; it is there to be used.

The Greek episode notwithstanding, the European Convention has worked very well and has been of considerable value.

Accordingly, the experience gained in the decade during which the Convention has been in operation has proved its value. It now requires the amendments indicated. Bearing in mind the deficiencies mentioned, it can form a useful pattern for similar regional conventions in other regions of the world. The areas selected need not be very large, indeed initially such conventions might be adopted more conveniently by small groupings of States rather than large ones; others could then subsequently adhere.

The adoption of such regional conventions does not in any way obviate the need for a Universal Court of Human Rights; any more than the existence of State Supreme Courts in the U.S. obviates the need for the Federal Supreme Court.

As we have with us at this Nobel Symposium some distinguished jurists from Eastern Europe may I avail of the occasion to suggest they might well consider the possibility of formulating a regional Eastern European Convention for the Protection of Human Rights and Fundamental Freedoms which would spell out the rights enunciated in the Universal Declaration and which would provide for judicial implementation machinery. Such a Convention could run on parallel lines to the European Convention but taking into account the defects to which I have drawn attention.

If desired, the emphasis could be placed on economic and social rights. This could be an example and an encouragement to us in the Western world to emulate what can be done in regard to social and economic rights in Eastern Europe. I feel that the stage has been reached when the Communist States of Europe should also encourage and give an example to the Western part of the world. Human rights must not be allowed to become the monopoly of the Western world. The Eastern European countries have their own concepts of human rights; they may be somewhat different from ours, but this should not prevent the adoption of a regional convention and of regional implementation machinery in Eastern Europe. If this were done, it might become possible, ultimately, to envisage a link between the two jurisdictions and a common jurisprudence in regard to certain human rights. Is this not an idea worth examining?

Protection at universal level. At the universal level the United Nations and its specialised agencies have done a great deal in promoting the adoption of international conventions—for example, on the elimination of all forms of racial discrimination, on the prevention and punishment of the crime of genocide, on the status of refugees, on the rights of women, on slavery and forced labour, on discrimination in education. Most recently, the United Nations have adopted two conventions designed to implement the Universal Declaration of Human Rights in its entirety, the International Covenant on Economic, Social and Cultural Rights and the International Covenant on Civil and Political Rights.

Of all these conventions, only the last two—the Covenants on Human Rights, as they are known collectively—and the International Convention on the Elimination of all forms of Racial Discrimination contain any form of implementation machinery. These have not yet come into operation since none of them has yet received sufficient ratifications to enter into force; and even when the machinery does come into operation it is far from adequate or satisfactory.

The machinery provides for the submission of periodic deports by States Parties to the conventions on the state of implementation within their country. In the case of the Covenant on Economic and Social Rights they go to an 18-member Human Rights Committee elected by States Parties to the Covenant, and under the Convention on Racial Discrimination any State Party may bring a complaint alleging violation of its provisions against any other State Party. Such complaint is heard and investigated by the appropriate committee which, if it is unable to bring about an amicable solution, is confined to reporting on its findings, and, under the Racial Discrimination Convention, the Committee may also make recommendations. Reports of the Racial Discrimination Committee are also communicated to all other States Parties to the Convention; this is not so in the case of reports of the Human Rights Committee, which are only communicated to the States Parties concerned.

This complaints procedure only applies to States that are Parties to the Covenant on Civil and Political Rights if they have made a declaration accepting the competence of the Human Rights Committee to receive and consider such complaints. Similarly, the right of individual petition may be recognised by States Parties to that Covenant, or to the Convention on Racial Discrimination, but the competence of the two committees in relation to petitions by individuals is limited to forwarding its "views" (Covenant on Civil and Political Rights) or "suggestions and recommendations" (Convention on Racial Discrimination) to the State Party and the petitioner concerned.

It is thus clear that the great defects of the present efforts of the United Nations to provide implementation machinery are that it is piecemeal and disjointed and that it is likely to be political rather than judicial. Effective implementation machinery should conform to judicial norms, it should be objective and automatic in its operation, and it should not be *ad hoc* nor dependent on the political expediency of the moment.

U.N. Committees or Sub-Committees are not the ideal bodies to be charged with implementation. They are subject to the prevailing political and ideological controversion: they do not have to have a judicial approach to the problems with which they are dealing. They regard themselves as the political spokesmen of their governments and often use Committees as a convenient arena in order to gain kudos for themselves or their governments. In some cases they are not really qualified to deal with the problems under discussion and in some cases they do not even consult their governments. On some important issues government representatives have been known to express views which are not in accord with their own governments policy. Decisions of such U.N. Committees are also sometimes influenced by power politics and "horse trading" bargains. Such U.N. Committees and Sub-Committees are necessary and valuable for the purpose of discussing and preparing new Conventions and proposals but not for the purpose of serving as an implementation authority. They have not the necessary time or attributes for such a function. It is accordingly necessary to provide implementation machinery of a completely different type.

If we are serious about the protection of Human Rights, the time has surely come to envisage the establishment of a Universal Court of Human Rights analogous to the European Court of Human Rights, with jurisdiction to pronounce on violations of human rights. Even if its judgments were initially to be only declaratory, they would be of considerable moral value and would help to create judicial norms in the field of human rights. Its findings would certainly carry far more weight than those of transient and often ill-equipped part-time U.N. committees or subcommittees, selected on a political basis.

The jurisdiction of such a Court should be two-fold. In areas where there already exists an effective international regional Court of Human Rights its function should be that of an appellate Court. In areas where there is no effective regional machinery it should have original jurisdiction to hear complaints by governments, groups or individuals.

It is true that the creation of a Universal Court of Human Rights or of a criminal jurisdiction to deal with Crimes against Humanity would involve an acceptance of some degree of supra-national jurisdiction. I have already dealt with the necessity to modify the old "taboos" based on a narrow view of absolute national sovereignty in dealing with universally recognised Human Rights. The extent of the acceptance of such supra-national jurisdiction could be regulated at first by optional clauses and specific reservations.

The reasons for the need of international judicial machinery in the field of human rights are many, the most important is to ensure objectivity and independence on the part of the tribunal which decides the issues. We all know only too well that often the political authorities—particularly in periods of stress—are not above using patronage, pressures and even coercion against judges to secure their subservience.

International jurisdictions of the kind suggested must be "automatic"—that is, must be free to act and be capable of acting on receipt of a complaint without the intervention of a government. This is one of the defects of the European Convention in regard to those States which have not subscribed to Art. 25 (the right of individual petition) and 53 (the compulsory jurisdiction of the Court) of the Convention. In any international jurisdiction which is created, it is essential that the individual aggrieved should have the direct right of petition or complaint to the instances created. It is important to ensure that a complaint will not be stifled by a government or be made dependent upon the prevailing political alignments.

The composition of any international court or tribunal set up must be above suspicion of bias. Its members should as far as is possible be selected on a non-political basis; they should not be merely functionaries of their governments but should be jurists of high standing who would command respect.

General assistance to advance protection of human rights

A U.N. high commissioner for human rights. Independently of any international judicial implementation machinery, there is at the moment a vitally important proposal for the establishment of a United Nations High Commissioner for Human Rights with a status somewhat analogous to the High Commission for Refugees. This proposal does not and cannot be said to involve any even remote infringement of national sovereignty or element of supra-national jurisdiction.

This proposal, if adopted, will provide the United Nations with a modest but useful instrument for the fulfilment of its mandate, under Art. 13 (1) of the Charter, to assist "in the realisation of human rights and fundamental freedoms for all". It does not go so far as to provide machinery for the implementation of the Universal Declaration of Human Rights. The High Commissioner is not intended to form part of the machinery for the implementation of existing or future international instruments relating to human rights, and his powers and functions will not be such as to clash with any existing or future machinery for their implementation, but will rather be complementary to such machinery.

The High Commissioner's power to give advice and assistance to United Nations organs which request it, will be of considerable value to bodies such as the Commission of Human Rights, which is not organised in such a way as to enable it to undertake detailed examinations of particular problems and at the present time has no independent authority available to which it could entrust such a task. Further, the High Commissioner, being independent of government influence, would be in a position to act completely impartially in any assistance he might give to United Nations organs.

One aspect of the proposal which is of considerable importance is the power given to the High Commissioner to render assistance and services to governments when requested to do so. Governments, particularly of newly independent states, are frequently faced with complex problems affecting human rights in regard to which they require advice and assistance. At the moment there is no United Nations body to which they can turn. The result has been that non-governmental organisations, such as the International Commission of Jurists, have received requests from governments for assistance. In 1965 the International Commission of Jurists, at the request of the government of British Guiana, set up a Commission of Inquiry into certain racial problems which had to be solved prior to the granting of independence; further requests have been received since from governments for assistance, but non-governmental organisations are not the ideal bodies to carry out this sort of mission; they have not the necessary resources to undertake this work; nor are they always politically acceptable. This is a function which would be much better performed by a High Commissioner appointed by the General Assembly, with all the moral authority that he would have as representative of the General Assembly. There is a considerable field in which, for lack of an appropriate United Nations authority, the non-governmental organisations are the only bodies to take an active interest. The appointment of an independent and objective High Commissioner would provide a United Nations authority able to perform some of the functions now being discharged by non-governmental organisations. Non-governmental organisations are often overwhelmed by demands on their services; they are just unable or ill equipped to cope with all the situations in which their assistance is sought.

It is really those governments which level criticism at non-governmental organisations generally, or which accuse them of bias, that should be foremost in supporting the proposal for the creation of the post of a High Commissioner for Human Rights. Paradoxically, however, it is these governments which, so far, have opposed the proposal.

The High Commissioner, through his report to the General Assembly, could play an important part in encouraging and securing the ratification of international conventions relating to human rights. At the same time, the High Commissioner's powers and functions are so defined and limited that his office will in no way encroach upon national sovereignty. He cannot intervene in the internal affairs of any state. He cannot undertake an investigation against the will of the state concerned; he can only act in relation to the internal affairs of a state, if he is requested to render assistance by the government of that state. He cannot issue any binding orders or directions.

Modest though it is, the proposal for the institution of a High Commissioner for Human Rights is, in the view of the international non-governmental organisations most closely involved in human rights problems, worthy of the support of those anxious to promote the cause of human rights. It would make a useful contribution to the protection of human rights acceptable to the large majority of the member states of the United Nations, since it in no way can be said to encroach up their national sovereignty and, while providing them with an institution to which they may turn for assistance if they desire it, refrains from any unsolicited interference in their domestic affairs.

As the six principal Non-Governmental Organisations concerned with human rights issues pointed out in expressing their support:

"The functions proposed for the High Commission fall short of those which the undersigned international organisations would wish to have assigned to such an independent Office. They do, however, appear to represent the maximum likely to be acceptable to a number of governments in the present circumstances."

It would be a tragedy and a cynical disregard for the Universal Declaration if this proposal were not adopted at least in 1968, it has now been under active consideration for three years.

Ratification of international conventions. One of the obvious immediate tasks upon which all efforts should be concentrated is the ratification of all United Nations conventions and covenants in the human rights field. In many cases governments which have supported, and even signed, international conventions have failed to ratify them. Sometimes this is due to bureaucratic inertia; sometimes to political feel-dragging by governments or parliaments. Whatever the reason, a special effort should be made in 1968 to secure the ratification of these international conventions. Some of these have been under discussion for close on twenty years; some of them have been adopted unanimously by the General Assembly.

The contribution of international courts and tribunals to the protection of human rights under international customary law

By Bin Cheng

University College, London, England

In their joint dissenting opinion in the First Phase of the *SW Africa Cases* before the International Court of Justice, Judges Sir Gerald Fitzmaurice and Sir Percy Spender expressed some doubt as to "whether the issues arising on the merits are such as to be capable of objective legal determination".[1] This doubt, which might well have been the real cause of the Court dismissing the applications of Ethiopia and Liberia,[2] relates in particular to the applicants' submissions E–H, namely that the defendant South Africa had "failed to promote to the utmost the material and moral well-being and social progress of the inhabitants of the Territory" in violation of Art. 2 of the SW Africa Mandate and Art. 22 of the Covenant of the League of Nations (Submission E), especially by its policy of *apartheid* (Submission F), its laws "which are by their terms and in their application, arbitrary, unreasonable, unjust and detrimental to human dignity" (Submission G), and its suppression of "the rights and liberties of the inhabitants of the Territory essential to their orderly evolution toward self-government" (Submission H).

It is true that in this regard the relevant sections of Art. 2 of the SW Africa Mandate and of Art. 22 of the Covenant appear essentially exhortative, and that compliance with them leaves much discretion to the mandatory and depends largely on its good faith. Yet, it may be wondered whether, even where an international court has jurisdiction, international law in no way provides any objective criteria whereby alleged violations of fundamental human rights can be assessed.

The problem appears to be one of special interest in the present discussion on the international protection of human rights. For, apart from the fact that some of the provisions of the two international Covenants on Human Rights seem to be even more exhortative in their formulation, if one is to protect human rights, it is obviously important to know what is the position of international law vis-à-vis such rights and whether it provides means whereby alleged violations of fundamental human rights may be determined.

It is not the purpose of the present paper to go into the merits of the *SW Africa Cases* or to deal with the problem of human rights under international customary law as such. All it seeks to do is to put forward for discussion the proposition that the method which international courts and tribunals have hitherto adopted for ascertaining the international standard in the treatment of foreigners may well be used for determining alleged violations of fundamental human rights. It is hoped that a few salient examples will suffice to show that international tribunals have so far not found the task impossible.

First of all, it may be of interest to mention what international courts and tribunals conceive to be the relationship between international law and human rights. The Central American Court of Justice in the case of *Fornos Diaz* v. *The Government of Guatemala* (1909) had this to say on the subject:

"The fundamental rights and powers of the human individual in civil life are placed under the protection of the principles governing the commonwealth of nations, as the international rights of man."[3]

This view was very much shared by Max Huber as sole arbitrator in the *Palmas Case* (1928) and he further indicated the role of territorial sovereignty in this context. According to him,

"Territorial sovereignty ... serves to divide between nations the space upon which human activities are employed, in order to assure them at all points the minimum of protection of which international law is the guardian."[4]

The right to exclusive jurisdiction which territorial sovereignty implies carries with it "as corollary a duty":

"the obligation to protect within the territory the rights of other States, in particular their right to integrity and inviolability in peace and in war, together with the rights which each State may claim for its nationals in foreign territory."[5]

The first part of the duty consequently is to respect the right of other States, within their borders, to self-determination and non-interference by others.

The second part of this duty is to protect the rights of foreign nationals. It is probably in this field that modern international courts and tribunals during the last 170 years have made the most significant contribution towards the elucidation and development of the rules of international customary law. Especially notable from this point of view has been the protection which international courts and tribunals have afforded to life, liberty and property.

The subject of the treatment of foreigners is of course well known. What may perhaps not have been sufficiently noted is the basis of the international standard which is applied. Of special significance is the fact that, while the obligation to protect foreigners according to an international standard is derived from a rule of international law, the specific standard to be applied is based on notions which are at once more profound and general.

Thus, in a number of cases of shooting by frontier guards, the Mexican-United States General Mixed Claims Commission (1923) resorted to what it conceived to be a universal and self-evident tenet, "the respect that is due to human life", in order to determine the international legality of the acts of the guards.[6] Therefore, although the claim was an international one concerning the proper treatment of the nationals of one State by another State, the Commission in no way tried to find a specific standard applicable only to the treatment of foreigners. Instead, as the Commission said in one of the cases:

"The Commission makes its conception of international law dependent upon the answer to the question, whether there exists among civilized nations any international standard concerning the taking of human life. The Commission not only holds that there exists one, but also that it is necessary to state and acknowledge its existence because of the fact that there are parts of the world and specific circumstances in which human practice apparently is inclined to fall below this standard ...

"Authoritative writers in the field of domestic penal law in different countries and authoritative awards have emphasized that human life may not be taken either for prevention or for repression, unless in cases of extreme necessity ...

"If this international standard of appraising human life exists, it is the duty not only of municipal authorities but of international tribunals as well to obviate any reckless use of firearms."[7]

What has been said with regard to human life, applies equally to personal liberty. Both constitute basic values to be upheld, as the Commission said, by municipal laws and by international law, subject to certain imperative needs of society. If from the respect that is due to human life, there is evolved an international standard applicable to the taking of human life, from the respect that is owed to individual liberty, there emerges also an international standard of due process. Thus the French-Venezuelan Mixed Claims Commission (1902) in the *Pieri Dominique & Co. Case* (1905) said:

"The arrest and imprisonment of the claimant, on the 8th day of October, 1896, on the oral order of the civil chief without warrant, his detention for twenty-four hours in prison, and his subsequent discharge on payment of the jail fees without intervention of a court or tribunal of any character is a serious assault upon the liberty of the individual and the sacredness of his person, is wholly unjustifiable, and is the proper subject of indemnity."[8]

These and other cases which may be cited serve to show that in respect of two basic human rights, the right to life and the right to personal liberty, international courts and tribunals have found no difficulty in ascertaining and applying the operative international standards.

These standards are international in three different meanings of the word. First, they are enforced by international law in so far as the treatment of foreigners is concerned. Secondly, they are standards applicable to all States and not specific to a country, such as the standard of national treatment. Thirdly, they are standards which are common to, and upheld by, all civilised nations *in foro domestico.*

For this reason, these standards have also been referred to as the standards of civilization. Thus F. K. Nielsen, in a separate opinion in the *Neer Case* (1926) before the same Commission said:

"It may perhaps be said with a reasonable degree of precision that the propriety of governmental acts should be determined according to ordinary standards of civilization, even though standards differ considerably among members of the family of nations, equal under the law."[9]

As is evident from the above opinions, however, the standards referred to are by no means the highest common factor of the practice of States, but rather what is generally expected at a given time of a well-governed State, *le bon père de famille,* the *bonus paterfamilias.* "Civilised state", an expression which has caused a great deal of discussion,[10] in this context appears to mean no more than *bona civitas.*

What is of particular interest from our point of view is that these standards are not based on how civilised nations treat foreigners, but how they intend all individuals within their jurisdiction to be treated. Thus, the United States-Venezuelan Mixed Claims Commission (1903), while it recognised the right of every State to punish all individuals, national or foreign, for violations of its laws, quickly added:

"provided always that the laws themselves, the methods of administering them, and the penalties prescribed are not in derogation of civilised codes".[11]

Even more explicitly, F. K. Nielsen said in his dissenting opinion in the *Salem Case* (1932) between Egypt and the United States:

"International law requires that, in connection with the execution of criminal laws, an alien shall be accorded certain rights, such as are guaranteed under the laws of civilised countries generally both to aliens and nationals . . .

"The proprierty of any law or of any institution must, I assume, be determined in the light of comparisons with other laws and institutions, in order to reach a conclusion whether ordinary standards of civilization have been outraged."[12]

It is, therefore, the internal laws and practices of civilised nations which provide us with the applicable international standards.

It follows also that these standards are not static ones, but must evolve with current developments in the community of nations. This points is well illustrated by several cases involving slavery and the slave trade which came before international arbitral tribunals. Four such cases came before the British-United States Claims Commission of 1853.

In one of these cases, the *Lawrence* (1855), an American ship which put into a British port for repairs was seized and condemned for being found in a British port equipped for the slave trade. Dismissing the claim put forward on behalf of the owners for the value of the ship and its cargo, the Umpire held:

> "The African slave trade at the time of this condemnation, being prohibited by all civilized nations, was contrary to the law of nations, and being prohibited by the laws of the United States, the owners of the *Lawrence* could not claim the protection of their government."[13]

In the other three cases, slavery having been abolished in most parts of the British Empire in 1833, three American ships, the *Enterprize,* the *Hermosa* and the *Creole,* entered various British ports in distress with slaves on board, respectively in 1835, 1840 and 1841. The slaves were freed by the British authorities. In awarding damages to their owners, the Umpire of the Commission said:

> "No one can deny that slavery is contrary to the principles of justice and humanity, and can only be established in any country by law. At the time of the transaction on which this claim is founded, slavery existed by law in several countries, and was not wholly abolished in the British Dominions. It could not, then, be contrary to the law of nations, and the *Enterprize* was as much entitled to protection as though her cargo consisted of any other description of property. The conduct of the authorities at Bermuda was a violation of the laws of nations, and of those laws of hospitality which should prompt every nation to afford protection and succor to the vessels of a friendly neighbor that may enter their ports in distress."[14]

The premise, or what the British Commissioner Hornby called in his minority opinion the "fallacy", of this argument consisted, as Hornby said, "in ignoring the slave as a man . . . As a man, the slave is as much entitled to appeal to the protection of our laws as his owner".[15] The Umpire treated them merely as "cargo" like, as he said, "any other description of property", even though he recognized that to do so was "contrary to the principles of justice and humanity". Apart from basing his award primarily on the limited immunity enjoyed by ships in distress,[16] the Umpire justified his premise by reference to the positive law of individual nations.

It must consequently be recognised that while the standards of civilisation enforced by international courts and tribunals do not mean the highest common factor of the practice of States, they are also not necessarily those set by the most progressive States, and still less some idealistic ones *de lege ferenda*. The system of values accepted by international courts, like any court, must perforce in the long run be those prevailing among the majority of the subjects of the community in which they operate, or perhaps one may say, those accepted by the dominant section of the community.

Whether or not the decisions in the cases of the *Creole, Enterprize* and *Hermosa* are open to criticism on other grounds, such as their exaggerated notion of what constitutes distress and the extent of the immunity which it confers,[17] it is significant that some twenty years later in 1875, in the case of the *Maria Luz* between Japan and Peru, Alexander II of Russia upheld the refusal of Japanese courts to recognise and enforce contracts entered into with Chinese coolies who were apparently being shanghaied from Macao to Callao on board the *Maria Luz* which had to put into a Japanese port on account of the weather.[18]

The British-United States Claims Commission, in the cases of the *Enterprize, Creole* and *Hermosa,* treated the problem ultimately as one of protecting the property of nationals abroad. Subject to what may or may not be the legitimate object of private ownership, the protection of private property or acquired rights in general may also be viewed as a problem of human rights. Thus Max Huber in the *British Claims in the Spanish Zones of Morocco* (1928) was of the view that any denial of justice is a negation of human personality. If one were to deny States the right of diplomatic protection in respect of their nationals and their property, he said:

"on arriverait à des conséquences inadmissibles: on désarmerait le droit international vis-à-vis d'injustices équivalent à la négation de la personnalité humaine: car c'est à cela que revient tout déni de justice."[19]

In subsuming the protection of property also under the concept of human personality, the Rapporteur came near to the view that property is a mere extension of human personality. The dictum foreshadows also that passage in the preambles of both human rights Covenants where it is recognised that "the rights derive from the inherent dignity of the human person".

This is hardly the place to go into a study of the decisions of international courts and tribunals regarding the protection of foreign property rights. Suffice it to say that here again international courts and tribunals have done much to assist in finding a just equilibrium between the rights of individuals and the demands of society. Even at the height of laissez-faire economy, international tribunals have seldom, if ever, asserted the absolute sacrosanctity of private property. They have always recognised the right of the community to take private property for public use, provided that fair compensation is paid and that there is no undue discrimination.[20]

As regards the quantum of compensation, international courts and tribunals appear to have found the relevant international standard in the very rationale of compensation for expropriation. Two factors are of particular relevance. First, in a taking of individual property for public use, the community has been enriched at the expense of one or more of its members. Secondly, where the sacrifice of those affected is not being shared equally by the rest of the community, compensation is required in order to spread the incidence of the sacrifice fairly throughout the community.[21] Once again, international courts and tribunals have derived these considerations from the practice of States, and these considerations appear to be eminently in accordance with universal concepts of justice.[22]

Looking back at the decisions of international courts and tribunals on the protection of nationals abroad, what conclusions can be drawn?

1. First, in the matter of the treatment of foreigners, international law does not itself specify the content of the standard to be applied, but refers instead to the current standard of civilisation.
2. International courts and tribunals have experienced little difficulty in determining the content of this standard.
3. They do so by reference to the practice of civilised States. Yet, the yardstick is far from being simply the highest common factor of State practice. Rather, it appears to be that of the *bonus paterfamilias*—hence, the qualification "civilised". On the other hand, the standard is one of current practice and not an ideal one yet to be achieved.
4. Even though their task is to deal with the treatment of foreigners, the standard they seek and apply is usually a general one, namely that which civilised States would normally apply to all individuals in like circumstances.
5. In other words, the international standard used by international courts and tribunals is in fact a general standard of civilised treatment of individuals, even though it is applied by international courts and tribunals merely to the treatment of foreigners.
6. This restricted application of the standard is merely due to the fact that the jurisdiction of international law and of international courts and tribunals normally extends only to individuals whose treatment by a State can be the subject of complaint by another subject of international law.
7. Consequently, if this jurisdiction is broadened by consent, there is nothing to prevent the same standard of civilisation being applied to other individuals, including stateless persons and nationals of the State concerned.
8. From the substantive point of view, international courts and tribunals have so far concerned themselves almost exclusively with those international standards that deal with the life, liberty and property of individuals.

9. In these matters, international courts and tribunals have in general shown themselves jealous guardians of the rights inherent in the dignity of the human person. The very institution of diplomatic protection of nationals abroad and of their property has sometimes been considered as one designed to prevent and to remedy denials of justice and, thereby, to safeguard the rights of the individual. International law and law in general merely serve the purpose of assuring a minimum of protection to human activities throughout the world.

10. Perhaps ultimately the crux of the problem of protecting human rights is how to strike a reasonable balance between the rights of the individual and the demands of society. From this point of view, the work of international courts and tribunals shows their anxiety to find within the practice set by States a desirable equilibrium. The treatment of property in particular illustrates their endeavour to conform to the requirements of social, commutative and distributive justice.

11. The fact that international courts and tribunals have not dealt with other than civil rights is merely because so far they have had little occasion to do so, since under international customary law, foreigners are not required to be given political rights, or other rights hitherto considered as inuring solely to members of the national community.

12. But assuming the jurisdiction of the tribunal to have been widened, there seems to be no reason why, not only *ratione personae,* but also *ratione materiae,* international tribunals may not be able to resort to the same international standard in fields other than civil rights.

13. In other words, the standard of civilisation is seen as providing a workable measure of the conduct of States in the matter of human rights, in fields not only civil, but also political, social, economic and cultural.

14. Coming back thus to the question raised at the beginning of this discussion, one may wonder therefore whether the doubt as to whether international law provides the necessary criteria to judge the obligations of States such as those contained in Art. 2 of the SW Africa Mandate is completely justified.

15. Furthermore, it is submitted that this standard, which is based on the positive laws and actual practice of the *bona civitas* of the world society, will in fact afford any international jurisdiction that may be called upon to judge the conduct of States in the matter of human rights not only a well-tried and realistic yardstick for translating abstract concepts into concrete terms but also a means of avoiding the Scylla of following the highest common factor of State practice and the Charybdis of pursuing utopian ideals purely *de lege ferenda.*

NOTES

[1] *ICJ Rep. 1962*, p. 319, at p. 466; see generally pp. 466–467.

[2] See B. Cheng, The 1966 SW Africa Judgment of the World Court. *Current Legal Problems* (1967), vol. 20, p. 181, at p. 212.

[3] *Am. J. of Int. Law* (1909), vol. 3, p. 737, at p. 743.

[4] Scott, *Hague Court Report*, vol. 2, p. 83, at p. 93; *UN Rep. of Int. Arb. Awards* (hereinafter *UNRIAA*), vol. 2, p. 829, at p. 839.

[5] Ibid.

[6] *J. H. McMahan Case* (1929), *Op. of Com. 1929*, p. 235, at p. 238; *UNRIAA*, vol. 4, p. 486, at p. 489.

[7] *García and Garza Case* (1926), *Op. of Com. 1927*, p. 163, at pp. 165–166; *UNRIAA*, vol. 4, p. 119, at pp. 120–121.

[8] Ralston–Doyle, *Report*, p. 185, at p. 205, *UNRIAA*, vol. 10, p. 139, at p. 155.

[9] *Op. of Com. 1927*, p. 71, at p. 78; *UNRIAA*, vol. 4, p. 60, at p. 65; see also same Commission: *Harry Roberts Case* (1926), *Op. of Com. 1927*, p. 100, at p. 105: "The test is, broadly speaking, whether aliens are treated in accordance with ordinary standards of civilisation."

[10] Cf. G. Schwarzenberger, The Standard of Civilization in International Law. *Current Legal Problems* (1955), vol. 8, p. 212.

[11] *H. C. Bullis Case*, Ralston, *Ven. Arb. 1903*, p. 169, at p. 170; *UNRIAA*, vol. 9, p. 231, at p. 232.

[12] *UNRIAA*, vol. 2, p. 1161, at pp. 1213–1214.

[13] Moore, *Int. Arb.*, vol. 3, p. 2824, at p. 2825.

[14] Moore, *Int. Arb.*, vol. 4, p. 4349, at p. 4373.

[15] At p. 4369.

[16] See B. Cheng, *General Principles of Law as applied by International Courts and Tribunals* (1953), p. 75.

[17] Cf. A. V. Freeman, *Denial of Justice* (1938), p. 238; see, however, opinions of British Law Officers of the Crown of the same period, referred to in B. Cheng, The Rationale of Compensation for Expropriation, *Grotius Society Transactions* (1958, 1959), vol. 44, p. 267, at p. 297, note 97.

[18] Moore, *Int. Arb.*, vol. 5, p. 5034.

[19] *UNRIAA*, vol. 2, p. 615, at p. 641.

[20] See further B. Cheng, op. cit. in note 16 above, pp. 36 et seq., and loc. cit. in note 17 above.

[21] See further B. Cheng, loc. cit., in note 17 above, pp. 298 et seq.

[22] See further B. Cheng, Justice and Equity in International Law. *Current Legal Problems* (1955), vol. 8, p. 185.

Régionalisme et universalisme dans la protection des droits de l'homme

Par Roger Pinto

Université de Paris, Paris, France

Principes

L'universalisme européen et la réaction des Etats nouveaux. Historiquement, les relations internationales se sont établies au sein de civilisations et de sociétés isolées les unes des autres, qui ont élaboré les règles de conduite nécessaires. A l'époque contemporaine, l'Europe devient une région privilégiée dont l'expansion mondiale entraîne celle de ses principes éthiques et juridiques. Cependant, d'autres régions, avant de subir l'intervention et l'influence européenne, avaient créé leur propre système de relations et de droit — la Chine, l'Inde, le Sud-Est asiatique, l'Amérique pré-colombienne. Le « monde » européen, à son tour, se différencie et se divise — avènement de l'Amérique puis constitution dans l'Est européen d'Etats qui rejettent le principe de l'appropriation privée de l'économie. On assiste plus récemment au réveil des régions subjuguées. La décolonisation façonne en Asie et en Afrique des sociétés nouvelles qui renouent d'anciennes traditions. Elles opposent leur conception du monde à celle d'une Europe qui prétendait jusqu'ici exprimer seule l'universel. A côté de l'égalité des Etats s'impose l'égalité des civilisations et des systèmes juridiques dont le statut de la Cour Internationale de Justice, comme déjà l'ancien, prescrit qu'ils doivent être représentés, dans l'ensemble, parmi les Juges.

Notre monde fini retrouve ainsi la « primauté » du fait régional, politique, économique et social autrefois imposée par l'absence de relations. L'universel subit la pression du régional dont il exprime les convergences, vraies ou fausses, ou constate les antinomies irréductibles. Les droits de l'Homme n'échappent pas à cette emprise.

Valeur universelle du principe de respect des droits de l'Homme. Pourtant le caractère universel de la protection des droits de l'Homme est affirmé par toutes les civilisations et par tous les systèmes juridiques. Le respect des droits de l'Homme est placé au rang des principes exceptionnels du droit international public de caractère impératif (*jus cogens*) auxquels les Etats ne peuvent déroger par convention.

Le président Cassin qui a toujours exprimé la philosophie universaliste en a marqué indirectement les limites :

« A cet égard, je n'ai jamais changé d'avis. Je suis et je demeure convaincu que si les grands principes sont communs au monde entier, si les droits de l'Homme ont et ne peuvent avoir qu'un caractère universel, il doit être permis aux groupes de nations plus avancées; plus développées sur le plan de la technique juridique ou même seulement de l'habitude du respect des libertés de devancer les autres pays. » (Colloque de Strasbourg, 1960, Dalloz 1961, p. 30.)

En fait la communauté internationale dans son ensemble constate, reconnaît et consacre l'existence d'un minimum de règles humanitaires, protectrices de droits élémentaires. Ces règles sont codifiées dans les quatre conventions de Genève sur les conditions d'emploi de la force armée dans les relations internationales et les guerres civiles, les conventions sur le génocide, sur l'esclavage et le travail forcé, la traite des femmes et des enfants. Malgré la convergence des mouvements spirituels dans une éthique universelle, les sociétés politiques se limitent au plus petit commun dénominateur et ne l'atteignent pas toujours. L'universel n'est conçu et pensé que par des minorités capables de dominer les contingences des appartenances historiques. L'influence de ces minorités sur les gouvernants est certaine sinon décisive. L'adoption en 1948 de la Déclaration Universelle des Droits de l'Homme et, dix-huit ans plus tard, en décembre 1966, par l'Assemblée Générale de l'ONU des pactes sur les droits de l'Homme en apporte la démonstration.

Portée et limites de la Déclaration Universelle et des Pactes internationaux relatifs aux droits de l'Homme. L'inspiration des Pactes des Droits de l'Homme comme de la Déclaration est universaliste. Mais en se précisant, dans les Pactes, les principes sont limités par la notion d'ordre public, nulle part définie. Sous réserve du minimum incoercible exprimé par des règles élémentaires d'humanité (droit à la vie, interdiction de la torture, de l'esclavage, de la servitude ou du travail forcé, de la prison pour dette), les droits et la liberté sont le plus souvent énoncés en termes si généraux que le législateur national conserve le pouvoir de les restreindre gravement.

Le jugement sévère porté sur ces tentatives par le professeur Alf Ross doit être rappelé :

« There is hardly any subject that has produced such a spate of words or left such a depressing impression of insincerity and lack of substance behind these words ... the profound differences between the cultural traditions and economic and political ideologies of the different peoples and States ... make it difficult, without resorting to untruths, ambiguities or camouflage, to draw up definitions acceptable to all. » (The United Nations : Peace and Progress, 1966, p. 350.)

Le Comité des Droits de l'Homme, créé par la Convention, peut, il est vrai, dans les rapports particuliers qu'il établit sur les mesures arrêtées par chaque Etat pour donner effet aux droits reconnus par le pacte relatif aux droits civils et politiques, estimer que les législations et les pratiques nationales ne sont pas conformes aux dispositions conventionnelles. Mais le désaccord de l'Etat partie sur de telles conclusions du Comité laisse les choses en l'état. Le Comité n'a pas compétence pour donner une interprétation authentique du pacte qui s'impose aux Etats parties. Aucune autorité n'est désignée pour trancher le différend. A plus forte raison les Etats parties ne peuvent faire l'objet de « plaintes » émanant d'autres Etats ou de personnes privées à moins qu'ils n'aient accepté par déclaration facultative en ce qui concerne

« les communications sans lesquelles un Etat prétend qu'un autre Etat ne s'acquitte pas de ses obligations. » (Art. 41.)

et par adhésion au Protocole facultatif en ce qui concerne les

« communications émanant de particuliers relevant de sa juridiction qui prétendent être victime d'une violation quelconque des droits énoncés. » (Art. 1.)

Dans les deux cas, la procédure n'aboutit pas à une décision obligatoire. Adoptée l'année précédente par l'Assemblée Générale, la Convention sur l'élimination de toutes les formes de discrimination raciale comporte un mécanisme de contrôle moins inefficace qui permet au Comité d'être saisi par tout Etat partie et d'adopter un projet de règlement. (Art. 11–13.)

A l'exception des quatre Conventions de Genève qui lient tous les Etats du monde, les conventions universelles portant sur des problèmes particuliers n'obtiennent pas le nombre de ratifications qui permettrait de constater l'universalité du principe qu'elles mettent en œuvre. (Génocide : 68; esclavage : 65, travail forcé (No. 29 OIT) 99; travail de nuit des adolescents (non industriels) (No. 79 OIT) 15; liberté syndicale et protection du droit syndical (No. 87, OIT) 75; travail de nuit (femmes) (No. 89 OIT) 44; travail de nuit des enfants (industrie) (No. 90 OIT) 30; abolition du travail forcé (No. 107 OIT) 78; populations aborigènes et tribales (No. 107 OIT) 20. Source : Primauté du Droit et Droits de l'Homme, CIJ, Genève, 1960; et C. W. Jenks, infra.)

Cette ambiguité des pactes universels, l'absence de contrôle international efficace, le nombre limité d'Etats parties reflètent des réalités regionales divergentes.

Réalités, divergences et exigences régionales. Malgré l'assentiment universel de principe, on constate, en fait, à travers le monde et ses régions politiques, un inégal développement et des oppositions profondes quant au contenu et aux conditions de mise en œuvre des droits de l'Homme et des libertés fondamentales.

A la conception universaliste, exprimée par le Professeur Cassin, s'oppose le réalisme prudent du Professeur Friedmann :

« While in theory such fields as the protection of human rights as formulated in the U.N. Declaration of Human Rights of December 1948, is a universal concern of mankind, in fact, the disparity of standards, systems and value is too great to make an effective international organization possible in this field. » The Changing Structure of International Law (1964, p. 63).

Sans doute les textes constitutionnels d'origine et d'inspiration souvent universelle se réfèrent aux droits de l'Homme, les énumèrent dans un préambule solennel et même les consacrent par dispositions expresses. Mais le contrôle de l'application des textes n'existe pas ou demeure limité. La suspension des droits et libertés est facilement prononcée en vertu ou en l'absence de dispositions légales. Si le pouvoir appartient à un parti unique ou à l'armée, les droits des opposants sont généralement méconnus. Que des troubles intérieurs surgissent, leur vie, leurs biens ne sont plus protégés. La résistance au pouvoir établi par ses méthodes terroristes fait écho aux excès et aux tortures des forces de l'ordre. Tel ou tel groupe ethnique de la population est massacré au hasard des combats. Les gaz toxiques retrouvent leur emploi. Qu'une puissance industrielle intervienne dans la guerre civile et utilise sans restriction les bombardements aériens, la destruction des récoltes, les techniques de la terre brûlée, les non combattants deviennent les plus nombreuses victimes des ces carnages.

La communauté internationale universelle ne se préoccupe guère de faire respecter les règles élémentaires des conventions de Genève. Le Comité International de la Croix Rouge panse les plaies et tente discrètment de limiter leur extension. Les Etats et leur gouvernement demeurent silencieux s'ils n'ont pas de motifs politiques d'agir. L'intervention d'humanité apparaît ainsi liée aux intérêts nationaux. La bonne conscience des Grandes puissances qui, selon les circonstances, ignorent ou invoquent les principes du droit humanitaire et la protection des droits de l'Homme, donne excuse aux nouveaux Etats. L'universalisme défaillant maintient le régionalisme insuffisant. Comme l'a reconnu le Secrétaire Général de la Commission Internationale de Juristes :

« Les facteurs à considérer varient de pays à pays selon leur stade de développement. Ce qui serait indéfendable dans une société évoluée et prospère, peut devenir admissible dans une société qui s'efforce de lutter contre la faim. » (Rapport à la réunion plénière de Genève, 1966, Bulletin No. 28, Décembre 1966, p. 5.)

A un double point de vue, l'action et l'organisation régionale pour la protection des droits de l'Homme paraissent paradoxalement nécessaires : tant pour tenir compte de la diversité des structures sociales que pour rappeler les exigences de l'universel.

Faits

La division du monde en régions géo-politiques. La diversité des structures sociales est trop évidente pour qu'il soit besoin de la décrire. Elle est liée à l'inégal développement économique qui oppose sociétés technologiques et urbaines et sociétés manœuvrières et rurales, au maintien de traditions religieuses qui imprègnent la société politique toute entière; au rôle de la famille — étendue ou limitée au couple et à ses enfants; à l'existence d'ethnies non encore fondues en nation : au niveau de vie individuel ou familial; au contenu du droit de propriété privée comprenant les moyens de production et d'échange ou seulement les biens d'usage personnel; au degré d'instruction et d'alphabétisation; à l'interaction sur les pays en voie de développement des pays hautement industrialisés; à la subordination des intérêts immédiats des individus à l'avenir de la collectivité envisagé selon une certaine conception du monde et au développement d'un nouvel ordre social.

Ces lignes directrices permettent de diviser le monde en régions relativement homogènes capables de mettre en œuvre une déclaration des Droits de l'Homme conforme aux aspirations et à la structure des pays membres.

L'Europe Occidentale et la Convention-pilote du Conseil de l'Europe. L'Europe Occidentale a, la première, choisi cette voie. La Convention Européenne de sauvegarde des droits de l'Homme et des libertés fondamentales de 1950 offre un exemple, et une leçon. L'exemple tient dans le catalogue des droits civils et politiques exactement adapté aux possibilités de la région; les droits « sociaux » relèvent de conventions européennes différentes (Charte Sociale Européenne de 1961).

La tendance « universaliste » de la Convention Européenne, dont pratiquement chaque article se rattache à l'article correspondant de la Déclaration Universelle de 1948, est évidente. Sur ce point même, la leçon commence. Les gouvernants européens de l'Occident n'ont pas consacré le droit des individus de choisir librement leur nationalité, ni ceux des étrangers de résister aux expulsions arbitraires et jouir de libertés essentielles (liberté d'expression, de réunions, d'associations). Surtout, ils ont refusé les droits et libertés proclamés à ceux qu'ils considèrent comme les ennemis de leur philosophie de la liberté (Art. 17). Cette disposition pourrait apparaître comme une expression de régionalisme politique si l'on ignorait qu'elle est inscrite dans la Declaration Universelle et le Pacte international sur les droits civils et politiques[1]. Mais cette « entorse » à l'universalisme acceptée par ceux-là même qui en sont les champions déclarés, préfigure le particularisme nécessairement plus accentué des autres régions.

La seconde leçon qu'apporte la convention européenne concerne le mécanisme de contrôle de l'application de la Convention. Entre Etats parties, des voies de recours qui conduisent à une décision finale obligatoire diplomatique ou facultativement juridictionnelle sont bien établiees. Onze Etats sur dix-huit membres du Conceil de l'Europe ont accepté ainsi de comparaître devant la Cour européenne des droits de l'Homme. L'Italie, la Grèce, la Turquie, Chypre et Malte, parties à la Convention, la France et la Suisse qui ne l'ont pas ratifié, ont ainsi refusé la compétence juridictionelle. De plus, les loups ne se mangent pas entre eux. En fait, les Etats parties à la Convention n'ont jamais pris l'initiative de plaintes devant la Commission Européenne des droits de l'Homme pour assurer la protection des individus. Les évènements récents de Grèce confirment cette carence et montrent que l'action régionale ne peut suffire[2]. La Convention européenne a prévu une garantie efficace mais facultative — le droit de recours individuel devant la Commission Européenne des droits de l'Homme. Onze Etats sur dix-huit l'ont accepté.

On imagine mal — tout en le souhaitant — que d'autres pactes régionaux puissent renforcer le caractère obligatoire des recours. On conçoit plutôt que les clauses facultatives de compétence ne seraient acceptées que par un nombre d'Etats plus faible encore.

L'unité régionale canadienne et américaine du Nord. Les Etats-Unis et le Canada constituent ensemble une région politique qu'il serait difficile de rattacher au Sud du Continent de structure sociale et de tradition juridique très différentes. On hésite à souhaiter la création d'un pacte régional englobant ces deux pays. Ils possèdent à la fois une déclaration des droits et de voies de recours affectives — au plan régional. Par contre, si le projet de Commissions régionales des Nations Unies pour les droits de l'Homme était acceptable, une telle commission inter-américaine et continentale devrait être créée pour assurer les liaisons indispensables sur le plan interrégional et universel.

Ainsi les griefs que pourraient faire valoir les républiques latino-américaines contre des actes des Etats-Unis, ou ceux que des personnes privées et groupement reprocheraient aux gouvernements latino-américains pourraient être entendus, au-delà du système régional et interrégional, dans un cadre universel. De même, dans la mesure où l'intervention américaine au Vietnam met en cause l'application du droit humanitaire et la protection des droits de l'Homme, l'action régionale — inter-américaine ou sud-asiatique — si elle se révèle inefficace doit s'appuyer sur un système universel.

Le système inter-américain et les Républiques d'Amérique Latine — La Commission Interaméricaine des Droits de l'homme. Les éléments d'un système inter-américain de protection des droits de l'Homme commencent à apparaître. Une Déclaration des droits et des devoirs de l'Homme est adoptée le 8 mai 1948, lors de la neuvième conférence internationale des Etats américains (Res. XXX, 43 AJIL (1949) Sup. 133). Dix ans plus tard, la cinquième Réunion de consultation des ministres des affaires étrangères de l'OEA invitait, d'une part, le Conseil de l'Organisation à créer une commission interaméricaine des droits de l'Homme et, d'autre part, la Commission inter-américaine de justice à préparer un projet de Convention (Résolution VIII, I et II 1959).

La Commission interaméricaine des droits de l'Homme a été constituée et ses membres désignés par le Conseil de l'OEA en 1960. Elle a progressivement étendu sa compétence du domaine des consultations, des études, des enquêtes par pays et des recommandations générales et particulières à l'examen, après épuisement des recours internes, de petitions individuelles, relatives à certains droits (vie, liberté, sécurité et intégrité de la personne, droit à une bonne administration de la justice) en vue d'adresser des recommandations à leur sujet aux gouvernements intéressés. (Statut du 25 Mai 1960, OEA, Doc. Conseil, c. a. 371), amendé le 8 Juin (id. c. a. 373) et en Octobre 1965 par la dixième conférence interaméricaine de Rio de Janeiro, cono. Scheman, The Inter-American Commission on Human Rights (59 AJIL (1965) 335); K. Vasak, La Commission inter-américaine des droits de l'Homme, son rôle et son importance pour les pays en voie de développement. (Travaux du colloque de Berlin sur les droits de l'Homme, Oct. 1966.)

Tout récemment, lors de la guerre civile à St. Domingue, la Commission a reçu mandat des parties à l'Acte de Saint Domingue des 2 et 3 Septembre 1965 de demeurer en République Dominicaine jusqu'aux élections prévues. La Commission a rédigé un projet de convention sur la liberté d'expression, d'information et d'enquête qui devait être soumis à la XIe Conférence Inter-américaine (OEA/Sér. L/V/II, 8, Doc. 15).

Le projet de Convention inter-américaine des droits de l'Homme a été également adopté par la Commission des Juristes de l'OEA lors de sa quatrième session à Santiago de Chili (8 Sept. 1959, Acte final, Doc. OEA/Ser. C/IV, 4, CIJ-43 et Rev. de la Commission Internationale des Juristes, Vol. IV, No. 1 (été 1962).) Plus de huit années se sont écoulées. La Convention n'a pas encore vu le jour. On a expliqué cette carence par l'arrivée au pouvoir de Fidel Castro (Introduction to « Comparative Texts of Drafts of Regional Conventions on Human Rights », p. 3, International Commission of Jurists, Geneva, 3 d). On aperçoit mal la corrélation.

On peut se demander si le problème ne se rattache pas aux divergences de conception existant entre les Etats-Unis et les Républiques latino-américaines (voir les réserves américaines en Annexe II à la Résolution VIII (1959) et en annexe VI au projet de Convention à Santiago (1959).) Dans ce cas, une convention régionale limitée à ces Républiques aurait plus de chance de succès.

Un projet de convention entre les cinq Etats d'Amérique Centrale a été préparé par un groupement privé. Ses promoteurs font état de l'identité de nature, des traditions, intérêts et aspirations de ces pays et rappellent qu'ils avaient autrefois constitué une Cour de Justice Centre-Americaine (ibid. p. 3). Le projet est soutenu par l'association Freedom through Law (New York). Il a été publié dans le document précité avec le texte du projet de Convention interaméricaine et celui de la Convention Européenne.

Le dernier état du projet de Convention de l'O.E.A. Cette évolution s'est manifestée lors de la 2ᵉ conférence interaméricaine de Rio (1965). La conférence a examiné non seulement le projet de la Commission des Juristes mais deux nouveaux projets, déposés l'un par le Chili (OEA/Sec. E/XIII. 1, Doc. 35, 30 Sept. 1965) rapprochant les droits politiques et sociaux des libertés traditionnelles, et l'autre par l'Uruguay (id. Doc. 49 du 19 Novembre 1965). Ces deux projets s'inspirent du texte de la Commission des Juristes de l'OEA. La Conférence a renvoyé l'ensemble du problème au Conseil de l'OEA, chargé d'élaborer dans le délai d'une année, un texte unique qui soit être soumis à une conférence ad hoc (Resolution XXIV, ibid., Doc. 150, 30 Novembre 1965, pp. 55–57).

La Commission interaméricaine des droits de l'Homme, appelée à donner son avis, a établi un texte unique de convention qui tient compte notamment de son existence et de son expérience propre (OEA/Sec. L/II/15, Doc. 26 du 15 Novembre 1966; ibid, Sec. L/V/II, 16, Doc. 8 du 24 Avril 1967).

Le Conseil de l'OEA a confié l'examen de l'avis de la Commission Interaméricaine des droits de l'Homme ainsi que la Résolution XXIV de la Conférence de Rio à sa Commission des affaires juridiques et politiques. Celle-ci a soulevé dans un rapport du 31 Mai 1967 (OEA/Ser. G/IV-C-2 787, Rév. 3, 7 Juin 1967) le problème du conflit entre une convention interaméricaine et les pactes des droits de l'Homme adoptés par l'assemblée générale des Nations Unies en décembre 1966. Elle a suggéré au Conseil de l'OEA de poser aux Etats membres les deux questions suivantes :

1. Désirent-ils que soit établie une *règlementation* universelle et uniforme

des droits de l'Homme ou considèrent-ils possibles la coexistence et la co-ordination des Conventions universelles et des conventions régionales sur les droits de l'Homme?

2. Au cas où l'idée d'une réglementation universelle des droits de l'Homme serait retenue, faut-il alors se borner à instituer un mécanisme interaméricain de *protection* des droits de l'Homme, comprenant la Commission et éventuellement une Commission inter-américaine des droits de l'Homme?

Cette procédure ratifiée par le Conseil de l'OEA remet en question l'adoption, à échéance prévisible, d'une convention inter-américaine. En vérité, le véritable régionalisme consisterait à constater l'existence d'une région latino-américaine dont les conceptions politiques, économiques et sociales ne sont pas le reflet de la vision du monde nord-américaine[3].

Cependant, il convient ici encore de marquer les limites de l'action régionale. Dans la mesure où les gouvernements établis se maintiennent au pouvoir grâce à l'intervention des forces militaires, ils sont peu disposés à assurer effectivement le respect des droits de l'Homme. A plus forte raison s'ils sont aux prises avec une résistance armée ayant recours aux actes terroristes, ils estimeront légitime d'exercer des représailles incompatibles avec le droit humanitaire. Pour tenter de redresser cet état de fait fréquent, l'appel aux institutions inter-américaines et universelles est indispensable.

Le régionalisme africain et les mouvements non gouvernementaux. Le Continent Africain pose des problèmes analogues. Comme l'écrit M. Karel Vasak dans un rapport présenté au Congrès des juristes africains francophones

« un homme de bonne foi ne peut considérer le problème des droits de l'Homme de la même manière et dans les mêmes termes en Afrique et en Europe. » (Dakar, Janvier 1967, D. 15. 818. 05.12, Les Droits de l'Homme et l'Afrique.)

Les Africains éclairés entendent bien placer leur continent sous la protection des grands principes.

Le Congrès africain non gouvernemental sur la primauté du droit, réuni à Lagos en janvier 1961, sous les auspices de la Commission Internationale de Juristes, a réaffirmé les exigences de l'universalisme. La même inspiration s'inscrit dans les constitutions africaines. La réalité sociale est bien différente. Les droits de nombreux individus sont nécessairement limités par ceux de la famille et de la tribu. L'existence d'un parti unique, d'un gouvernement militaire prive les opposants de leurs libertés politiques. Le développement économique impose une organisation du travail souvent à base de contrainte. La liberté d'expression, le droit à l'information, dans leurs formes modernes, ne sont pas et ne peuvent pas toujours être respectés. Ils doivent s'insérer dans un système traditionnel (information de bouche à oreilles, palabres villageoises). L'affirmation constitutionnelle du principe de non discrimination est devenu sans effet pratique. De sanglants carnages ont mis aux prises les ethnies libérées. (Burundi, Ruanda, Congo) La constitution fédérale au Nigéria confia aux tribunaux la garde des droits de l'Homme et des libertés fondamentales. Elle n'a pu assurer le règlement des conflits entre tribus. Le massacre des Ibos en 1966 a conduit à la guerre de sécession.

La protection des droits de l'homme dans les chartes constitutives des organisations africaines. La protection des droits de l'Homme ne tient guère de place dans les chartes régionales africaines. La charte de l'Organisation de l'Unité Africaine (OUA — 1963) mentionne simplement l'adhésion des Etats membres à la Déclaration universelle. Parmi les principes énoncés à l'article III que les Etats s'engagent « à respecter scrupuleusement » ne figure pas le respect des droits de l'Homme. Sur un point particulier et significatif, la charte énonce parmi les principes fondamentaux de l'Organisation : « la condamnation sans réserve de l'assassinat politique. » (Art. III. 5). Une commission de juristes, créée en 1964 avec statut de commission spécialisée de l'OUA, aurait pu affirmer sa compétence en matière de sauvegarde des droits de l'Homme. Elle n'a pas été constituée faute de crédits.

Le projet de Convention africaine des droits de l'homme d'origine non gouvernementale. La « loi de Lagos », adoptée en 1961 par le congrès africain (non gouvernemental) sur la primauté du droit, invitait les gouvernements africains à « étudier la possibilité d'adopter une convention africaine des droits de l'Homme prévoyant notamment la création d'un tribunal approprié et de voies de recours ouvertes à toutes les personnes relevant de la juridiction des Etats signataires. » (Point 4) L'idée a été reprise par la République de Somalie, dans ses observations présentées à l'ONU sur les pactes universels. Son gouvernement a souligné qu'en ce qui concerne le droit de l'Homme, les différences entre régions sont souvent plus prononcées qu'à l'intérieur de ces régions et qu'il serait plus facile pour les Etats d'une région donnée de se mettre d'accord sur la garantie des droits de l'Homme entre eux plutôt qu'avec tous les membres des Nations Unies. Le gouvernement Somalien évoquant l'expérience européenne et américaine déclarait souhaiter l'établissement d'un système analogue en Afrique dans le cadre de l'Organisation des Etats Africains. (A/5411/Add. 2, 25 Octobre 1963.)

Dans le rapport qu'il a présenté au Congrès des juristes francophones, M. Karel Vasak a suggéré, lors de la rédaction d'une convention africaine, d'une part d'établir une liste et une définition des droits de l'Homme tenant compte des conditions particulières propres à l'Afrique et, d'autre part, de prévoir un mécanisme de contrôle progressif, initialement fondé sur de simples rapports généraux et se développant par périodes successives de cinq années, pour aboutir à la création de voies de recours ouvertes aux individus. (Rapport précité, pp. 21–23.)

Le Congrès de Dakar a souhaité dans ses conclusions que soient examinées « l'opportunité et la possibilité de créer un système de protection des droits de l'Homme, fonctionnant dans le cadre africain dont une commission interafricaine des droits de l'Homme dotée de compétences consultatives et de pouvoirs de recommandation, pourrait ... constituer le premier élément. » (Art. VI (3) proposé par la Commission I, Bulletin de la Commission Internationale de Juristes, No. 29, Mars 1967, p. 11.) Mais la Déclaration de Dakar confirme plutôt l'adhésion des juristes africains francophones à une profession de foi universaliste. Elle porte en effet

« que la dignité de l'Homme africain exige des normes aussi hautes que celles reconnues ailleurs; que l'effritement de cette notion serait le signe d'une régression inadmissible. »

En même temps, elle reflète plus exactement la réalité en estimant

« que partout et toujours doit être préservé ce minimum imprescriptible au dessous duquel la dignité de l'Homme n'existe plus ».

De même, la Déclaration affirme :

« que les exigences fondamentales 'de la primauté du droit' ne sont pas différentes des celles acceptées ailleurs, que les difficultés économiques, sociales, culturelles de l'Afrique d'aujourd'hui ne sauraient pas justifier l'abandon des principes fondamentaux de la primauté du droit » (loc. cit. pp. 5–6).

Régionalisme et universalisme au stade actuel de l'évolution africaine. Il apparaît que la protection des droits de l'homme en Afrique exige un relai régional. Toutefois, la carte des régimes politiques africains, aujourd'hui bouleversée et toujours instable, exige peut-être plusieurs relais régionaux. L'unité du régionalisme africain est, au stade actuel, menacé par les conflits internes et la formation de plusieurs régions politiques et politico-ethniques qui s'ignorent et se combattent.

Dans l'immédiat, les groupements les plus solidaires pourraient plus facilement créer, à leur échelle, les instruments régionaux de défense et de protection des droits de l'Homme.

Dans ces circonstances, le cadre régional strict ne permet pas, en Afrique comme ailleurs, de résoudre tous les problèmes. Les atteintes aux droits de l'Homme dont la région est complice muette ou spectatrice impuissante, relèvent de la communauté internationale organisée toute entière.

La volonté des élites africaines de ne pas isoler l'Homme d'Afrique de l'Homme tout court exigerait en tout cas le recours à l'universel.

La Ligue Arabe et la protection des droits de l'Homme. Les Etats arabes sont unis au sein d'une organisation particulière. Il leur serait possible de prévoir dans ce cadre une protection régionale des droits de l'Homme. Ici encore l'opposition des régimes politiques et sociaux en présence rend difficile — malgré l'identité originelle d'inspiration religieuse et culturelle — l'expression d'une doctrine commune et l'acceptation de mécanismes de contrôle. Même, entre Etats islamiques, l'organisation régionale ne suffit pas. A plus forte raison, le règlement de problèmes avec un Etat géographiquement voisin, dont l'existence est niée par tous, exige l'intervention de l'organisation universelle.

Les problèmes de l'Asie et du Pacifique. L'immense Asie du sud-est, avec l'Inde, les Philippines, et le Japon, n'a pas constitué d'organisation régionale générale susceptible de servir de support à un système de protection des droits de l'Homme. Ce vide régional est étroitement lié au niveau de vie d'une grande partie de la population du sud-est asiatique. Aux frontières de la famine, les droits de l'Homme perdent leur sens. Pourtant, le droit humanitaire maintient ses exigences. Les massacres de paysans, tels ceux qu'a connu l'Indonésie, en 1965, en l'absence de condamnation régionale, devaient être dénoncés devant l'opinion publique universelle. Le terrorisme et le contre-terrorisme, les moyens d'anéantissement de la population mis en œuvre au Vietnam, à défaut d'institutions régionales compétentes, ne peuvent échapper à la connaissance des organisations mondiales.

Comme en Europe, en Afrique et en Amérique, dans l'Asie du sud-est et le Pacifique la « région » est en réalité divisée en groupes d'Etats de structures économique et sociale opposées. La République Populaire de Chine et la République Démocratique du Vietnam forment une région politique particulière. La différence de régimes politiques existant entre les autres Etats ne facilite pas, en ce qui concerne la protection des droits de l'Homme, la création d'une organisation régionale commune.

L'action non gouvernementale en faveur d'une convention asiatique des droits de l'Homme. Deux congrès non gouvernementaux tenus à Bangkok (1965) et à Ceylan (1966) sous les auspices de la Commission Internationale de Juristes, ont souhaité l'adoption d'une convention des droits de l'Homme pour l'Asie et la zone du Pacifique, et la création d'un groupe d'étude auprès de la Commission des Droits de l'Homme de l'Organisation des Nations Unies, chargé de la conseiller pour ce qui concerne cette région. Le congrès de Bangkok s'est déclaré favorable à la constitution d'un Conseil de l'Asie et du Pacifique sur le modèle du Conseil de l'Europe (Bulletin précité, n° 26, juin 1966, pp. 11, 13, 17).

La protection régionale des droits de l'Homme dans l'Europe de l'Est socialiste. Nous retrouvons l'Europe avec l'Europe de l'Est — celle des pays à économie centralement planifiée et au parti politique unifié. Elle n'a pas suivi l'exemple occidental. La question commence à être discutée en doctrine et devant les instances politiques.

Il existe, avec des nuances, une conception régionale des droits de l'Homme (cf. sous la direction de I. Szabo, l'ouvrage collectif : « Socialist Concept of Human Rights »), dont la formulation dans une convention contribuerait non seulement au développement et à la protection des droits de l'Homme dans la région mais à une utile confrontation avec les autres régions politiques. L'essentiel d'une telle convention réside dans les conditions et garanties d'application. Une convention liant les pays socialistes devrait prévoir des voies de recours tenant compte du système politique. On pourrait concevoir une cour composée des présidents des Cours Suprêmes nationales dont l'intervention serait subordonnée à l'enquête par un parquet représentant chacune des procuratures. Les mécanismes adéquats — à défaut de modèle universel — doivent être élaborés par les hommes politiques et les juristes de la région[4].

Il serait utile de disposer d'une étude réaliste de l'état des droits de l'Homme dans l'Europe de l'Est, fondée sur les principes mêmes du système politique existant. (Sur les attitudes soviétiques à l'égard de la coopération régionale non militaire : consulter la thèse de K. Törnudd : « Soviet Attitudes towards Non-Military Regional Cooperation », Helsingfors 1961, spécialement sur l'opposition doctrinale entre Lénine et Trotski quant à la collaboration régionale, pp. 67–69.) Dans un article intitulé « On the Slogan of the United States of Europe » (août 1915), Lénine condamne l'organisation régionale de l'Europe par des Etats capitalistes comme réactionnaire, tandis que Trotski considère que l'unification européenne doit être poursuivie, pour assurer le triomphe de la révolution, même si cette union doit être réalisée d'abord entre Etats « bourgeois » (ibid. p. 263; cf. Trotski, « Le désarmement et les Etats-Unis d'Europe », Ecrits 1928–40, I. 289–90, Paris, 1955). A l'étape actuelle de l'évolution politique des pays socialistes, ceux qui souhaitent un développement nouveau de la protection des droits de l'homme estiment que l'action nationale est préférable. Plus précisement, ils craignent les dénonciations abusives, à travers les organes de contrôle établis dans le cadre des Nations Unies, à l'occasion de cas réels ou supposés de violation des droits de l'homme dans les Etats socialistes. De telles dénonciations vont à l'encontre du but recherché et sont de nature à freiner l'évolution constatée[5].

Conclusions

Absence de liaison avec la protection régionale dans les pactes des Nations-Unies. Malgré, ou doit-on dire, en raison de l'existence de la Convention européenne, malgré l'existence d'un projet intergouvernemental de convention américaine, malgré les vœux maintes fois répétés d'organisations non-gouvernementales des pays du tiers monde, les pactes internationaux de 1966 n'établissent aucune liaison entre la communauté œcuménique et les régionalismes.

Une discussion très confuse s'est déroulée devant la IIIᵉ Commission de l'Assemblée Générale (XXIᵉ session), sur un projet d'amendement demandant qu'il soit tenu compte dans la mise en œuvre du pacte sur les droits civils et politiques de l'existence d'autres instruments, notamment régionaux. Certains pays afro-asiatiques manifestèrent une opposition assez vive à la possibilité d'une subordination des pactes des Nations Unies aux conventions régionales, et en particulier à la Convention Européenne des Droits de l'Homme. (A/C 3/SR Nʳˢ 1432 à 1434.)

Le texte finalement adopté (Art. 44), s'il n'interdit pas aux Etats de recourir à d'autres « procédures instituées en matière de droits de l'Homme » ne se réfère expressément qu'aux procédures adoptées « aux termes ou en vertu des instruments constitutifs et des conventions de l'Organisation des Nations Unies et des institutions spécialisées ». Les conventions régionales des droits de l'Homme sont passées sous silence.

Apports du régionalisme à la protection des droits de l'Homme et ses limites. Le tableau qui précède permet de mesurer l'apport du régionalisme à la protection des droits de l'Homme et aussi ses limites.

La prise de conscience régionale permet de définir des droits et libertés adaptées au degré d'évolution matérielle (économique et technique), et à l'idéologie propre au groupement d'Etats en cause. Elle implique la coexistence de déclarations régionales des droits de l'Homme qui développent avec précision et certitude dans tous les domaines ou dans certains seulement, en fonction précisément de chaque niveau régional, les principes généraux et nécessairement vagues des pactes universels. Elle n'interdit pas d'aller au-delà de ces pactes et d'apporter une protection plus exigeante et plus étendue partout où les circonstances le permettent. On peut penser que les données particulières à certaines régions serviront de guide aux autres. La protection régionale des droits de l'Homme facilite le progrès en établissant un système susceptible d'être effectivement appliqué. Elle permet la création de mécanismes de contrôle plus facilement acceptés parce qu'ils opèrent « entre soi ». Elle favorise une émulation générale entre les régions.

Toutefois, elle ne saurait suffire. Elle risque en effet de cristalliser les règles existantes défavorables aux droits et libertés. Elle peut planter un simple décor dissimulant d'atroces réalités avec l'accord tacite des gouvernants régionaux. La solidarité politique, plus forte que le souci de respecter les droits de l'Homme, incitera les gouvernants à ne pas réagir malgré la violation de principes élémentaires.

L'existence de la Déclaration et des pactes universels ouvre un droit de regard sur la région. Elle fonde le droit de la communauté œcuménique d'être exactement informée, de s'informer directement et d'intervenir si nécessaire. Les principes universels, même méconnus par les Etats, sont généralement reconnus par eux. Ils ne les contestent pas mais prétendent les avoir observés. Les Etats et leurs gouvernants peuvent être dénoncés devant l'opinion publique internationale et ses institutions organisées.

Nous constatons ainsi une action et une interaction constantes entre le régional et l'universel. Il n'est pas possible de les dissocier. Sous cette réserve, nous voudrions souligner notre accord avec les conclusions générales du professeur Landheer. Au terme d'une récente enquête sociologique (On the Sociology of International Law and International Society, La Haye, 1966), Landheer conclut :

« The theory of social evolution points to an intermediary level of regional organization rather than to the emergence of a world society in the foreseeable future » (p. 73).

La structure réelle du monde actuel le conduit à suggérer le développement d'organisations régionales et inter-régionales d'un nouveau type et la simplification des organisations globales purement formelles. Il affirme ainsi la primauté contingente du régional :

« We should accept the regional and emerging large states as the focal point of world power... The regional state or group of states should basically limit itself to its own region » (ibid. p. 72).

Cette analyse vaut pour l'organisation de la protection internationale des droits de l'Homme.

Simultanéité et interaction nécessaires de l'action universelle et régionale.
La grande misère de la protection des droits de l'Homme doit inciter à faire feu de tout bois. Le rôle des mouvements privés nationaux, régionaux et universels, est essentiel. Qu'ils agissent comme forces permanentes religieuses ou philosophiques, politiques ou syndicales, ou comme « commandos » de la liberté et des droits de l'Homme pour faire échec à tels abus concrets. Il importe aussi d'utiliser toutes les institutions publiques existantes. Le Comité International de la Croix Rouge se doit d'être discret. La Fédération

Internationale des sociétés nationales de la Croix Rouge a vocation pour dénoncer toutes les atteintes au droit humanitaire. Mais les sociétés nationales, fidèles à leur mission, ne devraient pas hésiter à faire front contre leur propre gouvernement s'il oublie des engagements solennels. Dans le cadre des Nation Unies, la Commission des Droits de l'Homme a déjà établi une procédure de rapports des Etats, susceptibles d'être mis en cause devant l'Assemblée Générale. La ratification des pactes universels consacrera cette procédure en la développant. On peut craindre que la ratification ne soit lente et loin d'être universelle. L'institution par l'Assemblée Générale d'un Haut Commissaire des Nations Unies, proposée par la Commission des Droits de l'Homme des Nations Unies, ne sera pas inutile. On souhaiterait cependant que son mandat soit élargi de façon à lui permettre d'entrer en relation avec, et éventuellement d'assister les organisations régionales.

Il conviendrait au surplus d'inciter l'Assemblée Générale à créer des commissions régionales des droits de l'Homme à l'image des commissions économiques et sociales. Ces commissions joueraient un double rôle. Elles inséreraient l'universel dans la région. Elles permettraient le cas échéant un dialogue entre les groupements d'Etats de régimes politique, économique et social, différents, au sein de la région, ainsi en Europe et en Amérique. Elles favoriseraient la préparation de conventions régionales (Afrique, Asie du sud-est et Pacifique). Elles constitueraient des centres d'information et de publicité pour la protection des droits de l'Homme — nécessaires dans la double perspective régionaliste et universelle.

Ces commissions des Nations Unies n'exclueraient ni ne remplaceraient, loin de là, les conventions régionales de sauvegarde des droits de l'Homme et des libertés fondamentales. Ces conventions régionales sont aussi indispensables que les pactes universels.

NOTES

[1] Art. 30 de la Déclaration Universelle et 5 (1) du Pacte international relatif aux droits civils et politiques (1966).
[2] Toutefois, plusieurs pays scandinaves viennent de déposer une plainte contre la Grèce devant la Commission Européenne des Droits de l'Homme.
[3] Les développements qui précèdent ont été informés par M. K. Vazak qui prépare un ouvrage sur la commission inter-américaine des droits de l'Homme qui sera publié en français et en anglais.
[4] La Pologne a accueilli en 1967 un séminaire des Nations Unies relatif à la protection des droits économiques et sociaux.
[5] Voir infra les interventions des professeurs Szabó et Bystrický.

An investigation of the influence of the European Convention on Human Rights and Fundamental Freedoms on national legislation and practice

By Ulrich Scheuner

Universität, Bonn, West Germany

I. *Aims and characteristics of the European Convention*

A. Different systems of implementation for the protection of human rights

1. International instruments for the promotion of fundamental liberties have different aims and vary in the extent of control to which they submit their signatories. We may distinguish three types of declarations or conventions:

(*a*) The *first* kind of proclamation or treaty is mainly destined to set up an international standard for international and national practice without being concerned with the implementation of its rules. It does not put upon the signatory states definite obligations or a system of control. But it can serve as an example for the development of protective measures in the constitution of states, and it provides an orientation and to some extent a legal basis for international political or legal action in the defence of human liberties. This is the role played by the Universal Declaration of Human Rights, which has exercised a considerable influence on recent constitutions in Africa and elsewhere.[1]

(*b*) A *second* type of international instrument creates legal obligations for the signatory states to observe and to adjust their own national legal order to the rules of the international convention. Such instruments also institute a system of control either by demanding periodical reports from member states or by admitting complaints from other member states against a government failing to do its duties. Their measures of implementation do not, however, include judicial control or applications from individuals. Even if the ultimate purpose of such a convention is the promotion of the civil, social, or cultural position of the individual within the member states, there are only created legal obligations for the states. These conventions entrust to governments the task of passing on the benefits of the convention to individuals.

(*c*) For the *third* kind of convention, the position of the individual is the essential element. The international document is so constructed as to grant immediate legal protection to the individuals within the member states and to procure effective guarantees that governments will observe its rules. A supervisory mechanism is introduced which gives the individual direct access to an international organ and submits the states to judicial control by an international court or a quasi-judicial body. For that purpose the convention not only engages the states to the observance of its general principles for the promotion of human freedoms; it also equips the individuals with material rights and with procedural status before international organs. These rights belong to the international legal order, but they can be transferred to the interior order by action of the member states. At this stage, the international conventional order permeates the national sovereignty and opens a direct communication between the individual and international instances.

2. Mr. Golsong has shown that a system of periodical reports by the single states to international institutions can assure effective control of obligations undertaken by governments. However, this holds only if the reports are followed up by careful examination through an international agency or body of experts which might take up further questions with the member state.[2] The public sanction inherent in such a scheme will in most cases prove sufficient to induce the states to accept the international agency's suggestions and observations. This method of international institutional control can be completed by the right of member states to bring cases of alleged violation of the conventional obligations to the attention of a Committee of Experts, which may then carry out further investigations and finally report on the matter. This is the method chosen by the recent Covenant on Civil and Political Rights of the U.N. (Art. 41.)

The European Convention on Human Rights and Fundamental Freedoms has even gone further in its measures for protecting human liberties. It has created a system of quasi-judicial supervision by an international organ directly accessible for individuals, and has given the member states and the European Commission of Human Rights the right of appealing to an international court.

The reasons which led to the acception of a system of quasi-judicial and judicial control are twofold. *First,* it was felt that within the region of the European nations strongly connected by a common heritage of legal traditions the purpose of a convention should not be limited to a supervision of the governments by an international organ; rather, it should be extended to an examination of individual complaints laid before the international instances by individual petitioners themselves. Declarations of human liberties in national constitutions confer rights to individuals which they can invoke before courts and administrative authorities. The European Convention intends to provide a similar measure of protection on an international basis.[3] The *second* idea which led to the elaboration of the European Convention was a wider political conception within the context of the movement for European Unity after the Second World War. The Council of Europe started its work with the hope for a closer union of the European states. It was in this connection that the creation of effective guarantees for human rights as a foundation of a democratic order within Europe received its particular political importance.[4] Although the idea of a united Europe has now lost some of its former impetus, it is still an essential factor for the appreciation of the European Convention on Human Rights. This agreement rests upon the recognition of a democratic interior order by all its members. The Permanent Commission of the Assembly of the Council of Europe had in mind this fundamental feature of the Convention when it carried on June 23, 1967 a resolution on the situation in Greece, expressing its concern about the deviation of the Greek government from the obligations accepted in the European Convention and citing Art. 24 of the Convention, which empowers any signatory state to bring to the attention of the European Commission of Human Rights violation of the Convention perpetrated by another member.[5]

B. Importance of individual access to international organs in the system of the European Convention

3. The admission, in the framework of the European Convention on Human Rights, of individual applications to the European Commission of Human Rights opens a new dimension in the defence of human liberties. The individual complaints bring to the attention of the international organs charged with the supervision of the Convention the whole spectrum of problems concerning the execution of the rules of the Convention within the states. The European Commission of Human Rights has now decided over 3000 cases; and even if the number of really important affairs is much smaller, the broad access to the basic material alone gives a comprehensive impression of how the rules of the Convention are observed in the practice of the member states of the human rights community.

4. The control exercised by the examination of reports from governments can in some instances lead to the discussion of individual grievances. But it will in the main rest centered on general questions. The right of signatory states to apply to international organs against the violation of contractual obligations by another state (as foreseen in Art. 41 of the Convention on Civil and Political Rights of the U.N.) is a means of control quite different from the individual petition. Most states will resent being brought to the

attention of international instances for non-fulfilment of treaty obligations by other governments. It follows that a government will hesitate to employ its right to focus the attention of an international organisation upon failures of other nations to comply with their obligations from a treaty and indeed will do so only if its own interests are at stake. The European Convention, in Art. 24, gives member states the faculty to refer to the Commission of Human Rights another state's alleged breach of the provisions of the Convention. Only rarely has such a step been taken. On two occasions action was taken by a state directly involved because of interests of its nationals or of a group of persons to which it had a special affiliation. In 1956 and 1957, Greece introduced two complaints against Great Britain about some legislative and administrative measures taken by the British authorities in Cyprus. The applications were not further pursued after the conclusion of the Zürich and London agreements of 1959.[6] In 1960 Austria lodged a complaint against the Italian government, claiming a violation of Art. 6, § 1, 2, and 3 (d) and 14 of the Convention. Austria's reason for taking up this case was its interest in the individuals concerned, fourteen persons belonging to the German-speaking minority in South Tirol (Alto Adige), who had been tried before Italian courts on a murder charge arising out of a local brawl.[7] The case ultimately failed; the Commission and the Committee of Ministers rejected the complaints directed against the procedure of the Italian courts.[8] The control exercised over the observance of the European Convention by the means of a state application according to Art. 24 will in most cases bear a decidedly political character. Most states, reluctant to cite another government before an international instance for a breach of the Convention, will take up a cause only if their own political or legal interest is involved —as will be the case in a matter of ill-treatment of one of their own nationals.

Recently, the complaints of several Governments[9] against the Greek Government, directed against the stern restrictions imposed upon civil and political liberties after the establishment of the military regime in April 1967, represent an example of an action under Art. 24 of the European Convention undertaken not in the own national interest but for the preservation of the foundations of the European Convention itself. This collective application proves that the rules of a convention can be effectively defended by the action of member states; but we must not forget that in this case fundamental issues regarding the whole purpose of the convention are at stake.

The individual petition offers the most efficient means for the protection of human liberties. Under normal conditions, individuals can be expected to make use of this faculty to refer complaints against their own government to an international organ. The situation will be different under the rule of an authoritarian government. If a national government resents being drawn before an international authority and is resolved to bring pressure upon individuals or even to punish them, no complaints will be forthcoming from that country. It can therefore be misleading to conclude from the number of individual petitions issuing from a particular country that conditions must be at fault there.[10] As numerically the greatest number of applications under the European Convention come from persons who are serving prison sentences, quite the contrary may be true.[11]

The European Convention does not make obligatory the admission of individual applications against the own government for its members. A signatory state has to declare expressly that it recognises the competence of the Commission to receive individual petitions in order to become the object of such applications by individuals or groups (Art. 25). Of the present 17 members of the European Convention only 10 have accepted the competence of the Commission to receive individual applications.[12]

5. The introduction of individual petitions into the system of implementation of a convention must have important repercussions upon the substance of its substantial provisions.

(*a*) A convention creating individual rights and opening the way for individual complaints to international agencies has to be drafted precisely, distinguish clearly between those of its provisions which proclaim general principles only laying obligations upon the states but not constituting a foundation for individual claims, and those norms which directly confer rights to individuals. The difficulties which may arise here can be observed in the application of the Treaty of the European Economic Community. This agreement contains a number of provisions of general character which were often held to bind only the member states and not the individual citizen. The European Court at Luxembourg, however, has shown a tendency to regard some of these dispositions as immediately applicable in the interior order of the states.[13] The problem is still under discussion for several provisions.[14]

(*b*) The European Convention is written with the intention that its provisions can be incorporated into the national legal order of member states.[15] Also this circumstance demands a clear and precise wording of its articles.

In those countries where this transfer of the Convention into domestic law is determined by the constitution or other legal dispositions, the question arises whether the single articles of the Convention are intended to create rights and duties directly enforceable by individuals in the courts of this state. It has to be decided for each particular provision whether its text is capable of immediate application by the courts or whether it only confers obligations to the member states, in other words, whether it is self-executing.[16] Among the dispositions of the European Convention, Art. 13 is now generally recognised as a norm binding only the member states.[17] Other dispositions were initially regarded as non-self-executing (Art. 5), but the practice of the Commission has rightly taken another view.[18]

(*c*) The intention to create individual rights defended by individual petitions has—besides other reasons—induced the authors of the European Convention to limit the rules of the Convention—as in the Conventions drafted under the auspices of the U.N.—to general guarantees of a social and cultural standard, The authors of the European Convention have deliberately elaborated a convention containing rather a minimum standard of essential individual freedoms.[19] They have refrained from including into the Convention economic and social rights, because these seemed too controversial and too difficult to enforce.[20]

6. Nations sometimes remain sensible to such intercession by international authorities. If the organs of the European Convention have acted, especially in the first years, with great circumspection,[21] their attitude has showed regard of this difficulty. While some authors are inclined to exhort the Commission to a broader interpretation of the scope of conventional rules, I still hold that a cautious attitude would be wiser. The Commission recognises this point by leaving the states a considerable "marge d'appréciation" for their legislation as well as for the application of the Convention in their administration and judicial order.[22]

There is another point where this regard to the sensibility of nations is still visible in the practice of the Commission and the Court. If amiable settlement in a case is reached (Art. 28) or the dispute under examination is solved in some other way, a decision on the merits of the case is avoided, The same method is applied if a case is settled through an alteration of the law in the defending state or an agreement out of court. I have formerly— as did Judge Ross—expressed some doubts whether the European Court on Human Rights was right in the de Becker case to strike the affair off its list when new legislation had supported the most substantial demands of the petitioner.[23] I am now inclined to approve this procedure, which has been followed since in a number of other cases.[24] In the Niekisch case, the applicant complained about several procedural and material violations of the Convention during the examination of his demand for compensation for persecution suffered under the Nazi regime in Germany. Pending the request the applicant concluded an agreement with the authorities of the Federal Republic of Germany and informed the Commission of his wish to withdraw his petition. The Commission therefore struck the affair off its list. But it made the following observation, which seems to me a just and necessary statement:

> Que la Commission state que nulle considération d'ordre général touchant au respect de la Convention de Sauvegarde des Droits de l'Homme et des Libertés Fondamentales ne s'oppose en l'espèce à la demande de radiation formulée par le requérant.[25]

It seems adequate that the Commission retains ultimate control of the affair, and not leaves it entirely to the individual and the state concerned to terminate a procedure which could give occasion to general observations.

II. *Domestic law under the influence of the European Convention on Human Rights*

A. Implementation of the European Convention in the legal order of member states

7. In a deeper sense, the close relationship between the rules of the European Convention and national guarantees for human liberties is quite natural. The idea of protection of individual rights and freedoms has not originated in the international order. The concept dates back to the constitutional development in some Western countries—England and France as well as the United States—where from the 17th century onwards the idea of individual liberties first found expression in literary writings and later, in the 18th century, was introduced into the text of constitutions and legal declarations.[26] I cannot here deal with the history of human rights and the problems connected with it. But it can be said with confidence that all the general principles and values recognised in this field by international law are always the reflection of the development of conceptions of law and justice within the nations that form the international community. At all times the legal conceptions of international law are founded upon a common basis of legal principles acknowledged by all nations. As W. Jenks has pointed out,[27] international law and its general principles have to be deduced from a common legal conscience of the international community uniting the nations despite differences in existing legal systems and traditions. Human rights, even in a regional context, are a most illustrative example of this deeper connection of the legal foundations of the international order with a common legal conscience of the international community. The influence of the European Convention on Human Rights upon the national legal systems can never be one-sided. The international rules reflect the prior formation of common legal principles within the legal systems of the European nations. Progress in national law for the protection of human liberties is also of importance

for the application of the international convention. Members of the Commission and of the Court of Human Rights rely naturally on the experience of their own national law for the interpretation of particular freedoms and of the restrictions added to them. International and national order are thus mutually dependent.

8. The extent to which the European Convention directly influences the domestic order of member states depends on the general conceptions prevailing in each national order about the relation of international law to municipal law. There are two fundamental issues on which the states themselves have to make a decision, and by their decision they determine to what extent the rules of the Convention have a direct impact upon the national legal order. *First* each member state must decide whether it will accept the competence of the European Commission of Human Rights to receive individual applications directed against its own non-execution of the Convention (Art. 25). This point is of the greatest importance. Without being exposed to individual complaints, a state will not come into close relation with the Convention in a day-to-day practice. The government will acknowledge its obligation to take care that the interior law does not violate the provisions of the convention. But cases in which the harmony of the national order with the demands of the European Convention is questionable will not so easily be brought to attention if it is not possible to follow the procedure opened in Art. 25.

A *second* issue is of equal importance. We may say that the European Convention intended to have its rules transferred to direct application by national courts and authorities.[29] However, the attitude of member states towards an incorporation of conventional law into their domestic legal order shows two possible solutions.

(*a*) In seven countries which have acceded to the Convention (Austria, Belgium, Greece, Italy, Luxembourg, the Netherlands and the Federal Republic of Germany) the rules of the Convention receive the character of binding elements of the internal legal order as soon as the consent of Parliament is given and ratification has taken place.[29] They are applied by courts and other official agencies, and they immediately create rights and duties for individuals.[30] In one country, Austria, the rules of the Convention have now (since 1964)[31] the quality of constitutional law (as from the beginning of their transfer into the national order).[32] It seems that the same precedence is recognized for the rules of the Convention in Luxembourg and Cyprus.[33] In the Netherlands, the directly applicable rules of a convention have priority over municipal law, if they are "binding to any person" (Constitution Art. 66).[34] In all other countries the norms of the Convention are incorporated into the internal order with the rank of normal statutory law only. The consequence is that a later statute which does not comply with the Convention is binding for the courts, which have to give it priority over the rules of the Convention (even in their quality as incorporated internal law) and have to leave it to the government to find a way out of the resulting impasse.

(*b*) In six countries (Denmark, Great Britain, Iceland, Ireland, Norway, Sweden) the rules of the Convention are binding for the state as every international convention, but are not immediately applicable within the domestic order by courts or administrative authorities. They find no direct execution within the state and do not form an element of the internal legal system.[35]

The question whether the rules of the Convention are incorporated into the internal law is decided by the constitutional law of each state. The Convention itself favors the acceptance of its rules into the domestic order, but it does not oblige member states to introduce its rules into their municipal legal system.[36] It only demands from each signatory government to bring its internal order into compliance with the rules of the Convention. By which method this result is secured, the Convention leaves to the discretion of member states.[37]

In the Federal Republic, a discussion has been going on in recent years whether the rules of the Convention incorporated into the national legal order have not obtained priority over the statutory law. We can dismiss those authors who claim a priority for the Convention because they regard it as higher natural law. But other scholars defend the opinion that the European Convention belongs to the general rules of international law accepted by the civilised nations which, in Art. 25 of the Federal Constitution of 1949, are given priority over normal statutory law.[38] These views, however, have not prevailed in the German discussion and, so far as I can see, they have no counterpart in the literary findings in other countries. They can therefore also be dismissed as individual opinions which have not been confirmed by judicial decisions.

9. In following the impact of the European Convention upon national law we meet also some problems of interpretation. Art. 6 of the Convention, a norm often invoked, assures to the individual "a fair and public hearing within a reasonable time by an impartial and independent tribunal". But this applies only to cases regarding "the determination of civil rights and obligations or of any criminal charge". What, then, is the meaning of "civil rights"? The Commission has justly refused to leave the definition of this term to each national system, as the result of such a reference to national law could be arbitrary. The conception of "civil rights" must be taken to

be autonomous in the context of the Convention "even though the general principles of the domestic law of the High Contracting Parties must necessarily be taken into consideration in any such interpretation".[39] The term "civil rights" can include also administrative procedures which tend to protect rights of the individual.[40]

The Commission is not inclined to accept the procedural dispositions of a national system as decisive. Even if a certain complaint has to be lodged with an administrative organ or court it may nevertheless be regarded as belonging to the area of "civil rights"; therefore, the administrative board which has to decide on the case will be bound to observe the rules of Art. 6, § 1 of the Convention.[41] On the other hand, the Commission has consistently excluded from the field of application of Art. 6 all complaints concerning taxation.[42] It is possible that the procedure chosen by the national law for the settlement of a dispute can be of importance for the applicability of Art. 6: German courts have decided that Art. 6, § 1 does not apply to administrative courts,[43] an opinion which cannot escape some criticism. The interpretation of Art. 6, § 1 is still to some extent under discussion. If a "civil right" in the sense of an individual position is involved, the qualification of the alleged right, not the procedure prescribed in the national legislation, decides the issue.[44] The suggestion of Doehring to include under Art. 6, § 1 all complaints before administrative tribunals is attractive, but it would transgress the limits of even a liberal and functional interpretation.[45]

10. To a certain extent, national courts may be inclined to a wider interpretation of the European Convention than the organs of the Convention themselves. In a number of cases, national decisions have rather extended the sense of the rules of the Convention, as shown by the following two examples.

A German District Court found that a provision of the Penal Code (§ 161) depriving a person found guilty of perjury of civil rights for a certain amount of time could not be deemed compatible with the European Convention. It regarded this preventive measure inflicted upon the convicted individual an "inhuman and degrading" treatment (Art. 3 of the Convention).[46] However, another Court did not share this opinion. It found that temporary deprivation of civil rights did not violate the Convention, and that only the permanent loss of the capacity to take an oath could be, if applied to cases of minor misdemeanours, an infringement upon the Convention.[47] I am not sure whether the European Commission would have found any exception with this provision of the Penal Code.

In the Netherlands, the courts have tended to show a remarkable respect for extreme interpretations of religious freedom. They have discussed but finally declined the objections of a pastor of the Reformed Church against a contribution imposed upon him under the Old Age Pension Act. He complained that this assessment interfered with his religious freedom, because imperative prescriptions given by a divine law to provide for old people, especially ministers of religion, made such provision an element of free Christian activity, whereas, the state imposed an obligatory measure of welfare.[48] The Commission shared the view of the Dutch courts.[49]

B. Influence of the European Convention upon the application and interpretation of national law

11. The European Convention determines a certain standard for the protection of human rights, to which the internal order of the member states must comply. Control that this standard is in fact complied to is the task of the organs of the Convention and, if the rules of the Convention are incorporated into the domestic order, also that of the national courts. To perform this task the international agencies or the national courts have to make comparisons between the rules of the Convention and the municipal law which regulates the same individual liberties. As the municipal norms on human freedoms are independent of the European Convention in origin and content, this examination must regard not so much the wording of the provisions as their substance. The decisive question is whether the provisions of the internal order assure at least the same amount of protection for human rights as the rules of the Convention. The task of international and national instances is slightly different.

In most cases, the Commission of Human Rights (and also the Committee of Ministers or the Court) will have to compare a part of national statutory law or the decision of a court with the corresponding rule of the Convention. They have therefore to interpret not only the provisions of the European Convention but to a certain extent also the internal law. They have, in other words, to examine the norms of the national legislation as legal rules. The well-known dictum of the International Court of Justice that national laws are but facts for an international court[50] does not apply to the European Commission or the European Court of Human Rights.[51] To ascertain whether, for instance, an article of a national constitution guaranteeing a certain individual freedom corresponds to the European Convention's provisions for the same right, the international organ has to apply and interpret the municipal law. This is especially so in examining whether the requirement of the exhaustion of local remedies is fulfilled. Before the national court, the applicant has naturally founded his complaint upon the provisions of the municipal order, and it may well be that he has not even cited the corresponding provision of the European Convention.[52] It falls upon the international organs to decide whether national procedure regards the same liberties as are involved in the case before them.[53] If it comes to the interpretation of municipal law, the European Commission, however, follows an established rule: So far as possible it avoids preparing its interpretation of national law of its own but tends to follow closely the leading opinion on the question which has been formed in the country concerned.[54]

In every case, this interrelation between international and national law in the application of the Convention leads to an influence of the former upon the latter. The natural tendency of international organs as well as of the national courts will be to adapt interpretation of the national statute to the demands of the international engagement under which it comes to be examined.

12. There is one point in which national legal systems may even exercise a certain influence upon the interpretation of the international rules. Sometimes the European Convention employs legal terms which may be elucidated in the light of the meaning of the same term in municipal law. One could perhaps refer to the term "normal civic obligations" in Art. 4, § 3 (d), "legal assistance" in Art. 6, § 3 (c) or the term used in Art. 9, § 2 "public order, health and morals". It is a common practice of the Court of the European Communities to interpret such terms in the light of common solutions found in the various national legal systems.[55] If national statutes or jurisprudence reveal a concurring opinion, this may be a strong incitement for the international organ to follow this interpretation of a legal term.[56]

C. Uniformity of interpretation

13. For every international engagement which receives application by various international and national instances, there arises the problem of safeguards for a cohesive and so far as possible uniform interpretation. The European Convention provides no express solution for this problem, nor does it even solve the question of whether the Commission is bound to follow the decisions of the European Court of Human Rights. I am inclined to assume that the Commission is bound by the sayings of the Court, because in the legal order of the European Convention it is the Court which has the ultimate decision.[57] In practice, of course, the Commission will generally accept the directive which a decision of the Court indicates.

On the other hand, national courts are certainly not bound by the decisions of the European Court of Human Rights. For practical reasons they will respect the opinions of the Court and the Commission. But is the legal practice within the member states really well aquainted with the decisions of the European Court and the Commission? Until now, references to the opinions of the international organs of the Convention are rather an exception in decisions of national courts, even if they deal with matters decided by Court or Commission. One reason for this situation is obvious. In those countries which do not speak either of the two official languages of the institutions of the Convention, translations are necessary to give the decisions of the European organs a wider effect. Here there certainly exists a gap which should be filled in some way.

When the European Commission applies national law, it tends, as we have seen, to follow the usual national interpretation. But how can the rules of the Convention receive the same interpretation in various countries where they are applied by national courts? Will there not be considerable differences in interpretation according to the various legal schools of thought existing within the conventional community? The Treaty of the European Economic Community provides—as did already the Treaty on the Coal and Steel Community (Art. 41)—that national courts, if their decision is final, have to bring all questions concerning the interpretation of the Treaty before the Court of the European Communities (Art. 177).[58] In this way the European Communities tend to assure a uniform interpretation of the Treaty to which national courts are bound. Should this solution be applied also to the system of the Convention on Human rights?

I am not inclined to recommend a new disposition in the framework of the European Convention which would compel the national courts to submit questions regarding the interpretation of the Convention to an international authority.

If a state has submitted to the competence of the Commission according to Art. 25 of the Convention, an individual complaint can always refer the case to the cognicance of the Commission, and an erroneous interpretation of a national court can be corrected. Only when a member state has incorporated the rules of the Convention into its internal law, but has not submitted to Art. 25, does the decision of a national court, interpreting the Convention obtain a final character. Only in this case can the national interpretation of the European Convention not be corrected by the Commission of the Court of Human Rights. For these cases it would be important if national courts were under obligation to refer questions of interpretation of the European Convention to the international organs of the Convention. But even under these circumstances the idea meets objections. It would be akward if the considerable number of cases in which national courts refer to the articles of the Convention, should in many instances be suspended during an appeal to the Commission or the Court for interpretation of rules of the Convention. National courts might become cautious in the citation of the Convention. The international organs, on the other hand, would be overwhelmed with questions of interpretation. Introducing an appeal for interpretation would rather obstruct the free and fast growth of a body of national jurisprudence. The present situation produces some differences in the interpretation of the Convention by national courts, but this is, it seems to me, at the present time tolerable. During the Vienne Colloquium, Mr. Golsong was of the opinion that a national judge should interpret the Convention in the light of his national legal tradition.[59] I would not share his view, but at the present stage it is more important to make the Convention directly applicable in the internal legal order than to secure an uniform interpretation.

Finally, another point may be mentioned briefly. It is a duty of the national judge when applying national law in view of the rules of the Convention, to interpret it in a sense favorable to the Convention. Such practice corresponds to a well-known rule of international law that national legislation should be constructed so as to avoid a conflict with international engagements.[60]

III. *The impact of the European Convention on National legislation*

14. In the preceding section we have regarded the influence exercised by the rules of the European Convention and by their application by international organs upon the formation of a national body of interpretation of the same rules. In this final section we shall examine the impact of the European Convention on the national legislation and its further development, and the elaboration of a common legal tradition in all member states based upon a comparative study of the legal systems within the community of the Convention. In building up common principles for the protection of human rights among the members of the Convention, a certain process of harmonization is begun which corresponds entirely with the purpose of the Convention.

The impact of the Convention on national legislation comes to be felt in three different ways:

First, the Convention plays a preventive role. Before signing the Convention, governments will muster their national code and eliminate any elements evidently in conflict with the obligations to which they intend to subscribe. If they do not choose the method of a reservation[61] they will have to make alterations in their law. For this attitude examples can easily be cited.

The Norwegian Constitution (Art. 2) prohibited the activity of Jesuits on

Norwegian soil. The Norwegian Government, when signing the Convention, added therefore a reservation in this respect,[62] because this prohibition clearly derogated from Art. 9 of the Convention. In 1956, Norway amended its Constitution, suppressing Art. 2, and thereby renounced to this reservation.[63] The Swedish Government introduced into Parliament a bill to alter an ordinance of 1873 providing for the withdrawal from the Swedish Church (an established Church), but only by accession to another Christian community.[64] At the present time this preventive impact of the Convention is an obstruction to the accession of Switzerland. The Federal Constitution retains from the 19th century some articles which derogate from religious freedom (Art. 50, § 4; 51; 52). They prohibit the activity of the order of Jesuits, in Church and school, the foundation of new religious orders or of new convents, and submit the institution of new dioceses to the admission of the Federation. For a long time these articles have been practiced with great discretion but as their abrogation would necessitate a plebiscite, they are still on the statute book.[65] There is a second point. The movement to give women the right to vote in the federal, cantonal and communal elections is now well under way. But it has not reached its goal, and so Art. 14 of the Convention is not fully observed.[66]

15. The member states are committed to alter their legislation if Court or Commission find that any norm is not consistent with the Convention. In most cases, governments have preferred to forestall an unfavourable decision by proceeding to alter their statutes as soon as an individual application has been accepted by the Commission, and before the Commission has even given its decision. Several examples can be given.

On June 9, 1958 the Commission accepted the application of Mr. de Becker, a Belgian journalist, against Art. 123 sexies of the Belgian Penal Code, which deprived him for life from any participation in the administration, editing or printing of a newspaper or any other publication. The Belgian Government found it difficult to proceed with a legislative measure because of the highly political character of the provisions involved (condemnation for collaboration during World War II), so that the case passed the Commission and was brought by the Commission before the Court. At this stage finally the Belgian Parliament voted on June 30, 1961 an alteration of Art. 123 sexies limiting the restrictions. The applicant declared himself satisfied and withdrew his application.[67] The Court then struck the case off its list.

Four applications from Austria, the cases Ofner, Hopfinger, Pataki and Dunshirn,[68] criticized Art. 294 and 296 of the Austrian Code of Criminal procedure. These provided for an appeal in criminal cases to the Supreme Court over which the Court decided in a closed hearing in the presence of the Attorney-General but not of the parties. The Commission did not regard this procedure as fulfilment of the demands of Art. 6, § 3 of the Convention for "equality in arms", because no contradictory hearing was held. In the two cases of Ofner and Hopfner, the Commission found no violation of the Convention, because the individuals concerned were not actually prejudiced by this procedure. In the two other cases, the violation was recognized by the report of the Commission and by the Committee of Ministers.[69] The Austrian Government moved immediately an iniatated an amendment to the Code which replaced the former procedure by a new settlement of strict equality for both sides.[70] Moreover, further law was enacted on April 5, 1963[71] which reopened appeal proceedings for those persons whose applications against the former law had been declared admissible by the Commission. This new legislation enabled the Commission to conclude all pending applications in so far as these concerned the same grievance.[72]

A last series of applications which has resulted in some legislative measures and will perhaps necessitate further action is now pending before the Court of Human Rights. In these cases the applicants complain of the length of preventive detention pending trial and of that of the trial itself (Art. 5, § 3 and 6, § 1 of the Convention).[73] The Commission has dealt with these problems in many former decisions.[74] It meets here a particular difficulty stemming from the different attitude of different legal systems. In continental countries, especially Austria and Germany, a criminal procedure takes a long time because a long stage of examination precedes the hearing before the court. If the accused is arrested, a considerable period of detention before trial can ensue (in one case of five cited, more than 3 years). This seems inadmissible to the English tradition, which regards such delays as unreasonable and excessive.

On December 19, 1964, the German Code of Criminal procedure was amended by a law altering a great number of its provisions.[75] The German Government had used also the opportunity to insert into the new law revised provisions on preventive detention (§ 112–126 a). Continuation of the preventive detention over six months requires now a special decision of a higher court and must be justified by strong reasons. At any time, the individual can demand that the reasons for the detention pending trial be examined by a court. No provisions of the new law are concerned with the length of the trial itself. The decisions of the Court on the four cases still pending before it—they can be expected for 1968—will perhaps induce further legislative changes.

The amendment to the German Code of Criminal Procedure took also into consideration another point in the practice of the Commission. The Commission has stressed the right of an accused individual to receive free legal assistance during his trial.[76] The German law of 1964 extends therefore in its provisions (§ 140–142) the right of the accused to receive the help of counsel by way of legal assistance.

The Government of the Netherlands has also taken into account the rules and practice of the European Convention for its future legislation. On many occasions Ministers have mentioned the Convention in the debates of the Chamber when introducing new legislation.[77]

16. The application of the European Convention by international organs can influence the internal order in a third way. The first ten years have shown the states that the possible area of conflict between the domestic law and the requirements of the Convention is more extended than governments previously presumed. Therefore, authorities responsible for legislative development in member states tend now to take notice of the rules of the Convention when preparing reforms in the existing law. The German Government, when introducing the reform of the Code of Criminal procedure in 1962, expressly referred to the demands of the European Convention.[78] The bill asking the approval of Parliament for the ratification of the Protocol No. 4 to the Convention on Human Rights, which was laid before the Bundestag on April 21, 1967, was accompanied by a report of the German Government, examining in detail whether any provisions of the German law needed to be altered.[79] A reason to amend national legislation can also be provided by decisions of national courts which declare a norm of the internal order to be in violation of the European Convention. It seems that no examples can be cited for this effect of the practice of national courts, but such cases might be expected in the future.

17. Returning to a point already mentioned briefly, we may add to the comparative method some observations which can be of use for the interpretation of a regional engagement as the European Convention on Human Rights. The Court of the European Communities is familiar with this method. When referring to general principles in the interpretation of the Treaty, the Luxembourg Court quite often evolves them from a common legislation or legal practice in all the member states. If the Court finds in each national order the same conceptions and the same solutions for a certain problem it feels itself strengthened to apply these rules also within the law of European Communities.[80] Clearly, the economic cooperation of the Six creates a closer community between its members than the European Convention on Human Rights. But I see no reason why the comparative method, elaborating legal principles from the common legal conscience and practice of the European states, should not be valuable also in the framework of the European Convention on Human Rights.

The Commission took recourse to a comparative method in the Iversen case when determining the sense of the term "forced or compulsory labour" by reference to the practice of the ILO.[81] Examining the length of the period of detention preceding the first access of the accused to a judge in the Dutch Code of Criminal Procedure, the Commission approved the Dutch system after comparison with the law in other European states.[82] The Commission said in this decision:

"Whereas the Commission finds that the Dutch provisions as applied in the present case do not exceed this margin of appreciation and are otherwise consistent with the general tendency of other members of the Council of Europe ..."

A broad application of a comparative method can be observed in the recent pleading before the Commission in the *Televizier* case. The *Televizier* argued that by withholding the compilations of broadcasting programmes from newspapers, the broadcasting corporations tended to acquire a monopoly in the news services on radio and television, thereby violating the freedom of information guaranteed in Art. 10 of the European Convention. The Commission declared the application of the publishers of Televizier admissible and accepted it. One of the arguments of the application was that a copyright protection of pieces of writing without distinctive or personal nature (as these broadcasting programmes are) cannot be found in other democratic countries or in the Berne Convention. The Commission took no sides but mentioned that a number of important issues concerning the interpretation of the Convention was raised in the case.[83] Finally I may mention the application of a minister of Jehovah's Witnesses against conviction for not fulfilling the service required of him as an alternative to compulsory military service, because he had been accepted as a conscientious objector. In this case, the applicant cited decisions of the American courts and in a dissenting vote a member of the Commission made express reference to a comparative method for determining the conception of a "democratic society" in the meaning of Art. 10, § 2 of the Convention.[84]

18. From the application of the European Convention by international instances and national courts there slowly emerges a series of general principles which will be accepted also in the internal legal order of the signatory states. The common heritage to which the preamble of the European Convention alludes will not only be preserved: it will be enlarged and strengthened through a continuous practice in the field of human freedoms. Already a concept like "fair trial" has become widely understood and accepted within the conventional community. The purpose of the European Convention on Human Rights is not, as it is in the European Economic Community, active

promotion of harmonization and unification of the legal order among member states. But in the field of individual liberties and personal freedom, a common legal conscience will evolve from orientation towards an effective international system of protection and control. The impact of the Convention will be felt less in those countries which have neither submitted to individual petitions nor recognised the rules of the Convention as a part of their internal order. There the Convention will remain more a remote reality, a concern of the government, not of the courts of the legal profession in their normal work.

The European Convention on Human Rights as a system of regional guarantees for human freedoms shows clearly the advantages of a regional solution. Within a community of states united by a common heritage of values and legal traditions, it is easier to develop common principles and standards for the protection of human rights. International control can be made more effective within a limited area of nations. The institution of a Commission and of a Court of Human Rights is feasible only in a regional community where a common interest outweights the sentiments of national pride and sovereignty. Tensions between a regional mechanism and a universal system need not arise: it is necessary only to provide a clear system of priorities and to avoid contradictory decisions or double work. We must hope that delimitations between the regional and universal sphere can be worked out in the framework of the new conventions of the United Nations. Effective protection of fundamental human rights is a task which will need continuous support and patient effort for a long time to come. Here there is ample room for the work of both regional and universal institutional arrangements.

NOTES

[1] For the importance of the Universal Declaration in this direction, see E. Schwelb, *Human Rights and The International Community*, pp. 50 ff., Chicago, 1964.

[2] See H. Golsong. *III Recueil des Cours* (1963), p. 34; W. Jenks, *Human Rights and International Labour Standards*, London, 1960.

[3] On the emphasis on individual protection during the stage of the drafting of the European Convention, see G. Weil, *The European Convention on Human Rights*, p. 25, Leyden, 1963; W. J. Ganshof van der Meersch, *Organisations Européennes*, vol. I, p. 260, Paris, 1966.

[4] For the political ideas behind the Convention, see K. Vasak: *La Convention Européen des Droits de l'Homme*, p. 9, Paris, 1964; the same in *Menschenrechte im Staatsrecht und im Völkerrecht. Vorträge und Diskussionen des Zweiten Internationalen Kolloquium über die Europäische Konvention zum Schutz der Menschenrechte und Grundfreiheiten*, p. 24, Karlsruhe, 1967; Golsong, loc. cit., p. 55.

[5] The resolution invokes Art. 24 und urges governments to refer the matter to the European Commission according to its rules. See Information of the Council of Europe, June 26, 1967, No. D 19 102.

[6] See *Yearbook of the European Convention on Human Rights* (henceforth cited as

Yearbook), vol. I, p. 129; vol. II, pp. 175 and 179 (Cases Nos. 176/56 and 299/57). See on these cases Ganshof van der Meersch, op. cit., p. 316.

[7] Case 799/60, *VI Yearbook*, p. 740.

[8] See C. C. Morrisson, Jr., *The Developing European Law of Human Rights*, p. 85, Leyden, 1967.

[9] An application was made by the Governments of Denmark, Norway, and Sweden on September 20, 1967. Later on the Governments of Luxembourg and Belgium acceded.

[10] For the number of applications and their national composition, see *VII Yearbook*, p. 378.

[11] In some cases the Commission had to insist that no inhibition be laid upon the access and correspondence to it by prison authorities. See No. 1593/62, *VII Yearbook*, p. 163; No. 2764/66 *Collection of Decisions* (henceforth cited as *Coll.*), vol. 22, p. 89. These cases show the influence exercised by the Commission through its dealings with national authorities, even before decision is made.

[12] See *VII Yearbook*, p. 4849.

[13] See especially the decision in the Van Gend and Loos v. Netherlands case from February 5, 1963, *Recueil des Décisions de la Cour Européenne*, vol. 9, p. 1. Cf. Th. Buergenthal in *The European Convention on Human Rights*, p. 82. Published under the Auspices of the British Institute for International and Comparative Law (Publ. No. 11), London, 1965.

[14] See for a special chapter of the E.E.C. Treaty (the law on admission of aliens from member states), K. W. Platz, *EWG-Niederlassungsrecht und individuelle Rechtspositionen*, p. 66, Köln, 1966.

[15] The Convention does not oblige the member states to incorporate its provisions in their domestic legal order. See K. J. Partsch, *Die Rechte und Freiheiten der europäischen Menschenrechtskonvention*, p. 37; Berlin, 1966; H. Golsong, *Das Rechtsschutzsystem der europäischen Menschenrechtskonvention*, p. 8, Karlsruhe, 1958; Weil, op. cit., p. 209.

[16] See K. Vasak, op. cit., p. 228; Morrisson, Jr., op. cit., p. 189; my observations in the *Wiener Kolloquium*, p. 208.

[17] See Partsch, op. cit., p. 42; Buergenthal, *Wiener Kolloquium*, p. 180; decision of the Hooge Rad in the Netherlands of February 24, 1960, *Ned. Jurisprudentie* (1960), p. 1121; M. J. van Emde Boas, *Ned. Tijdschrift voor Intern. Recht* (1966), p. 347.

[18] Art. 5 was regarded as not immediately applicable by national courts (not self-executing), see the Austrian Constitutional Court, *VerfGE* of October 14, 1961 *Jurist. Blätter* (1962), p. 145. Against this view, Ermacora, *Jurist. Blätter* (1962), p. 118. Buergenthal, *Wiener Kolloquium*, p. 154. See also cases No. 858/60, *IV Yearbook*, p. 236; No. 1404/62, *VII Yearbook*, p. 109; No. 2077/63, *VII Yearbook*, p. 275, for the application of Art. 5 by the Commission.

[19] See G. L. Weil, op. cit., p. 28.

[20] See G. L. Weil, loc. cit.

[21] See Morrisson, Jr., op. cit., p. 33. This attitude of the Commission has evoked some critical observations. See Morrisson, p. 204, and H. Mosler, *Festschrift für H. Jahrreiss*, p. 289, Köln, 1964.

[22] See cases No. 2306/64, *Coll.*, vol. 21, p. 33; No. 2792/66, ibid., p. 67; No. 2894/66, ibid., p. 71.

[23] My observations, *Festschrift H. Jahrreiss*, p. 374. Dissenting vote of Judge Ross: de Becker Case, *Publications* of the European Court Series A, p. 32. See Morrisson, Jr., op. cit., p. 178.

[24] An example is the settlement of the case Boeckmans v. Belgium. See *VI Yearbook*, p. 445, and report of the sub-commission of February 17, 1965 (see Morrisson, Jr., op. cit., p. 46). Also the case of Angelika Kurtz, *Council of Europe Legal News* of 31.7.1967, D 19 621, p. 14.

[25] No. 1470/62, *Coll.*, vol. 21, p. 7. The formulation of this decision is similar to the conclusions of the Court in the de Becker case.

[26] For the history of human rights, see H. Lauterpacht, *International Law and Human Rights*, p. 73, London, 1950; G. Oestreich, Die Entwicklung der Menschenrechte und Grundfreiheiten in Bettermann-Neumann, Nipperdey, *Die Grundrechte*, vol. I/1, p. 1, Berlin, 1966; J. Bohatec, *England und die Geschichte der Menschenrechte*, Köln, 1956.

[27] C. W. Jenks, *The Common Law of Mankind*, pp. 7 and 43, London, 1958.

[28] This opinion is held by H. Golsong, *Das Rechtsschutzsystem der europäischen Menschenrechtskonvention*, p. 7, Karlsruhe, 1958; Velu in *Wiener Kolloquium*, p. 39.

[29] For Luxembourg, see Partsch, op. cit., p. 54. The same seems to be true for Turkey and Cyprus. For the last two countries there are no clear national decisions to allow a precise answer. See Th. Buergenthal, *The European Conventions on Human Rights*, British Institute for International and Comparative Law 1965, p. 81; and Partsch, p. 54.

[30] For a general survey on the attitude of national legal systems to the application of the Convention as part of the internal order, see Buergenthal, op. cit., p. 84; Ganshof van der Meersch op. cit., p. 365; Partsch, op. cit., p. 47; my observations in *Wiener Kolloquium*, p. 206.

[31] Some insecurity about the status of the Convention was solved by the Bundesverfassungsgesetz of March 4, 1964 (BGBl. Nr. 59), altering the Constitution in this respect (Const. Art. 50, Law 1964, Art. II).

[32] See on this legislation Partsch, op. cit., p. 55; Kunst, *Oest. Juristenzeitung* (1964), p. 197.

[33] See the authors cited in note 29.

[34] The formula "binding on any person" represents a certain restriction for the immediate application of rules of the Convention as internal law. See M. J. van Emde Boas, *Ned. Tijdschrift* (1966), p. 343.

[35] See Buergenthal, p. 84; Partsch, p. 51.

[36] K. Vasak, op. cit., p. 234; Sørensen in *Wiener Kolloquium*, p. 24.

[37] See Weil, op. cit., p. 209; Ganshof van der Meersch, op. cit., p. 357.

[38] See for this opinion H. Guradze, *Der Stand der Menschenrechte im Völkerrecht*, p. 172, Göttingen, 1956; Meyer–Lindenberg, *Berichte der Deutschen Gesellschaft für Völkerrecht* (1962), vol. 4, p. 105; and Guradze in *Wiener Kolloquium*, p. 57.

[39] See case No. 1931/63, *VII Yearbook*, p. 223.

[40] See Morrisson, Jr., op. cit., p. 106.

[41] See Case No. 2145/64, *Coll.*, vol. 18, p. 17.

[42] No. 2248/64, *Coll.*, vol. 22, p. 27.

[43] Oberverwaltungsgericht Münster, *Neue Juristische Wochenschrift* (1956), p. 1374; Bundesverwaltungsgericht, *Monatsschrift für Deutsches Recht* (1957), p. 697.

[44] See Buergenthal in *Wiener Kolloquium*, p. 173.

[45] See Doehring, p. 55, also case No. 2793/11, *Coll.*, vol. 23, p. 128.

[46] Amtsgericht Wiesbaden, *VII Yearbook*, p. 516.

[47] Oberlandesgericht Köln, p. 522.

[48] Hooge Rad, *Ned. Jurisprudentie* (1960), Nr. 436.

[49] No. 1492/62, *V Yearbook*, p. 287, and more recently No. 2065/63, *Coll.*, vol. 18, p. 40.

[50] The leading statement of the Court is in the German interests in Upper Silesia Case 1926, *P.C.I.J.* Series A, p. 18/19. See further Judge Badawi diss.op. in the Norwegian Loans Case 1957, *I.C.J.*, p. 32, and Judge Read in the Nottebohm Case 1955, *I.C.J.*, p. 35/36.

[51] A valuable critical examination of the real importance of this doctrine is to be found in C. W. Jenks, *The Prospects of International Adjudication*, p. 547, London, 1964.

[52] A complaint before national courts is not bound to cite expressly the rules of the Convention in order to be recognized as having exhausted local remedies in the sense of Art. 26 of the Convention. See case No. 712/60, *IV Yearbook*, pp. 387, 406; case No. 1983/63, *Coll.*, vol. 20, p. 76; and my observations in *Wiener Kolloquium*, p. 209; M. J. van Emde Boas, *Ned. Tijdskrift* (1967), p. 12.

[53] This can lead to an exhaustive comparative examination of international rules and municipal law. See case No. 2686/65, *Coll.*, vol. 22, p. 9/10; case No. 2742/66, *Coll.*, vol. 23, pp. 101, 113.

[54] See case No. 1068/61, *V Yearbook*, p. 285/86.

[55] See cases Nos. 8/57, 9/57, 10/57, 11/57, 12/57, 13/57, *Decisions of the Court* (German ed.), vol. 4, pp. 408, 445, 483, 523; case No. 23/60, *Decisions*, vol. 7, p. 421 (General Advocate Roemer). Cf. to the questions involved in this method of compara-

tive evolution of common principles Bernhardt, *ZaöRuVR* 24 (1964), p. 448; and *Die Auslegung völkerrechtlicher Verträge*, p. 156, Köln, 1963.

[56] The European Court on Human Rights has sometimes applied the same method. In the de Becker case it referred to provisions of the Penal Code common to many European legal systems (ECHR Series N 1962, p. 99) and in the Lawless Case the Court mentioned some common principles of judicial procedure in the member states (ECHR Series A, p. 13).

[57] Cf. Morrisson, Jr., op. cit., p. 58.

[58] From the abundant literature on this procedure of authoritative interpretation I cite only H. van Heuvel, *Prejudiciele vragen en bevoegdheidsproblemen in het europeese recht*, Deventer, 1962; Steindorff, *Rechtsschutz und Verfahren im Recht der europäischen Gemeinschaften*, p. 66, Baden-Baden, 1964; Chr. Tomuschat, *Die gerichtliche Vorabentscheidung nach den Verträgen über die europäischen Gemeinschaften*, Köln, 1964.

[59] *Wiener Kolloquium*, pp. 62, 239.

[60] For this general rule, see D. P. O'Connell, *International Law*, vol. I, p. 52, London, 1965.

[61] Art. 64 of the Convention. See the list of reservations *I Yearbook*, p. 40.

[62] *I Yearbook*, p. 41.

[63] *I Yearbook*, p. 42. See Morrisson, Jr., op. cit., p. 188.

[64] See Partsch, *ZaöRuVR* (1956), vol. 17, p. 97.

[65] The history of these articles is given by William E. Rappard, *Die Bundesverfassung der Schweizerischen Eidgenossenschaft 1848–1918*, Zürich (1948), p. 296; Z. Giacometti, *Schweizerisches Bundesstaatsrecht*, Zürich (1949), p. 354. These "konfessionelle Ausnahmeartikel" are now generally regarded as discriminatory. See Jean-François Aubert, *Traité de droit constitutionnel Suisse*, vol. II, p. 722, Neuchâtel, 1967.

[66] See Aubert, op. cit., vol. II, pp. 405, 640.

[67] See No. 214/56, *II Yearbook*, p. 215, and the Decision of the Court in *ECHR* Series A (1962). See further *IV Yearbook*, p. 436; *V Yearbook*, p. 321. Cf. for this case Partsch, op. cit., p. 205; Morrisson, Jr., op. cit., p. 139.

[68] No. 524/59, *III Yearbook*, p. 322; 617/59, *III Yearbook*, p. 370; No. 596/59, *III Yearbook*, p. 356; No. 789/60, *IV Yearbook*, p. 186.

[69] See *VI Yearbook*, pp. 677, 715.

[70] See the text of this "Strafprozessnovelle" (Federal Law of July 18, 1962, BGBl, p. 1128), *VI Yearbook*, p. 341. Cf. on the cases Partsch, p. 151; Morrisson, Jr., p. 126.

[71] See the text in *VI Yearbook*, p. 804. This law was prior to the decision of the Committee of Ministers in the cases Pataki and Dunshirn of September 16, 1963.

[72] See the Report of the Commission on 14 cases and the decision of the Committee of Ministers to take no further measures in *VII Yearbook*, p. 387. Cf. the cases Ganshof van der Meersch, op. cit., p. 318, Partsch, p. 151, and Morrisson, Jr., p. 126.

[73] Two cases are against Germany: No. 2122/64 (Wemhoff), *VII Yearbook*, p. 280, and No. 2294/64 (Gericke) *VII Yearbook*, p. 348. The latter one has been closed in the meantime by amiable settlement. Three cases are against Austria: No. 1963/63 (Neumeister), *VII Yearbook*, p. 224; No. 1602/62 (Strögmüller), *VII Yearbook*, p. 168; No. 2178/64 (Matznetter), *VII Yearbook*, p. 348. Cf. on these cases Morrisson, Jr., p. 112, Partsch, p. 132. See further *Legal News of the Council of Europe* D 19, 621 of July 31, 1967, pp. 3 and 11.

[74] See the report on them in Morrisson, Jr., p. 108.

[75] Gesetz zur Änderung der Strafprozessordnung *BGBl.*, part I, p. 1067.

[76] See Morrisson, Jr., p. 120.

[77] A detailed survey is given by M. J. van Emde Boas, *Ned. Tijdschrift* (1966), p. 360, and (1967), p. 9.

[78] *Report to the Bundestag*, Document IV/178 of July 2, 1962, pp. 17 and 25.

[79] *Report to the Bundestag*, Document V/1679 of April 21, 1967, p. 9.

[80] I refer to my observations in *Wiener Kolloquium*, p. 200, for further elaboration of this point.

[81] See No. 1468/62, *VI Yearbook*, p. 306. For a strong criticism of this decision, see

Partsch, p. 113; H. G. Schmermers, *Ned. Tijdschrift,* vol. 12, p. 366. I approve the decision of the Commission because the short and remunerated period of service in the north of Norway did not fulfil the elements of a forced labour. The Norwegian legislator could have made this time of practical service a presupposition for the admission to the dental practice in Norway.

[82] Case No. 2894/66, *Coll.,* vol. 21, p. 71.

[83] See No. 2690/65, *Coll.,* vol. 21, p. 90, and M. J. van Emde Boas, *Ned. Tijdschrift* (1966), p. 355.

[84] See Report of the Commission of December 12, 1966, p. 41 (vote of Prof. Eustathiades).

Practical application of the European convention

By A. B. McNulty

The European Commission of Human Rights, Strasbourg, France

The celebration of the International Human Rights year of 1968 will involve a general stock-taking of the situation regarding the protection of human rights. This provides an opportunity to report on the work of the European Commission of Human Rights since it achieved in 1955 its competence to receive 'individual' applications under the European Convention on Human Rights (Art. 25).

This optional competence has now been recognised by 11 Parties[1] to the Convention while its competence to receive inter-State applications (Art. 24) is obligatory as between all Parties.[2]

Briefly, the procedure is that the Commission sits at two stages: to decide on the admissibility of an application (Art. 26, 27) and, if admitted, to ascertain the full facts and attempt to reach a friendly settlement between the Parties (Art. 28, 29). At the first stage its role is judicial in the sense that its decision is final. At the second stage, unless a settlement is achieved (Art. 30), it sends a report to the Committee of Ministers (Art. 31) with an opinion as to whether there has been a violation of the Convention. The case may then be referred to the Court of Human Rights (Art. 48) for a decision on the issue of violation and, if not referred, the Committee of Ministers will take a decision (Art. 32). The Commission's proceedings are *in camera* and the case files are confidential but its decisions on admissibility and, nearly always, its reports are published.

What is the concrete value of the protection given by the Commission to individuals and by what procedure has it been achieved?

I do not now intend to examine the Commission's jurisprudence but have simply attempted to collate in systematic form the factual results.

First, regard must be had to the statistics in order to see this question in the right perspective.

At the end of September 1967, the Commission had registered 7 cases brought by one member State against another member State (Art. 24) and 3350 cases brought against States by individuals or groups of individuals (Art. 25).

The 7 inter-State cases can in fact be considered as three: 2 brought by

Greece in 1956/57 against the United Kingdom concerning the situation in Cyprus; one by Austria against Italy in 1960; 3 identical applications recently lodged against Greece by Denmark, Norway and Sweden, and one substantially the same by the Netherlands.

As regards individual cases, about 95 % of the total have been declared inadmissible or struck off the list of cases without being communicated by the Commission to the Government concerned. Although a number of these cases have produced important developments in its jurisprudence, the Commission has finally, in all these cases, felt that their non-admissibility was so clear as not to require any comments from the Government complained against. Cases struck off the list are those where applicants have failed to pursue their claim before the Commission or, very rarely, have shown themselves unrepentantly abusive. It is the remaining 5 %, or about 140 cases, which now concern us. Of these, some 90 cases have been rejected after obtaining the written and/or oral observations of the Government concerned, while the remaining 50 cases have been declared admissible and consequently dealt with by the Committee of Ministers or Court of Human Rights or are still pending.

Again, of these 50, some 30 represent groups of cases, i.e. 19 against Austria (criminal appeal proceedings), 8 against Belgium (linguistic cases) and a further 3 against Belgium (vagabond cases). The real figure here is, therefore, about 23 cases.

The real total to be considered is accordingly 3 inter-State and about 110 individual cases, many of which affect categories of people of whom the actual applicant is only an example. It is against this background that we should regard the results achieved.

First, as to the inter-States cases:

In 1956 and 1957 two cases were brought by *Greece against the United Kingdom.* In the first (No. 176/56) it was alleged that a series of emergency laws and regulations introduced in Cyprus by the United Kingdom were incompatible with the Convention. This application was declared admissible in June 1956 and, after investigation by a Sub-Commission, some of whose members had visited Cyprus to make enquiries on the spot, the Commission made its report. In the meanwhile, some of the measures complained of were suspended and finally, in 1959, the Zurich and London Agreements produced a solution to the Cyprus question. In April 1959, the Committee of Ministers, at the joint proposal of Greece and the United Kingdom, decided that no further action was called for.

In the *second Cyprus case* (No. 299/57) the Greek Government referred to 49 cases of "torture or maltreatment amounting to torture" which allegedly took place in Cyprus and for which the British Government was allegedly responsible. The Application was declared admissible in respect of 29 cases and the Sub-Commission met several times in 1958 and held 2 hearings of the Parties. However, again in view of the Zurich and London Agreements, the Commission decided, at the joint request of the Greek and the United Kingdom Governments, to terminate the proceedings without examining the merits. A report was sent to the Committee of Ministers which, in December 1959, decided that no further action was called for. The Commission's reports in these cases were not published.

The third inter-State case was brought by *Austria against Italy* (No. 788/ 60 lodged in July 1960) and concerned criminal proceedings leading to the conviction of 6 young men for the murder of an Italian customs officer in the German-speaking part of South Tyrol. The Austrian Government alleged that these proceedings were not compatible with the provisions of the Convention (Art. 6) which lay down rules concerning the proper administration of justice and the protection of an accused person's rights.

This application was declared partly admissible in 1961 and, in 1963, the Commission sent its report to the Committee of Ministers with the opinion that there had been no violation of the Convention. In October 1963, the Committee of Ministers itself decided that there had been no violation and, at the same time, transmitted to the Governments concerned the Commission's wish that clemency should be shown to the prisoners. The youngest of the accused had, in fact, been pardoned shortly beforehand.

The last four inter-State cases are those recently brought by *Denmark, Norway, Sweden and the Netherlands against Greece* (Nos. 3321/67, 3322/ 67, 3323/67 and 3344/67). They allege generally that the present Greek Government has violated its obligations under the Convention. They refer to the suspension of certain articles of the Constitution and allege that, regardless of any individual or specific injury, this affects corresponding articles in the Convention. They also submit that the derogation by the Greek Government under Art. 15 of the Convention is not justified. The Commission has decided to give priority to these cases and, on December 14, 1967, to hold a hearing of the Parties on their admissibility.

Secondly, insofar as the 110 individual cases have yielded results, they fall into 4 categories: cases where the Commission considered a violation had occurred; cases where a Sub-Commission achieved a friendly settlement; cases withdrawn by the Applicant following some form of unofficial arrangement with the Government concerned; pending cases where there is some indication of a possible solution.

The Commission has so far, in 4 cases, or groups of cases, stated its opinion that there was violation of the Convention.

In the *de Becker case* (No. 214/56 v. Belgium) the Commission in its report stated the opinion that the particular provisions of the Belgian Penal Code (paras (e) (f) (g) of Art. 123 sexies), insofar as they affected the freedom of expression, were not fully justifiable under the Convention (Art. 10). In April 1960 the Commission brought the case before the Court of Human Rights and, on June 30, 1961, an Act was passed amending the provisions concerned. The Commission referred the Court to the explanatory memo-randum of the Bill which expressly mentioned the Government's intention of "bringing our legislation into line" with the Convention. The Belgian Government then submitted to the Court in October 1961, that, by virtue of the new Act, M. de Becker had achieved his purpose. M. de Becker con-firmed this to the Commission stating that his claim for restitution of the right of free expression had now been met. In January 1962 the Comission submitted that the case, if regarded on the basis of the new Act, should be struck off the list and the Court, in March 1962, took this course.

In the cases of *Pataki and Dunshirn* (Nos. 596/59 and 789/60 against Austria) and 15 other similar cases, the applicants had complained that, under the existing Code of Criminal Procedure, the procedure before the Criminal Court of Appeal violated the right to "fair trial" in that the applicants had no right of representation in these *in camera* proceedings whereas the Public Prosecutor himself was present. The Commission in its report of March 1963 stated the opinion that the "equality of arms", i.e. the procedural equality of the accused with the prosecutor, was an inherent element of "fair trial" and that the proceedings concerned were not in conformity with the Con-vention (Art. 6). However, the Commission then took note of new Austrian legislation of July 1962 and March 1963 which respectively amended the Code of Criminal Procedure and, in *ad hoc* and retroactive form, gave to the applicants the possibility of new appeal proceedings under the amended procedure. The Commission according proposed that no further action should be taken in these cases and, in September 1963 and June 1964, the Com-mittee of Ministers so decided after expressing its satisfaction at the new legislative measures.

In the *Belgian linguistic cases* (Nos. 1474/62, 1677/62, 1691/62, 1769/63, 2126/64) now pending before the Court of Human Rights, 6 groups of applicants, being francophone residents in the Flemish part of Belgium and the Brussels periphery, claim that the linguistic system for education in Belgium under the 1932 and 1963 Acts is incompatible with the Convention. The Commission in its lengthy report of June 1965 considered in effect that the 1963 Acts were in various respects incompatible with the first sentence of Art. 2 of the Protocol: "No one shall be denied the right to education . . ." read in conjunction with Art. 14 (protection against dis-criminatory treatment). The Commission's report has been published and a hearing on the merits will take place before the Court on November 25, 1967.

Three other 'linguistic' cases are still pending before the Commission. Two of them have been declared admissible (Nos. 2013/63, 2209/64) and may be the subject of some sort of settlement.

In two other cases (Nos. 1936/63 v. Austria, 2122/64 v. Federal Republic of Germany) the applicants, *Neumeister and Wemhoff,* each submitted that the period spent by them in detention on remand (Neumeister 26 months; Wemhoff 3 years) violated the provisions of the Convention guaranteeing to a detained person the right to trial within a reasonable time or to release pending trial (Art. 5, para (3)) as well as the right of a person to a hearing within a reasonable time for the determination of any criminal charge against him (Art. 6, para (1)). The Commission, in its reports of May and April, 1966, stated that there had been a violation in each case of Art. 5, para (3) and, in the Neumeister case, also of Art. 6, para (1).

These two cases are now pending before the Court which has fixed hearings for January 1968. The cases of *Stögmüller and Matznetter* (Nos. 1602/62 v. Austria, 2178/64 v. Austria), where the Commission's reports have not yet been made public, are also before the Court. It should here be observed that, in the Federal Republic of Germany, an Act of 1964 amended the Code of Criminal Procedure and Judicature Act by providing that remand in custody should not exceed 6 months except in special circumstances.

As a postscript to this category, it should be added that the *Lawless case* (No. 332/57 v. Ireland) was concerned with the detention in an internment camp of the Applicant under an Order of the Minister of Justice under the 1940 Offences Against the State Act. The Commission, in its report of December 1959, stated the opinion that such arrest or detention was on various grounds an infringement of the right to personal liberty (Art. 5) but it also found that, by reason of the Irish Government's derogation (Art. 15), there had finally been no violation of the Convention. The Court's decision of July 1961 was also that there had been no violation. It may be noted that Lawless was in fact released during the proceedings before the Commission and that, since this case, such measures have apparently not been reintroduced.

The next category of cases is where a Sub-Commission has effected a friendly settlement between the parties (Art. 28, 29). In these cases, as in those in the following category, the Commission always has regard to possible elements of "public interest" before deciding to terminate the proceedings.

In the *Boeckmans case* (No. 1727/62 v. Belgium), the Applicant, who had been convicted of theft, complained that remarks made at his trial in

February 1962 by the President of a Chamber of the Court of Appeal were inconsistent with the protection of certain rights of accused persons, e.g. impartial tribunal (Art. 6, para (1)), presumption of innocence (Art. 6, para (2)), right of defence (Art. 6, para (3) (c)). Under the settlement the Belgian Government, while stating that the validity of the sentence could not be questioned, agreed to pay Boeckmans 65,000 Belgian Francs for compensation for remarks which were such "as to disturb the serenity of the atmosphere during the proceedings in a manner contrary to the Convention and may have caused the applicant a moral injury".

In the *Poerschke case* (No. 2120/64 v. Federal Republic of Germany), the Commission admitted his application insofar as it related to the length of his detention pending trial (Art. 5, para (3)) and of the legal proceedings (Art. 6, para (1)). The terms of settlement effected by the Sub-Commission in December 1966 were (Government) Poerschke's immediate conditional release and (applicant) waiver of proceedings before the Commission and of any civil proceedings before the Berlin courts.

The next category is those cases which have been withdrawn by an applicant in view of some form of arrangement with the Government concerned.

In the case of *Niekisch* (No. 1470/62 v. Federal Republic of Germany), the applicant, who had been refused compensation as a victim of Nazi persecution, claimed that court proceedings in November 1961 violated the guarantee of "fair trial" (Art. 6, para (1)). The Commission, which had adjourned the case during the domestic appeal proceedings, finally noted the terms of a settlement whereby Land Berlin recognised him as a resistance leader since 1933 and awarded him a pension under the Federal Compensation Law. The applicant, on his side, waived all right to further compensation proceedings and withdrew his constitutional appeal and his application before the Commission.

Another similar case brought by *Mr. and Mrs Gericke* (No. 2294/64 v. Federal Republic of Germany) was admitted by the Commission insofar as it concerned the length (3 years) of Gericke's detention on remand (Art. 5, para (3)). The case was withdrawn and the proceedings terminated by the Commission in May 1966 after it was satisfied that, following the *Wemhoff* report, reasons of public interest did not demand its retention. Gericke, who had been convicted as an accomplice of Wemhoff and had not appealed from his conviction, was in February 1966 pardoned and released on probation.

The next case (No. 2707/66 v. Federal Republic of Germany) was lodged in the names of *Angelika Kurtz,* a child born in 1956, her father Mr. Seltmann and her grandmother Mrs Seltmann. In 1957, Mrs Kurtz entrusted the guardianship of her illegitimate daughter to Mrs Seltmann and in 1959, went to the Soviet Occupied Zone of Germany where she married Mr. Klauert. From February 1962 onwards, a series of proceedings took place before the Berlin courts as to whether her mother, father or the juvenile office should determine her place of residence and the final decision of the District Court (Amtsgericht) in August 1966 was in favour of Mrs Klauert.

The applicants' claim was that the compulsory removal of Angelika Kurtz to the Soviet Occupied Zone of Germany would deprive her of various rights and freedoms protected by the Convention and, in particular, would violate her right to liberty (Art. 5). The Commission was informed that negotiations between the East-West authorities were taking place in order that Angelika Kurtz should, with her grandmother, make a trial trip to her mother in the Soviet Occupied Zone. This took place about February 1967 but the child returned with her grandmother to live permanently in West Berlin as some agreement appears to have been reached within the family. The Commission, which had repeatedly adjourned its proceedings, struck the case off its list in April 1967.

The last case is that of an Austrian insurance company *Wiener Städtische Wechselseitige Versicherungsanstalt* (No. 2076/63 v. Austria). The case was complicated and, in general, concerned Austrian post-war legislation for the restitution of property seized under the Nazi régime. The issue, which would have been raised, was the absence of judicial proceedings in the determination of a civil right and thereby a possible violation of Art. 6, para (1). The Company informed the Commission of an *ad hoc* Act of July 1966 which enabled it to acquire the required shareholding at an acceptable price. The Commission decided, in May 1967, to strike the case off its list.

The last category concerns certain current cases of special interest.

The case of *M. Delcourt* (No. 2689/65 v. Belgium) concerns the role of the Procureur Général in proceedings before the Court of Cassation.

The applicant was convicted in September 1964 on charges of fraud and abuse of trust and sentenced to one year's imprisonment and a fine. The Court of Appeal, to whom the case had been referred by the Public Prosecutor and by the applicant, increased his sentence to 5 years, confirmed the fine and added a 10-year sentence of preventive detention. His subsequent appeal was rejected in June 1965 by the Court of Cassation. In April 1967, the Commission declared admissible his application insofar as he alleged that the presence of the Procureur Général at the Court of Cassation *in camera* deliberations, from which he himself was absent, violated the principle of "equality of arms" which forms part of the right to a fair hearing (Art. 6). It also referred to the reports in the Pataki/Dunshirn cases mentioned above.

The case of *Baouya* (No. 2396/65 v. Federal Republic of Germany), an Algerian serving a prison sentence in West Berlin for offences of theft, concerns his threatened deportation to Algeria where he is allegedly threatened with reprisals as a result of having served there as a conscript in the French army in 1960–62.

The Convention does not guarantee any right of residence in a particular country and therefore extradition or deportation are not, as such, covered by the Convention. However, the case before the Commission raises a possible violation of the right to be protected from torture or inhuman treatment or punishment (Art. 3). The Commission has repeatedly adjourned the case pending efforts by the German authorities to find a solution and, in the meanwhile, Baouya has not been deported to Algeria. A hearing is to take place in December 1967 and Baouya has been granted legal aid by the Commission for his representation.

Also pending are 3 cases lodged by *MM. de Wilde, Ooms and Versyp* (Nos. 2832/66, 2835/66, and 2899/66 v. Belgium) and about 7 other similar cases. These all relate to the applicants' detention in an institution ("maison de refuge" or "depôt de mendicité") by order of a "juge de paix" under an 1891 Act "pour la répression de vagabondage et de la mendicité". Their principal complaint is that, as the "juge de paix" apparently acts in an administrative character, they had no possibility of obtaining a court decision as to the lawfulness of their detention as provided for in Art. 5, para (4) of the Convention. The first three of these cases was admitted in April 1967, legal aid having been granted to the applicants, and there is now some question of amending legislation or, of the Conseil d'Etat being, after all, competent to hear appeals from a decision of the "juge de paix".

In the case of *Mr. Alam,* a Pakistani, and his son (No. 2991/66 v. United Kingdom), it is alleged that the latter was refused entry into the United Kingdom in July 1966 by the immigration authorities at London Airport acting under the 1962 Commonwealth Immigrants Act. The applicants allege violations of the right to family life (Art. 8) and the right to receive a fair and public hearing by an independent and impartial tribunal in determination of their civil rights (Art. 6, para (1)).

After a hearing of the parties in July 1967, at which the Solicitor-General appeared on behalf of the Government, the Commission declared the case admissible. A Sub-Commission has now been set up. In the meanwhile, it has been announced that a governmental committee, the Wilson Committee on Immigration Appeals, has recommended the setting up of a two-tier appellate structure for hearing appeals from such decisions of the immigration authorities.

The next case was brought by the *N. V. Televizier* company (No. 2690/65 v. Netherlands) which is a weekly magazine, "Televizier", containing information and comments on forthcoming radio and television programmes.

Proceedings were brought against Televizier before the Dutch courts for having derived its information from compilations of programmes made by an organisation called the "Centraal Bureau voor den Omroep in Nederland" thus allegedly committing a breach of copyright. In June 1965, the Netherlands Supreme Court considered that the compilations concerned were subject to copyright under the Dutch Copyright Act. The applicant company considers that the Supreme Court's decision resulted in an infringement of the right freedom of expression (Art. 10) as well as the right to freedom from discriminatory treatment (Art. 14).

The application was declared admissible by the Commission in December 1966 but, at the request of the applicant company, the Sub-Commission has adjourned its proceedings as some form of settlement appears to be imminent.

The above summary indicates some tangible results achieved so far in cases which, it must be repeated, have often affected far more people than the applicant himself. Three observations, again factual, remain to be made.

First, until now there has been no confrontation between the Court of Human Rights or the Committee of Ministers and a Government in the sense that in no case has either organ yet found a violation of the Convention. This may certainly constitute a threat but, so far, all that has been, or is being achieved, has been initiated at the Commission stage where proceedings are throughout confidential and, after admissibility, fact-finding and conciliatory rather than judicial.

This is, in my opinion, clear evidence of the effectiveness of the indirect or moral sanction particularly in those cases mentioned above where national legislation was enacted *ad hoc* applications before the Commission. I think that this has a special interest in view of the discussion on universal action or regional action as alternative systems for the protection of human rights. It may be that the particular interdependence of the Member States of the Council of Europe contributes to the force of this sanction and is an argument for the regional system.

Secondly, 11 States, as opposed to the original 6 in 1955, have now accepted the Commission's optional competence to receive individual applications (Art. 25), while the rate of cases, and of important cases, is increasing. I should add that the United Kingdom Government has this month extended to 21 overseas territories the right of individual application.

Thirdly, certain States have accepted the presence of the Commission or of some of its members to carry out investigations in their territory and have given full co-operation for this delicate task. In 1958, members of a Sub-Commission in the first Cyprus case carried out an investigation on the spot for 3 weeks and this year the whole Sub-Commission visited a prison and heard evidence in West Berlin in regard to a case (No. 2686/65) where ill-treatment was alleged. In 1966 and 1967, delegated members of 2 Sub-Commissions heard evidence in Austria and, I myself, at the suggestion of the Federal German Government and with the Commission's approval, visited the applicant, Baouya, (mentioned above) in 1966 in order to settle a procedural point.

Finally, then, it is, I think, a reasonable deduction that the Commission is securely establishing itself in the confidence both of the public and of the Parties to the Convention. It is particularly this basis of co-operation between the Commission and Governments, rather than a relationship of prosecutor and accused, which has brought this about and generally made the Convention workable at this first stage of its existence.

NOTES

[1] Austria, Belgium, Denmark, Federal Republic of Germany, Iceland, Ireland, Luxembourg, the Netherlands, Norway, Sweden, United Kingdom.
[2] Ditto, plus Cyprus, Greece, Italy, Malta, Turkey. France and Switzerland have not yet ratified the Convention.

Human rights, social justice and peace
The broader significance of the I.L.O. experience

By C. Wilfred Jenks

International Labour Office, Geneva, Switzerland

Historical perspective

No one culture and no particular political or legal tradition can claim a copyright in the concept of human rights or hold a patent for its practical application. The validity of the concept and the breadth of its appeal arise from its being a synthesis of all the great moralities, the most varied cultures, and diverse political and legal traditions. The course of history during recent centuries has nevertheless been a decisive factor in determining the precise form and content of the concept of human rights as it has now found expression in the Charter of the United Nations, the Universal Declaration of Human Rights, and the United Nations Covenants on Human Rights. The concept includes two complementary elements, freedom from fear guaranteed by civil, political and religious liberties, and freedom from want, guaranteed by economic, social and cultural rights. The roots of all these rights lay far back in primitive, ancient and medieval thought, but their formal recognition by law in the world at large in the manner which has given them the connotation which we now attach to the rights of man is a development of the last three centuries. They have gradually become, by stages merging into each other, rights by common law, rights by constitutional law, and rights by international law. The civil, political and religious liberties and the economic, social and cultural rights have achieved this status at different stages of historical development, in different societies, and in different political contexts. The "liberties" are in large measure the legacy of the English revolutions of the seventeenth century and the American and French revolutions of the eighteenth century. They became common currency with the progress of constitutionalism during the nineteenth century and especially after the "war to make the world safe for democracy".[1] The economic, social and cultural rights came to be given legal form as the result of the Mexican and Russian revolutions of 1917 and the German revolution of 1918; they found legal expression in the Mexican Constitution of 1917, the Weimar Constitution of 1919, and the successive constitutions of the R.S.F.S.R. and the U.S.S.R. This second tradition precipitated, rather than arose from, the revolutions as the result of which it was given legal form; it was shaped by Robert Owen, Proudhon, Marx and their successors as clearly as the earlier tradition was the legacy of Milton and Locke, Montesquieu and Jefferson, Voltaire and Rousseau; it was profoundly influenced by the West European trade union movements;[2] by the time of the Second World War it was reflected in the constitutional charters of many countries; it has become an accepted part of the political outlook of the emerging countries; during the last three-quarters of a century the Papal Encyclicals from *Rerum Novarum* to *Populorum Progressio,* and more recently the Report on Church and Society of the World Council of Churches,[3] have raised it to the level of a spiritual quest with an oecumenical appeal transcending boundaries of confession and faith.

On the international plane the process of historical development has been reversed. The Constitution of the International Labour Organisation anticipated by almost thirty years, and the Declaration of Philadelphia which subsequently amplified it by nearly five years, the Universal Declaration of Human Rights, and the creation of the International Labour Organisation in 1919 provided the machinery for "continuous and concerted" international effort to achieve the purposes set forth in its Constitution. Only for such special cases as mandates, minorities and certain areas subject to a special international regime was any comparable (and even so for the most part less effective) provision made at that time for the promotion and protection of civil liberties. It was the challenge of totalitarianism before and during the Second World War which made the protection of civil liberties a major and urgent issue of international policy.[4] We have, therefore, in the promotion of economic and social rights by the International Labour Organisation, a unique case of almost fifty years of experience of the opportunities and problems of international action for the promotion of such rights. How far has this experience any significant bearing on the wider effort to promote and protect human rights and fundamental freedoms initiated in pursuance of the Charter of the United Nations?

The I.L.O. tradition and experience has, it is submitted, already contributed to the wider movement the two fundamental concepts on which it is based; it includes an imposing body of precedent which is a valuable guide for further action; and it also includes an unwritten wisdom which can season the whole effort with a maturity of temper essential to its success.

The first of the two fundamental concepts is that human rights find fulfilment in, but are an essential element of, social justice; civil liberties give no real freedom to stunted lives, but bread and circuses are no substitute for personal freedom. The vocation to social justice was from the outset the keynote of the Constitution of the I.L.O.; the commitment to human rights was, as of 1919, more implicit; they were, so to speak, taken for granted by the I.L.O. in the same manner in which they were taken for granted by the League of Nations. The Constitution declared that labour was not a commodity and proclaimed the right of association for all lawful purposes by the employed as well as by the employers, but otherwise its concern was with conditions of life and work in the field of social policy. By 1944, when the aims and purposes of the I.L.O. were restated in the Declaration of Philadelphia, the inter-dependence of human rights and social policy had been brought into sharper focus by the events of the inter-war period and the Second World War. Freedom of expression and of association were declared to be essential to sustained progress and the Declaration proclaimed the right of every human being, irrespective of race, creed, or sex to seek both spiritual fulfilment and material well-being in conditions of freedom and dignity, economic security and equal opportunity. The greater concern with civil liberties reflected in the I.L.O. was paralleled, primarily as the result of the Great Depression, by the manner in which the social objectives of the I.L.O. had become central preoccupations of national and international policy.[5] The confluence of the keener concern for civil liberties and the wider recognition of the central importance of social policy gave us the United Nations approach to the international protection of human rights. Historically the experience and advocacy of the I.L.O. played a significant part in broadening the thinking which found expression in the Universal Declaration of Human Rights to include economic and social rights as the corollary of civil liberties.

The second fundamental concept is that human rights and social justice are essential constituents of a lasting peace. The I.L.O. was designed from the outset to place peace-keeping on a solid foundation of peace-building.[6] The Preamble to the Constitution affirms that there can be no lasting peace without social justice. The multifarious activities of the Organisation have impinged at many points on the creation of a sense of world community which reaches back into the lives of the common people. The I.L.O. contribution to the building of peace has been manifold. Its important institutional aspect[7] has included the pioneering of the compromise between responsible majority decision and the search for a general consensus which has replaced the principle of unanimity as the basis of the rules of procedure of contemporary international conferences,[8] the whole specialised agency concept on which virtually all of the significant work of the United Nations family in the economic, social and cultural fields is now based, the initial formulation of the basic principles on which much of the co-operation between the United Nations and the specialised agencies has been based,[9] and the reaffirmation, when the United Nations and the new specialised agencies were taking shape, of the indispensability of an impartial international civil service.[10] These are all major matters; orderly procedure in the transaction of international business by consensus or majority decision, the widening of areas of co-operation beyond the paralysis of politics, the concept of a United Nations family of autonomous organisations each retaining its own vitality but all acting in a close partnership, and the element of continuity, specialised knowledge and disinterested objectivity represented by a professional international service with an exclusive allegiance to mankind as a whole are all vital bonds of world community. Politically the I.L.O. was the bridge whereby the United States passed from the isolation of the rejection of the Covenant to world co-operation; historically this was the turning point which made possible the whole United Nations system. But no other element in the I.L.O. contribution to the building of peace has been comparable in importance to the fundamental concept that peace must be built by continuous and concerted effort to promote the common welfare. Throughout the life and decline of the League of Nations the I.L.O. remained the living embodiment of this concept which was to find fuller expression in the United Nations in the economic and social provisions of the Charter.

The standards and procedures evolved by the I.L.O. for the promotion and protection of human rights and social justice are a leading example of the manner in which concrete expression has been given to this general concept. To estimate the extent to which they are of wider significance and the importance of their contribution to building the foundations of peace we must review their nature, scope and operation.

The I.L.O. standards and procedures

Neither the Constitution of the International Labour Organisation in its original form as negotiated in 1919 nor the Declaration of Philadelphia, which restated the aims and purposes of the Organisation in 1944 and was incorporated in the Constitution in 1946, purport to be or is a declaration or covenant of human rights. They are constitutional instruments designed to establish and consolidate the position of a world organisation with a mandate to make human rights and social justice effective in practice as a contribution to peace. This approach had its critics both in 1919 and again in 1944. There was a school of thought in 1919 which regarded the inclusion in the peace treaties of labour clauses affirming certain rights and principles as more important than the creation of a permanent organisation. There was a school of thought in 1944 which wished to redraft the Declaration of Philadelphia as a statement of rights rather than a mandate for continuing action by the I.L.O. Happily the institutional school of thought which attached primary importance to the creation and development of the permanent international machinery necessary for a continuous and concerted effort to implement a broad mandate prevailed on both occasions.

The machinery created in 1919 in the form of the I.L.O., and fortified in 1944 and 1946 by the adoption of the Declaration of Philadelphia and the amendment of the Constitution, has six features which were wholly novel in 1919 and have remained highly distinctive as the I.L.O. approaches its fiftieth year.

The first of these features is the clear and specific mandate given to the I.L.O. to carry out a positive programme for human rights, social justice and peace, in matters immediately affecting the everyday lives of ordinary folk from the cradle to the grave; the protection of motherhood and childhood; work, wages, leisure and social security; retirement, widowhood and orphanage. The mandate includes the more equitable distribution of wealth and welfare; the development and deployment of the human resources and skills necessary to match need and rising expectations with production; and the development of the social institutions necessary for the achievement of these purposes. In 1919 this mandate, already clearly outlined though not stated as fully as in more recent years, was a revolutionary departure in world organisation; it is now paralleled by the mandates of the Economic and Social Council, some of the other specialised agencies (notably U.N.E.S.C.O., F.A.O. and W.H.O.) and some of the regional organisations; but it still touches the everyday life of ordinary folk with a special intimacy at an exceptionally wide range of points. The I.L.O. has played a vital role in transforming our image of the world community from a world of States into a world of peoples; it has redefined the fundamentals of international politics by shifting the emphasis which commends itself to enlightened opinion from power and prestige to freedom and welfare; and its leadership in this general direction remains vigorous.

The second feature is the unique structure of the Organisation. The International Labour Organisation does not represent governments alone. It is unique among the organisations of the United Nations family in granting the living forces of production, management and labour a status in its counsels and deliberations equal to that of governments. Both the International Labour Conference and the Governing Body are composed upon a tripartite basis. This unique composition has profoundly influenced their methods of work and approach to problems; it has dethroned the arrogance of sovereignty and made possible imaginative initiatives which could not have been taken in purely governmental bodies which take their tone from current official thought; it has given a special importance to the role of the International Labour Office as the impartial servant of all three groups working in a close partnership of mutual confidence with the Conference and the Governing Body. Nothing comparable exists in any of the regional bodies, though the Council of Europe and the European Communities have broken new ground in a different manner in their interparliamentary assemblies. The far-reaching changes in economic and social structure which have taken place in so many countries have presented acute problems in regard to the application of the tripartite principle, but progress is being made in resolving these problems, and the principle remains the corner stone of the Organisation.[11] The severest critics of the tripartite system are to be found chiefly among those with least experience of its practical operation and of the dynamic manner in which the Organisation has constantly adapted its programme and methods of work to changing needs in a changing world. The evolution of all societies, irrespective of their economic and social structure or ideological background, is giving a new importance to a stable partnership between government and the twin forces of production. The I.L.O. is the instrument for such a partnership on the world scale. On the success of such a partnership in the pursuit of dynamic policies of economic growth and social justice both the coexistence in freedom of different economic and social systems and the bridging of the gap between affluence and embitterment may in large measure depend; and without such coexistence and the bridging of the gap there can be no peace.

The third feature is the importance of the quasi-legislative functions of the I.L.O. The International Labour Conference has no legislative power, but Members of the Organisation have under its Constitution an obligation to submit Conventions and Recommendations adopted by the Conference by a two-thirds majority for the consideration of the national authorities competent to give effect to their provisions and this is construed as meaning normally the legislature. The obligation applies irrespectively of whether or not the government of the Member voted for the Convention. The fulfilment of this obligation is reviewed regularly and zealously by the International Labour Conference. In 1919 this was a radical innovation; the whole conception of a convention being adopted by an international conference by a two-thirds majority instead of being signed by plenipotentiaries was new; and the obligation to submit conventions so adopted for parliamentary consideration was unprecedented. The adoption of conventions by international conferences has now become a commonplace and the constitutions of a number of the specialised agencies provide for such adoption but the position of the I.L.O. in the matter remains unique in two respects, the scale of its quasi-legislative action, and the fact that only in the I.L.O. is there an obligation, widely effective in practice, to submit Conventions and Recommendations for parliamentary consideration. The fact that we have no world legislature is one of the fundamental weaknesses of the structure of the world community; the problem is so difficult that we may well have to be content for a generation or more to come with creating more effective international legislative procedures rather than a world legislature; in this perspective the quasi-legislative functions and procedures of the I.L.O. may be the germ of one of the ingredients of more far-reaching action indispensable to the future of human rights, social justice and peace.

The fourth feature is the procedures provided for in the Constitution of the I.L.O. for international supervision of the implementation of Conventions and Recommendations: regular reporting on the fulfilment of the obligation to submit Conventions or Recommendations to the competent authority and the decision taken by the authority and on the measures taken to give effect to the provisions of Conventions which have been ratified; reporting at intervals as requested by the Governing Body on the law and practice relating to the provisions of Conventions which have not been ratified and Recommendations; consideration by the Governing Body of respresentations by industrial organisations that a ratified Convention is not being applied; commissions of inquiry to consider complaints by governments which have ratified a Convention that another party to the Convention is not fulfilling its obligations; compulsory jurisdiction of the International Court of Justice on matters relating to the interpretation of Conventions. Not all of the full scheme is in constant application but the reporting arrangements are, and all parts of the scheme have been put to the test of practical application and served a useful purpose at some time and are potentially of continuing value in the future. In their comprehensiveness and effectiveness the I.L.O. arrangements for the international supervision of the implementation of some 120 international Conventions with some 120 different States as parties are unique.[12] The world community has no greater structural weakness than that which arises from the difficulty of making its decisions effective. The I.L.O. arrangements for international supervision of the implementation of Conventions and Recommendations are a significant contribution in a particular field to the solution of this fundamental structural problem.

The fifth feature is that these constitutional arrangements have not been regarded as a rigid framework created by the Constitution and therefore unchangeable; they have been supplemented by a whole series of developments not specifically contemplated by the Constitution which have been made possible and become effective because they have been evolved within the general framework of these constitutional obligations. The reconciliation of stability and adaptation to change in a process of dynamic growth which does not erode the existence of clear-cut obligations is one of the fundamental problems of international institutional development; the history of the constitutional development of the I.L.O. has an important bearing on this problem.

The sixth feature is the extent to which, in the I.L.O., policy formulation, standards, industrial relations functions, quasi-judicial responsibilities, informational and promotional activities, education and training, research, advisory services and operational programmes are mutually complementary to each other. This is characteristic of the I.L.O. as a whole and of special importance in its impact in the field of human rights. In the world community, as in the State, the effectiveness of public policy depends on the extent to which the different functions of government effectively complement and reinforce each other.

In none of these respects can we reasonably claim more than that the tradition and achievement of the I.L.O. represent a trend, the further development of which would greatly strengthen the vitality of purpose and institutional structure of the world community, but in all of them the trend is clear and significant, the impact already apparent is appreciable, and the potential results of further developing the trend can extend far beyond those already achieved.

Through this unique constitutional framework the I.L.O. has evolved a unique *corpus juris* of social justice.[13] As of 1967, 128 Conventions and 131 Recommendations had been adopted by the International Labour Conference. Conventions, when ratified, constitute a body of obligations binding upon States; Recommendations are guides to national legislation, collective negotiation, and administrative action; Conventions frequently operate as Recommendations in relation to States which have not ratified them. As of 1 August 1967, 110 of the 128 Conventions were in force for numbers of States varying from 2 to 99 and 3312 ratifications distributed over 122 Conventions and 118 countries had been registered; to these must be added 1191 declarations applying the provisions of Conventions to non-metropolitan territories, giving a total of some 4500 international engagements. Nothing on a comparable scale exists in any other field of economic or social policy. Taken together the Conventions and Recommendations constitute what has come to be known as the International Labour Code. This is not a code in the sense of being binding anywhere in its entirety or being a definitive formulation of a branch of the law of which the outstanding characteristic is that it is in process of constant growth and adaptation. "The International Labour Code is not primarily a code of international obligations, but a code of internationally approved standards, certain of which are capable of becoming, and have in many cases become, binding upon States by reason of the ratification by those States of the relevant international Labour Conventions, and in respect of all of which members of the

Organisation have an obligation to report on the position of their national law and practice at appropriate intervals as requested by the Governing Body."[14] But the term "code" is not a misnomer for so unprecedented and beneficent an achievement.

The ground covered by the Conventions and Recommendations includes basic human rights (including freedom from forced labour, freedom of association and freedom from discrimination), human resources development (including employment policy, employment services, and vocational guidance, training and rehabilitation), general conditions of employment (including employment security, wages, hours of work, and leisure), industrial relations, the employment of children, young persons and women, industrial health, safety and welfare, social security, migration, and labour administration and statistics. There are special provisions where appropriate for industry, mining, transport, agriculture, and the special problems of developing countries.

There has been a tendency in some quarters to suggest that Conventions and Recommendations are no longer as important as they may once have been and that the need today is for practical action. This is a dangerously myopic view. Practical action is not an end in itself; it is a means of achieving an end in practice; and the end to be achieved must first be defined by a consensus which commands general assent. This is the function of Conventions and Recommendations. Legislation remains a major instrument of social policy throughout the world and virtually every member of the I.L.O. is constantly enacting new social legislation on matters within its field. There are, it is true, acute divergences of view concerning the proper or best relationship between legislation and other forms of action in particular contexts, and these may clearly have a bearing on the desirability or otherwise of particular Conventions or Recommendations or the inclusion therein of particular provisions. There will also continue to be controversy concerning the extent to which particular matters can appropriately be dealt with internationally. But such controversies relate to particular cases and afford no warrant for the view that we have passed beyond the legislative phase of international action in matters of labour policy. I.L.O. standards remain the backbone of the multifarious activities and functions of the I.L.O. and their constant revision in the light of changing needs is among the major tasks and responsibilities of the Organisation. Even among the critics of I.L.O. standards there are many who are at pains to make it clear that their criticism is not intended to apply to the standards which they recognise as relating to fundamental human rights.

Virtually all of the I.L.O. Conventions and Recommendations are in some measure a contribution to the promotion and protection of human rights in the broad sense in which the term is used in the Charter of the United

Nations, the Universal Declaration of Human Rights, and the United Nations Covenant on Economic, Social and Cultural Rights, for even the most technical of them may be regarded as measures for the implementation of the right to just and favourable conditions of work affirmed by the Universal Declaration and recognised by the Covenant on Economic, Social and Cultural Rights. There is, however, a limited group of Conventions which have come to be regarded as being in a special sense the human rights Conventions of the I.L.O. This group consists essentially of six Conventions relating to freedom from forced labour, freedom of association, and freedom from discrimination, but is sometimes enlarged to include some of the other Conventions. The six Conventions in question have an important common feature; "they all have a close bearing on personal freedom, not only in the enlarged sense of freedom from fear and from want (fundamental as such freedom may be) but in the primary sense of freedom from arbitrary restraint upon the action and opportunities of the individual".[15] They have also been particularly widely ratified. As of August 1, 1967 the Forced Labour Convention, 1930 had been ratified by 99 States; the Abolition of Forced Labour Convention, 1957, by 78 States; the Freedom of Association and Protection of the Right to Organise Convention, 1948, by 75 States; the Right to Organise and Collective Bargaining Convention, 1949, by 82 States; the Discrimination (Employment and Occupation) Convention, 1958, by 60 States; and the Equal Remuneration Convention, 1951, by 55 States; this gives an average of 75 ratifications by Convention for the Conventions in this group of six.

The extent to which the Conventions have been ratified, which compares impressively with the position in respect of other international conventions, may be attributed in a considerable degree to the obligation of member States under Art. 19 of the Constitution of the Organisation to submit Conventions adopted by the Conference to national competent authorities and to inform the International Labour Office of the action taken. On the basis of this obligation the Governing Body and the Conference review regularly the progress of ratifications; they have before them each year a report on the manner in which the obligation has been discharged in respect of Conventions generally and give special consideration from time to time to the position in respect of the human rights Conventions. The crux of the matter is the principle, which has been insistently and, in the main, successfully maintained by the I.L.O., that the competent authority to which Conventions must be submitted is the legislative authority competent to make their provisions fully effective;[16] the effect of the obligation, so construed, is to by-pass executive inertia and bureaucratic conservatism by ensuring that the matter is considered both at a higher executive level and beyond the executive in such a manner that broader attention is focused on the issues of wider policy involved and the strength of the case which may exist for dynamic action inspired by and based upon an international standard.

The value of ratifications is enhanced by the fact that reservations to ratifications of international labour Conventions are inadmissible.[17] The majority of the Conventions permit a substantial flexibility in their application but the measure of such flexibility is determined by the terms of the Conventions and not unilateral action by the parties. This gives the obligations resulting from the Conventions a solidity which they would otherwise lack.

This far-flung network of obligations would nevertheless be of uncertain and debatable value in the absence of effective arrangements for international supervision of their application. The strength of the I.L.O. system of supervision lies in the fact that it combines provision for a continuous routine examination year by year of reports from governments with a wide range of procedures, some of them provided for in the Constitution and others evolved to meet special needs, to inquire into alleged violations and special situations, and provides for the association with all of these arrangements in some appropriate way of parties with a real and direct interest in securing effectiveness of application.

Reports on ratified conventions. Art. 22 of the Constitution of the Organisation provides that each Member having ratified a Convention shall make an annual report to the International Labour Office, in such form and containing such particulars as the Governing Body may request, on the measures which it has taken to give effect to the provisions of the Convention.

When the ratifications required to bring a Convention into force have been registered, the International Labour Office submits to the Governing Body for its approval a draft form of annual report for the Convention. When approved by the Governing Body, this form becomes the standard form of annual report for the Convention prescribed by the Governing Body under Art. 22 of the Constitution and members bound by the Convention are under a legal obligation to furnish the particulars of the measures which they have taken to give effect to their obligations which are specified in the form.

A summary of these reports is submitted by the Director-General to each session of the International Labour Conference, together with a report by a Committee of Experts consisting of independent persons of the highest standing, enjoying in practice complete security of tenure as members of the Committee, having outstanding qualifications in the legal or social field, including persons with an intimate knowledge of labour conditions and of the application of labour legislation, and so chosen as to ensure that they have collectively a wide and authoritative knowledge of the varying degrees of industrial development and the variations of industrial methods to be found among the Members of the Organisation.

These arrangements are highly effective for the purpose of ascertaining whether the law of the Member is in compliance with its obligations under Conventions; they are in the nature of the case less satisfactory for the purpose of ascertaining the extent to which there is full *de facto* compliance, but both the Committee of Experts and the Conference Committee began to be acutely preoccupied with this aspect of their task as early as 1927. The Constitution, as amended in 1946, requires that governments shall communicate copies of their reports to the representative organisations of employers and workers; the form of report approved by the Governing Body asks whether any observations regarding the practical application of the Convention have been received from employers' and workers' organisations; and the employers' and workers' representatives take part in the Conference Committe on the application of Conventions and Recommendations and have the fullest opportunity there to state their views. The report forms also request information concerning statistics, legal decisions and, in appropriate cases, official reports concerning the manner in which the Convention is applied. A special survey of the problem involved in the examination of the practical application of Conventions was made by the Committee of Experts in 1963.[18] The procedure therefore affords considerable guarantees of reasonable effectiveness even in respect of questions of *de facto* application.[19]

In recent years the Committee of Experts has listed in its report cases in which governments, in response to its earlier comments, have introduced changes in their law and practice in order to give fuller effect to ratified Conventions. During the years 1964–1967 close to 300 such instances of progress came to the Committee's attention. There is nothing comparable in the experience of any other international organisation.

Reports on unratified conventions and recommendations. As amended in 1946 the Constitution of the Organisation provides that where a Member does not ratify a Convention it shall report to the Director-General of the International Labour Office, at appropriate intervals as requested by the Governing Body, the position of its law and practice in regard to the matters dealt with in the Convention, showing the extent to which effect has been given, or is proposed to be given, to any of the provisions of the Convention by legislation, administrative action, collective agreement or otherwise and stating the difficulties which prevent or delay the ratification of such Convention. There is a similar obligation in respect of recommendations. The Governing Body selects each year a limited number of Conventions and

Recommendations on which it requests reports in a prescribed form in accordance with these provisions.

The Governing Body has exercised this special power by requesting reports on all of the six Conventions which are regarded as constituting the human rights group. On the basis of these reports the Committee of Experts has been in a position to submit to the Conference comprehensive surveys of the impact of the Conventions relating to forced labour,[20] freedom of association,[21] discrimination in employment and occupation,[22] and equal remuneration,[23] covering as many as 168 countries for forced labour, 160 for freedom of association, and 138 for discrimination. The surveys have proved to be an invaluable instrument for invigorating and intensifying action to make the provisions of the Conventions effective.

Among the other Conventions in respect of which such surveys have been made are those relating to a number of the other social rights enunciated in the Universal Declaration of Human Rights and the United Nations Covenant of Economic, Social and Cultural Rights, including the right to social security,[24] the right to reasonable conditions of work (hours of work,[25] weekly rest[26] and holidays with pay,[27] the protection of motherhood,[28] and the protection of young persons.[29] In the nature of the case no precise measurement of the effect of the general surveys is possible, but it is apparent that they have furnished the occasion for reporting a great deal of positive action which in the absence of such a stimulus might not have taken place or would have tended to take place more slowly.

It is upon the reporting procedures provided for in Art. 19 and 22 of the Constitution that the I.L.O. relies for regular and continuous supervision of the implementation of Conventions and Recommendations, but further procedures for serious cases of non-compliance are provided for in Art. 24 and 26.

Representations under Art. 24. Under Art. 24 of the Constitution any "industrial association of employers or of workers" may make a "representation" to the International Labour Office that "any of the members has failed to secure in any respect the effective observance within its jurisdiction of any Convention to which it is a party" and in any such case "the Governing Body may communicate the representation to the government against which it is made, and may invite that government to make such statement on the subject as it may think fit". The development of this procedure has passed through three stages. The earliest representations were considered by the Governing Body in plenary sitting; the outcome in the second case which was considered in 1931 was a somewhat confused discussion, embarrassing to all parties and quite unfruitful.[30] The Governing Body therefore adopted in 1932 Special Standing Orders concerning the Procedure for the Discussion of Representations which provided that the Governing Body should be advised at each stage of the procedure by a Committee of Three; these committees acted judicially and submitted for the approval of the Governing Body reports containing their findings and recommendations. A number of cases, but none of outstanding importance, were dealt with in a businesslike manner under this procedure in the course of the 1930's.[31] The procedure then appeared for a quarter of a century to have become obsolete. It was in any case highly formalistic in character. When it was next invoked in 1965, in a representation made by the Association of Federal Servants of the State of Sao Paulo concerning the application by Brazil of the Labour Inspection Convention, 1947, the Governing Body extended the powers of the Committee of Three and empowered it to deal with all stages of the case until it was ready to submit findings and recommendations to the Governing Body. The report of the Committee of Three in this case, submitted in 1967, contained valuable findings and recommendations.[32] The Sao Paulo case may therefore be regarded as having reaffirmed the usefulness of the procedure of representation and furnished a new pattern of action for any future cases which may arise.

Complaints under Art. 26. Art. 26–29 and 31–34 of the Constitution provide for a considerably more elaborate procedure for the examination of complaints. Any member may file a complaint with the International Labour Office if it is not satisfied that any other member is securing the effective observance of any Convention which both have ratified. The Governing Body may, after previous communication with the government in question if it thinks fit, appoint a Commission of Inquiry to consider the complaint and to report thereon; it may also adopt the same procedure either on its own motion or on receipt of a complaint from a delegate to the Conference. Members agree that, in the event of the reference of a complaint to a Commission of Inquiry, they will each, whether directly concerned in the complaint or not, place at the disposal of the Commission all the information in their possession which bears on the subject matter of the complaint. The Commission of Inquiry is to prepare a report embodying its findings on all questions of fact relevant to determining the issue between the parties and containing such recommendations as it may think proper as to the steps which should be taken to meet the complaint and the time within which they should be taken. Any government concerned in a complaint which does not accept the recommendations contained in the report of the Commission of Inquiry may refer the complaint to the International Court of Justice, which may affirm, vary or renounce any of the findings or recommendations of the Commission of Inquiry. In the event of any member failing to carry out within the time specified the recommendations, if any, contained in the report of the Commission of Inquiry, or in the decision of the International Court of Justice, as the case may be, the Governing Body may recommend to the Conference such action as it may deem wise and expedient to secure compliance therewith.

For many years this procedure appeared to be a dead letter. A complaint concerning the application of the Hours of Work (Industry) Convention, 1919, to Indian railways was submitted by the Indian Workers' delegate to the Conference in 1934, but the Governing Body did not consider it necessary to appoint a Commission of Inquiry.[33] The procedure was not invoked again until 1961.

Ghana then submited a complaint alleging failure by Portugal to fulfil its obligations under the Abolition of Forced Labour Convention 1957. The Governing Body appointed a Commission of Inquiry to consider the complaint and it fell to that Commission to put the flesh upon the bare bones of constitutional provisions which, prior to its appointment, had come to be widely regarded as obsolete and inoperative. The Commission heard witnesses for both parties and visited Angola and Mozambique.

The report of the Commission,[34] which was unanimous, contains its findings of law and fact and far reaching recommendations for further remedial action; these included a recommendation that the Committee of Experts on the Application of Conventions and Recommendations should be kept regularly informed of progress. There has continued to be political controversy concerning the matter but the report was accepted by both parties and substantial progress appears to have been made in implementing the recommendations of the Commission; a special report on the matter was made by the Committee of Experts in 1966.[35]

While the proceedings in the Ghana-Portugal case were pending, Portugal initiated what were in effect counter-proceedings by charging Liberia with failure to fulfil her obligations under the Forced Labour Convention, 1930, and a second Commission was appointed by the Governing Body to consider this new complaint.

The Commission, in a unanimous report, formulated its findings of law and fact on the allegations submitted to it and made recommendations, some of them quite far-reaching in character, for appropriate remedial action. The recommendations were accepted by both parties and action to implement them is in progress; the report, like that of the Ghana-Portugal Commission, included a recommendation that the Committee of Experts on the Application of Conventions and Recommendations should be kept regularly informed of the progress made; the Committee of Experts reviewed the position in 1966.[37]

How important the procedure of complaint under Art. 26 of the Constitution will be in future remains unforeseeable, but the Ghana-Portugal and Portugal-Liberia cases have set solid precedents for its future application.

These regular constitutional procedures have been supplemented by a variety of special procedures and measures of *ad hoc* or continuing character.

Forced labour inquiry. A special inquiry into forced labour was held during the period 1951 to 1953 by a United Nations-I.L.O. Ad Hoc Committee under the chairmanship of Sir Ramaswami Mudaliar. The Committee held four sessions, examined thoroughly the relevant legislation in twenty-four countries and territories concerning which allegations had been made, considered information supplied by forty-eight governments in reply to a questionnaire, and heard and questioned representatives of fifteen organisations which had submitted information to it; it issued a comprehensive report[38] containing general conclusions and its findings concerning individual countries and territories. The report had a considerable impact and gave the impetus which resulted in the adoption by the International Labour Conference of the Abolition of Forced Labour Convention, 1957, now as we have seen, in force for 78 countries. Further inquiries affording independent confirmation of the findings of the Ad Hoc Committee and reviewing later developments were subsequently made by an I.L.O. committee under the chairmanship of Mr. Paul Ruegger.[39]

Freedom of association procedure and inquiries. For freedom of association matters the regular constitutional procedures are supplemented by a special procedure for the examination of allegations of trade union rights established by agreement between the United Nations and the International Labour Organisation in 1950. The procedure originally consisted of provision for the reference of such allegations with the consent of the government concerned to a Fact-Finding and Conciliation Commission of independent persons. When it became apparent that such consent would rarely be given the Governing Body of the I.L.O. established in 1951 a Governing Body Committee on Freedom of Association to make a preliminary examination of allegations and the desirability of requesting the government concerned to consent to their being referred to the Fact-Finding and Conciliation Commission. The Governing Body Committee, with the co-operation of governments in all parts of the world, rapidly developed into a body which makes a substantive examination of the allegations and submits to the Governing Body its findings concerning the extent to which the allegations are justified and recommendations concerning any action to redress the alleged grievances which should be taken by the government concerned. Upwards of 500 cases had been considered in this manner by 1967; the Committee had developed an imposing body of consistent precedent on a wide range of questions by which it is guided; and many governments had accepted and given effect to recommendations by the Committee.[40] The procedure inevitably poses delicate problems in every new phase of its application, but the measure of confidence which has been created by the thoroughness and fairness with which it has been operated has made such problems less insoluble than they would have been if they had become more acute in the earlier stages of its development.

In 1964 Japan consented to the reference to the Fact-Finding and Conciliation Commission of a major case relating to freedom of association for government employees. The Panel of the Commission to which it was referred modelled its procedure on that of the Commissions of Inquiry approved by the Governing Body to consider complaints under Art. 26 of the Constitution. The Panel received elaborate written statements from the complainants and the Government, had prepared on its behalf by the International Labour Office a comprehensive analysis of the relevant legislation, held full hearings in Geneva in private but in the presence and with the participation of both complainants and Government, and visited Japan for discussions with all concerned. While in Japan the Panel submitted certain preliminary proposals to the Minister of Labour and the General Council of Trade Unions of Japan; it subsequently made a comprehensive and voluminous report[41] embodying its findings and recommendations which was accepted by both parties as the basis of further discussions which are still in progress. While not all of the questions at issue have been finally resolved, the report is widely regarded as a landmark in the history of industrial relations in the public sector in Japan.[42]

Among other special inquiries into freedom of association matters, the Committee on the Freedom and Independence of Employers' and Workers' Organisations (the McNair Committee), which, after reviewing, on the basis of replies from governments to a questionnaire and monographs submitted to governments for comment, the position throughout the then membership of the Organisation, reported in 1956[43] was of special importance.

There can be little doubt that the impact of these special procedures and inquiries, though not susceptible of precise measurement, has been far-reaching. A partial reflection of it is to be found in the fact that the Freedom of Association and Protection of the Right to Organise Convention, 1948, is now in force for 75 States and the Right to Organise and Collective Bargaining Convention, 1949, for 82 States.

Discrimination and apartheid. There are no special arrangements comparable to the freedom of association allegations procedure for discrimination questions. The regular constitutional procedures are applicable in respect of the Discrimination (Employment and Occupation) Convention and Recommendation, 1958, but a special procedure of general application for the examination of allegations of discrimination has been thought unwise by reason of the nature and scale of the problem and its political aspects.[44] In general, the I.L.O. has preferred to supplement the Convention with a vigorous promotional and educational programme.[45]

It has, however, always been recognised that extreme cases call for special measures. The strongest condemnation of discrimination has always been in the tradition of the I.L.O. Thus the Conference was emphatic in its condemnation, on June 20, 1938, of discrimination against workers belonging to certain races or confessions, an unveiled rejection of Nazi racism at the height of its ascendancy. The Declaration of Philadelphia first formulated in an authoritative international instrument the principle that human rights transcend differences of race, creed and sex which has now become the keynote of the Universal Declaration of Human Rights and the United Nations Covenants of Human Rights. The Declaration concerning *Apartheid* and I.L.O. Programme for the Elimination of *Apartheid,* adopted unanimously by the International Labour Conference on July 8, 1964, is a further expression of this tradition.

The Declaration and Programme set forth a specific programme of reform, concentrating on three broad areas, namely, equality of opportunity in respect of admission to employment and training, freedom from forced labour (including practices which involve or may involve an element of coercion to labour) and freedom of association and protection of the right to organise. They indicate precisely the changes in labour policy necessary to eliminate *apartheid.* A series of subsequent annual reports keep the matter under continuous review.[46] No success can as yet be claimed for the action of the I.L.O. against *apartheid* but it has at least the merits of a reasonable policy through which *apartheid* could be eliminated.

Jurisdiction of the International Court. Art. 37 of the Constitution of the Organisation provides that any question or dispute relating to the interpretation of the Constitution or of any Convention shall be referred for decision to the International Court of Justice. The I.L.O. referred six cases to the Permanent Court of International Justice for an advisory opinion but has not found it necessary to seek an advisory opinion since 1932. Only one of the six cases, that relating to the *Interpretation of the Convention concerning the Employment of Women During the Night,*[47] referred to the interpretation of a Convention, though three of the earlier cases, those relating to the *Competence of the I.L.O. in respect of Conditions of Agricultural Labourers,*[48] the *Competence of the I.L.O. in respect of the Organisation and Development of the Means of Agricultural Production,*[49] and the *Competence of the I.L.O. to Regulate, Incidentally, the Personal Work of the Employer,*[50] referred to the competence of the I.L.O. to adopt certain Conventions and Recommendations. Art. 37 is binding upon all Members of the International Labour Organisation, the Constitution making no provision for membership on the basis of incomplete acceptance of its obligations.[51]

General effect of I.L.O. standards and procedures. The I.L.O. experience in the field of human rights has been so extensive and varied, and has touched at many points questions of policy of so fundamental a nature which still represent crucial dilemmas of contemporary society, that it is difficult to distil from it any general conclusions. It may be a generation before we can see the whole picture in perspective and form a valid judgment of the long-term impact of the I.L.O. standards and procedures. But we have the elements for at least a provisional judgment. The I.L.O. standards and procedures have been a main thrust in the freedom and dignity campaign of twentieth-century man. Even if we limit our estimate of their significance to the immediate range of influence of the I.L.O. they represent one of the most imaginative and determined contributions of the last fifty years to the quest for human rights, social justice and peace. How far have they a still greater potential? What further contribution can they make to the new crusade for human rights, social justice and peace in which, on the occasion of International Human Rights Year, the United Nations is endeavouring to enlist the dedicated energies of all mankind? To pursue the inquiry further we must consider the forms which more vigorous international action for the protection of human rights is taking or is likely to take and the possible relevance of the I.L.O. experience to the varied possibilities which lie before us.

The I.L.O. experience and the future

Future progress in the international protection of human rights will require a wide range of mutually complementary measures and approaches.

The Universal Declaration of Human Rights will remain the intellectual, and to some extent the political, framework of the whole undertaking. It is of vital importance that the political, moral and, in some measure, legal authority which the Declaration has gradually acquired[52] should not be impaired by any delay or difficulty which there may be in bringing generally into force the provisions of the United Nations Covenants.

The United Nations Covenants of Human Rights provide the basis for a comprehensive body of firm obligations transforming the legal standards of the Universal Declaration (which may well be, and should increasingly be, regarded as having the force of customary law but remain inchoate as obligations) into legal rules formally accepted by States as binding upon them. The Covenants are still, however, an opportunity rather than an achievement.[53] Whereas the Universal Declaration of Human Rights became operative as such by virtue of adoption and proclamation by the General Assembly, the Covenants become operative as such only in relation to States which ratify or accede to them and each Covenant requires thirty-five ratifications to bring it into force. Both substantive and procedural reservations to the provisions of the Covenants appear to be freely admissible and the effect on the obligations resulting from the Covenants of any reservation or objection thereto remains somewhat indeterminate; there is therefore a real danger that the Covenants may disintegrate into series of bilateral agreements expressed in two common instruments but binding in different degrees between different parties. The Covenants make no provision for adjudication and arbitration in the event of any disagreement concerning their interpretation, and subject to the measures of implementation for which they provide each party therefore remains the judge of the nature and extent of its obligations. These deal with matters concerning which there have been varying, and in some cases conflicting, concepts concerning the fundamentals of civil liberties and social policy. The measures of implementation applicable to all parties by virtue of their acceptance of the Covenants provide for a general appraisal of the progress made in implementation but appear to be designed to exclude any review of the fulfilment by individual parties of their obligations; they provide for the review of general reports. In the case of the Covenant on Economic, Social and Cultural Rights, there is no provision for the consideration of complaints by States that a party has failed to fulfil its obligations or of communications from individuals claiming that the rights enumerated in the Covenant have been violated. In the case of the Covenant on Civil and Political Rights, claims by one party that another party is not fulfilling its obligations may be considered only as between States parties which have made special declarations accepting such a procedure; communications from individuals may be considered only if they relate to States having accepted an Optional Protocol; the rules in respect of claims by a party and communications from an individual are different but in both types of case the powers granted to the Human Rights Committee are strictly limited. The entry into force of the Covenants can, by reason of their comprehensive scope and unequivocal character as legal obligations, be an epoch making advance in the international protection of human rights, but their immediate practical value will depend on the extent to which they are promptly and widely ratified without reservations which detract significantly from the obligations which they embody and on how far the procedures of implementation are applied, within the limits resulting from the fact that they provide primarily for a general appraisal of the progress made and only exceptionally for the examination of particular cases, with the highest standards of thoroughness and objectivity.

Whatever measure of practical success the Covenants may attain, both their substantive and their procedural provisions need to be supplemented to define with greater precision the obligations assumed, to secure the widest possible spread of uniform or comparable obligations, and to provide for more effective procedures for the implementation of particular rights in specific cases. The further action of this nature which is required may be expected to take three main forms, each of which would represent a natural development of existing precedents or action already in progress.

The United Nations may find it desirable to sponsor a series of special Conventions defining in more precise detail particular rights proclaimed by the Universal Declaration and embodied in the Covenants, specifying some of the modalities of the national action necessary for the effective implementation of the right in question, and establishing an appropriate international procedure to ensure that the right is fully respected in practice. There is a precedent for such action in the International Convention on the Elimination of All Forms of Racial Discrimination of January 19, 1966. It may be specially desirable to have a series of such Conventions establishing the presumption of innocence until proof of guilt, precluding guilt by association, prohibiting retroactive penalties, providing procedural safeguards for freedom from arbitrary arrest or detention and for prompt trial, and guaranteeing freedom of religious observance.[54]

Most of the substantive rights provided for in the Covenant on Economic, Social and Cultural Rights fall, as the procedural provisions of the Covenant recognise, within the competence and specialised experience of one of the specialised agencies. The fuller implementation of these rights is therefore likely to require the conclusion of further special Conventions under the auspices of the appropriate specialised agencies. The widespread network of the international labour Conventions, already described,[55] affords an obvious prototype for such action, with the U.N.E.S.C.O. Convention against Discrimination in Education of 1960 affording a further illustration.

Regional action may be a valuable anticipation of, a powerful reinforcement of, or a necessary substitute for, universal action under the auspices of the United Nations, the International Labour Organisation, or another specialised agency such as U.N.E.S.C.O. A pattern for regional action of a comprehensive nature is afforded by the European Convention for the Protection of Human Rights and Fundamental Freedoms and the European Social Charter.[56] The European Commission of Human Rights and European Court of Human Rights established by the European Convention provide a type and degree of protection for civil liberties unparalleled in the United Nations system or, as yet, in any other region. An Inter-American Convention on Human Rights has existed in draft since 1959 but has still not been adopted; meanwhile the Inter-American Commission on Human Rights established by the Council of the Organization of American States receives allegations of violations of human rights in the American Republics, hears evidence, and makes reports and recommendations.[57] The Organization of African Unity also has the matter under consideration.[58] These comprehensive regional approaches may be supplemented in course of time by special arrangements in respect of particular rights.

The Charter of the United Nations, the Universal Declaration, the United Nations Covenants, and the special and regional Conventions, represent the core of the international law of human rights. No less important than the law is the practice. During the period when the adoption of the United Nations Covenants seemed problematical a series of alternative approaches, including the establishment of United Nations advisory services in the field of human rights, the institution of a system of annual reports on human rights by governments, and the initiation of a series of studies of specific aspects of human rights, were approved by the Economic and Social Council on the proposal of the Human Rights Commission at the initiative of the United States;[59] these arrangements will doubtless be continued. More recently the General Assembly has had under consideration a proposal for the appointment of a United Nations High Commissioner for Human Rights to assist in furthering the realisation of human rights and the observance of the Universal Declaration.

The I.L.O. experience has some bearing on virtually all of the main elements of such a comprehensive programme of mutually complementary measures to secure the more effective international protection of human rights.

The relevant I.L.O. experience consists, as already indicated, partly of a body of formal precedent readily reducible to cold print and partly of an unwritten wisdom born of much experience by which the appropriate authorities of the I.L.O., the Governing Body, the Director-General, the Committee of Experts on the Application of Conventions and Recommendations, Commissions of Inquiry, the Freedom of Association Committee, the Fact-Finding and Conciliation Commission on Freedom of Association, and in the last resort the International Labour Conference, are guided in practice.

The formal precedent takes the form of constitutional provisions, Conventions, Recommendations and other I.L.O. standards, established procedures, findings and recommendations contained in innumerable reports, and decisions taken by the Governing Body and the Conference on the basis of such reports. A general account of this body of formal precedent has already been given.[60] It is available as a model for all who may wish to be guided by it independently of any formal co-operation with the I.L.O. in drawing upon it, but such co-operation is normally available to all who care to seek it.

The unwritten wisdom of the I.L.O. in matters of human rights[61] is essentially a body of experience guided by certain fundamental principles: firm adherence to accepted international obligations and standards; a scrupulous thoroughness; the strictest objectivity; recognition of the need for a sympathetic understanding of what lies beyond the letter of the law, of problems of timing, and of practical difficulties; and acceptance of the duty to observe the highest standards of tact and courtesy in the evaluation of complex and delicate problems.

Let us first consider the bearing of the body of formal precedent afforded by the I.L.O. experience on the varied approaches necessary for an effective comprehensive programme for the international protection of human rights. In some respects I.L.O. precedents are being followed; in others they are not being, and in certain cases cannot be, followed; in a number of major respects how far the I.L.O. experience will be turned to good account on a wider basis remains an open question. In some cases I.L.O. precedent is being or may be taken as a model for independent action by other bodies; in other cases the active co-operation of the I.L.O. is being or may be sought to make wider use of a unique experience; in some cases I.L.O. action is in practice an important or even indispensable complement to the action of other bodies.

The Universal Declaration of Human Rights enunciates the right to freedom of association and a series of economic and social rights including the right to social security, the right to work, to free choice of employment, and to just and favourable conditions of work and remuneration, the right to rest and leisure, the right to an adequate standard of living, and the rights of motherhood and childhood to special care and assistance. As is emphasised in the statement of Essential Human Rights prepared on behalf of the American Law Institute in 1943,[62] from which the formula "everyone has the right" to each of the economic and social rights specified in the Declaration was derived, each of the economic and social rights presupposes a correlative duty of the State. None of the economic and social rights is, or can be, self-executing. They all require the adjustment of conflicting interests and positive measures of implementation by legislation or administrative action. To give any definable international content to these rights, conventions and recommendations which provide the common core of uniform or at least comparable legislation and administrative action are therefore necessary. This common core exists in the I.L.O. Conventions and Recommendations which constitute the International Labour Code.[63] There are now major international labour Conventions covering all of the economic and social rights within the field of the I.L.O. enunciated in the Universal Declaration; the extent to which these Conventions are in force inevitably varies but even where they are not binding as obligations they tend to be influential as standards and their practical impact is greatly increased by the arrangements which exist for the systematic international review and appraisal of their application.[64]

This situation was well understood when the United Nations Covenant on Economic, Social and Cultural Rights was drafted. It is therefore not surprising that this Covenant should provide that the Secretary-General shall transmit to the specialised agencies copies of the reports to be made by the parties to the Covenant which relate to matters falling within the responsibilities of the said agencies in accordance with their respective constitutional instruments, and that the Economic and Social Council may make arrangements with the specialised agencies in respect of their reporting to it on the progress made in achieving the observance of the provisions of the Covenant falling within the scope of their activities, including particulars of decisions and recommendations on such implementation adopted by their competent organs. The Covenant authorises the specialised agencies to submit comments to the Economic and Social Council on any recommendation made by the Commission on Human Rights and empowers the Council to bring to the attention of the specialised agencies concerned with furnishing technical assistance any matters arising out of the reports which may assist them in deciding on the advisability of international measures likely to contribute to the effective progressive implementation of its provisions. The Covenant also specifies that nothing contained therein is to be interpreted as impairing the provisions of the Charter of the United Nations and of the constitutions of the specialised agencies defining the respective responsibilities of the various organs of the United Nations and of the specialised agencies in regard to the matters dealt with therein. The effect of these provisions is that potentially the specialised agencies, and in particular the I.L.O. by reason of the number and importance of the economic and social rights falling within its field, become the executing agencies of the Covenant on Economic, Social and Cultural Rights with a major share of the responsibility for its effective implementation.

The full co-operation of the I.L.O. in the implementation of the Covenant on Economic, Social and Cultural Rights in accordance with its terms was pledged by the Governing Body immediately after the adoption of the Covenant by the General Assembly, and the International Labour Conference, at its 51st Session, renewed this pledge and invited the Governing Body to undertake a comparative study of the relevant provisions of the Covenant and the corresponding Conventions and Recommendations with a view to assessing how the I.L.O. could best assist in further promoting the protection of fundamental human rights.

The potential role of the I.L.O. as the most effective executing agency of much of the Covenant on Economic, Social and Cultural Rights is greatly increased by the fact that the standards, structure, constitutional powers, and procedures of the I.L.O. make it possible to remedy many of the weaknesses of the procedure of implementation provided for in the Covenant. The I.L.O. standards are so much more definite and detailed than the provisions of the Covenant that they permit of a far more thorough and discriminatory appraisal of the extent to which the obligations assumed are being fulfilled. The tripartite structure of the I.L.O. ensures a full and equal voice in both the determination and the operation of the I.L.O. arrangements concerning implementation to elements which have a real and keen interest in effective implementation and do not share the common interest of governments in protecting each other against criticism. The constitutional powers of the I.L.O. enable it to secure more thorough and precise reporting than is provided for in, or seems probable under, the Covenant and ensures a more thorough and informed but nevertheless more objective examination of reports. The Covenant on Economic, Social and Cultural Rights makes no provision for the examination of complaints or allegations of particular violations of its provisions; in the I.L.O. such procedures are available. The full use by the I.L.O. of its own constitutional powers and procedures and the synchronisation and intermeshing of such action with its collaboration in the reporting system provided for in the Covenant on Economic, Social and Cultural Rights can therefore secure an effectiveness in reviewing the progress made in the implementation of the Covenant which would otherwise be wholly unattainable.

The Covenant on Civil and Political Rights does not envisage any comparable role for the specialised agencies as executing agencies of the Covenant. It establishes a Human Rights Committee of members serving in a personal capacity to consider reports on its application and, to the limited extent to which they are receivable, claims from States and communications from individuals relating to alleged violations of its provisions. This is not unnatural as the matters covered by the Covenant on Civil and Political

Rights, in contrast to those covered by the Covenant on Economic, Social and Cultural Rights, fall primarily within the responsibility of the United Nations rather than within that of the specialised agencies.

There are, however, in the Covenant on Civil and Political Rights provisions concerning forced labour and freedom of association for trade union purposes which are related to and to some extent reflect, but afford substantially less protection than, the provisions of the relevant international labour Conventions. Thus the Covenant reproduces the general prohibition of forced or compulsory labour contained in the Forced Labour Convention, 1930, but maintains the exceptions provided for in the definition of forced labour contained in that Convention, the general effect of which is to permit the exaction of forced labour by the State in a wide range of cases as a penalty for a criminal offence or a civic obligation; there is no equivalent in the Covenant for the provisions of the Abolition of Forced Labour Convention, 1957, which prohibits without any corresponding exception the use of forced labour for such purposes as political coercion or education, economic development, labour discipline, strike breaking, and racial or social discrimination. Similarly, the Covenant grants such a wide power to place restrictions on the right of freedom of association for trade union purposes which it purports to recognise that it was necessary to specify that nothing contained therein prejudices the stricter obligations of the Freedom of Association and Protection of the Right to Organise Convention, 1948, for the parties thereto.

In these circumstances it is not surprising, and is highly satisfactory, that the Covenant should provide that its provisions concerning implementation "shall apply without prejudice to the procedures prescribed in the field of human rights by or under the constitutional instruments and the Conventions of the United Nations and the specialised agencies and shall not prevent the States parties to the present Covenant from having recourse to other procedures for settling a dispute in accordance with general or special international agreements in force between them".[65] In forced labour and freedom of association matters there will generally be two good reasons for having recourse to the I.L.O. procedures rather than the procedure for the implementation of the Covenant, that the obligations of the Covenant concerning them are almost nominal in view of the scope of the permitted exceptions, and that the I.L.O. procedures permit of complaints by governments, and of representations or (in freedom of association matters) allegations by individual organisations, without any limitation to cases in which the government charged with violation has made a special declaration or accepted a special protocol. Without, therefore, having any formal status as an executing agency of the Covenant of Civil and Political Rights in respect of these provisions, the I.L.O. will tend to be in fact, through the normal application of its own procedures, the effective watchdog of their application. There is, however, no formal provision permitting the I.L.O. to invoke or participate in the procedures of the Covenant of Civil and Political Rights in respect of these or any other matters of concern to it, though it could in virtue of the Agreement between the United Nations and the I.L.O. participate in the discussion of the annual report of the Human Rights Committee in the Economic and Social Council or the General Assembly. In any case in which the effectiveness of the I.L.O. procedures proves to be limited because, for instance, a question arising in relation to freedom of association resolves itself into one of freedom from arbitrary arrest, detention or exile, the right to a fair and public hearing by an independent and impartial tribunal, or the presumption of innocence until proof of guilt,[66] this may prove to be one of the most appropriate manners in which the I.L.O. can seek complementary action by the United Nations.

For the implementation of special Conventions sponsored by the United Nations or other specialised agencies the I.L.O. experience of both reporting and allegation and complaint procedures may to some extent serve as a prototype, though the extent to which it can do so is limited by the difficulty of creating in the United Nations or other specialised agencies any real equivalent for the manner in which the I.L.O. system combines the special knowledge represented by the continuous studies of the Office, the independent judgment of experts of the highest standing, and the practical experience and outlook of the representatives of the affected interests participating in the Governing Body and the International Labour Conference with the same status as government representatives. The I.L.O. procedures have, moreover, been shaped by, even when they are not based upon, the specific powers of the Governing Body and Conference and the specific obligations of governments under the Constitution of the I.L.O.; there are only shadows of these, and no full equivalent for them, in the more general provisions of the Charter and of the constitutions of the other specialised agencies responsible for matters covered by the Covenants. Apart from these basic structural and institutional difficulties the I.L.O. tradition owes its strength and vitality to the fact that it has developed and matured during a period of almost half a century; the growth of such a tradition has been made possible by the scale of the problem in the I.L.O. which stands in sharp contrast to the position in agencies with few Conventions relating to human rights, and by the political forces which have sustained the I.L.O.; such a tradition cannot readily be transplanted to a *milieu* where it would be an alien growth. Nevertheless, some elements in the I.L.O. tradition may be of wider interest. In particular regular periodicity of reporting, the usefulness of a standard form of report, the value of a committee of independent experts, thorough staff work to enable the experts to raise the right questions, and the practice of precise requests to governments for explanation, further information, or remedial action, may be susceptible of wider application in respect of Conventions for which there are still only inchoate reporting systems; in respect of future Conventions it may sometimes be possible to make provision for some of these matters in the Convention itself. Similarly, the I.L.O. allegations and complaints procedures may afford precedents for other Conventions, notably in the manner in which they have set a pattern for the meticulous examination of conflicting contentions on the basis of consistent principles and the formulation of a comprehensive body of recognised jurisprudence.[67]

Only in Europe are regional conventions concerning human rights yet in force. The European Convention on Human Rights and Fundamental Freedoms contains provisions relating to forced labour and freedom of association for trade union purposes which are subject to the same criticism as the corresponding provisions of the United Nations Covenant on Civil and Political rights;[68] the Convention contains no reference to the possible obligations of parties under the relevant international labour Conventions and the I.L.O. has no organised relationship to the European Commission and Court of Human Rights in respect of the application of these provisions, but when the Commission was called on to consider an allegation that an obligation placed upon dentists by Norwegian legislation to serve for a period in outlying areas was forced labour within the meaning of the European Convention it sought from the I.L.O. information concerning the application of the Forced Labour Convention, 1930, before finding that there had been no violation of the European Convention. The absence of an organised relationship does not therefore preclude practical co-operation with the Commission in respect of matters arising from provisions of the Convention which reflect provisions of international labour Conventions; it might make it more difficult to arrange for any such co-operation at the stage of any such matter coming before the European Court of Human Rights. The position in respect of the European Social Charter is entirely different. The Charter was the outcome of co-operation between the Council of Europe and the I.L.O.; its provisions relate to matters many of which are dealt with in greater detail in international labour Conventions; and it specifically provides that the I.L.O. shall be notified in the same manner as Members of the Council of Europe of ratifications, amendments and denunciations of the Charter and that the I.L.O. shall be invited to nominate a representative to participate in a consultative capacity in the deliberations of the Committee of Experts to be appointed under the Charter to examine the reports of governments concerning the application of the provisions of the Charter which they have accepted. There is therefore a formal link whereby the Council of Europe can draw on I.L.O. experience in respect of matters of common interest which may arise in connection with the application of the Charter. The experience of modalities of co-operation between the I.L.O. and regional bodies, acquired in this manner, may be of value if and as regional arrangements for the protection of economic and social rights are developed in other parts of the world.

To define clearly the I.L.O. contribution to the promotional and operational activities of the United Nations in the field of human rights involves problems of definition which become almost insoluble.

The I.L.O. has not organised advisory services in the field of human rights as a distinctive activity, but all of its advisory services to member States in respect of the subject matter of the economic and social rights enunciated in the Universal Declaration and in the United Nations Covenants may be regarded as being in some measure advisory services in the field of human rights.

To the studies of various aspects of human rights initiated by the Economic and Social Council and other United Nations bodies, the I.L.O. has made, and may be expected to continue to make, a substantial contribution. It has presented periodically general reports on developments in regard to human rights falling within I.L.O. competence[69] and special reports on I.L.O. action in regard to discrimination in employment and occupation;[70] it has also prepared for special meetings reports on human rights in developing countries,[71] on the realisation of economic and social rights,[72] and on *apartheid*.[73] To the studies prepared for the Commission on the Status of Women, the I.L.O. has contributed, each year, in a more general report to the Commission on its activities relating to women,[74] an account of its work concerning discrimination in employment and occupation, and, at two-yearly intervals, a progress report on equal pay for work of equal value.[75]

What contribution the I.L.O. could make to the work of a United Nations High Commissioner on Human Rights would depend on his terms of reference and mode of operation. It would be important to avoid any harmful duplication and feasible to work out arrangements whereby they could assist each other, particularly in matters not covered by the binding obligations of one of the Covenants or a convention in which the general terms of a United Nations standard require more precise definition by the I.L.O. to make them meaningful or the effectiveness of one of the social freedoms enunciated by the I.L.O. presupposes effective procedural protection in the field of civil liberties.

The potential contribution of the unwritten wisdom of the I.L.O. tradition and experience applies in a more general manner irrespective of the distinctive modalities of different procedures. It consists essentially of a spirit, a method and a discipline. The spirit is one of a passionately dispassionate respect for truth expressed in the highest standards of thoroughness and objectivity, unclouded by prejudice of any kind, undaunted by the magnitude or complexity of any task, and wholly unmoved by fear or favour, no matter how charged with political tension or distrust the issue may be. The method is one of scrupulous and relentless examination of all of the available and findable facts, of the most rigorous testing of the reliability, force and consistency of all the evidence, and of the fullest application of the principle that every interested party should be fully and fairly heard or have the opportunity to be heard; the rigour of the method is guaranteed by a complex of institutional devices, notably the importance of the part played by bodies of independent persons chosen for their integrity, wisdom and standing on the initiative of the Director-General of the I.L.O., the declaration made by the members of such bodies that they will discharge their duties honourably, faithfully, impartially and conscientiously (in effect an oath of office which is based on that taken by judges of the International Court), the servicing of such bodies by a highly-trained, experienced, and disciplined staff chosen for detachment and loyalty, and appropriate procedural guarantees of full and fair hearing; the relentlessness of the method is made palatable by the authoritative and objective character of the standards applied and the tradition of applying them with tact, courtesy and a sense of proportion. The discipline which makes the whole undertaking possible is both emotional and intellectual; it is a collective discipline which requires complainants, governments complained against, independent bodies, international staffs, and representative international organs and assemblies to show a common restraint and collective sense of mutual obligation in seeking and pursuing truth rather than political advantage and agreement for the future rather than justification regarding the past.

The basic dilemma

The challenge to promote and ensure on the world scale human rights, social justice and peace is often thought to pose a basic dilemma—that of reconciling faith in fundamental human rights and in the dignity and worth of the human person with the duty to practice tolerance and live together in peace with one another as good neighbours in a world of divergent moral values and conflicting political and economic interests, in which the mortal combat of good and evil remains the essence of personal, national and international life. So formulated, the dilemma is more apparant than real.

Fundamental human rights and the dignity and worth of the human person cannot be secured without tolerance, peace and good-neighbourliness; tolerance, peace and good-neighbourliness involve respect for fundamental human rights and the dignity and worth of the human person. The true dilemma is the challenge of evil which denies both fundamental human rights and the dignity and worth of the human person and the duty of tolerance, peace and good-neighbourliness. Such a denial is not limited to any one ideology; it tends to clothe itself, in all ideologies, with considerable self-righteousness; it rarely grasps the real issues and never senses the unprecedented opportunities of a world and age of cataclysmic change. Human rights, social justice and peace have an appeal which transcends all ideologies and a core of common meaning which can be enlarged by common action. If we are inhibited by fear or prejudice from enlarging the core of common understanding by common action we will inevitably freeze divergences of view and conflicts of interest which will arrest the whole process of further development.

NOTES

[1] Agnes Headlam-Morley, *The New Democratic Constitutions of Europe,* Oxford University Press, 1929.

[2] L. L. Lorwin, *Labor and Internationalism,* New York, 1929.

[3] *World Conference on Church and Society Official Report,* World Council of Churches, Geneva, 1967.

[4] H. Lauterpacht, *International Law and Human Rights,* Stevens & Sons, London, 1951.

[5] International Labour Office, *The I.L.O. and Reconstruction* (1941); *Future Policy, Programme and Status of the I.I.O.* (1944); *Reports of the Conference Delegation on Constitutional Questions* (1946).

[6] On the whole matter, see Edward J. Phelan, The Contribution of the I.L.O. to Peace. *International Labour Review,* vol. LIX, June 1949, pp. 607–632.

[7] For the details see Phelan, op. cit.

[8] For the part of the I.L.O. in the process of development, see C. Wilfred Jenks, Unanimity, the Veto, Weighted Voting, Special and Simple Majorities and Consensus as Modes of Decision in International Organisations. *Cambridge Essays in International Law: Essays in Honour of Lord McNair,* pp. 48–63, Stevens & Sons, London, 1964.

[9] International Labour Conference, Twenty-Seventh Session, Paris 1945, *Report IV(1), Matters Arising out of the Work of the Constitutional Committee: Part I. The Relationship of the I.L.O. to Other International Bodies.*

[10] Cf. C. Wilfred Jenks, Some Problems of an International Civil Service. *Public Administration Review* (1943), pp. 93–105.

[11] On the whole matter, see C. Wilfred Jenks, *The International Protection of Trade Union Freedom,* pp. 67–87, 109–132 and 512–529, Stevens & Sons, London, 1957.

[12] E. A. Landy, *The Effectiveness of International Supervision: Thirty Years of I.L.O. Experience,* Stevens & Sons, London, 1966.

[13] C. Wilfred Jenks, The *Corpus Juris* of Social Justice. *Law, Freedom and Welfare,* pp. 101–136, Stevens & Sons, London, 1963.

[14] International Labour Office, *The International Labour Code 1951,* vol. I, p. LXX; for the more recent Conventions and Recommendations, see International Labour Office, *Conventions and Recommendations 1919–1966.*

[15] C. Wilfred Jenks, *Human Rights and International Labour Standards,* p. 9, Stevens & Sons, London, 1960.

[16] The I.L.O. position is defined in "The Nature of the Competent Authority Contem-

plated by Art. 19 of the Constitution of the International Labour Organisation", Memorandum by the Legal Adviser of the International Labour Office. International Labour Office, *Official Bulletin*, vol. XXVI, No. 2, December 1, 1944, and see also International Labour Conference, Twenty-Ninth Session, *Reports of the Conference Delegation on Constitutional Questions*, pp. 35–43; it is restated in a *Memorandum Concerning the Obligation to submit Conventions and Recommendations to the Competent Authorities* approved by the Governing Body in 1959 which records the unanimous acceptance by the International Labour Conference at its Thirty-Sixth Session of the position.

[17] On the whole matter, see *The International Labour Code 1951*, vol. I, pp. XCIX–CIV; and C. Wilfred Jenks, *The International Protection of Trade Union Freedom*, pp. 542–547, Stevens & Sons, London 1957.

[18] International Labour Conference, Forty-Seventh Session, Geneva, 1963, Report III (Part IV), *Report of the Committee of Experts on the Application of Conventions and Recommendations*, pp. 8–16.

[19] For a fuller account of the procedure and its operation, see Landy, op. cit.

[20] International Labour Conference, Forty-Sixth Session, Geneva, 1962, Report III (Part IV), *Report of the Committee of Experts on the Application of Conventions and Recommendations*, pp. 191–245; reports were received in respect of 168 countries, 94 member States and 74 non-metropolitan territories.

[21] International Labour Conference, Forty-Third Session, Geneva, 1959, Report III (Part IV), *Report of the Committee of Experts on the Application of Conventions and Recommendations*, pp. 101–137; reports were received in respect of 160 different countries, 74 member States and 86 non-metropolitan territories.

[22] International Labour Conference, Forty-Second Session, Geneva, 1963, Report III (Part IV), *Report of the Committee of Experts concerning the Application of Conventions and Recommendations*, pp. 171–262; reports were received in respect of 138 countries, 90 member States and 48 non-metropolitan territories.

[23] International Labour Conference, Thirty-Ninth Session, Geneva, 1956, Report III (Part IV), *Report of the Committee of Experts on the Application of Conventions and Recommendations*, pp. 148–156; reports were furnished by 46 governments.

[24] 1961; 56 member States.

[25] 1967; 123 countries, 93 member States and 30 non-metropolitan territories.

[26] 1964; 147 countries, 90 member States and 57 non-metropolitan territories.

[27] 1964; 150 countries, 92 member States and 58 non-metropolitan territories.

[28] 1965; 135 countries, 93 member States and 42 non-metropolitan territories.

[29] 1960; over 100 countries, the number varying for different Conventions and Recommendations.

[30] *The International Labour Code 1951*, vol. I, pp. 761–762.

[31] International Labour Office, *Official Bulletin*, vol. XXI, No. 1, April 15, 1936, pp. 16–19; vol. XXII, No. 2, July 15, 1937, pp. 61–69; and vol. XXIII, No. 2, June 30, 1938, pp. 60–61; and *The International Labour Code 1951*, vol. I, pp. 687–689.

[32] International Labour Office, *Official Bulletin*, vol. L, No. 2, April 1967, pp. 267–278.

[33] International Labour Office, *Official Bulletin*, vol. XX, No. 1, April 30, 1935, p. 15.

[34] International Labour Office, *Official Bulletin*, vol. XLV, No. 2, April 1962, Supplement II.

[35] International Labour Conference, Fiftieth Session, Geneva, 1966, Report III (Part IV), *Report of the Committee of Experts on the Application of Conventions and Recommendations*, Appendix.

[36] International Labour Office, *Official Bulletin*, vol. XLVI, No. 2, April 1963, Supplement II.

[37] International Labour Conference, Fiftieth Session, Geneva, 1966, Report III (Part IV), *Report of the Committee of Experts on the Application of Conventions and Recommendations*, pp. 59–61.

[38] United Nations and International Labour Office, *Report of the Ad Hoc Committee on Forced Labour* (1953).

[39] International Labour Office, *Official Bulletin*, vol. XLII, 1959, No. 6, pp. 236–346.

[40] For a fuller account, see C. Wilfred Jenks, *The International Protection of Trade Union Freedom*, Stevens & Sons, London, 1957, and for more recent developments

Jenks, The International Protection of Trade Union Rights, *The International Protection of Human Rights* (ed. Evan Luard), pp. 210–246, Thames & Hudson, London 1967.

[41] International Labour Office, *Official Bulletin*, vol. XLIX, No. 1, Special Supplement, January 1966.

[42] See also as regards Greece, International Labour Office, *Official Bulletin*, vol. XLIX, No. 4, Supplement No. 1, July 1966.

[43] International Labour Office, *Official Bulletin*, vol. XXXIX, 1956, No 9.

[44] C. Wilfred Jenks, *Human Rights and International Labour Standards*, pp. 85–86, Stevens & Sons, London 1960.

[45] See, for instance, International Labour Office, *Minutes of the 159th Session of the Governing Body* (1964), pp. 128–130, "Future Programme of the I.L.O. in the Field of Discrimination".

[46] International Labour Office, *Apartheid in Labour Matters: I.L.O. Statements and Reports concerning Apartheid in Labour Matters in the Republic of South Africa, 1964–1966*, Geneva, 1966; International Labour Office, *Third Special Report of the Director-General on the Application of the Declaration concerning the Policy of Apartheid of the Republic of South Africa*, Geneva, 1967.

[47] 1932, P.C.I.J. Series A/B, No. 50, pp. 365–390.

[48] 1922, P.C.I.J. Series B, Nos. 2 and 3.

[49] 1922, P.C.I.J. Series B, Nos. 2 and 3.

[50] 1926, P.C.I.J. Series B, No. 13.

[51] International Labour Office, *Official Bulletin*, vol. XXXVII, No. 7, December 31, 1954, pp. 229–231.

[52] Egon Schwelb, *Human Rights and the International Community*. Quadrangle Books, Chicago, 1964.

[53] I have attempted to analyse their importance and limitations more fully in C. Wilfred Jenks, The United Nations Covenants Come to Life, *Recueil d'Etudes de Droit International en hommage à Paul Guggenheim*, 1968, pp. 765–773.

[54] I have discussed the desirability of such a series of Conventions more fully in *Law in the World Community*, pp. 28–29, Longmans, 1967.

[55] pp. 10–12 above.

[56] See A. H. Robertson, *Human Rights in Europe*, Manchester U.P., 1963; the original provisions of the European Social Charter are described in The European Social Charter and International Labour Standards. *International Labour Review*, vol. LXXXIV, Nos. 5–6, November–December 1961.

[57] Inter-American Institute of International Legal Studies, *The Inter-American System: Its Development and Strengthening*, pp. 39–68, Oceana Publications, New York, 1966.

[58] Gaius Ezejiofor, *Protection of Human Rights under the Law*, pp. 146–147, Butterworths, London, 1964.

[59] For a critical discussion of these approaches, see Sir Samuel Hoare, The U.N. Commission on Human Rights, *The International Protection of Human Rights* (ed. Evan Luard), pp. 79–88, Thames & Hudson, London, 1967.

[60] pp. 6–33 above.

[61] I have attempted to discuss somewhat more fully this acquired and, at times, subtle wisdom in The International Protection of Trade Union Rights, *The International Protection of Human Rights* (ed. Evan Luard), pp. 235–246, Thames & Hudson, London, 1967.

[62] *Essential Human Rights*, The Annals of the American Academy of Political and Social Science, vol. 243, January 1946.

[63] International Labour Office, *The International Labour Code 1951*, and for the more recent texts, *Conventions and Recommendations 1919–1966*.

[64] On the whole matter, see C. Wilfred Jenks, *Human Rights and International Labour Standards*, Stevens & Sons, London, 1960; and especially "The *Corpus Juris* of Social Justice" in *Law, Freedom and Welfare*, pp. 101–136, Stevens & Sons, London, 1963.

[65] Art. 24.

[66] Cf. C. Wilfred Jenks, *The International Protection of Trade Union Freedom*, pp. 485–486, Stevens & Sons, London, 1957.

[67] See, for instance, as regards freedom of association C. Wilfred Jenks, *The International Protection of Trade Union Freedom*, pp. 235–476, Stevens & Sons, London, 1957.

[68] pp. 21–29 above.

[69] Reports relating to the periods 1954–56, 1957–59, 1960–62, and 1963–66, published respectively as documents E/CN.4/758/Add. 1, E/CN.4/811/Add. 1, E/CN.4/861/Add. 1 and E/CN.4/918/Add. 1.

[70] See, for example, documents E/CN.4/Sub.2/257 (1965), E/CN.4/Sub.2/272 (1966), and E/CN.4/Sub.2/284 (1967).

[71] United Nations Seminar on Human Rights in Developing Countries, Kabul, 12–25 May 1964, Background Paper C, prepared by the International Labour Office; and, United Nations Seminar on Human Rights in Developing Countries, Dakar, February 8–22, 1966, Background Paper D, prepared by the International Labour Office (SO216/3(7) AFR 1966).

[72] United Nations Seminar on the Realisation of Economic and Social Rights contained in the Universal Declaration of Human Rights, Warsaw, August 15–28, 1967, Paper I, prepared by the International Labour Office (SO216/3(12) EUR 1967).

[73] United Nations Seminar on *Apartheid,* Brasilia, August 23 – September 4, 1966, Paper I—"The I.L.O. and Apartheid", prepared by the International Labour Office (SO216/3(11) LA 1966).

[74] See, for instance, Commission on the Status of Women, 20th Session (1967). I.L.O. Standards relating to Women's Employment: Report of the International Labour Office, chapter I, paragraphs 4–9, E/CN.6/465.

[75] See, for instance, Commission on the Status of Women, Equal Pay for Equal Work: Progress Report of the International Labour Office, E/CN.6/468.

Discussion

I. *The foundations of human rights*

On the basis of the papers by Castberg and Szabó a number of interventions were made concerning the foundations of human rights and the transformation of the factors underlying these rights into positive law. In the debate, the following aspects were mentioned: The geographical origins of the natural law conceptions, the degree of immutability of these conceptions, the relationship between social and economic factors on the one hand and ethical factors on the other, and the process of transformation of such factors into positive law.

1. *Adegbite* gave a number of examples to show that human rights conceptions with various contents were held far back in African civilization, and he therefore rejected the belief that human rights had a basically European origin.

Scheuner supported him on this point. Conceptions of human rights could be found in most civilizations. He referred in particular to Muslim legal doctrine, where some basic ideas had been prominent which expressed the desire to guarantee human rights, ideas which had influenced the application of Muslim law. Sometimes the same ideas were expressed in different terms in different civilizations. During the preparation of the Universal Declaration of Human Rights, a Chinese delegate had referred to the protection of human rights as a question of good manners. Thus one could see how such conceptions, though differently formulated, could be found throughout the world.

In reply, *Castberg* agreed that such ideas were held far beyond the European civilization. In this context, he referred to a decision by the Hague Academy to invite a number of scholars from different Asian cultures to lecture at the Academy on fundamental principles of law in their respective cultures. From the lectures so far given, his impression had been strengthened that there was a wide consensus between representatives of different cultures on the basic human rights.

2. *Scheuner* pointed to the reference made by Castberg to the thinking of Thomas Aquinas, particularly on the right to revolt against a tyrant. Similar ideas could be found also in the writings of others. It was possible to find some general principles which are considered immutable. On the

other hand, the emphasis changes from time to time, like a beam of light at night now illuminating one area, now another. For instance, nobody today would subscribe to the idea, expressly formulated in the French Declaration of 1789, that private property was inviolable. Recent developments show far less emphasis on this aspect.

Schreiber was in some doubt concerning the concept of immutability of human rights. Though some of them might be eternal, the same accent was not placed on all of them all of the time. There were presently some new ones coming to our mind which it was important to define and give the proper priority and weight. That was a major purpose of the International Year of Human Rights of 1968 and of the great number of confrontations which it was hoped were going to take place then.

As an example, he pointed out that the rapid development of modern techniques made it necessary to protect the individuals of our time against new factors, which represented dangers to man's integrity and dignity. Some recent studies had been made in the United States and in Europe on these problems. A Nordic meeting had focussed on the respect for the right of privacy, which was becoming particularly significant in our time— partly as a consequence of the development of modern technology. The problem of economic underdevelopment of large areas of the world to which our generation had become aware—thought it had existed for a very long time—did also establish certain priorities in our thinking. And what about the protests against abusive use of force and violence? He was ready to accept that human right were immutable, but he also believed that we should scrutinize from time to time what was particularly important in each epoch to study, to codify and to implement.

In this context, he also quoted the following excerpts from an address by Dag Hammarskjöld held in 1956 in the state of Virginia, at the commemoration of the Virginia Declaration of Human Rights.

"Some days ago I returned from an assignment in the Middle East. I had to negotiate questions connected with the implementation of the armistice agreement between Israel and her Arab neighbour states. In the first articles, those armistice agreements establish the right of each party "to security from fear of attacks". In a political atmosphere of the utmost significance this clause recognizes a human right which in a broad sense may be said to sum up the whole philosophy of human rights. What is the right to security? Is it not the right to the free development of individual and national life within the limits set by the rights of the other parties to the same securities?
What is the right to freedom from attack? Is it not the right to freedom from fear? Thus we see how close the links are between the philosophy reflected in the recognition of the rights of the individuals and the basic principles

which may decide the issue of war and peace. We all know how, when moved by fear, people may act against what others see as their own best interests. We know how, when people are afraid, they may even act against their own fundamental will. We have seen how, when influenced by such actions, the course of events may take on aspects of inexorable fatality up to the point where out of sheer weariness resistance to the gravitation towards open conflict no longer seems possible. This is a constantly repeated pattern of tragedy. Why is war and the fear of war in the headlines of every day's papers? Is it not because man fears man or nations fear nations? Could there be a more eloquent sign of how far we are from the recognition of the philosophy behind the principles of the human rights on which alone peace can be built? Can there be a greater challenge for us to work for such a recognition for the dignity of man and to eliminate that fear?"

Castberg agreed with these views. His task had been to sketch the historical development of the natural law thinking on human rights, but it had not been his intention to present the view that these rights were eternal or immutable. Some of them might possibly be so, but for many others their contents depended on the conditions and opinions prevailing in the given society at the given time. For instance, the principle of democracy was fundamental to present natural law conceptions of human rights. Nevertheless, it could not be considered as eternal and immutable in its more specific contents, since many states confronted great difficulties in their efforts to practice democracy. Thus, the contents of some norms are probably eternal and immutable, but the contents of others vary with time and social conditions.

3. *Capotorti,* referring to the paper presented by Szabó, accepted the view that economic and social conditions of a given society were of fundamental importance for the laws of that society. In his opinion, however, there were also other factors working rather independently of these and which also had great influence on the degree of protection of human rights. Among these, ethical attitudes and ideas play a prominent role. These ethical ideas had been developed through philosophical conceptions which only to a limited extent could be ascribed to social and economic conditions.

Szabó agreed that other factors were also operating. He was of the opinion, however, that the foundations of all those others were property relationships and other economic factors.

4. Concerning the relationship between the underlying factors and the contents of positive law, *Capotorti* underlined the fact that this was never an automatic one, but a more or less deliberate process where political forces were the agents. Therefore, the aims and conceptions of these political forces

were of great importance for the legal protection of human rights. Since the human rights protection was basically a question of the relationship between the state organs and the individuals, the conceptions held by the dominant political forces of the state and its role achieved great significance. To illustrate, he mentioned that when political forces with Nazist ideology controlled the state organs, the degree of protection of human rights was by necessity low.

Elaborating on the point that the question of human rights was, in the final analysis, the problem of the relationship between these individuals and the authorities, he referred to the example mentioned by Castberg that Catholic thinking had at an early stage accepted, within some limits, the right to revolt against authorities which were abusing their powers. This could be seen as the origin of the concept of human rights as a limitation of the power of the authorities. At that time and in the subsequent development of the human rights philosophy, the emphasis had been on the freedoms and rights of the individual, and this philosophy therefore gave expression to civil and political rights only. These rights defined, primarily, what the state organs were *not* entitled to do in relation to the individual. In more recent times, however, there had been a growing awareness that it was also necessary to place duties on the state as to what it *should* do to enable all its subjects to enjoy fully their rights. Such duties were the basis of what were called economic, social, and cultural rights.

The relationship between the state and its individuals had first of all to be defined by the state itself, through positive law. The conception of state and law had been realised through norms limiting the activities of the state by the positive law inside the states themselves. Positive law served as a necessary link between the underlying factors—economic and social as well as ethical—and actual protection. In legal application of human rights, one could not refer directly to natural law, but only to established, positive norms. The protection was achieved through certain guarantees in the constitutional framework and in the legislation.

It was insufficient, however, to give the states complete discretion in defining its relationship to the individuals. The human rights protection of states had sometimes been more formal than real, and its content had not always conformed to international standards. For this reason it was necessary to achieve *international* rules and guarantees, again on the level of positive law, in order to create a measure to which the states had to conform in their relationship to the individual.

Scheuner said that though ethical conceptions were widely held and formed the content of natural law, they could not as such be directly applied in practical jurisprudence except in special circumstances. Normal, positive law had to be the source on which legal decisions drew. Only when the norms of positive law became violations of general principles could these be cited immediately. In all other cases, only normal law as it was shaped into positive law could be cited by the judicial organs.

Bystrický referred to the view presented by Castberg that human rights could be listed among so-called suprapositivist principles. In his own opinion, human rights were historical rights in the same way as other rights. Their contents were determined by the conditions of life of the people, and by certain social circumstances.

But having said this, he did not deny that in the general development of human society at all times in history, there were human rights and liberties which were and should be common for the whole human community. Therefore, there were some universal principles of human rights, but it was more correct to speak of universal, fundamental principles of positive international law than of supra-positive principles. To the point made by Castberg that in Germany some war criminals had been punished not on the basis of positive law but on the basis of natural law, Bystrický claimed that their acts had been violations of positive international law existing at the time when they were committed.

5. On the basis of the presentation by Szabó, some discussion took place on the distinction between human rights and citizens' rights. In his presentation, Szabó had declared i.a.: "The Socialist concept will speak in a uniform manner of citizens' rights, because it considers every positive right as being created by the state." Some had got the impression that in the Socialist doctrine, human rights protection extended only to citizens of the state in question.

MacBride thought that this was a problem of semantics and doubted that in Eastern Europe the view was held that only citizens could enjoy human rights. In Western Europe, he claimed, the European Convention applied to all irrespective of citizenship.

Scheuner said that it was necessary to be clear on this point. It was not correct to say that all human rights must belong to all human beings. For some of the essential human rights it would be true, e.g. in relation to life and liberty. In relation to other rights, even the international instruments permitted discrimination in favour of the citizens. In the European Convention it was made possible to reserve certain rights for citizens, such as the right of assembly and of association. In the field of economic and social rights the same applied — e.g. the right of admission to certain professions are guaranteed only for citizens. This was not a limitation of human rights, but an expression of economic and social factors. On this point, he agreed with Szabó. No state was prepared to give access to all professions to everybody, including aliens. It was an important aspect of the European Community that efforts were made to open almost all professions to citizens of at least the six states members of the Community. But in positive law the distinction between citizens and aliens was still important.

Szabó pointed out that he had a different question in mind than the one raised in the discussion. He wanted to emphasize, however, that Socialist countries *did* recognise the rights also of aliens, and agreed with the view presented by Scheuner.

The idea he (Szabó) had wanted to present was this: that from the point of view of internal law, the rights of man were claims, and the positive laws were the realisation of these claims or exigencies. On the level of international law, human rights were partly claims and partly positive international law—and the latter were, in turn, claims directed at the states and for these to materialise through positive law. The Hungarian constitution accepted the citizens' rights, and with a paragraph added to the effect that the same rights were recognized in relation to aliens who were living permanently in Hungary, except in regard to elections. Thus, the concept of "citizens' rights" may include aliens as well as nationals of the state in question.

6. Referring to the various views presented in regard to the foundations of human rights, *Cassin* pointed out that in the preparation of the Universal Declaration, no one particular doctrine had prevailed. The efforts would have been in vain if everybody had wanted to have his respective doctrine succeed. The Declaration carried the traces of the transactions and compromises which the delegations had accepted. It had for instance been proposed to use the word "natural" in Art. 1, but there had been opposition to this, and the question had therefore been dropped. Some had argued that the human being had a divine origin and wanted a formulation to this effect introduced into the Declaration. Everybody knew that if this had been persisted in, no declaration would have been adopted. In connection with Art. 22, two lines of thought had been clearly discernible—one conceiving human rights as being the inalienable prerogative of all human beings, the other conceiving them as rights of members of society (citizens' rights). After difficult negotiations, a synthesis had been arrived at. This had also demonstrated that the Universal Declaration was based on genuine aspirations. Originally, it had been conceived as a protection against the Hitlerite barbarism, but in the end it became the expression of universal aspirations for the future. The success was assured because, while no author was neglected, on the other hand, no particular point of view was preferred.

II. *Purposes behind the efforts to protect human rights. The relationship between human rights and war and peace problems*

In various connections, the participants discussed the purposes underlying the efforts to create a more universal and effective protection of human rights. The following aspects were brought into the discussion: The role of human rights in the efforts to maintain and strengthen peace, and the place of human rights in armed conflicts.

1. *Schreiber,* commenting upon the remarks made by Schou at the opening of the Symposium, drew attention to the reference made to our divided world—divided politically, religiously, racially, by tradition, by philosophy and in other ways. Recently much thought had been given in the United Nations to the general impact of the work of the organisation in the field of human rights, not only as regards the effectiveness of the protection of these rights everywhere, but also in relation to the achievement of the other purposes of the organisation, for the maintenance of peace and security or for the economic and social development of the world. In the first article of the Preamble to the Universal Declaration, later reproduced in the Covenants, the conviction was expressed that the recognition of the inherent dignity and of the equal and inalienable rights of all members of the human family was the foundation not only of freedom and of justice but also of peace. The whole experience of the last twenty years strongly confirmed that assertion. In this light, the standard-setting activities of the United Nations and of the most important of the specialized agencies mostly concerned took on a special significance. This was indeed a divided world, and not only by political doctrines. There were other divisions, perhaps going deeper. The world was divided according to the degree of economic development of the various peoples, and divided according to ethnic origins and race. The danger was there that the division was parallel between these two factors, the division according to economic development and according to the colour of the skin. In the United Nations many, including Schreiber, felt that what was important was to build bridges to create common aspirations and common objectives for action so that the aims of all who inhabited one world should have as much as possible in common. Therefore, the unanimous adoption in 1966 of the International Covenants on Human Rights by the vote of 106 and then 107 Members of the United Nations without a negative vote, without abstentions, was of tremendous importance. In the Introduction to his Annual Report to the General Assembly, the Secretary-General, U Thant, had stressed that point, saying among other things:

A gradual development is taking place within the United Nations of a common philosophy regarding the right of every individual, without distinction as to race, sex, language or religion, to secure respect for his dignity as a human being whether in the political and civil, or the economic, social and cultural fields.

Schreiber regarded this as an essential factor in the progressive attainment of the Charter goals of universal peace as well as of peaceful economic and social cooperation and development.

Bystrický held that the theoretical foundation of *international* protection of human rights was to be found in the close, inextricable links between peace and security, on the one hand, and the enjoyment of human rights, on the other. In this he was supported by *MacBride,* who claimed that the sources of international conflicts in our days stemmed less from questions of boundaries or from economic domination than from differences in political philosophies, largely based on differences of opinion on human liberties. To reduce these differences would be essential for world understanding and peace in the future.

Jenks stressed that all participants shared the opinion that full respect for human rights was an essential prerequisite for peace and could make a major contribution to peace. Since we live in a divided world, the contribution that human rights could make to peace depended on the extent to which they bridged gaps instead of creating gulfs in the respective attitudes towards the problem confronting us: the further promotion of human rights.

Andenæs had some doubts on this point. It had been presented as an undeniable fact that the protection of human rights was a good thing for peace—that it was a prerequisite for peace. This was such a sympathetic proposition that he felt uneasy to doubt it. But he had some difficulties in accepting it flatly without elaborating it a bit more. In his opinion there were at least two questions which should be kept apart. *One* was the promotion of civil rights inside each individual state. That this would be beneficial for peace was obvious, he felt. Thus, if every country could do away with all kinds of racial prejudice, that would greatly enhance the prospects of peace.

But it was *another* question whether *international* protection of human rights had a positive value for peace. If by international protection we were thinking of some kind of interference from outside, interference into the treatment of citizens of the different countries, it seemed to him *prima facie* that under certain circumstances such protection might increase international tension. It was possible that the prevalent attude, which was to leave to each country to do what it liked inside its own territory, might be better for peace.

If his doubts were justified on this point, that did not mean that the international protection of human rights was undesirable, but such protection would have to be based on another aspect—another foundation than the promotion of world peace.

2. *MacBride* had raised in his paper the problem of the place of human rights protection in armed conflict. This caused some interventions where highly different opinions were displayed.

Bystrický thought that to speak of protection of human rights in armed conflicts was a *contradictio in adjectio*. War was a negation of human rights. If there existed a right to kill and to destroy, it was very difficult to speak of human rights. *Inter arma silent leges*. Granted, there were some rules regulating conduct of war, some *"jus in bello"*, but that was something else.

Pinto expressed his disagreement with this view. The Geneva Agreements were part and parcel of the human rights protection, since the states now have given up their former freedom to wage war and have outlawed offensive use of force. The Geneva Conventions can be compared partly to the rule governing the conduct of the police internally and also to those rules of the criminal code making it a further offence for a violator to use certain means. It was important to maintain the Geneva Conventions in the human rights protection, and machinery for its enforcement existed and should be used. The International Red Cross as well as governments and non-governmental organisations should try to obtain enforcement of the Conventions. He had some years ago asked the International Commission of Jurists to look into the way the Vietnamese war was being fought, and the answer he got was—strangely enough—the same Latin sentence as that cited by Bystrický, *"Inter arma silent leges"*. Over the last years, however, a revolution had taken place in the thinking on this question. It was no more regarded as outside the competence of the Internation Commission of Jurists to see to it that human rights are protected in time of international and civil wars.

III. *The universality of human rights and the widening agreement on their contents*

On the basis of the papers by Adegbite and Bystrický, some discussion took place concerning the universality of human rights and the prospects for reaching a higher degree of agreement on their contents. The discussion centered on the different emphasis in different parts of the world on social, economic, and cultural rights, on the one hand, and civil and political rights, on the other, the interrelationship between these two categories, and the trends towards more comprehensive conceptions of human rights in all parts of the world.

1. *Jenks* thought it desirable, for the purpose of paving the way for more effective practical measures in the future, to achieve a fuller understanding of the respective approaches to the topic, and more particularly to avoid using a language so general that it could be used in different senses. There were, in his opinion, some superstitions which tended to emerge in the course of discussions of the human rights problems, and some of these superstitions had even been voiced in the Symposium. Among these superstitions was the belief that economic, social, and cultural rights, on the one hand, and civil and political rights, on the other, had so different origins that they represented the contribution to the universal protection of human rights of wholly different economic and social philosophies. In this context it had frequently been claimed that civil and political rights had originated in the Western world, while economic, social, and cultural rights had emerged particularly in the Socialist countries. This belief, he maintained, was simply not in accordance with facts.

Asking from where the economic and social rights originated and reached their present prominence in international discussions, he argued that the answer was that they were not formulated in any one quarter. They gradually came to acquire acceptance in the 19th century and increasingly so in the 20th. Karl Marx had made an important contribution to the discussion and many Marxists believed that he made the *only* important contribution. But there were also others, such as Proudhon and Robert Owen. When taking a look at the evolution of the idea during the century that followed, we could see currents that ultimately flowed together to create a large tide. In the English-speaking world a whole series of social thinkers could have been mentioned, from William Morris down to Sir William Beveridge. In the United States, some of the most important contributions to the status which economic social rights acquired had been given by outstanding judges of the Supreme Court, in the tradition of Holmes and Cardozo.

This very diverse body of social thought began to find expression in constitutions long before any attempt were made at formulating it in detail in international documents. This constitutional incorporation of economic and social rights started first in Mexico, and almost the whole intellectual background to the far-reaching references in Latin-American constitutions stem from the Mexican Constitution of 1917. Shortly thereafter, the Weimar Constitution of Germany included a very large proportion of the provisions relating to economic and social rights which appeared in the Western countries in the course of the inter-war period. And about the same time first in the Socialist Federal Republic and then in the Union of Soviet Socialist Republics, where, however, the rights in the form of *legal* rights as different from political manifestos did not find clear expressions until the constitution in 1936. All these tendencies had little effect on the English-speaking world until the Irish Government from 1922 took a close interest in these experiments, an interest which did not materialise into constitutional provisions until the adoption of the Irish Constitution in 1937. That proved to be an imporant departure, however, since that constitution influenced i.a. the Indian Constitution.

On the international scene, one of the most important initiatives was taken by the United States, in the speeches by President Roosevelt in 1941 of the "Four freedoms", in which the emphasis on the freedom from want was the unquestionable departure for the whole of the subsequent effort to write the economic and social rights into any post-war declaration of the rights of man. Jenks had a vivid recollection of the follow-up work, since the American Law Institute had invited him in 1942 to participate in the working-out of a detailed draft. This draft had been at the disposal of the Commission of Human Rights of the United Nations when it first set out to consider the framing of the Universal Declaration. It was the first draft in which there was some balance between the economic, social, and cultural rights, on the one hand, and the civil and political rights, on the other. The British draft, which had been worked out under the guidance of Lauterpacht, had for very good reasons of policy put the emphasis on civil liberty.

The fact that the initiative came from the United States was frequently overlooked, for very understandable reasons: It was a very controversial proposal on the United States political arena at that time, and in a country with complete freedom of speech and a legal profession which by and large was rather conservative, it was perhaps not unnatural that the volume of criticism subsequently voiced in the United States should have distracted the attention from the original initiative.

Szabó agreed that superstitions should be dispelled; in addition, he thought there was little point in discussing who was the initiator of these rights, whether it was Karl Marx or somebody else. In the French Constitution of 1848, the right to work was included, and one cannot accuse Marx of having been the author of that constitution. But Szabó wanted to underline three elements which he considered to be of importance in this context.

In the past, it had always been the socialist forces which had fought for the economic, social, and cultural rights, and this was only natural since these forces represented the working classes. The same socialist forces had been at work in Germany to include some economic and social rights, however weak, in the Weimar Constitution.

In U.S.S.R. it was not the Constitution of 1936 which entered the economic and social rights for the first time in the legal system of the state. It was the Constitutional Act of 1917 contained in the Proclamation to the Russian People. The Constitution of 1918, moreover, introduced economic and social rights. In the United Nations, it had been the Socialist countries which had insisted upon the introduction of social and economic rights in the human rights system of the world organisation.

2. The paper presented by *Adegbite* on African attitudes to the international protection of human rights caused some discussion on the role of civil and political rights in countries undergoing a revolutionary development. In his description of attitudes prevalent among African politicians, he had pointed out that many of these felt that civil and political rights should be protected only to the extent that this did not represent brakes on the economic and social development.

Schreiber had the impression that the attitude referred to by Adegbite was not so widely shared by present-day African political leaders. During the last several years, the African representatives had participated patiently and persistently in the negotiations which led to the drafting of the Covenants. It might well be that without their faith and insistence there would have been no covenants. The International Covenants on Human Rights were as much theirs as those of anybody else. They had the wisdom not to want to go back on many provisions which had been adopted before they became Members of the United Nations. They could have done so because of their voting strength, but they wanted to have the Covenants and they wanted to have them last year (1966). If the Covenants had not then been adopted one would have had to wait much longer or the Covenants might never have been adopted.

African spokesmen had sometimes presented their views along the following lines: That they had been forced to concentrate the efforts of their generation on obtaining independence—because without independence, in their opinion, no other rights nor the dignity of individuals was really conceivable. But since independence now had been achieved, they had gradually come to discover that they had a number of other problems to solve. In societies which came out of the colonial regimes, they had to find a balance between the rights of individuals and those of the rulers— and their rulers were of their own race now—but they were nevertheless rulers with their own pressing preoccupations. A certain equilibrium had to be found between the rights of the individual and those of his ethnic group and between the ethnic groups *inter se*. A new Africa had to be built, with a new structure of the society, and they were therefore very much interested in problems of contemporary rights. It was not something which they wanted to copy from others, though they were quite willing to accept from others the lessons of their experiences, but it was primarily something which they wanted to adapt to their own situation in the post-colonial era.

Schreiber added that it was difficult to accept the view that during revolutionary periods of national and economic development the protection of human rights should be considered a luxury which could not be afforded. History demonstrated that the great landmarks of human rights had been achieved precisely during revolutionary eras. In his opinion the practice of human rights was an element making the achievement of other aims more feasible. There was no inherent contradiction between revolutionary change and protection of human rights.

Cassin supported Schreiber on this point. One might deplore the long time which elapsed before the Covenants were adopted and the changes which were made, but the benefit of this was that the young states came to participate for ten years in the drafting of the Covenants and that hence the Covenants were theirs as much as anybody else's. If they had been adopted by the "old" states only, these young states might not have felt themselves so attached to the Covenants. Some African delegates played prominent roles in the drafting. It was unwise to persuade the Africans that they did not need the same protection of human rights as others did. Sometimes African leaders seemed to have stressed human rights before independence, but afterwards they had been arguing that because of their culture, the economic development and so on, a strong discipline was needed and that therefore the conditions did not allow for a rigid protection of human rights. Cassin thought that such a position should not be encouraged. It was necessary to emphasize that the citizens inside the new states had the same right as others to have full enjoyment of all human rights. This equality of all peoples throughout the world should be considered fundamental.

Jenks listed as one of the superstitions which should be discarded, the belief that if one has a social system which is regarded as satisfactory, the civil liberties can take care of themselves. This belief presupposed that if the state organs were dedicated to the welfare of their people, it was unnecessary to make any special provisions for the protection of civil liberties of the individual citizens. In his opinion, much of what had been said both in the present discussion and in the invaluable volume edited by Professor Szabó on Socialist conceptions of human rights, regarding present trends and difficulties in preventing personality cults, demonstrated the need for provisions within the society for the exercise of some of the classical civil rights if any long-term stability of the society should be achieved.

Adegbite answered these remarks by pointing out that the task he had set before himself was that of a reporter—to convey to the participants the attitudes taken in Africa, without by necessity subscribing to these. Regarding the plea of economic necessity which many of the African leaders put forward as a defence for not securing effective protection of civil and political human rights, he (Adegbite) himself did not consider this plea valid. In his opinion, the social and economic aims could not and should not override the civil and political rights. If human rights in the classical sense were enjoyed in good measure, economic and social progress would also take place. In his opinion, it was a *contradictio in adjectio* to speak of economic and social rights, it was more adequate to conceive of them as de- sires or aims. It should be made clear that they were lamp-post guides which governments should bear in mind in carrying out their civil policies. On the other hand, experience had shown that too much emphasis on political free- dom made one forget to advance the welfare of the totality of the commun- ity. He referred to the statement by Harold Laski that economic progress is essential and that freedom of speech has a limited value in a society which has not achieved material well-being for all its citizens, since those wanting to speak out might lose their jobs. In this context, it could be useful to heed some of the statements made by President Nyerere. The latter had stated that it is comparatively easy to build a nation of well-fed robots with no ideas of their own, and also a society where everyone can talk while starving. The aim should be something more pretentious—to work at all stages for economic and social progress of all members of the community while at the same time protecting also the civil and political rights. At present, however, it had to be accepted that in general terms the freedom for all to live a decent life must take priority—that means that economic develop- ment must be considered first.

In Adegbite's opinion, there was no antithesis between social and political freedoms. But many African leaders believed so, and one should not ignore their feelings.

3. The possibilities for bridging the gap between the conceptions and making human rights fully universal were the subject of a number of the interventions following *Bystrický's* presentation.

Cassin pointed out that the preparation of the Universal Declaration and the Covenants took the form of compromises between different ap- proaches and different doctrines. On the basis of the experience of the preparation, he would predict a considerable convergence in the field of human rights. This was due to the unity of mankind. This unity had been thought of by philosophers and others, but as long as the human society had consisted of states separated from each other and when there were also great gulfs inside the states, it had been impossible to arrive on the legal level at this unity of mankind. Now, however, after twenty years of work on human rights in the United Nations, the material unity of mankind had become a reality due to communication and technological change. This had also the result that the vast, former differences in legal systems and customs were gradually eradicated through a uniformation process. This development had been quickened after the independence of more than fifty new states.

These factors enhanced the unification and widening of the human society, and it might be that this would result in a synthesis, a new doctrine. In any case, he was convinced, on the basis of the experience of the past twenty years, that on the legal level we are marching towards an epoch where there is not only state law—though for practical reasons one must obviously for a long time to come have human rights primarily guaranteed by the states—but where there is also a universal law which will be growing in strength. As to the question of the implementation—as different from the substance—of this law, we are also witnessing the development of regional systems, and thus we will have a synthesis of national and regional law and, at the summit, universal law. Cassin was confident that before long, real progress would be made in this direction.

MacBride shared the opinion that there was a trend towards convergence in attitudes. Looking ten years back, it was not considered desirable in the Eastern European countries to discuss civil and political human rights. The greatest differences had been on the freedom of association and expression. In this field, considerable progress had taken place over the last years. Conversely, in Western Europe ten years ago, social and economic rights were not given much emphasis, but today nobody would deny that these rights form part of the fundamental human rights, and the opinion is now generally shared that there is little point in civil and political rights as long as the masses of the population are hungry. Thus, even though on the level of doctrine there may still be considerable disagreement, on the level of practical arrangements the consensus is already great and growing.

Schreiber referred to the remarks made by Szabó on the primary role ascribed by some to economic, social and cultural rights. There were undoubtedly reasons of doctrine and belief in the Socialist countries for establishing this kind of relationship. It was also true that a number of the new states had come to the United Nations—to the whole family of United Nations organizations—saying something like this: "Well, all that you propose on international standards in the field of human rights is very noble, but as long as we don't have schools and medical services, please don't press us about freedom of speech, freedom of expression, or the other freedoms." It was also true that in the United States, the whole concept of not very well defined economic, social and cultural rights was difficult to insert in the legal thinking. He believed, however, that this contrasting process was not resorted to so much anymore, and in any event he had not heard much of if in the United Nations for some time. He thought it was accepted by everybody that economic and social development was needed in order to have real civil and political rights respected and guaranteed. In that connection he wanted to recall a remarkable statement by the American member of the Commission of Human Rights. Speaking in the Commission in the spring of 1967, Mr. Abram had referred to the American approach to economic rights, to minimal health services and to the right to education and to work. He had said that there was a new understanding of the meaning of the economic and social policies in terms of the rights of a citizen. After all, the struggle against poverty in which the present United States administration was engaged, was a governmental policy and action to ensure the minimal economic, social and cultural rights. On the other side, there was also a greater understanding that economic or social development by itself had no deep meaning if it did not lead in fact to ensuring a greater degree of dignity to human beings. He thought this had been generally accepted by now and that this was what had led to the unanimous acceptance by countries from Western Europe, North America, as well as the countries of Africa, Asia, Latin America and Eastern Europe, of the very far-reaching principles and rules which were contained in the two Covenants.

IV. *The role of international customary law and international courts and tribunals in the protection of human rights*

Ensuing primarily from the paper presented by *Cheng,* a discussion took place on the role of international customary law and of courts and tribunals in the protection of human rights. The following points were in focus of the discussion: whether or not the Universal Declaration or part of it had aqcuired the character of international customary law, the scope of traditional international law in the protection of human rights, and the approach taken by and contribution given by international courts and tribunals to the protection of human rights.

1. *MacBride* referred to a view widely held among international lawyers,

to the effect that the Universal Declaration had by now become part of customary international law and thus was binding upon all states. Six arguments supported this view: *Firstly,* that the Declaration had been adopted by the large majority of the states, and that though there were some abstentions at the time of the adoption, these had been motivated by the view that the Declaration did not go far enough. These abstentions had been waived since then by implication because the Declaration had frequently been referred to in United Nations resolutions without abstentions. *Secondly,* because the Declaration to a large extent had been a restatement of established usages, laws of humanity, and dictates of the public conscience of the present century. *Thirdly,* because the Declaration had been adopted by implication by a number of international conventions throughout the world. *Fourthly,* because the Declaration had been included in a great many state constitutions in various parts of the world. *Fifthly,* since there had been a great number of references and utilisations of the Declaration in judicial decision-making. And *sixthly,* because the view that the Declaration had acquired the status of international customary law had now been accepted by a great many experts on international law. The Declaration, therefore, should be taken as the positive law starting point, and arguments as to the foundations of human rights were of little practical interest.

Capotorti declared his doubts on this point. In his opinion, the Declaration had neither been a restatement of the usages established, nor the laws of humanity or a reaffirmation of anything which already were in existence in the conscience of mankind. The Declaration should rather be considered a new fact, though clearly related to Articles 55 and 56 of the Charter— but these Articles were definitely new facts. Traditional customary law had not dealt with the human rights in general, it took care only of citizens of certain states from the point of view of diplomatic protection. The very idea of protecting man and his rights and dignity as a human being was one of the great new achievements of the Charter and the Declaration. Therefore, the continuity claimed to exist between the Declaration and the previous laws of mankind could not be established.

2. In his paper *Cheng* had discussed the role of international courts and tribunals under international customary law and had presented the view that their most important contribution had been the use of the standard of civilization. Though these had been applied by the courts only in dealing with the treatment of foreigners, the standard they had been applying had been a general one, that is the one which civilised states would apply to individuals in like circumstances.

Capotorti argued that in view of the fact that the scope of adjudication by international courts in the field of human rights had been limited to the treatment of foreigners, their practice could therefore not amount to the formation of any international customary law protecting human rights in general. It could not even be considered as an element for the formation of such customary law. To arrive at a customary law one must be able to deduce from the behaviour of states that they consider themselves obliged to treat their citizens in a certain way. On the basis of present behaviour, such a deduction could not be made.

Cheng answered that what he had wanted to say was that though these standards had been applied only to the treatment of foreigners, they were capable of being employed also concerning the relationship between the state and its citizens. In the South West Africa case it could thus have provided the means by which the International Court of Justice could have made a decision on the merits.

3. The relative role of international courts and international customary law formed the subject of an intervention by *Opsahl* following the paper presented by Cheng. Opsahl argued that the primary aim of international action should not be to have a machinery for condemning violations but rather to create conditions which would stimulate compliance with the conventions. The organs dealing with the protection of human rights should therefore act primarily as diplomats and only secondarily as judges, a pattern which he hoped would be followed also in the Greek case. In his opinion, and despite Professor Cheng's demonstration of the potentialities of the international courts and tribunals, their function should not be given too much emphasis, although the courts might affirm standards which could be used in this field. This function would be a supplementary and minor one, since the tendency was towards the relatively quick quasi-legislation rather than the painstaking and time-consuming development of case law.

Cheng warned against the concept of quasi-legislation. There was nothing more pernicious than the conception held in particular by some American lawyers on some "soft" law, which was not exactly binding. This conception should be sumarily dismissed as mere pseudo-law, it was nothing but a game of make-believe. The second category of watered-down law consisted of what could be called toothless conventions. He referred to the remark by Opsahl that international conventions could be good even without international jurisdiction. But this acceptance of half loaves could lead into impasses, they were crumbs which were not even worth gathering. Using the Genocide Convention as an illustration—if one took away the jurisdiction clause from that convention, the whole convention would be meaningless. That example would be bad to follow. Though international jurisdiction implies some weakening of state sovereignty, it was wise to be aware that one cannot protect human rights without making some sacrifices. And cheap law would be likely to drive away good law.

Opsahl stated that by quasi-legislation he had meant simply conventions, which were alternatives to customary law—and the most practical alternative. Cheng had himself stated that before the courts could play a larger role they had to have their jurisdiction extended. This could not be done by customary law—it would have to be done by conventions. Therefore, the role of courts would be dependent on a conventional basis and the substantive law which the courts should apply would then also more naturally be included in the conventions.

4. In connection with the problems of the role of international courts, some interventions were also made concerning the decision of the International Court of Justice in July 1966 in the *South West Africa Cases*. In his paper, *Adegbite* had pointed out that African states interpreted this decision as a European expression of support for South Africa even though the Court declined to pronounce on the merits of the case. *Petrén* argued that one should not read more into the judgment than what was already in it. The court had made its decision entirely on procedural matters, and the International Court of Justice did not by the decision accept *apartheid.* The same point was stressed by *Cheng.* Since the Court did not go into the merits of the case, one could not say that the Court rejected human rights under international customary law.

Bystrický supported the criticism made by Adegbite on the South West Africa Cases, and referring to what Petrén had said about the decision being made only on a procedural basis, he argued that procedure was very important because the substance of law lived in the form of procedure. If a court dealt during six years only with procedural questions, and rejected the claims on procedural aspects, this had to shake the confidence of the large masses of people. In this connection, there had been considerable discussion concerning the problem whether or not the international community was ripe to have legal organs to decide on political issues. The International Court of Justice was in his opinion a political organ, an organ of the United Nations, and one should not forget that in cases like that of South West Africa, the life of a large community inside a state was involved. Nor should one forget that there existed a Universal Declaration of Human Rights, and it seemed that after six years to concentrate on a procedural question meant that the political conscience was not ripe enough. He wanted to say, *bona fide,* that the judgment had not been criticised in Socialist countries to the same extent as in the Western world, since judges who had to judge in international affairs must be and should be not only lawyers but also statesmen, politicians: that was what one expected from them. Frankly, he would say that though he was a friend of international jurisdiction, and though he recognised the merits of the International Court of Justice for the progressive development of international law, the question was overestimated. It was important to have international jurisdiction, but it was not of primary importance. What had it to do with the problems of hungry people in South America, of Peru, of Chile, of Colombia, to give them a code when they did not have bread to eat?

V. *Sovereignty, domestic jurisdiction, and international protection of human rights*

Following the paper presented by *Marcović* an exchange of views took place concerning the limitations on international protection caused by the sovereignty of states as expressed in the concept of domestic jurisdiction.

MacBride claimed that in spite of considerable progress towards consensus between the Socialist and non-Socialist states in the field of human rights, fundamental differences seemed to remain regarding the concept of sovereignty and the place of the individual in international law. It seemed that the Socialist legal doctrine still did not accept the individual as subject of international law, though the traditional concept of international law as regulating only the relationship between states had been abandoned by the minority protection arrangements in the inter-war period and had been still further pushed aside by later developments, such as the European Convention on Human Rights. In his opinion, the non-flexible attitude of the legal doctrine in the Socialist countries in this connection was the outcome of excessive statism and of a rather outworn conception of sovereignty.

Bystrický did not consider the concept of sovereignty to be outworn, he thought it was very important also in present-day international law. He asked the participants to furnish him with a single example showing that sovereignty had been an obstacle to international cooperation. This had never happened, according to his opinion. On the contrary, obstacles to international cooperation could be formed by the oppression of the sovereignty of one state by another. Sovereignty as such was not outworn, it was an objective necessity. The ideal was to let everybody live his own life and at the same time to realise that there were also others who wanted to live their own lives. He was of the opinion that the idea that sovereignty was outworn was an idea for export—to small countries. No great power was prepared to renounce its sovereignty. If any of these did so, that might furnish an example which might make it sensible for others to follow suit. If anybody was capable of persuading President de Gaulle or Prime Minister Harold Wilson or President Lyndon B. Johnson or Prime Minister Kosygin that they should renounce the sovereignty of their respective states, then it could be a basis for discussion.

It did not represent a limitation on sovereignty to become a party to a treaty. To enter into international agreements was no (partial) renunciation of sovereignty, but simply an exercise of sovereignty. Only sovereign states had the capacity to enter into treaties. He was in favour of international jurisdiction, but the importance of it was overestimated. International jurisdiction could solve only a limited part of the problems of human rights. What was most important was to follow the guideline of the preamble of the Charter: to establish conditions under which justice and the respect for obligations could be preserved. Proper international protection of human rights consisted in the obligation of states to cooperate closely so that human rights could be protected not only within the boundaries of the state but on the universal level.

To maintain the importance of sovereignty did not mean to claim that any state was entitled to close itself into any kind of Chinese wall. The Charter made it an international obligation to cooperate, but sovereignty only meant that every state should be master on its own territory. Any narrow-minded nationalism was very far from his mind, and he did not think there were any important differences between his opinion and those of the other participants in the Symposium on this question.

Capotorti declared his agreement with the propositions made by Bystrický that the importance of state sovereignty would remain because it formed the basis for international agreements, and that to enter into international agreements did not imply a limitation of sovereignty. The real problem which had caused the discussion on limitations of sovereignty was whether states were willing to subordinate themselves to the authority of certain international organisations. There was a considerable difference concerning sovereignty between entering into traditional international agreemets, on one hand, and to accept the intervention by international organisations, on the other. This resulted partly from the fact that while the interpretation of "traditional" international agreements could be made by the parties themselves, the intervention from international organisations signified, first and foremost, a form of control. The claim by Bystrický that no great power had denounced any part of its sovereignty was therefore not fully acceptable: France was a member of the European Community, whose organs had considerable competence to intervene, and United Kingdom was applying for membership. Members of the Council of Europe had also accepted some limitation on their sovereignty by the fact that they had accepted intervention by the Commission of Human Rights. In particular, this was the case for those states which had accepted the system of petitions from individuals. Some limitation of sovereignty was also made by those states which had accepted the compulsory jurisdiction of the International Court of Justice. Thus the question was not whether the states had waived their sovereiginty or not—since all states are sovereign in the context of international law—but the problem was the extent of the limitations. States were willing to sign international agreements on human rights since these implied only a minor limitation of sovereignty, but they were considerably more reluctant when there was a question of intervention by international organisations in order to implement the agreement.

Sovereignty implied also some kind of equality between states, and it was in other words necessary to face the problem of *equal* limitations. To take one example: The competence of the United Nations to deal with the *apartheid* policies of South Africa was widely accepted because of the South African attitude to human rights. But one should not take completely different attitudes to the violations of human rights elsewhere. If one accepted the intervention of international organisations for the protection of human rights, one should accept it as a general principle. This did not mean that there could not be different degrees of intensity of intervention due to different degrees of gravity of the situations.

VI. *Self-determination and human rights*

In his paper, *Fawcett* had argued that the United Nations action in the field of self-determination had diverted the organisation from what he considered to be its proper task in the protection of human rights. This caused a number of interventions, partly dealing with the question whether and how self-determination should be classified as a human right, and partly whether it was reasonable to single it out for praticular treatment and criticism.

1. *Schreiber* referred to the concept of "directing principles" as different from "enforceable rights", borrowed by Fawcett in his presentation from the Constitution of India. There might be a considerable degree of legal subtlety in this distinction. But out of India and going around the world came also another concept, namely the principle that good government was no substitute for selfgovernment. This had now been accepted everywhere, except in the rather reduced parts of southern Africa. There were

applied only in regard to those states which were prepared to accept that procedure themselves—and to accept it in regard to the whole list of civil and political rights. Consequently, the states which would be entitled to raise any questions in Art. 1, would only be those which were themselves prepared to accept the same procedure in respect to the whole list of other articles of the Convention. That secured in practice a very real measure of reciprocity. It made it possible to institute a kind of cross-action which could include investigation of conditions of human rights also in countries which had instituted the proceedings.

Schwelb said that the adoption of the Declaration on the Granting of Independence to Colonial Countries and Peoples had given the United Nations human rights program a new impetus. It provides that all states, not only states administering dependent territories, shall observe faithfully and strictly the provisions of the Charter, the *Universal Declaration of Human Rights* and the anti-colonial Declaration itself. It was the basis for the establishment, in 1961, of the comprehensive machinery for its implementation. To recognize the tremendous precedent thus created, one did not have to approve of all the activities of the Committee of 24, particularly not, to give an example, what he considered a clear aberration of that Committee: that a population of 24,000 people (Gibraltar) should be placed under the jurisdiction of the only surviving fascist government of the inter-war period against the practically unanimous wish of its population. The struggle against apartheid and racial discrimination and segregation brought about fundamental changes in the tasks given to the United Nations Commission on Human Rights. In 1947, the Commission and the Economic and Social Council had ruled that the Commission on Human Rights had no power to take any action in regard to any complaints concerning human rights. This often criticized ruling remained in force for almost twenty years. In 1966 and 1967, in view of the necessity to try to act against racial discrimination, an inroad into this self-denying ordinance was made. Certain circumscribed powers to act on violations of human rights were given to the Commission. The General Assembly and the Economic and Social Council were careful to stipulate that these powers of the Commission, while primarily motivated by the situation in the South of the African Continent, shall be directed towards putting a stop to violations of human rights *wherever they may occur.*

Schreiber referred to the view taken by Fawcett that human rights were less important than ideologies in the United Nations. Schreiber did not follow him on this point. Firstly he believed in human rights as an ideology of itself, though there were other ideologies and preoccupations which took respect of human rights into consideration in varying degrees. He would hope that political expediency would not count for more than respect for human rights in the United Nations. Generally speaking it was probably true to say that the concern for human rights was on the increase in the United Nations. This had been frequently expressed, e.g. in the Middle East crisis. Referring to the criticism by Fawcett of the dealing of the United Nations with the South Arabia question, Schreiber thought that this was not very adequate. This had been a situation where the responsible governments had waited to the very last moment when a harmonious solution was very difficult to find before the matter was brought before the United Nations. On the argument that self-determination led to fragmentation he wanted to draw attention to some other factors. It was a problem not only for the United Nations but also for those governments which had administered the territories to see to it that the world did not become too much fragmented. The problem was there. The Secretary General had drawn attention to the microstate problem in his last annual report. Several very small territories, sparsely populated, might present, upon independence, special problems if they claimed membership in the United Nations. There would be certain possibilities for membership in the specialized agencies of the United Nations which could open the possibilities for the small states to benefit from United Nations technical assistance, or some other form of associate membership could be found.

VII. *The Covenants on human rights of December, 1966: The substantive law and the implementation*

Following the papers presented by *Schwelb* and *Capotorti,* a discussion took place which focussed mainly on the problems of implementation.

1. *Cassin* thought that the most important task ahead was to have the conventions ratified by as many states as possible at the earliest possible time. It was true that there were deficiencies in the system created by the United Nations, particularly with regard to implementation. A variety of systems had been created for the different conventions adopted by the United Nations itself and by UNESCO and ILO. Much money and efforts had been dispersed by this variety of approaches, and though efforts had been made to prevent it, these had not succeeded. Nevertheless, the best thing now would be to ratify the conventions, one after another. At a later stage one could try to unify the implementation systems, but today and looking at the years needed before the Covenants were adopted, the primary emphasis should be on ratification of the texts as they now stood. The participants of the Symposium should see it as their duty, whether they

were placed in education or in administration, to influence the political leaders to ratify.

Jenks was of the opinion that the whole future of the international protection of human rights depended on what now happened to the Covenants —firstly, on the extent of ratification, without many reservations, and secondly, the extent to which the Covenants, when ratified, were effectively applied. There were a number of difficulties which had to be overcome. Among these were the provisions of self-determination which to colonial or ex-colonial countries seemed to become something of a stumbling-block for ratification, though in his opinion this was a misplaced apprehension— these states would have very little to fear. A second problem was the reluctance of certain states, particularly the United States, which had considered human rights as being inappropriate for international treaty regulations. It was therefore important to bring influence to bear on these states to modify their views.

Schreiber also stressed the importance of the ratification of the international instruments on human rights by a sufficient number of states as soon as possible so that they could come into effect. The movement was relatively fast. The Convention on the Elimination of All Forms of Racial Discrimination adopted in 1965 had by now 16 ratifications. Eleven more were needed before that Convention could come into effect, and he hoped that next year, in the course of the International Year for Human Rights, the necessary ratifications would be obtained, and that the Committee envisaged in the Convention, this first new machinery in the field of human rights which the United Nations would create since the time immediately following the adoption of the Charter, would come into being.

One form of resistance came from countries which believed that it was not necessary to ratify these instruments, or not necessary to hurry, because in fact they felt that they already effectively guaranteed these rights on the national level. To that the Secretary-General in the Introduction to his Annual Report had said the following:

"Those countries which may believe that it is not necessary for them to become parties to these instruments, because they have already adequate guarantees of the rights proclaimed in the United Nations Conventions, should realize that their active preparation in this United Nations long-term effort is also an important part of the contribution to international solidarity and the efforts to attain the Charter objectives of peace, economic solidarity and the harmonization of the action of nations."

Declaring his agreement with Cassin and Schreiber, *Bystrický* said that the Covenants were landmarks in the international protection of human rights, that many new conceptions had got their legal expression there, such as self-determination, the prohibition of propaganda for the incitement of war, and some seven or eight very important economic, social and cultural rights. With all their faults, the Covenants were documents of the greatest importance, and he wanted to assure this colleagues that the scientific workers of the Eastern European countries would do their best to have the Covenants ratified.

2. Discussing the means to be used, *Fawcett* underlined the difference between compulsory and voluntary implementation. The procedures in the European Convention and also those contemplated in the Covenants were to some extent mixtures of both. Fundamental for implementation was, in his opinion, publicity, and this was a compulsory means. That this was so was due to the results of the Universal Declaration of Human Rights and the immense discussions which had gone into the preparation of the Covenants and many other influences in the last years which had made it very difficult for any government to defend either in the United Nations or in its own parliament conduct inconsistent with those declarations. It was of the utmost importance to know what was going on. In this connection he paid tribute to the press, to which the greatest debt was due for its incessant efforts to bring information in spite of enormous difficulties in many instances. Publicity was a real force which governments were not easily prepared to ignore.

He raised the question whether the reports under Art. 41 and 42 of the Covenants were to be published—the drafting seemed to be somewhat obscure in that regard. It might be a matter of interpretation. He thought it very important that these reports were published since this would strengthen implementation.

Schwelb said that it was difficult to give a definite answer to the question concerning the weapon of publicity as a means of implementation in relation to Art. 41 of the Covenant on Civil and Political Rights and to Art. 4 of the Optional Protocol. Neither of these were very clear on the subject. But there had been a very involved debate on this in the Third Committee. The provisions of Art. 45 providing for the Human Rights Committee to make an annual report to the General Assembly, and the provision in Art. 6 of the Optional Protocol that the Committee shall include in the annual reports referred to in Art. 45 a summary of its activities, did not preclude (to say the least) that the Committee include the giving of details of cases dealt with. The situation was therefore not very different from that under the European Convention, which expressly provides that the states are not free to publish the reports, a provision which has in fact been set aside in many cases. This was the outcome of the decision of the

Commission itself that when it considered the admissibility or non-admissibility of petitions it was exercising a judicial function and that consequently the decisions had to be made public. The Council of Ministers had in several cases authorised publications of reports of the Commission and the Court had amended its Rules of Court to allow for publication.

3. Various suggestions for improved means of implementation were put forward in the discussion, particularly as a response to the paper presented by *MacBride*. These suggestions which included the appointment of a High Commissioner for Human Rights and a more perfect system for individual petitions will be summarized under IX (below).

4. *Fawcett* expressed his surprise that the use of economic sanctions as a means of implementation had not been mentioned. The Rhodesia situation was basically a case of violation of human rights, and the measures taken by the Security Council could therefore be seen as efforts to enforce human rights. If it had been predicted fifteen years ago that states through their international organisations would resort to sanctions to enforce human rights, this would not have been believed. However, there were some comments to be made regarding these efforts.

Firstly, economic sanctions were the maximum pressure which could be used by the international society short of force. Looking at how sanctions were working in the Rhodesia situation, one was struck by the almost incredible economic interdependence in the world, and secondly by the lack of control by governments over private business inside their own country. This was a very good illustration of the weaknesses of sovereignty. In states where the government had more control over these elements, it might be easier to take the view (which Bystrický had taken) that sovereignty was not outworn. The weakness of the sanctions against Rhodesia was not due to lack of will but to lack of actual control by some Western governments over very intricate economic arrangements. Each country might impose barriers, but there were many ways of circumventing these.

Adegbite pointed out that most African states believed that the United Kingdom had chosen the economic sanctions approach because the government knew that it had no power to compel those of their citizens who traded with Rhodesia to abstain from doing so. He thought that if the United Kingdom had the will to do so, it would have the power to do what it had done in other African territories where the political leaders had defied the British government, i.e. to use military force. This was not done in Rhodesia. Was the reason that the use of force was by now taboo forever?

Fawcett agreed that economic sanctions were not effective, this was exactly what he had wanted to point out. The United Kingdom was not alone in not being very efficient in this regard; the Security Council had not established a commission for supervision of the sanctions. In the long report by experts presented in 1964 on the problems of economic sanctions against South Africa, the experts were unanimous in their insistence that sanctions would never work without a commission of supervision reporting regularly to the Security Council. This one step the Security Council had omitted in the Rhodesia resolution. Therefore, it was not very surprising that the sanctions against Rhodesia were working in a very piecemeal way.

VIII. *Regionalism and the protection of human rights*

The paper presented by *Pinto* was the starting-point for a very extensive discussion on the desirability of regional arrangements for the protection of human rights. Some of the participants argued that it was desirable to begin "at the grassroots", to take into account the fact that there are different political, social and economic systems which may make it more feasible to create operative systems on a regional basis rather than on a universal one, at least in the short run, and that some states were willing to go further than others and should be permitted to do so through the vehicles of regional organisations. Some claimed, on the other hand, that the further proliferation of regional arrangements would imply a fragmentation of the world, that it would slow down the progress achieved by the United Nations in this field and make ratification of the Covenants less likely. It was also argued that political conditions inside a region might make effective protection of human rights less feasible there than in the universal forum, i.e. the United Nations.

1. *Wold* stressed the importance of beginning at the grassroots. The experience of one area of region, as positivised in human rights law, could not easily be generalised and transplanted to other parts of the world. The conventions had to be the creations of the regions themselves. He did not deny the importance of the United Nations efforts in this field. But if it had taken twenty years to agree on the Covenants, how many more years would be needed for the implementation of these? The European Convention, though far from perfect, was in operation, but great difficulties still had to be overcome. How, then, could it be hoped that a universal convention should be effectively operated? It was necessary to start on the regional level because the rights could not be separated from their practical implementation. Only on the regional level was it possible to obtain precise agreements. In the European Convention, precise definitions had been

agreed upon. This was possible because the level of development, political as well as social and cultural, was fairly similar within the region. Since the development was very different in different parts of the world, the human rights had by necessity to have different contents. When Norway became an independent democratic state 150 years ago, its democracy was very poorly developed, but now, 150 years later, it has gained considerably in richness.

Petrén shared the opinion of Wold on this point. There was already in existence one regional system which worked; one could not exclude the possibility that other systems could be developed that might also work. The European Convention did not give less than the Covenants. There might be problems because there were different formulations and different machineries for implementation (where such machineries existed at all). The case law of the different organs might lead to discrepancies in the substance of the law. Thus, there might be different jurisprudence in the different regions, and there might be difficulties concerning jurisdiction. Solutions would have to be found to these problems, which should not be seen as obstacles to the development of regional arrangements for the protection of human rights.

Castberg said that there were and would always be some states which were willing to go further than others in the protection of human rights, and they should have the opportunity to make arrangements between themselves such as had been done within the framework of the Council of Europe. He referred in particular to the system of individual petitions which had been accepted by some of the states in the Council of Europe—that such an option was open for those states which wanted to avail themselves of it, could only be useful.

Adegbite did not think that there was any serious danger in proliferation of regional systems for the protection of human rights. Even bilateral arrangements would be good, because so much denial of human rights was taking place that all efforts to protect them should be welcomed, though there should always be a link with the United Nations machinery. He expressed some criticism of the European system, however, which he thought to be excessively regional. It would, in his opinion, have been more fruitful and have encouraged better understanding if any state anywhere in the world could become associated with the European arrangement, in the same way as association was possible for outside states to the European Common Market. It would not do much harm to allow for such association, though it was far from obvious that e.g. African states would avail themselves of the possibility.

He also pointed to the fact that states members of the Council of Europe were entitled to extend the protection also to their overseas territories and that some had done so, but when these territories had become independent they had fallen out of the protection.

2. *Schwelb* was very much opposed to proposals which had been made, among others, by the International Commission of Jurists for new regional human rights conventions and commissions and, additionally, also separate machinery and separate instruments for "sub-regions". The Commission had assisted in the project of drafting a private proposal for a Central American Court of Human Rights and a Central American Commission, which would be additional to the contemplated Inter-American Convention on Human Rights and the United Nations Covenants.

If these efforts were successful, they would create a nightmarish situation of overlapping procedures and institutions and inconsistent provisions of substantive law. Years of procedural disputes would have to elapse to establish where a certain complaint should go and which rules of substantive law should govern it. Taking a case relating to Guatemala as a hypothetical example, he pointed out that it might become a choice between three different systems of substantive and adjective law — the Central American, the Inter-American and that of the United Nations. He was an admirer of the system created by the European Convention on Human Rights and had said so repeatedly before, but he was strongly opposed to creating new regional machineries and to the fragmentation of the international effort to protect human rights and fundamental freedoms for all. Every effort should now concentrate on achieving the ratification of the Covenants of December 1966. This would be made much more difficult if, at the same time, international and national energies were devoted to creating competing new regional instruments each with its own machinery.

Scheuner held that the regional and the universal systems both had their right of life and could exist side by side. He could very well understand the fear expressed by Schwelb that a proliferation could have greatly disturbing effects. But a distinction already made by Cassin should be kept in mind here—that between substantive rights and implementation. If there were differences in substantive rights this might be deplorable, but in the matter of implementation the only difficulty was that there could be two systems of implementation, and it would probably be possible to insert some provisions in the conventions and covenants about the solution of such problems. In the Optional Protocol attached to the Covenant on Civil and Political Rights there was a provision whereby the Commission should not consider a matter which was presently under consideration under another procedure of international investigation or settlement. This settled the matter with regard to the Optional Protocol. Art. 44 of the Covenant on Civil and Political Rights itself referred only to United Nations procedures. But methods could be found to solve these difficulties. The solution would have to be based on some sets of priorities. It could not be the choice of one individual to invoke one or the other of the machineries, except in particular situations. As a general rule, he thought that the regional organs should have priority to deal with the cases emanating from that region and that the United Nations should at least await the outcome of the regional procedure.

3. In his paper, *MacBride* had presented as one of the possible roads to an improved protection of human rights the setting up of other regional arrangements similar to the European Convention, and he had specifically aked the participants from Eastern Europe whether they were inclined to consider the possibility in Eastern Europe of formulating a Socialist Convention on Human Rights, or whatever it would be called, in that region.

Szabó answered that after considerable reflection, he was inclined to be negative to the proposal. The major reason for this stand was that regional organisations tended to create fragmentation of the world. Such organisations were always set up by groups with some political affinities. The preamble of the European Convention spoke of states having common heritage of political traditions and ideals of freedom and the rule of law. Thus the organisation was made up of a group of states having the same economic-political systems, which had nothing to do with geographical regions. He referred to the Inter-American Commission which had been preoccupied with the Cuban question. These examples demonstrated that the regional organisations had political features which separated the states participating in the United Nations efforts to protect human rights. It was of course a fact that the world in one sense was divided between different political and economic systems, but from another perspective it was also one and indivisible in the sense that the different systems must coexist. Universal action enhanced coexistence, but this was not always the case with regional action.

Furthermore, he did not think positively of a Socialist regional convention if it was to be patterned on the same lines as the Western European one. Pinto had referred to the possibilities of a Socialist court to hear complaints from individuals. But in his own opinion, this was not the best starting-point for a multilateral action for the protection of human rights.

Bystrický also expressed his doubts on the proposal. He had not yet given much thought to the problem, but on the face of it he was inclined to take the same stand as Szabó. The most important problem today was to achieve unity. On the order of our time was to dissolve the NATO, the Warsaw Treaty Organisation, and so on. Which influence would the setting up of regional organisations for the protection of human rights have on this road to unity? He was not himself quite certain. If the countries of Western Europe thought it useful for them to have such arrangements, he would readily give his support to this, but he was not sure that the same pattern would fit in other places. The major task was, in his opinion, to find a system for the protection of human rights at all stages, and not ony in exceptional matters. Discussions were presently going on in Eastern European countries for the best approaches to these problems, mainly with reference to the protection of human rights by the individual states. Some argued in favour of a system parallel to the French "Conseil d'État" and others in favour of the British system with judicial control. There were protagonists of both views. Yugoslavia had already both a constitutional court and an administrative court. In Czechoslovakia, there was a desire to create something along these lines. But there were also opponents to this, pointing to the fact that in France, Austria and Germany a number of years—sometimes five, six or more—might lapse before the final decisions were reached. Therefore it was necessary to look for something better than that. Referring to the (Western) European Convention he did not want to pronounce himself on it, though Europe did not have its eastern frontiers at the Elbe. Many of the results obtained by means of the European convention were remarkable, and he declared that some of the Eastern European countries had neglected these aspects and were now studying the results obtained in the Western European system. But there were some bad examples which they would not like to follow, for instance the decision upholding the outlawing of the Communist party in Western Germany. This decision, while phrased in legal terms, was clearly political and undemocratic. In addition the European Convention had departed from the Universal Declaration in that the former did not include economic, social, and cultural rights. It had also departed from the Universal Declaration in that it was a closed system, open only to the members of the Council of Europe. He was therefore not in favour of copying that example.

4. *Cassin* argued that the goal now was to have human rights respected to the highest degree possible. There might be differences of opinion as to the best methods, but at the present moment the most immediate task was to obtain an immense effort by the people of the different states so that their governments ratified the Covenants. A new effort on regional arrangements before the states had ratified could not but contribute to a

delay in the ratification or to ratifications with reservations—some states might argue that they wanted to ratify only parts of the Covenants and that for the rest they intended to enter into conventions *inter se.* Particularly serious was the situation in the developing countries, where the position of women was rather miserable. They might become the victims of such regional or subregional approaches. The states in question might argue e.g. that the conditions for women in Africa differ greatly from the rest of the world and that they therefore should create a convention on the status of women in their own way. This would cause considerable delay. Speaking generally, he again stressed that there was nothing more important than to have a maximum of ratifications and that nothing should be done which could cause delay.

IX. *Future measures*

MacBride had dealt in his paper with further measures which could be taken in the future to strengthen the international protection of human rights. Some of the interventions related to this problem have been summarised under VII and VIII above. In addition, there were some interventions discussing his other proposals and some further ideas, such as setting up the office of a High Commissioner of Human Rights, creating arrangements for individual petitions, and intensifying the efforts within each country.

1. *Jenks* supported the proposal for a High Commissioner. This would be a valuable step forward because it would succeed in fulfilling in a unique way the function of concentrating the full weight of world opinion upon thorough, objective statements of facts. This view was also shared by *Wold,* who stressed the importance of having an *ombudsman* who could deal with these questions in complete independence from political ties.

Szabó referred to the statements by MacBride to the effect that the Socialist countries had been strongly opposed to the establishment of a High Commissioner. This was true. The reason for this was the following: There was at the present time a growing number of complaints against the Socialist countries for having violated human rights. He did not want to discuss the political motivations for these complaints. But all were in agreement that the conditions of human rights had improved over the last ten, five or three years. The attacks did not have any positive effect on this development. Furthermore, he doubted the value of having an international organ for the handling of individual complaints. What was more important was the general development of the human rights protection in the Socialist countries.

2. *Nørgaard* said that he had been encouraged by the progress reported in the papers presented by McNulty and Jenks of the Western European system and in I.L.O. for individual complaints. These results could be confronted with what had been said on the implementation of the Covenants, particularly the scepticism which had been expressed by Capotorti in his paper regarding individual petitions under the Optional Protocol. Perhaps the ideal solution, from a legal point of view, would be a court with compulsory jurisdiction to which the individuals had direct access. On the other hand, it was far from impossible that a number of cases could be better handled if the competent organs were allowed to use some "political wisdom" in the sense used by Jenks in his paper. This could best be done through a system of petitions, where the recommendations could be formulated with "political wisdom". It was much more difficult for courts to formulate their decisions in that way. He drew a parallel to municipal law systems for petitions. In Denmark and Norway, the individual who thought his rights violated by an administrative decision could bring the case before the courts. There was, therefore, a perfect system of judicial control. None the less, this system had been supplemented by a system of petitions to an *ombudsman,* who could tackle the question in a different way. Thus, when even within municipal systems judicial control had proved insufficient, and had to be supplemented with a system of petitions, this was certainly more important in the international society. In his opinion, therefore, the highest priority should be given to develop a more perfect system of petitions.

3. *Fawcett* said that the focus should not be exclusively on what could be done internationally. It was rather easy to talk about what was going on in other countries and what the people of those other countries had better do about it. But one ought not to forget to take action in one's own country. Each country had its own problems. He informed the participants that in the United Kingdom a committee had been in operation for more than a year, a part of whose program was to bring out information on human rights. But more important, the committee was going to focus on the problems of the United Kingdom itself, particularly trying to solve some of the problems connected with the large immigrant population. The committee was hoping to do something practical in this field in the coming year. More generally speaking, he thought that individuals engaged in the efforts to enhance the protection of human rights could achieve great re-

sults by trying to involve themselves in some practical work of this kind. There was always a certain degree of inertia and complacency prevailing in any society, but if somebody took efforts to do something practical it could bear fruits out of all proportions because there was a widespread, latent willingness to support such initiatives.

Wold considered one of the most important tasks to be to educate and influence the people to understand and support the protection of human rights. The mass medias should be used to bring the message to the great masses of people. Public opinion should be influenced and in turn influence the governments in the United Nations. In this way it would become a political necessity for governments to support the schemes for human rights protection. But it was necessary to get the message through to the public that human rights were the rights of every, individual human being.

Expression of thanks

Schreiber:

I should like to express my thanks to the Nobel Institute for having organised the Symposium, which has been a great success and an example for those who may wish to organise such gatherings in the future. Few could but respond positively, in spite of other engagements, to the invitation of the distinguished Institute and the associations which it invokes for us. The truest titles of nobility in our generation and our century have been awarded through the intermediary of this Institute.

Though I have spoken here in my personal capacity, I want to underline that in my view, this Symposium is an important response to the appeal by the General Assembly of the United Nations to all private and public organisations concerned to engage in discussions concerning human rights before and during the International Year of Human Rights. I believe this is the first manifestation which can be linked directly to the International Year. I would like to express to Director Schou and to the Institute the thanks of the Secretary General for having organised this Symposium.

Cassin:

Dear Colleagues,

As the *doyen* I have the honour and pleasure to thank the Institute and the Norwegian hosts for the excellent occasion they have provided for us to work together here. What was a hope when this Symposium started on Monday has become a reality now. We have worked in an exceptional way in an atmosphere of quietness, security, and confidence in the world which is common to us all. The papers presented have been very valuable, and there was not a single one which did not bring forward something new. Facing the discussions of the future, this experience in itself has given great promises. I would like to thank Director Schou, expressing our gratitude for the efforts made to bring the Symposium to a reality. All of us present here probably have the feeling that they can return with some fundamental ideas to work on for the future progress of human rights.